Bewilderments

Bewilderments

REFLECTIONS ON
THE BOOK OF NUMBERS

Avivah Gottlieb Zornberg

Schocken Books, New York

All rights reserved. Published in the United States by Schocken Books,
a division of Random House LLC, New York, and in Canada by Random House
of Canada Limited, Toronto, Penguin Random House companies.

Schocken Books and colophon are registered trademarks of Random House LLC.

*Some of the material in this book originally appeared, in slightly different form,
in the following publications:* Chapter 5: "Bewilderments," in *Answering a Question
with a Question*, vol. 2: *The Tradition of Inquiry in Contemporary Psychoanalysis
and Jewish Thought*, edited by Lewis Aron and Libby Henik (Academic Studies
Press, 2014); Chapter 7: "'From Another Shore': Moses and Korach," in *Radical
Responsibility: Celebrating the Thought of Chief Rabbi Lord Jonathan Sacks*, edited
by Michael J. Harris, Daniel Rynhold, and Tamra Wright (Maggid Press, 2013);
Chapter 8: "Heart of Stone, Heart of Flesh," in *Sanctification: Kedushah*, edited
by David Birnbaum and Benjamin Blech (New Paradigm Matrix, 2015);
Chapter 11: "'Let Me See That Good Land': The Story of a Human Life," in
*Answering a Question with a Question: Contemporary Psychoanalysis and Jewish
Thought*, edited by Lewis Aron and Libby Henik (Academic Studies Press, 2010).

Owing to limitations of space, acknowledgments to reprint previously published
material can be found following the index.

Library of Congress Cataloging-in-Publication Data
Zornberg, Avivah Gottlieb, author.
Bewilderments : reflections on the Book of Numbers / Avivah Gottlieb Zornberg.
pages cm
Includes bibliographical references and index.
ISBN 978-0-8052-4304-8 (hardcover : alk. paper). ISBN 978-0-8052-4305-5 (eBook).
1. Bible. Numbers—Criticism, interpretation, etc. I. Title.
BS1265.52.Z67 2014 222."   1407—dc23 2014011802

www.schocken.com

Jacket photograph: Har Harduf, Judean Desert, copyright © Neil Folberg
Jacket design by Abby Weintraub

Printed in the United States of America
First Edition

2 4 6 8 9 7 5 3 1

In order to arrive at what you are not
　　You must go through the way in which you are not.
　And what you do not know is the only thing you know

—*T. S. Eliot,* Four Quartets, *"East Coker," III, 142–44*

CONTENTS

ACKNOWLEDGMENTS

This book began as a series of lectures I gave to rabbinical students at Boston Hebrew College. Some of the students were in the classroom with me here in Jerusalem, while others sat in the College in Boston. The technology involved was in itself a source of considerable bewilderment for all concerned. Despite this, our journey into the wilderness evoked much valuable discussion and gave me the sense that a book might come of it. I am grateful to these students and to the two later generations of students with whom I shared my developing understanding of the biblical and midrashic texts.

I am grateful to Betsy Rosenberg for reading some chapters and for her dedicated attention to large and small aspects of the book. I am grateful to David Shulman and to Linda Zisquit for their generous readings of parts of my manuscript.

Special thanks to Adele and Ron Tauber for their warm hospitality in New York during my U.S. lecture tours. And to Altie Karper, my wonderful editor at Schocken, together with her devoted team; to Sharon Friedman, my agent; and to the many friends and students whose conversation has helped me on my journey.

My love and gratitude to and for Eric, my husband and friend, and our children, Bracha, Moshe-Yarden, and Avi; their partners, Paul, Yael, and Tali; and our grandchildren, Miriam, Aluma, Zohar, Shuvi, Yasmin, and Amir. They radiate the light by which I live and write.

PREAMBLE

BEWILDERMENTS

The Hebrew name for the book of Numbers is Sefer Bamidbar, the Book of (lit.) In-the-Wilderness.[1] Although the Israelite wilderness experience begins in Exodus and concludes in Deuteronomy, the book of Numbers claims the interior of this world of wilderness as its peculiar territory. It evokes not only geographical terrain, but also an inner landscape, an "inscape,"[2] as it were—a world of imaginative being.

Between Egypt and the Holy Land, the wilderness intervenes. As the Torah tells the story, this was meant to form a brief episode in the history of the Israelites, a passage between leaving Egypt— *yetziat Mitzraim*—and entering the Land. But the brief interlude suddenly and tragically swells to deathly proportions. In one traumatic moment, the divine decree goes forth: this interval will encompass the life and death of a whole generation. Those who left Egypt will sink into the sands of this wilderness. Only their children will see the Land.

What is the nature of this interim space, so terribly extended? The surface of the wilderness proves to hold vertical menace—"Into this wilderness your carcasses shall fall!" the Torah intones repeatedly. This is not simply a walking surface for the traveling people, but a quicksand ready to consume human bodies. The first such bodies figure in the macabre showdown of Korach's rebellion, where the earth "opens its mouth and swallows" Korach's followers. They "vanish" from the human landscape, into the netherworld: the hungry maw of the earth has removed them from the surface on which human acts are played out. Nothingness has triumphed over being.

This terrible image haunts the reader, who contemplates the

many vanishings of a whole generation. For this is the very nature of the *midbar*—of *this great and terrible wilderness*.[3] It is an environment that is inimical to human life. Jeremiah describes its singular horror when he reminds the people: "God has led you through the wilderness, through a land of deserts and of pits, through a land of drought and deadly darkness, through a land that no man passed and where no man dwelt" (Jer. 2:6).

This landscape does not yield to human demands: it frustrates the need for food and drink, but also the basic demand for direction, for markings to indicate a human mapping of blank space. No human steps have trod this sand, it stares back at the traveler indifferently— pathless, *bewildering* to the human imagination. A kind of horror besets the mind. Already traumatized by their Egyptian past, the Israelites, one by one, must be swallowed into this senseless space.

"A great and terrible wilderness": the experience of *midbar*, extended to the edges of life, suddenly becomes a total experience. These people will never know any other reality. But precisely here lies the central enigma of the narrative. For in its way of telling the story, the Torah creates an illusion of continuity, as though we are throughout reading about the same people who left Egypt. Till the second census in chapter 26, the reader does not clearly understand that thirty-eight years have passed, with their full harvest of death. Only when the text clearly states that in this census there are no survivors from the earlier census at the beginning of the book (26:64),[4] do we realize that, without our noticing, a generation has slipped into the sands. A great interruption has occurred; thirty-eight years have imperceptibly vanished. By chapter 20, in fact, the new generation is already in place. And yet, even then, even after the census and indeed throughout Deuteronomy, it takes an effort to convince ourselves that, in fact, the generations have changed.

At the heart of the wilderness story, then, there is a gap, which is masked by apparent continuities. As often in traumatic experience, the rupture is somehow elided from the official record. The record continues to register the human hubbub of complaint and rebellion to which we have become accustomed. But the fabric of national life has been ripped open; unremarked within that hubbub, ring the death cries and the sudden silence of a generation.

This macabre secret at the heart of the narrative is revealed only after the catastrophe is over. It becomes one of the central "bewilderments" of the book. The other "bewilderment"—also essential to this wilderness—is the lack of *emunah*, of *faith*, that continuously and repeatedly characterizes the people's utterances. Classic midrashic sources have suggested that *midbar* is closely associated with issues of *dibbur*, of language and utterance. *Ein midbar ela dibbur*, declares one such source—"Wilderness is nothing but utterance"[5]— cryptically playing with the roots for the two terms. In which case, we can say that the Book of the Wilderness yields a human language of querulous skepticism. Cries and whispers and rages and laments fill the air, a cacophony that God describes as issuing from lack of faith.

At the beginning of the Exodus narrative, Moses protests against his mission of redemption: "But they will not believe me, they will not listen to my voice! They will say, God did not appear to you!" (Exod. 4:1). Moses' basic sense of the people is that they are *unbelieving*. His words will fall on deaf ears; he has no power to impinge on their skepticism, which, in his mind, is radical, subversive of redemptive possibility.

God, too, protests at this recalcitrant trait in the Israelite character: "How long will they have no faith in Me, despite all the signs I have enacted in their midst?" (Num. 14:11). Not-believing and having no faith are different nuances of a fundamental posture indicated by the Hebrew word *emunah*.[6] This connotes solidity, stability, continuity, validity. God sees the people as *not-trusting*. In spite of all the signs, all the indications of His love and His benign purpose, His promise to bring them into the Land is, it seems, deeply *incredible* to them. "*Ad anna?* How long?" God asks: How inherently unstable is this condition of *no-faith, no-trust*![7]

The posture of *not trusting*, ironically, seems to affect Moses also. In the end, God will accuse him of "having no faith in Me, to sanctify Me before the eyes of the Israelites" (Num. 20:12). An epidemic of skepticism has apparently not spared Moses himself, whom God, at an earlier moment, had praised as uniquely *ne'eman*—"*faithful* in all My household" (12:7).

SKEPTICISMS

Strangely, the wilderness seems to bring out latent skepticisms, even in those who are also capable of moments of trust and faith. This same people, after all, did believe Moses' original message, as God had promised they would.[8] The "signs"—the leprous hand of Moses, his staff that changes into a snake[9]—do their work. And at the Red Sea, the Israelites do see God's mighty hand and "believe in God and in His servant, Moses" (Exod. 14:31). But this was before the Book of the Wilderness, in another world. In the wilderness space of bewilderment, their language expresses a "desert-sea" of skepticism, as the American philosopher Stanley Cavell, in a different context, describes this state of being.

For Cavell, modern skepticism is to be viewed against the history of an age-old philosophical posture that came to dominate European philosophy and literature from Descartes onward. As a philosophical position, skepticism questions our ability to know the world and its objects, including other minds. But, he adds: "skepticism with respect to the other is not skepticism but is tragedy." It is a moral stance "in the face of the other's opacity and the demand the other's expression places upon me; I call skepticism my denial or annihilation of the other."[10]

Cavell's descriptions of this moral posture are informed by psychoanalytic thought: it represents "world-consuming doubt, which is hence a standing threat to ... human existence";[11] an "unappeasable denial, a wishful uncertainty that constitutes an annihilation";[12] an "incurable malady."[13] Cavell traces the devastations of this malady through Shakespeare's *The Winter's Tale*—where a king refuses to acknowledge his own son—and through Kant's *Critique of Pure Reason*. It is a fanaticism, nihilism, that no knowing can oppose. At its heart, it wants "there to be nothing," if there can't be everything.[14] Its basic question is "How can I trust the basis upon which I grant the existence of the other?"[15]

The response that Cavell offers is drawn from Levinas: "To see a face is already to hear 'You shall not kill.'"[16] If for Kant the scandal of philosophy is that "the existence of things outside us ... should have to be assumed merely on faith," then for Cavell "the problem is to *recognize* myself as denying another. ... Here is the scandal of skepticism with respect to the existence of others; *I am the scandal*"[17] (my emphasis).

In the wilderness history of the Israelites, this scandal is most acutely expressed in the narrative of the Spies, who, with one word—*efes,* zero—obliterate their own faithful report of the "goodness" of the Land. *Efes,* usually translated "however," deletes at one stroke the beauty of the world and of God's promise. In Cavell's terms, it represents a failure of *acknowledgment*—perhaps even a wish for there to be nothing: not to be born, not to love or marry or acknowledge one's own son. In the absence of certainty, a core fantasy of disappointment dissolves the possibility of even partial knowledge. The only alternative to this fantasy of annihilation is accepting that the world and its people are separate from us, "as if gone," and "must be regained every day." Repeated mourning of this kind is the "condition of the possibility of accepting the world's beauty."[18]

THE DOUBLE NARRATIVE

Cavell's complex view of skepticism frames it as a malady that is also a liberation from dogmatism. In the biblical narrative, the questions that the Spies are commissioned to investigate begin with the radical question *Mah hi?:* "You shall see the Land.... *What is it?*" And again, "*What is* the Land? ... Is it good or evil? ... *What* are the cities? *What is the Land?* Is it fertile or infertile?" (Num. 13:18–20). The repeated *Mah?*—the "What is it?" question—expresses a necessity of the human mind: to question, to see, to articulate meanings. The Spies' mission, is, in a sense, to be *skeptical,* not to rely on hearsay, or even on God's original magisterial description of the Land: "a good and spacious Land, flowing with milk and honey" (Exod. 3:8). God Himself, after all, initiated the Spies' mission. This fact seems to validate a "good" skepticism, the inquiring spirit of those who want to know for themselves what can be known.

However, it seems that "good" and "bad" skepticisms may be expressed in the same words. The midrash[19] offers the analogy of a king who makes an excellent match for his son, only to have his son demand to see the bride for himself. The king is aggrieved at his son's doubting his word: "Because you did not trust me, you will never see her in your home—she will marry your son!" The prince wants to "see" the bride in order to ascertain her beauty. Is he justified in wanting to find out what only he can know—if she is beautiful *in his eyes*? Or is the father right to be aggrieved at his son's lack of trust?

Perhaps both positions are valid. In "real time," in Numbers 13:2, it seems that God underwrites the Spies' mission; but forty years later, Moses retells the story in such a way as to incriminate the people for initiating the project. "I told them it is a good land," God protests in Rashi's reading of the story.[20] But the goodness of the Land is ultimately a subjective matter, to be acknowledged, if at all, by the people who are to "marry" it. Is the bridegroom simply exercising the right of an adult to choose a lovable bride? Or is he moved by a nihilism that may reject the very possibility of love?

The double biblical narrative, as well as the midrashic parable, put on view the ambiguity of the issue of trust. This issue, with all its bewilderments, runs through the book of Numbers. The treachery of the Sotah, the woman suspected of adultery, is itself the subject of an uncertainty that the ordeal is to resolve. Is she guilty or innocent? *What is she?* But, it turns out, no absolute certainty is to be had. In human affairs, the field of inquiry is never sterile; the wife may have other virtues that cloud the issue, or the husband may have a history of his own that will similarly block the elegance of the proof. If she is innocent, an incomplete certainty frees her from suspicion. If she is guilty, she may confess, and thus avoid the (dis)solution of God's Name in the bitter waters. From the beginning of the book, the tone is set for the bewilderments of uncertainty, denial, and mistrust; for a bitter dissolution of meaning where certainty is not to be had.

NOT-BREAD FROM HEAVEN

The skeptical question *Mah hi?*—"What is it?"—gives its name to the manna, the bread from heaven, that feeds the people through the wilderness. *"Man hu?—What is it?"* the people ask, *"for they did not know what it was."* Moses answers: "It is God's gift of bread."[21] But it is the question, and not the answer, that names the unknowable substance. This manna, this "What-stuff," remains enigmatic—it may be a source of sensual variety and pleasure, but at the same time it remains ungratifying, imaginatively *indigestible*.[22]

Uncanny stuff, it is in the end remembered by Moses in his last speeches as the very essence of the wilderness experience:

> Remember the long way that God your God has made you travel in the wilderness these past forty years, that He might afflict and test you to know what was in your hearts: whether you would keep His commandments or not. He afflicted you and subjected you to hunger and gave you manna to eat, which neither you nor your fathers had ever known, in order that you might know that man does not live on bread alone, but that man may live on whatever issues from God's mouth. (Deut. 8:2–3)

The forty-year *midbar* journey was intended as a difficult odyssey of self-understanding, a reconnaissance mission into the human heart. The manna is essential wilderness food, unknown, uncanny; but precisely in its unknowability it will open a new kind of knowledge: "that man does not live on bread alone but on what issues from God's mouth." The sentence communicates the mystery of the manna: it stirs up the question—*What is it* that can sustain human life?

For manna is both bread and not-bread; it comes, not from the earth but from heaven, from God's mouth, like His utterances and the world they create. The manna is an intimate encounter with the otherness that issues from God's mouth. In a profound sense, the human being lives on language. (S)he comes to realize this by way of the strangeness, the uncanniness of the manna, which does not answer to the familiar needs of the human animal. A substance that tells of the unknown leads the consumer to *see through* its flimsy appearance. This is the essential *midbar* experience: the unknowable leads the traveler to an imaginative knowledge, which refigures, transfigures the world.

What *issues forth* (*motza*) from God's mouth speaks not to the senses but to the human capacity for language, which is intimately connected with the divine. Imagination, as a form of language, creates realities. Human consciousness also undoes such creations, turning back on itself; as David Shulman writes: "this movement back [is] the imaginative act par excellence."[23]

RETHINKING EXODUS

Here lies the central paradox of *yetziat Mitzraim,* of the Exodus: leaving Egypt, issuing forth from a place of death, connotes birth, the opening of closed places, new *expressions* of consciousness. In mystical sources, the Exodus represents the redemption from the condition of *Galut Ha-Dibbur,* the Exile of the Word. Mutely subjected to the Egyptian slavery, the people at first begin to groan, cry, scream, moan—inchoate vociferations of pain. Discovering their voice, they may now pray, sing, speak themselves in the presence of God.

However, from the very moment of *yetziah,* of that separation, that issuing forth, the people contemplate return to Egypt; they wish for it, and express their desire repeatedly. Essentially, they *dissolve* every expressive achievement back into the void, the undefined domain from which it was drawn.

The first intimation of this wilderness pattern arises in the mind of God. It is God who first foresees the likelihood of such a desire arising; in view of this, He makes actual return more complicated, to prevent the people from acting on their *midbar* thoughts. These thoughts are indicated by the expression *yinachem*—"The people will change their minds" (Exod. 13:17). The changeable human mind is set in sharp focus in Rashi's translation: the core idea of *nechamah* (usually translated as either "comfort" or "relief") is *machshavah acheret*—"another thought." What God knows about the people is that the thought of Exodus will be rethought as regression. And indeed, it does not take long for the people to cry out: *"What is this* you have done to us in bringing us out of Egypt?" (14:11).

The movement outward is coupled with a movement backward, at least in language. After the Song of the Sea, their voices modulate to a key of resentment. After bravely proclaiming at Mount Sinai, "We will do and we will hear!" they proceed to undo their own commitment. The Golden Calf, the blatant act of idolatry, is introduced by words, again the skeptical *What?* question: "We *don't know what* has happened to [Moses]!" (Exod. 32:1). Moses has vanished, dissolved—and with him all the words of Sinai, its meanings and apparent certainties.

THE FREEDOM OF REVERSIBILITY

This "rebound" movement, however, is the very matter of the *midbar* and its utterances. In the Book of the Wilderness, it is the people who continuously and turbulently *speak*. God's words, which occupy the heart of Exodus, are now spoken mostly in response to the people's speech. There are silent epiphanies of the glory of God; intermittently, these come to punctuate the outcries of the people. There are passages of laws, mysteriously related to the narratives of regression and despair. But it is the people's language, their dark expressiveness, that, in its intensity, constantly questions and dissolves, disrupts meaning and restores the void.

I suggest that we see this "destructive" pattern as part of a larger evolution of imaginative language. Rather than dismiss it as regressive, perhaps we can imagine it as returning meaning to the infinite potential of the unnamed. Every creative act objectifies; every named object presents limits and constraints that the imagination persists in reworking.

The child who spends many hours building an elaborate sand castle, safe against the tides, may, as the sun sets, kick it down with all his might. Susan Stewart remembers Shelley's "Ozymandias": "The lone and level sands stretch far away."

She writes:

Without the freedom of reversibility enacted in unmaking, or at least always present as the potential for unmaking, we cannot give value to our making. . . . By destroying the mere thing, and using all his physical might to do so, the boy seemed to be returning the power of the form back into himself. . . . Once the skills used in making the castle in its entirety were internalized, they were ready to be used again. Unwilling or unable to be the curator of his creation, the boy swiftly returned it to its elements, that is, to its pure potential.[24]

This is skeptical creativity in all its paradoxical force. Asserting a "freedom of reversibility," the imagination demolishes, with destructive passion, its own structures. Whatever "*issues* from the mouth of God" lives in the vortex of such opposite forces—eternal, fully formed, and yet subject to the flood of "other thoughts."

It should be no surprise, then, that the issues of the human imagination are expressed with similar tension. Exodus, expressiveness, the creation of forms, backlash into resentment, recoil, dissolution. Like the child with his sand castle, the people experience a strange delight in their very despair. This is the delight of consciousness coming to know itself, through its own languages: its own *motza peh*—its expressive utterances.

In the Book of the Wilderness, *yetziat Mitzraim*—the issuing forth from Egypt—is registered within the subjective consciousness of the Israelites; and within their own *issues,* their troubled utterances. God has offered them gifts—the Sabbath and the Holy Land.[25] Their response to the latter gift is recorded in this book. The question that haunts the book is *"What is it—for you?"* The question is embodied in the crystalline substance of the manna—the *What*-substance on which they must live. They eat in order to know: more pointedly, in order to speak themselves into being. Essential *midbar* goes in at their mouths and issues in bewilderment, anger, destructiveness— all the ruptures that beset human desire.

No one is exempt from this complexity. As Mei Ha-Shilo'ach[26] points out, all the protagonists of the difficult dramas of this book—including Moses and Aaron—bear great potential and great *wilderness* passion: the tension between the two poles of creativity and destructiveness must be lived as well as is humanly possible. "There is no righteous person on earth who does good and does not sin," declares Ecclesiastes (7:20). Yosef Albo reads this: "There is no righteous person who, *in doing good,* does not sin." Even in the good deeds, the loving acts, there remains a vestige of some proto-fantasy about self and the world. This constitutes a "missing of the mark"—the underlying meaning of "sin" (the Hebrew *chet*).

IN PURSUIT OF THE WILDERNESS

This is the issue that the wilderness exposes. A powerful midrash declares:

"And he drove the flock to the furthest wilderness" (Exod. 3:1): R. Joshua said, Why was he in pursuit of the wilderness? He saw that Israel were raised up from the wilderness, as it is said: "Who is this who rises up from the wilderness?" (Songs 3:6). They had the manna from the wilderness, and the quails, and the well, and the Tabernacle, and the Divine Presence: priesthood, kingship, and the Clouds of Glory. . . . *Wilderness* [midbar] *is, in essence, language* [dibbur]. [*Ein midbar ella dibbur.*] As it is said, "Your lips are like a scarlet thread, your mouth [*midbarech*] is lovely" (Songs 4:3).[27]

The *midbar* becomes precious in memory. For the prophets and, later, the Sages, it becomes the place of passionate revelations. Hosea, in particular, will speak of God's yearning for that original wilderness where divine seduction might again take place: "I shall lead her to the wilderness [*midbar*] and I shall speak [*ve-dibbarti*] with her heart" (Hosea 2:16). The words *midbar* and *dibbarti* are set together, in all their electric tension. They are the same, say the Sages. Out of this wilderness once issued the voice of divine revelation, as well as voices of human mistrust, which brought the core fantasies of the people into view. There, the people once heard its own voice as it struggled with God's word and His light. In this way, Israel came to know God in naked reality. How strange that God should long to return to that place, as though the people had responded there to God's words of love!

In the midrash, Israel is "raised up" in and from the wilderness. God's heavenly gifts, the utterances of His mouth, are bestowed there. Wilderness itself *is* utterance, the midrash cryptically declares, and proceeds to quote from the Song of Songs in praise of the "mouth" of the beloved; *midbarech* unfolds its ambiguity—"your speaking," "your mouth," on the one hand, and "your wilderness," on the other. Like the text from Hosea, the midrash plays with shockingly unrelated meanings; spins bridges across the chasm between them. The beloved and her beloved speech, her way of speaking, are linked with the wilderness and evoke a wilderness beauty precisely in the utterances of the people, as well as in those of God.

The wilderness is the source of Israel's exaltation. There she is incubated; and there she is endowed with divine gifts. But there, too, her truth, the reality of her wilderness being finds expression in all her utterances. The midrash begins with the proof text that describes Moses as "driving his flocks to the furthest wilderness [*achar ha-midbar*], where he came to Horeb, the mountain of God" (Exod. 3:1). The midrash reads *achar ha-midbar*—"He was *in pursuit* of the wilderness, because he saw that Israel was exalted by the wilderness." That is, even before God first speaks to him, Moses has a passion for the wilderness, sensing its "exalting" potential. How will Israel learn to speak in this stark place?

THE POSSIBILITY OF LOVE?

The darkest moment in this journey may be when Israel begins to doubt herself, her own capacity for love. The various expostulations of the people find their center in the *efes* (zero) moment of the Spies, when all meaning is annihilated. After that, and after the proliferating fantasy of the giants, which generates a grasshopper sense of self (Num. 13:28–33), there is the terrible night of weeping, in which a wordless "voice" rises up from the camp, modulating to weeping and then to the utterance of a Job-like wish to be already dead: "If only we had died in the land of Egypt, or in this wilderness if only we had died!" (14:2)

A poignant midrash[28] describes this moment of despair: "*Yatza libam*—Their hearts [lit.] *left them!*" Their hearts failed them. In this crisis of the history of *yetziat Mitzraim* (*leaving* from Egypt) they experience also this loss, this separation—between their hearts and themselves. Mei Ha-Shilo'ach[29] elaborates: they lose confidence in the real nature of their hearts. Perhaps, deep in their hearts, they will never *love the Land*? Therefore, at precisely this crisis of self-doubt, God commands the wine libation (Num. 15:5)—which signifies courage—to move them to a profound dialogue with their own despair.

Such a depth of experience breeds its own new language of hatred and love. Despair declares itself, in all the cries and laments and death-wishfulness of the people. Their words are suffused with the unspeakable pain that inhabits them. And yet precisely this intensity of self-expression may connect them to a faith that brings them again to life. Beyond what can be said, or known, there is an opening to the infinite.

The issue is the possibility of love. In the absence of certainty about God's love, can the human heart really love—God, the Land, others, itself? At heart, the issue about God is not about His power to bring them into the Land but about His love, His desire to bring them into full being. On this question, the mission of the Spies collapses. Hatred, and not love, declares itself; projected onto God, aggression rages. Disruptions, bewilderments erode the received formulas. If faith is to become real, catastrophe must be acknowledged and fully spoken.

As it turns out, it is only when hatred is acknowledged that the language of love begins to emerge. In Deuteronomy,[30] it is only after Moses has spoken to the people about their core fantasy of God's hatred—or, in Rashi's devastating reading, about their own projected hatred of God—that he can begin to utter words like *ahavah* (love), *cheshek* (desire), *chefetz* (delight).

Even desire and delight, it seems, have their terrors. The Revelation at Sinai perhaps aroused in the people an unbearably complex experience of bliss and terror.[31] We may even say that the subject of this Book of the Wilderness is the response of the people to this encounter with the divine. Stirred to the depths by God's voice, human beings give voice to the passion—attraction and repulsion—that tests the constraints of language and meaning.

God *gives* the Torah; now the issue is of the human *reception* of the gift. The Israelites are moved to partial revelations, each of which has its skeptical rejoinder. Imagination breeds questions, doubts that dissolve and re-form the revelation.

THE WILDERNESS VOICE

The American philosopher and psychoanalyst Jonathan Lear discusses the organizing power of fantasy. Unconscious fantasies, he writes, "tend toward the expression of an unconscious worldview. . . . The core fantasy has great organizing power and provides an imaginative answer to the question: Who am I?"[32] "It is a mark of the human that we do not quite fit into our own skins. That is, we do not fit without remainder into socially available practical identities . . . what lies 'outside' is a basic organizing principle, working around primordial human challenges."[33]

Because of this, when one verbally expresses one's anger, or one's self-hate—which is not simply to *avow* these emotions but to become "consciously angry"—one becomes aware of a disruption of one's conscious sense of self. Another organizing principle becomes visible when one speaks in the first person, putting oneself *into* words. One's fantasy then suffuses one's words. This is a moment of what Lear describes as "uncanny, anxious longing."[34]

We have seen a moment of this kind when, at least in the midrashic reading, the people become aware of the disruptive implications of their own words. *Yatza libam*—their hearts left them, separated from its usual certainties. If this is the *midbar* voice issuing from them, the Book of the Wilderness allows us—and them?—to hear this voice unremittingly.

Even the death of the generation does not interrupt this voice. Only retroactively, when forty years are almost over, we realize that a new population is now in view. The second census reveals the movement of time and its casualties. But, in reading of that deathly time, we are aware of a strange continuity, of a narrative in which time vanishes. The voice we hear is the voice of unconscious fantasy that knows no time. It is this intensity of imaginative language that carries us unawares through the changes and disasters of history.

For the reader, it requires a positive cognitive effort to remember the facts of time and change. The people's wilderness imagination continues to express itself, even after the dying is over, blurring our sense of transformation. Evidence of spiritual redemption, of integration, is in fact scant. The narrative of the daughters of Tzelofchad, culminating in God's splendid accolade to the five sisters, *"Ken—Finely, fairly* do the daughters of Tzelofchad speak!"* (Num. 27:7), offers perhaps the only clear suggestion that the wilderness struggle for utterance has, at least in this case, achieved felicity. But our desire for a confirmed progress narrative is largely frustrated. The Torah tells a longer, less gratifying tale.

THE ROSE AND THE SHADOW

However, the midrash[35] offers a poetic meditation on the development of the Israelite voice:

> "I am the Rose of Sharon [*chavatzelet ha-sharon*]": Said the community of Israel, I am she, and I am beloved [*chavivah*]! I am she that God has loved of all the seventy nations. . . . *Ha-sharon*— for I uttered song [*shirah*] before Him, through Moses, as it is said, "Then Moses and the Israelites sang" (Exod. 15:1).

> Another interpretation: I am the rose of Sharon, and I am beloved! I am she that was hidden [*chavuyah*] by the shadow of Egypt. Then in one instant, God gathered me in to Ramses, and I became full of sap with good deeds like a rose, and I sang in His presence!—as it is said, "For you there shall be singing, as on a night when a festival is hallowed" (Isa. 30:29).

> Another interpretation: I am the rose of Sharon, and I am beloved! I am she that was hidden in the shadow of the Sea. Then in one instant, I became full of sap with good deeds like a rose; and I pointed Him out, my Lord who was before me—as it is said, "This is my God and I shall glorify Him!" (Exod. 15:2).

Speaking in her own voice, in the first person, Israel figures herself as the rose of Sharon. Adopting the words of the beloved in the Song of Songs, she declares, "I am the rose of Sharon" (Songs 2:1). Playing with the unusual five-letter root *chavatzelet* (rose) the midrash generates a chain of associations. *Chav* evokes *chaviv ani*—"I am beloved, precious," while *tzel* (the second half of the word *chavatzelet*) means shadow. *Chav* also evokes *chavuyah*—to be hidden, covered over, buried. Israel brings herself to life by speaking of herself as precious, even though—or because—she is almost obscured, suppressed—by the menace of Egypt, of the Red Sea, of Sinai.[36] But then, like the rose, in one instant, she *emerges* and becomes full of sap, succulent with good deeds; then Sharon releases its hidden *shirah*—she sings her song to God: "I am the Rose of Sharon."

The image of the rose, its beauty once invisible, suddenly thriving and singing, present to the senses—sight, hearing, touch—in fact confuses the senses with its intensity. This is a visible, moist, singing rose: synesthesia takes the reader beyond the knowable.

Ultimately, all the external suppressive forces of history give way to God's redemption: the rose emerges from obscurity into brilliant blossom and song. In a further passage in the midrash, however, the shade under which the rose is obscured becomes "the shade *of herself*"—*chavuyah be-tzel atzma*. Undeveloped, the *chavatzelet* lives unseen within its green shade, the tight sheath of leaves that encases her; then she appears as a full-blown rose, a *shoshanah*. Israel identifies herself as that early bud, latent, inexpressive; and then, as the bloom in its fullness. She is her own shadow. It is all a matter of imagination, of potential blossoming: an astonishment of the natural world.

The rose of Sharon becomes a figure through which Israel can imagine herself and her potential. Threatened externally and internally, her rose reality almost extinguished, she contains unknown possibilities. In this way, the following passage in the midrash[37] implies, she resembles the wilderness itself, which is Israel's formative environment. Here it is the wilderness that speaks, under the imagery of the rose:

R. Berachia said: This verse was spoken by the wilderness. The wilderness said, I am wilderness, and I am beloved! For all the good things in the world are hidden in me—as it is said, "I will plant cedars and acacias in the wilderness" (Isa. 41:19)—God gave them to me in trust, and when He asks them of me, I will return the trust in full, and I will become full of sap with good deeds, and I will sing in His presence—as it is said, "The wilderness and the parched land shall rejoice" (35:1).

The earth said this: I am she, and I am beloved! For all the dead of the world are buried in me—as it is said, "Let your dead revive, let corpses arise!" (Isa. 26:19). When God asks them of me, I will return them to him, and I will become full of sap with good deeds like a rose, and will sing in His presence—as it is said, "From the end of the earth we hear singing" (24:16).

"All the good things in the world are hidden in me." Within her arid void, the wilderness holds much beauty, much moisture—as well as much death. (The last passage includes the revival of the dead in the chain of surrealistic association.) She is the container of infinite potential, held in trust against the moment she is required to restore it to God. Her very blankness holds untold imaginative possibility. The moment of realization is the moment when the wilderness itself breaks into song.

THE PENETRATING GAZE

Clearly, the wilderness that speaks and identifies itself with the latent beauty of the rose, awaiting its moment, is itself a metaphor for Israel. However, the wilderness as rose, or Israel as rose, is a creative act of imagination. To call it a metaphor is, in a sense, to dull the effective force of this kind of language. In such midrashic meditations, we engage with the mind of the Sages, who are poets intensely *thinking*—figuring the reality of Israel. The intensity of focus strips away conventional meanings and penetrates to a world of imaginative reality. This is what it means to *see* the potential flower within the bud. The shadows and sheaths of nature and history are both acknowledged and dissolved by the imaginative force of the poet. A hidden reality comes into being.

Such creative acts implicitly celebrate their own creativity. The full bloom of the rose will be achieved when it *sings*. Seeing through all the sheaths, the imaginative mind links Israel, the wilderness, the rose, and the song in which creation praises God. It is the penetrating gaze of the poet that dissolves all conventional differences.

In the same sequence of midrashic passages, Israel continues her meditation in the presence of God:

R. Abba said: The community of Israel said in the presence of God: "I am she [the rose], and I am beloved, for I am set in the deep places of suffering. But when God draws me out of these sufferings, I am full of sap like the full blooming rose, and I utter song before Him."

R. Acha said: The community of Israel said, "Master of the

World, at the moment when you *deepen Your gaze* upon me, I become full of sap with good deeds like the full blooming rose, and I utter song, as it is said: A Song of Ascents: From the depths I have called to You, O God!"[38]

Only if God "deepens His gaze" will He penetrate the "deep places"—*ma'amakim*—of suffering in which Israel is hidden. The creator discovers/creates the potential life. This is the greatest achievement of the creative mind—to plumb the depths of fantasy and draw forth the invisible. The poet-sages, created in God's image, draw on their own experience in order to evoke His power to bring their full being into expression.

A THERAPEUTIC JOURNEY?

At the end of the Book of the Wilderness, we read a list of all the separate journeys undertaken during these forty years:

These were the journeys of the Israelites who left the land of Egypt in their hosts, in the charge of Moses and Aaron. Moses wrote down the starting points of their journeys, according to the word [lit., mouth] of God. Their journeys, by starting points, were as follows . . . (Num. 33:1–2)

Rashi asks why the Torah makes a point of recording these stations in the wilderness, and offers a midrashic answer:

R. Tanchuma interpreted: This is like a king whose son was sick so he took him to a distant place to heal him. On their way back, his father began to enumerate all the separate stages of the journey. He told him, Here we slept, here we caught cold, here you had a headache etc.[39]

In the original midrash, the analogy for the king and his sick son is spelled out: God instructs Moses to record all the places where "they angered Me." In the Torah, a point is made of Moses' recording these stations of anger.

The *midbar* history as a history of *sickness,* to be recorded in detail like a logbook, may seem surprising. The child's sickness is recorded as a saga of suffering—fever, headaches. Why record these at all? What is the strange pleasure in lingering on each episode in this history of pain? Does healing change the past? Particularly in view of the midrashic "translation" of the sickness as "angering God," the question becomes sharper: why this emphasis on registering these vortices of sin and suffering?

Perhaps lingering on these particular painful memories, shared by father and son, conveys the sense that sickness itself is to be *seen through*, reimagined as part of a larger process. The poet Rilke writes in similar vein to a younger poet who is suffering from agitation, pain, sadness:

> If there is anything morbid in your processes, just that sickness is the means by which an organism frees itself of foreign matter, so one must just help it to be sick, to have its whole sickness and break out with it, for that is its progress. . . . You must be patient as a sick man and confident as a convalescent, for perhaps you are both. And more: you are the doctor too, who has to watch over himself.[40]

Through the imagery of freeing the body of foreign matter, Rilke figures sickness as a transition to a deeper health: *One must just help [the organism] to be sick.* In the midrash, the suffering is shared by father and son; the dynamic of human sin and divine anger works through its doleful repertoire until some kind of catharsis is achieved. Then, the stations of pain can be celebrated as particulars of a cleansing process. The people have had their sickness.

Of course, this midrashic story is in important ways a revision of the factual history. There, the sick child dies of his sickness: the people's inability to trust in God's love provokes for that generation a fatal divine anger. What moves the Sages to this therapeutic version of the wilderness narrative?

It is striking that, in a similar vein, Moses makes a point of reminding the people to remember the history of anger:

> "Remember, do not forget, how you angered God your God in the wilderness: from the day that you left Egypt. . . . At Horev,

you so angered God that God was furious enough with you to have destroyed you." (Deut. 9:7,8)

Why are the Israelites urged never to forget this period of terror? In fact, midrashic commentary extends this requirement of memory to oral narration of this painful saga.[41]

And again, in Psalm 95, God remembers:

"For forty years I strove with that generation. I said, 'They are a people whose hearts go astray, who have not understood My ways.' So I swore in My anger, 'They shall not enter My place of rest.'" (vv. 10–11)

One can say simply that we are to remember the sickness of the past in order to avoid a recurrence. But why does the Psalmist evoke this morbid vortex in a Song of Praise—chosen as the opening Psalm with which we welcome the Sabbath?

Perhaps, after all, the wilderness history with the hidden catastrophe at its heart is not about catastrophe but about a healing process in which, as Rilke suggests, the patient is to be also the convalescent, and even the doctor. This would suggest that in all their ravings, the Israelites are, in a sense, "watching over themselves." They are fulfilling the commandment of *lishmor mishmeret*:[42] they are keeping watch over the process of healing. In retrospect these vortices of sin-and-anger acquire a kind of transparency; they will have become a therapeutic process.

TRAVAILS AND UTTERANCES

In retrospect, God wants Moses to take account of these "starting places"—*motzaot*—that begin with the Exodus, with the moment of "starting out"—*yetziah*—from Egypt. We notice the repeated use of the *y-tz-a* root: all these starting points constitute the full history of that great starting point, the Exodus. That was the Great Foray that is spelled out in terms of many particular forays, cathartic episodes in which the people give expression to some of the accumulated traumas of history.

Particularly striking is the reversal of terms in Moses' record: "Moses recorded *the starting points of their journeys. . . . Their journeys, by starting points* were as follows. . . ." The Rabbi of Piacezna, Rabbi Kalonymus Kalman Shapira,[43] whose teachings under the shadow of the Holocaust record the stations of another trauma, addresses this passage.[44] He writes of the birth of the Messiah, the torment that ultimately yields new life. Of necessity, birth involves a kind of death, a dissolution of identity. As with the seed that decomposes in the ground, this process of "mortification" is the condition for the release of great potential.

"In pain you shall bear children," God says to Eve. Rabbi Shapira reads this as the laboring mother's surrender of her familiar body and its habitual strength. He quotes the Midrash:[45] "Ninety-nine groans tend toward death, while one calls out for life." Parts of the self must be relinquished if something new is to appear.

In this way, the Piacezna Rebbe refigures the sickness of his world. He reads all the journeyings of the sick son as birth pangs that will reveal divine light. While the people were still living through the journeys—the travails—the meanings were not obvious, so the text highlights the journeys, rather than the *motzaot,* the divine utterance. But when Moses recorded these events, after the journeyings were over, everyone could see *what had issued from God's mouth*—the *motzaot,* the utterances of God. *Malchut*—God's sovereignty—is brought into the world precisely by such "journeyings." So the text then speaks of the *motzaot,* the divine utterances, before the *journeyings.*

What *issues* from God's mouth has the power to illumine all the suffering. When Moses writes the story, redemptive meaning comes into being; now, God's mouth speaks. But in "real time," as we call it, the experience of trauma dominates consciousness. The self is dissolved, and only the groans of protest and pain fill the air.

PATIENT, CONVALESCENT, AND DOCTOR, TOO . . .

If this is, then, a progress narrative, it is a complicated one. There is little perceptible difference in the utterances—what issued from human mouths—of the first generation and the second. A "sickness" has to be uttered, put *into* words that bring to light a generative darkness. Ultimately, when the sickness resolves into birth, a different reading will become possible.

Rilke's advice to his poet friend resonates. "You must be patient as a sick man and confident as a convalescent; for perhaps you are both. And more: you are the doctor too. . . ." Perhaps we can say that the Israelites, even as they rebel and complain and express their deepest doubts, are somehow (latently) conscious of themselves as patient, convalescent, and doctor, too. If they *hear* their own utterances, if they are capable of that kind of attention, then a larger identity at least potentially becomes present. In imagination, they play all three roles. Or, to put it differently, if they can fully imagine the loving attention of the doctor, even in the moment of sickness, he becomes a live part of themselves.

In this sense, Moses records a fuller experience that encompasses both pain and birth, both mistrust and trust. Rilke again:

> We have no reason to mistrust our world, for it is not against us. Has it terrors, they are *our* terrors; has it abysses, those abysses belong to us; are dangers at hand, we must try to love them. . . . Then that which now still seems to us the most alien will become what we most trust and find most faithful.[46]

THE FIRST INTIMACY

"How long will they have no faith in Me?"—at the heart of the wilderness, God recognizes the core of dissolution, of *no-faith*. Mistrust of the world, of God's love, of the births yet to happen: this is the subject of the Book of the Wilderness.

What might serve as an image of faith, or trust, or, indeed, of love? Moses speaks for himself—and, obliquely, for the people—when, in the most powerfully imaginative moment in the narrative, he figures himself as a pregnant, then birthing, then suckling mother to his people.

Before we look more closely at this passage, however, I want to suggest that motherhood is the human reality that offers a vision of recovery from skepticism's annihilation of the world. Motherhood is an encounter with an other, who is both part of oneself and deeply unknown. Moreover, motherhood interrupts the continuities of life. Before and after birth, it shifts one's sense of self, exposing one to the absolute demands of the child. Something new erupts, transforming the surface of life. One is no longer, in any sense, at one with oneself. But this interruption has creative power, stripping away habitual structures.

The British psychoanalyst Christopher Bollas suggests that the mother is experienced by her infant as the source of cumulative transformations. This is made possible by the mother's ability to relinquish her familiar self and respond to the potential being of the child. Something, writes the British psychoanalyst Adam Phillips, "is unknowably evolving, as potential, between them. . . . The first intimacy is an intimacy with a process of becoming, not with a person." This intimacy has an impersonal quality that ignores the power difference between them and allows them to become "attuned . . . to what each is becoming in the presence of the other."[47]

If the Israelites, traveling and travailing in the wilderness, are to give birth to a divine light, the pulsations of their real experience are essential. The human pulse—tiny, insignificant in the larger scheme of things—is the sign of life. George Eliot describes the consciousness of one of her characters as "lighter than the smallest center of quivering life in the waterdrop, hidden and uncared for as the pulse of anguish in the breast of the tiniest bird."[48] But this "hidden . . . pulse of anguish" drums to the rhythm of life itself, even as it is manifested in larger historical moments. Here, in the pulsation, the impulses, compulsions, and repulsions[49] of human beings, terror and joy come into the world. In this personal/impersonal thrum of vitality, there is egotism and madness, the self at its most elemental.

In the wilderness, such pulsations reach us in the expressive cries and utterances of the Israelites. In this book, unlike the other books of the Torah, it is their voice that rings. This book is "their share in the Torah," as Sefat Emet puts it.[50] Their voice cries in the wilderness.

That voice, complex and often bewildered, holds at its heart Moses' most expressive cry to God:

"Why have You done evil to Your servant, and why have I not found favor in Your eyes, that You place the burden of this whole people upon me? Was I impregnated with this whole

people, did I give birth to it, that you should say to me, Carry
it in your bosom, as a wet nurse carries the suckling child—to
the land that You swore to its fathers?" (Num. 11:11–12)

In this passage of intimate fantasy, Moses imagines himself as
male wet nurse, nurturer, carrying the burden of the infant people, both before and after birth. It seems that he imagines this only
to reject its possibility. His questions are rhetorical, limning an
unthinkable thought: "Was I impregnated . . . ?"

And yet, at the same time, he is describing a possible reality, perhaps more real than the conventional kind. He gives voice—
incredulous, protesting voice—to his unimaginable *omen* role:
could he be the constant, dependable source of trust for his people? Acknowledging the ways in which this image defies belief, he
yet allows it expansive play. The "interruption" of motherhood ultimately appalls him; he defends himself against the madness it implies,
the dissolution of his being. In the end, he asks for death, rather than
suffer the loss of personal power, which is motherhood.[51] To *bear* life
means to relinquish some masterful force, some impervious sanity.

The voice with which Moses utters his death wish, like the
people's voice when they say, "If only we had died in the land of
Egypt . . ." (Num. 14:2), expresses the anguish of interruption. To
speak poetically is to release the voice that says nothing other than
itself. Unlike words that represent reality, this voice can express the
heights and depths of experience, like music and madness whose
work is to unwork the work.[52]

Like the woman in childbirth, Moses voices the "madness" of
labor, the way in which it will not be reduced to the avowals of sanity. There is a music to his utterance that takes us downward and
upward. The song that is consecrated is the larger work of writing
that is the Torah, which is called "the Song."[53] The "motherhood" that
interrupts this work punctures omnipotence. In this sense, Moses'
pulse beats to the same rhythm as that of his people. Something is
unknowably evolving between them.

In this book I adopt a "musical" strategy, in which I repeatedly circle back to certain key passages, rereading them in the light of the

immediate discussion. The biblical and midrashic words release spiraling meanings that gather with the movement of the narrative. This formal device seeks to express the double character of wilderness speech: the fatalistic litany of similar complaints, on the one hand, and the movement toward redemption, on the other.

Bewilderments

ONE

Flags in the Wilderness

TWO PERSPECTIVES

The book of Numbers is the narrative of a great failure. That is, at least, one view of the book. What should have been a brief journey from Mount Sinai to the Holy Land becomes a forty-year death march. The story of the Spies brings down God's anger upon the people; this divine anger, even when mitigated by Moses' prayer, is expressed in the decree of an *endless* journey: for this generation, its only end will be in the sands. Both before and after the catastrophe, the narratives of the book of Numbers center on the people's desire to return to Egypt, to undo the miraculous work of the Exodus. At their heart are speeches of complaint and lament, expressing a profound existential skepticism.

In direct contrast to this narrative is the narrative found in mystical and Hasidic sources. Here, the generation of the wilderness emerges as the generation of extraordinary spiritual experience, receivers of the Torah to the fullest extent, fed on miracles and nurtured directly by God: a generation of ecstatic faith. They are known as *dor de'ah*—a generation of *special knowledge*. The nineteenth-century Hasidic master Sefat Emet,[1] for instance, writes of the book of Numbers as a "celebration of Israel." Its true subject is the greatness of a people impassioned by God, human partners in an unprecedented conversation with Him. Where other books of the Torah are concerned primarily with God's acts or Moses' speeches or the lives of heroic individuals, this book gives voice to Israel herself.

Drawing on kabbalistic sources, the Hasidic master ignores the manifest narrative of the book—what we have called the "great failure." He depicts a people who transcend prudential considerations in order to follow God into the wilderness, and whose spiritual yearning comes to full expression in this book.

This view of the wilderness history may seem idealized, to say the least. But, I suggest, it invites us to a different kind of listening to the notorious *misspeakings* of the people, the many cries of distrust, lament, resentment, that issue from them throughout this book. It is these words that anger God: not rebellious actions but restless language. Is there a way to integrate this narrative of dark murmurings, of obsessive fantasies of return to Egypt, with Sefat Emet's celebration of a love-intoxicated wilderness discourse?

The question touches not only on the language the Israelites speak but on the very nature of human utterance. Who are these people? Who are we who listen to them? What effect does the cumulative trauma of slavery, of the miracles of Exodus, of the Revelation at Sinai, have on a nation that is beginning to speak?

COUNTING AND CATASTROPHE

The book begins with a census of the people. With ceremonious precision, the masses are tallied and choreographed for the march into the Land of Israel. Entry into the Land is imminent; the people are arrayed for battle. At the beginning of the book, this is the immediate future of the narrative.

The name of the book, therefore—in English (Numbers), in Latin (*Numeri*), in Greek (*Arithmoi*)—conveys just this memory of a moment of preparation for the fulfillment of God's grand narrative. In fact, this name is derived from the ancient Hebrew name *Chumash Ha-Pekudim*[2] (The Book of the Musterings). The people are counted twice, once at the beginning of the book and once toward the end (chapter 26). These two moments are thirty-eight years apart; and both, ironically, are in preparation for the imminent wars of conquest of the Land of Israel. Between these two moments, a whole generation dies. What separates the two moments of counting is a total shift in population.

The double census lends the Hebrew name a sinister cast. A book that begins in optimism shifts its meanings as the original generation is condemned to die in the wilderness. The obliteration of a generation is signaled by the numberings of *Before* and *After*. After the Sin of the Spies, God declared to Moses:

Your carcasses shall drop in this wilderness, while your children roam the wilderness for forty years, suffering for your faithlessness, until the last of your carcasses is down in the wilderness. You shall bear your punishment for forty years, corresponding to the number—forty days—that you scouted the land: a year for each day. Thus you shall know what it means to thwart Me. (Num. 14:32–34)

The two censuses, in effect, deal with two different populations, with no overlap between them:

These are the persons enrolled by Moses and Elazar the priest who registered the Israelites on the steppes of Moab, at the Jordan near Jericho. Among these there was not one of those enrolled by Moses and Aaron the priest when they recorded the Israelites in the wilderness of Sinai. For God had said of them, "They shall die in the wilderness." Not one of them survived, except Caleb son of Jephunneh and Joshua son of Nun. (Num. 26:63–65)

No one at all survives from the first census to the second. This statement is relentlessly repeated, leaving to the very end the two individuals who do in fact survive. Caleb and Joshua become a kind of afterthought, a gesture toward empirical accuracy. The repeated litany—*there was not one of those enrolled . . . not one of them survived*—intimates a tragic perspective. By the second census, the wilderness has reaped its total harvest of the dead, exactly as God had declared to Moses:

In this very wilderness shall your carcasses drop. . . . Your carcasses shall drop in this wilderness . . . until the last of your carcasses is down in the wilderness . . . in this very wilderness they shall die to the last man. (Num. 14:29,32,33,35)

The terror of the description encompasses precisely all those who had been so bravely counted in the first census. The double census intimates a great failure: an entire generation, with all its expectations, with the presence of God in its midst, with its tribal structures and its flags, has vanished into the sands. The book of Numbers is a narrative of great sadness, in which the *midbar,* the wilderness, swallows up all the aspirations of a generation—people who experienced the Exodus, the Revelation at Sinai, and the creation of a sanctuary for God.

As a collective, of course, the people of Israel continues. It is constituted by the young (under twenty) of the previous generation and by the new generation. In terms of sheer numbers, there has been no loss. Strikingly, however, there is no mention of births. In a sense, the apparent continuity only serves to emphasize the terror that is encompassed in this narrative. The living presence of *numbers* is transformed in the second census into the record of *absences* ("there was no person, no survivor . . .").[3] The tale of numbers, therefore, indicates both continuity and rupture, yielding an implicit narrative of catastrophe. In this sense, the book is well named Numbers, as though to indicate the tragic irony of altered expectations.

THE BOOK OF IN-THE-WILDERNESS

But there is another name for the book, Sefer Bamidbar, the Book of In-the-Wilderness. Awkward in English translation, this is its common Hebrew name; the word *Bamidbar* is simply the first usable word in the book. But the wilderness plays such a central role in the book: it is the great leveler, place of death, that which engulfs all these separate selves. Three times, God speaks of *"this* wilderness," conveying the uncanny horror of the place. All these carcasses will be referred to in later texts as *meitei midbar*—the dead of the wilderness.

The relation of the two names—Numbers and Bamidbar—creates a field of tension: between them, the failure of a great enterprise is positioned at the very heart of the book, in that physical and metaphysical space that is called *midbar.* The wilderness is more than context; it provides the tone and tension of a narrative of dying.

Once God's sentence has been spoken, all that remains for this generation is, in a sense, to die. One might even say that their main business is to die, to *complete the dying process:* ". . . until the last of your carcasses is down in the wilderness . . . in this very wilderness, they shall die to the last man" (Num. 14:33,35). The word *tom* (here translated "to the last man") is used twice to imply that a process is to be consummated. The journey of the people over these thirty-eight years has as its purpose its disappearance into the unmarked sands.

In ironic hindsight, the first census, its purpose, its inscription of individuals and their role in the nation—all this opens a narrative of *midbar,* in which the individual plays his role by dying. For only in the absence of this dying generation can a new and viable nation prepare once again to leave this wilderness and enter the Land.

What is this *midbar*? For that original generation of travelers, it was once intended as the transitional space between Egypt and the Land of Israel; now it has become something else—a clearing ground for the future. What can be said about the space that is to become a *dead end* for those who once embarked on a journey? Is this the very nature of the *midbar*—the unmarked surface on which no human trace is visible?

We remember previous and later references to "that great and terrible *midbar*." For instance, Jethro, Moses' father-in-law, makes his way from Midian "to Moses, *to the wilderness* where he was encamped, the mountain of God" (Exod. 18:5). Jethro's arrival in the camp is an arrival in the *midbar*. Rashi responds to the apparent redundancy ("We too know that Moses was in the wilderness!"), by reading Jethro's journey as a moral choice: "The text speaks in praise of Jethro, who was ensconced in all the glory [*kavod*] of the world when his heart moved him to leave for the wilderness, that place of void—*tohu*—in order to hear words of Torah."

The wilderness is the place of emptiness and void. Like the uncreated world, it lacks all *kavod,* all the density and structure of the settled world that Jethro comes from. What brings him on this strange journey—to a place where the human being is unknown and unhonored—is his heart's desire to "hear words of Torah." With such a wish, he will brave the voids of the *midbar*. Or, more strangely, perhaps this void is the only possible site in which his wish may be granted. Precisely in this silent, unmarked place, the voice of God will resound.

LANGUAGE IN THE WILDERNESS

Speech in the wilderness, *dibbur* in the *midbar* . . . The prophet Hosea
dreams of restored intimacy with his estranged wife, reconciliation
between God and his people: "Therefore, I will seduce her, lead her
through the wilderness—*ha-midbar*—and speak—*ve-dibbarti*—to her
heart" (Hosea 2:16). The word *midbar* is juxtaposed with *ve-dibbarti*:
wilderness and speech share the same root. But they are opposites:
this *midbar* lacks human markings, or human language. It is the non-
human space that Jeremiah speaks of: "They did not say, Where is
God who brought us up from the land of Egypt, who led us through
the wilderness, a land of deserts and pits, a land of drought and
darkness, a land no man had traversed, where no human being had
dwelt?" (Jer. 2:6)

The "land of deserts and pits" was once the site of one specific pit,
Joseph's pit, which his brothers explicitly describe as such: "Throw
him into *this pit which is in the wilderness*" (Gen. 37:22). Again, the reference to "the wilderness" seems redundant. Ramban elaborates on
Reuben's meaning: "That is, this pit is deep, so he cannot get out; and
it is in the wilderness, so even if he cries out no one will save him,
for no one passes by." This is a wilderness pit: the place where no
one passes by, as Jeremiah will later remind us. Human traffic avoids
such places. Joseph's cries will be forever unheard. The *midbar* is the
very world of such pits and such unheard cries.

It is this *midbar* that, at the heart of the Bamidbar narrative, will
swallow Korach and his followers. Since this rebellion probably
takes place after God's decree, it can be read as a kind of mise en
abyme, a concentrated dramatization of the thirty-eight-year pattern of unmarked disappearances into the sand. The cries of those
swallowed create panic in the rest of the people, who flee from
the horror of engulfment (Num. 16:34). The cries of the dying bring
them no aid; they serve only to stage the imaginative terror of such
spaces.

Dibbur ba-midbar—language in the wilderness: the paradox resonates strangely. The Sages go as far as to suggest that, in some sense,
the two—language and wilderness—are one: *Ein dibbur ella midbar*.[4]
The same midrash lists the divine gifts of the *midbar:* Miriam's well,
the Tabernacle, God's presence, the priesthood, royalty, and the

Clouds of Glory. And again: "One who makes himself like a wilderness, traversed by all—Torah is given to him as a gift."[5] Some essential link exists between this void place and the genius of language; here, God spoke to human beings and was acknowledged by them. Isaiah tells of it: "A voice rings out in the wilderness" (Isa. 40:3). And, again, Hosea: "I knew you in the wilderness, in a thirsty land" (Hosea 13:5).

Such knowledge in the wilderness is the drama recalled by the later prophets. But how are we to understand such a meeting of words and knowledge in a world of absence? For the wilderness *bewilders;* it undermines the very ability to speak, to know one's own experience. Its emptiness dwarfs the force of one's imagination. It is the burial site of the great enterprise of redemption that lies at the heart of this book.

"A fantastic effort has failed," the poet Wallace Stevens writes as he evokes a similar void: "We had come to the end of the imagination." But he, too, acknowledges, "Yet the absence of the imagination had / Itself to be imagined."[6] This secondary act of imagination, the attempt to behold the emptiness, "the nothingness that is not there and the nothing that is," requires a mind that Stevens describes elsewhere as "a mind of winter."[7] This snowman's mind is itself always making the world, however cold or blank. The plain sense of things is itself metaphorical, existing within a larger whole. The literary scholar Frank Kermode writes: "The imagination's commentary is a part of the text as we know it. . . . And the makings are themselves part of a reality more largely conceived. . . . The words of the world are the life of the world."[8]

The *midbar* evokes such an "end of the imagination," which has itself to be imagined. It is created in "a mind of *midbar*," which "beholds / Nothing that is not there"—that is, only what is there, beyond imagination and language, ". . . And the nothing that is"— where language creates the sound of silence, its "voice of nothing."

In *The Waste Land*, T. S. Eliot expresses his sense of the failure of poetry and of memory:

On Margate Sands
I can connect
Nothing with nothing.
The broken nails of dirty hands.

This failure to connect anything with anything is, in a sense, perfectly natural, is in fact *the* natural condition of man. The broken nails of dirty hands are a reminder of human labor in the world—the Egyptian slavery? The *midbar* is a starting place: *out of it,* language may emerge.

The *midbar* is the horizontal space, unbroken, unmarked. But out of it emerges Mount Sinai, bringing the people to a long standstill, while the living voice of God speaks and demands. From the *midbar,* too, emerges the Tabernacle, a human construction housing God's presence and voice. From here, the command comes to count the people. Here, six hundred thousand individuals are to be numbered in relation to their clans and tribes. In the end, these individuals, who constitute the structures of order and significance in the wilderness, will be defeated by the wilderness; one by one, to the last one, they will sink into the sands and vanish. In this world of *midbar*—where, in the end, *nothing counts*—how are we to think of the enterprise of *counting,* of creating significant connections and structures on the sand?

VANISHED GENERATION, VANISHED NARRATIVE

A new generation arises and, seamlessly, takes the place of the old. But just here is the strangest aspect of this book. In the "real world," the customary world of births and deaths that mark our trajectory through life, the movement of generations proceeds without operatic climax. Though particular deaths and births are significant to us personally, the replacement of the dying generation by the new generation is achieved gradually, over a long period.

By contrast, the biblical narrative emphasizes the forty-year period[9] as a critical time that has to run its course: the dying time of all adults of the dying generation. And yet the narrative that covers the thirty-eight crucial years after God's decree strangely conveys nothing of the experience of this period in real time. We are left to conjecture which chapters actually cover this time period—and at what point it ends.

Just as in real life, we might say, this text silences the narrative of the catastrophe of the generation. Not only the bodies of the dead vanish into the sands, therefore, but time itself. Thirty-eight years pass—but when? The decree is given in chapter 14, just nineteen days from the beginning of the book and the first census. The final chapters of the book (Num. 20:1–36:13) take place within the first five months of the fortieth year.[10]

Thirty-eight years apparently elapse within five chapters (which include the Korach rebellion and several laws). This foreshortened narrative structure generates a distinct unease in the reader. No time is allotted for this passage of time. No words specifically relate the sagas of dying. It is as though there is nothing to be said about this vanishing. If we are not alert to the dates offered by the text, we could remain unaware of the shift in populations that has occurred.

Silently, a generation slips downward. What has vanished is narrative itself. Those who had been counted, who, apparently, *counted*—the hosts of God—are untold as they disappear. It is only in the second census, as we have noticed, that two verses draw attention to total absence.

PRESENCE AND ABSENCE

Telling and counting are, of course, related; indeed, both involve *relating, recounting,* tallying, attending to loss and gain. Whenever God commands a count of His people, says Rashi, this becomes an expression of His love.[11] After historical crises, like the Exodus and sin of the Golden Calf, He counts in order to find out how many have survived; and when He comes to dwell among them, He likewise numbers them. God's love, it seems, is at its keenest in two opposite situations—in celebration and after catastrophe. Counting punctuates both presence and absence. It is a way of *paying attention*—for Rashi, loving attention—to the individual within society.

It is striking that the word *pakad,* which is used some twenty times to refer to the act of registering in the census, generates a larger field of meaning that includes paying attention, appointing, visiting, seeking, desiring, being interested, as well as depositing, committing, entrusting. At the same time, *pakad* refers to *absence;* it attends to a loss. For example, after the battle against the Midianites at the end of the book, the *pekudim*—those appointed to make the count of the survivors—report to Moses: "Your servants have made a check of the warriors in our charge, and *not one of us is missing* [*nifkad*]" (Num. 31:49).

The paradoxical meanings of *pakad* play off one another. This is Rashi's reading:

> *Lo nifkad:* no one is missing, as in Aramaic translation—*lo shaga*, which also means "not missing." So we find (1 Sam. 20:18): "if your seat is *empty* [*yipaked*]"—which means, if its usual occupant is missing.

A space has been left empty and the one who pays attention notices a gap. Rashi cites the story of Saul and David, where David's absence is remarked by Saul.

To count, then, is to tally, to tell, to recount those who are present and/or those who are absent, so that taking a head count may have its sinister as well as its gratifying significance. In celebrating what is present, one may encounter or even generate absence. Those who are counted in the first census are precisely those who are doomed to die in the wilderness.

On the words "Take a census of the whole Israelite community" (lit., "lift up the heads . . ."), the midrash comments:

> Why does it say this at the beginning of the book? Why precisely this expression, *Se'u et rosh*—"Lift up the heads"? Like a man who tells the executioner, "Take off his head"—that is, kill him, God speaks in ambiguous language: If they are worthy, let them rise higher—as we see [as Joseph told the butler], "Pharaoh will lift up your head and restore you to your position." But if they are unworthy, they will all die, as we see in the same story, "Pharaoh will lift your head from off you and hang you upon the gallows" (Gen. 40:13,19).[12]

This expression for counting lends itself to a double meaning: promotion or death. The proof texts point to the most striking example of this ambiguity, in the story of the butler and the baker, Joseph's prison companions, whose opposite fates are both indicated by this expression.

WHAT COUNTS?

In our narrative, too, the census opens up two possibilities. In being counted, the Israelites enter a field of promise and peril, for to count is to say *what counts*—that is, what fits, what matters, what belongs. It is to become part of everything that exists.

But it is also to notice "the nothing that is." In writing of "the mystery of human numbers," the essayist Annie Dillard reports a story about Ted Bundy, the serial killer: "After his arrest, [he] could not comprehend the fuss. What was the big deal? 'I mean, there are so many people.'" She also records an "unnerving fact: The human population of earth, arranged perfectly tidily, would just fit into Lake Windermere, in England's Lake District."[13] What Bundy is in fact saying is that there are *countless* people—why should a few more or less count? But to make his point, Bundy makes the futile gesture of counting.

In this way, throughout Dillard's book, she brings statistics to recount the dizzying relations of the individual with the world she lives in. She cites the figures released by the Hubble space telescope: "There are maybe nine galaxies for each of us—eighty billion galaxies. Each galaxy harbors at least one hundred billion suns. In our galaxy, the Milky Way, there are four hundred billion suns—give or take 50 percent—or sixty suns for each person alive." And again, "They say there is a Buddha in each grain of sand. . . . the universe 'granulated,' astronomers say, into galaxies."[14]

How can an individual count? The children of Abraham are to be like the sand on the seashore, or the stars in the heavens—these are the analogies that God makes in the course of His promises to the patriarchs. Numbers mean survival, power, blessing. But they also carry an undertow of melancholy, as each of us becomes a grain of sand, less than a speck among the immensities of the heaven. And yet, in the face of that granular reality, the prophet Isaiah cries: "Lift high your eyes and see: Who created these? He who sends out their host by count, who calls them each by name: because of His great might and vast power, not one fails to appear" (Isa. 40:26). A relation in which God names each star as He counts it is a relation of love, of appreciating its singularity.

As in English, the Hebrew words for counting and recounting are related: *li-spor* and *le-sapper* have the same root. To tell a tale is to acknowledge the value, the connection, in things. But how do we say what counts, especially in a *midbar* where nothing reaches out to mirror human desire?

The prophet Hosea touches on the issue of desire in the wilderness as he recalls the primal encounter of God and Israel: "I knew you first in the wilderness, in a land of great drought [*taluvot*]" (Hosea 13:5). This is the sole appearance of *taluvot* in the Scriptures; Rashi reads it: "In this context, this refers to a place [*tel*] where they desire [*ava*] all good things and find none." In keeping with this reading, Rashi reads the first part of the sentence: "I paid attention to know your needs and to satisfy them." Breaking up *taluvot,* Rashi understands the wilderness as the place of diffuse desires, which God acknowledges and fulfills. The tale that God tells of that time is a way of relating *what counts* for Him in that history, what He reads in it—which is precisely their unanswered/to be answered wilderness desire.

THE SCANDAL OF SKEPTICISM

However, in the book of Numbers, the question of counting in the wilderness acquires a singular paradoxical force. This is, I suggest, related to the larger question of skepticism that haunts the text. We hear in the people's voice a persistent tone that is variously called *massah, merivah, telunah, hit'onnenut*—complaint, quarreling, bewailing, a querulous ground bass—that, beyond its specific targets, speaks of a failure to fully know their own experience and speak it for themselves. They are possessed by a kind of chronic bewilderment. Their specific complaints convey a continual questioning whether *anything counts;* whether God's promise—or, more radically, whether language itself—applies to anything. It is as though the world given to them in the Exodus and at Sinai has in a sense abandoned them.

Stanley Cavell discusses the problem of skepticism as it figures in Shakespeare's *Winter's Tale,* in terms that will shed light on our exploration. Cavell writes: "I take us here to be given a portrait of the skeptic at the moment of the world's withdrawal from his grasp."[15] In Shakespeare's play, Leontes suffers, in the most dramatic form, from such a failure of knowledge. He cannot acknowledge his son as his own and condemns his wife to death for infidelity. He cannot be *certain* of his paternity and therefore cannot own his own child.

Of course, the biological connection between father and child is always, in a real sense, in question. For the skeptic, demanding certainty, hard evidence, there can be no full satisfaction. Leontes is tormented by his uncertainty. But his madness, says Cavell, is not simply "an ignorance but an ignoring, not an opposable doubt but an unappeasable denial, a willful uncertainty that constitutes an annihilation." This is "the portrait of the skeptic as a fanatic." More than that, Leontes "*wants* the annihilation that he is punished by." He cannot and will not be satisfied by merely human criteria of knowledge. "[He] *wants* not to count, not to own what is happening to him as his, wants for there to be no counting, which is to say, nothing."

Such a wish for there to be nothing—"the skeptic as nihilist"—is connected with his mad effort "not to count." "Counting implies multiplicity, differentiation. Then we could say that what he wants is for there to be nothing separate, hence nothing but plenitude." At base, the fantasy is the wish not to have been born, not to be mortal; Leontes wants no separation, no parturition, departures, partings. But life involves "seeing ourselves as apart from everything of which we are part, always already dissevered, which above all here means . . . that each is part, only part, that no one is everything, that apart from this part that one has, there is never nothing, but always others."[16]

Leontes's skeptical annihilation of the world carries him to sexual jealousy and the disowning of his child. To participate in bearing a child is to acknowledge one's wife as having a life beyond one's own, where "she can create a life beyond his and hers, and beyond plenitude and nothingness."[17]

For Cavell, the issue of paternity intimates the most personal experience of skepticism:

> I call skepticism my denial or annihilation of the other. . . . "How can I trust the basis upon which I grant the existence of the other?" . . . In the everyday ways in which denial occurs in my life with the other—in a momentary irritation, or a recurrent grudge . . . in a fear of engulfment, in a fantasy of solitude or of self-destruction—the problem is to *recognize* myself as

denying another, to understand that I carry chaos in myself. Here is the scandal of skepticism with respect to the existence of others; *I am the scandal.* [My emphasis.][18]

"I am the scandal": the skepticism that haunts the Israelite experience in the wilderness is, I suggest, of this order. It is a scandal of chaos and annihilation that is personal: that is, it is one we must recognize in ourselves. In the wilderness experience, the people cannot, perhaps will not, trust the basis on which they might acknowledge the Other, who is God, and who is at the same time all others. It is as though they can see or know nothing for themselves. In commanding a census, God asks them to account for the many others, to acknowledge that they count, to note their presences and absences. This is to take place *in the wilderness,* where skepticism undermines experience. The camp, numbered and ordered and bannered in tribal units surrounding God's Tabernacle, is to move through the wilderness as a gesture, precisely, of trust, of an almost flamboyant constancy and coherence. But how does this gesture affect the wilderness reality? How do the two realities meet each other?

SUSTAINING TRUST IN THE WILDERNESS

Addressing this encounter of skepticism and acknowledgment, the Torah uses the expression, "They observed God's mandate"— *ve-shamru et mishmeret*—a formula that occurs many times throughout the book of Numbers, usually with the meaning of observing, conserving, preserving. When applied to the Tabernacle, the root *sh-m-r* means "guarding," or "guard duty." It means guarding the Tabernacle from incursion by the people, and protecting the people from God's anger. When *mishmeret* refers to God, it means observing His prohibitions.[19] For instance, in Numbers 9:19, "They observed God's mandate" means resisting the desire to proceed on their journey until God gives His command: "And they did not journey on."

However, *shamar* is capable of more generative meaning. We remember, for instance, the story of Joseph's dream, which he relates to his father and his brothers. His father rebukes him for his absurd pretensions: "And his brothers were jealous of him, but his father *held the story in mind [shamar et ha-davar]*" (Gen. 37:11). On this, Rashi comments: "He waited in expectation for when it would come true, as in (Isa. 26:2), 'A nation that *keeps faith*,' and in (Job 14:16), '*Keep watch over my sin.*'"

Rashi elicits the dynamic implications of the root *sh-m-r*. He quotes texts in which the word comes to register *keeping faith*, the very movement that counters the "scandal" of skepticism. He notices the *future* implications of the word, the attention that is also an intention. In the midrash, indeed, Jacob is imagined as taking pen in hand and recording the date of the dream and its content: "I have seen things *me-mashmeshim u-ba'im*—gradually, slowly, gropingly moving toward realization."[20] He keeps an account of the dream, not only to preserve its memory, but to register the play of absence and presence in his mind. The fulfillment of the dream is at the moment unimaginable, but it is *feeling its way* toward him. He is vigilant, expectant, turned to past and future at once. In the French philosopher Maurice Blanchot's beautiful words, in a different context, he keeps watch over absent meaning.

Similarly, in the Zohar, the commandment to *keep—lishmor*—the Shabbat is interpreted as applying *mi-shabbat le-shabbat*. The Sabbath is not only to be observed, its prohibitions respected; to keep the Sabbath is to hold it in mind from one Sabbath to the next, in the in-between time of absence. This, again, is the intimation of the word *shamar*: to keep the Sabbath present in memory and desire.

To observe God's mandate in the wilderness, then, may imply: to be vigilant, actively absorbed in the future realization of a divine world not immediately present to the senses. It is to sustain a sense of trust in a relationship with the Other. The dual meaning of *shamar* covers a field in which guarding, preserving boundaries against encroachment, lives in fruitful tension with imaginative readiness for a future yet to evolve from the present.

THE DANCE OF THE CAMPS

At this point, we can turn back to the spectacle of the camp, arrayed in tribal order, representing meanings and intentions that defy skepticism—marching and camping at the word of God, covered by a cloud whose movements indicate His will. This human society with God at its center is marked by flags—a visual field of signs, colors, and shapes punctuating its massed blocs: "Each man by his flag, under the banners of their fathers' houses . . ." (Num. 2:2). According to Rashi, the colors correspond to the emblematic color of each tribe in the High Priest's breastplate.

If the first function of this display is preparation for battle, the flags nevertheless become in midrashic literature a vehicle of larger meanings:

> "Each man by his flag, under the banners": In allusion to this it is written, "Who is this that looks forth as the dawn, fair as the moon, clear as the sun, terrible as an army with banners. . . . ?" (Songs 6:10) Holy and grand were Israel beneath their banners! All the nations looked at them with rapt attention and wonder, thinking, "Who is this that looks forth. . . ." These nations said to them, "Return, return, O Shulamite. . . ." (Songs 7:1), "cling to us, come to us, and we will make you governors, generals, commanders, lieutenants, commanders-in-chief—Return, return, and we will look upon you!" "Look upon you" means "appoint you to power."
>
> Israel answers: "How will you 'look upon' the Shulamite? What grandeur can you give us? Can you give us the grandeur of the *dance of the camps,* such as God gave us in the wilderness, a flag for each tribe . . . ?" "How will you look upon the Shulamite? What grandeur can you give us? Can you give us the grandeur of the *dance of the camps,* such as God gave us in the wilderness, when we sinned and He forgave us and told us, 'Let your camp be holy'?"
>
> Even Balaam looked at them in resentment because he could not touch them, as it is said, "And Balaam lifted up his eyes. . . ." (Num. 24:2): this refers to the flags. He began speaking, "Who can touch these people, who know their fathers and their families," as it is said, "who dwell according to their tribes." From here, we learn that the flags [*degalim*] were grandeur [*gedulah*] and separation [*geder*] for Israel. That is why it is said, "Each man by his flag."[21]

The spectacle of the be-flagged hosts is shot through with the associations of the Song of Songs. The beloved woman has a terrifying beauty, *like an army with banners. Who is she?* Enigmatic, ferocious, she is Israel, who is "holy and grand." The nations are fascinated; they offer her all forms of worldly power, if only she will surrender her difference and "return" to them. Their blandishments fail to move her: what power can equal the grandeur of the "dance of the camps," the choreography of flags flying in the wind, each declaring an identity and a singular role in the collective destiny of the people?

The nations, for their part, wish to incorporate her, to clip the fierce wings that both attract and intimidate them. But she celebrates the grandeur of the wilderness, where *"we sinned, and He forgave us." Machal* means "forgiving"; but it also refers to the circle dance: the "dance of the camps" in the Song of Songs becomes a code for the profound wilderness experience that the people remember as the measure of grandeur and holiness. It is as though their very failures have moved them toward holiness, and as though any grandeur that the world may offer seems tawdry by comparison.

In the last passage, Balaam fixes his eyes upon the Israelites in hostile envy: "Who can touch these people, who *know their fathers and their families?"* The flags declare the confidence of each man that his world is knowable and may be represented with confidence in the emblems and colors of a collective identity. Playing with the consonants *g-d—degel, geder, gedulah* (flag, separation, grandeur)— the midrash captures the complex reaction (admiration? envy?) of Balaam to those who know themselves and their origins and their place in the world. The link with the past, "knowing their fathers," evokes the role of *trust* in the bonds of family and tribal identity.

Another midrash picks up the same theme—the nations' attempted seduction of Israel—this time using a different argument:

"That we may look upon you." The other nations say to Israel: How long will you die for your God and devote yourselves completely to Him?—as it says, Therefore they love you beyond death (Songs 1:3). And how long will you let yourselves be slain for Him?—as it is written, Nay, but for Your sake we are killed all day long (Ps. 44:23). And how long will you do good deeds for Him—for Him alone—while He requites you with evil? Join us, and we will appoint you governors, leaders, and generals. "And we will look upon you": as if to say, You will be the cynosure of the world—as it says, "And you will look out from among all the people" (Exod. 18:21).

Israel answers: "What will you see in the Shulamite, to compare with the dance of the camps?" Have you ever heard of Abraham, Isaac, and Jacob worshipping idols, that their descendants after them should worship idols? Our fathers did not worship idols, and we will not worship idols. And what can you do for us? Can you arrange such a dance for us as was provided for our father Jacob when he went out from the house of Laban? R. Berachia said in the name of R. Levi: Sixty myriads of angels danced and leapt before Jacob our father when he went out from the house of Laban.

Or can you arrange a dance for us like the dance that God will arrange for the righteous in the world to come? R. Berachia and R. Halbo and Ulla Bira'a and R. Eliezer b. Chanina said: In the future God will be at the center of a dancing circle of the righteous. . . . And they will point at Him in the center—as it is said, "For this is God our God forever. He will lead us beyond death [almut]" (Ps. 48:15). Also, in almut—in youthful agility, as in the dance of the righteous.[22]

On this occasion, the nations taunt Israel with its history of martyrdom. Their argument stages Israel's devotion to God as a historical folly. They attempt to rouse Israel's resentment, their *skepticism*—how is it possible to go on trusting the Other whose reactions are so unfathomable? The world that the nations offer is much more comprehensible.

But again, Israel answers with the "dance of the camps": those midrashic narratives of dancing camps of angels who celebrate the integrity of righteous fathers. That is, Israel celebrates its own grandeur in identification with, for instance, Jacob. What worldly grandeur can vie with this? The midrash culminates in the famous vision of the dance of the righteous in the world to come. Pointing fingers to the center, the dancers connect themselves to God, the part to the whole, periphery to center. These incomparable dancers—past and future—declare *what counts*.

In both of these midrashic tales of loyalty, the lure of skepticism is palpable. The nations appeal not only to the worldly ambition of Israel but to the "nihilism" that Cavell describes: the desire for certainty, for "nothing but plenitude." "We will look upon you—you will be the cynosure of the world, the center will be in you." But to be oneself the center is not to have been born, not to die. Through the imagery of the dance, Israel acknowledges that "each is part, only part, that no one is everything, that apart from this part that one has, there is never nothing, but always others."[23]

THE PROBLEM OF KITSCH

Balaam's envy of the Israelite camp focuses, essentially, on the trustworthiness of Israelite women—"Who can touch these people, who know their fathers and their families?" Their sexual purity is such that children can be confident of their fathers' identity.

Knowing one's father has always been a fraught issue. Only in the twentieth century have laboratory tests provided certainty on that score. But the question of paternity can be seen as *the* symbolic expression of the larger problem of the uncertainty of human knowledge. Human civilizations have had to find ways of living with this significant uncertainty. In the end, lineage is acknowledged—or not—on the basis of women's word or on the basis of *trust*, the underpinning of human society.

In these midrashic sources, the skepticism of the nations is related to their skepticism on the issue of lineage as well. Another midrash[24] is quoted by Rashi in his commentary on the second census, toward the end of the book:

> "The family of the Chanochites": Because the heathen nations spoke slightingly of Israel, saying, "How can these people trace their descent by their tribes? Do they think that the Egyptians did not master their mothers? If they mastered the bodies of the men, it is quite certain that they mastered those of their wives!" Because of this, God set His name upon them: the letter *Heh* on one side of their name and the letter *Yod* on the other side, to intimate: I bear testimony for them that they are the sons of their fathers![25]

Against the skepticism of the nations, God testifies by enclosing the name of the tribal father in His own name. Here, explicitly, the issue is the sexual purity of the women. The nations speak in the voice of a sophisticated knowingness: the Egyptian slavery, like all slaveries, obviously compromises the women who become subject to the domination of the master race. The claim to a pure, identifiable lineage is in this view wholly absurd.

In answer, God "wraps" His name around the clan name. In effect, this does not constitute hard evidence of the purity of the bloodlines. It is *testimony,* albeit divine testimony—made of words, letters, with all their associations. Belief still remains an issue: how does one know what, whom to trust? The woman's word, God's word: what is their valence in the face of the seductive nihilism of the nations?

From the concrete issue of biological paternity—knowing one's father, acknowledging one's son—we turn to the flags, those blazons of identity. In response to the Israelite celebration of relationship with past and future, between center and periphery, of grandeur (*gedulah*) and identity boundaries (*geder*), the nations invoke the reality of martyrdom, of a catastrophic history.

From their viewpoint, Israel's claim is absurd. It is, one might say, an example of what Milan Kundera calls *kitsch.* By this, he means the celebration of a self-indulgent sentiment that involves willful blindness to reality—like the improbable notion that the Israelite women resisted the sexual power of the Egyptians.

Kundera describes kitsch as the "aesthetic ideal" that "excludes everything from its purview which is essentially unacceptable in human existence."[26] Ugliness, filth is hidden from the gaze. "In the realm of totalitarian kitsch, all answers are given in advance and preclude any questions."[27] "[It] is a folding screen set up to curtain off death."[28] In *The Unbearable Lightness of Being,* Sabina, Kundera's heroine, goes so far as to hide the fact that she is Czech: "It was all merely a desperate attempt to escape the kitsch that people wanted to make of her life."[29]

Totalitarian kitsch is represented most grossly in the flags, the May Day parades—the fantasy of the Grand March: every display of individualism, every doubt, or irony, "must be banished for life. . . . In this light, we can regard the gulag as a septic tank used by totalitarian kitsch to dispose of its refuse."[30]

Through this lens of kitsch, what can we say about the "grand march" of the Israelites through the wilderness, "each man by his flag," laying claim to irreproachable ancestry, ignoring the realities of political and sexual domination? Do we have here yet another manifestation of what Kundera calls the "universal penchant" to kitsch? How does this celebration of grandeur and defined identity (*gedulah ve-geder*) respond to the cynical and skeptical voices from inside and out? What does it exclude? And to what septic (skeptic?) tank does it relegate the unthinkable?

Adam Phillips elaborates on the paradox of celebration and destruction. Perhaps rituals of celebration in fact often mask the destruction of memory? "Celebration, we can say—at least from a psychoanalytic point of view—is an ambivalent act pretending not to be one."[31] Quoting the German writer W. G. Sebald, Phillips asks, "What is there to celebrate, and what is it to celebrate, when 'confronted with the traces of destruction, reaching far back into the past'?"[32] Many moments in Sebald's work suggest that "our celebrations are dark reminders . . . as though the celebration itself is the registration of the forthcoming catastrophe."[33]

We are reminded of the ambiguities of celebration when we think of the first census in the book of Numbers—with its manifestations of coherence and identity, with its flags and its emblems bravely affirming pure bloodlines, with its "dance of the camps" embracing past and future. For no sooner are the formations of the hosts of Israel in place and the Grand March begins than catastrophe strikes. From these serried ranks, skeptical cries break forth, complaints, annihilations of the world. And these same numbered ranks are condemned to sink under the numberless sands. To count, then, to celebrate, may be to prepare for mourning, or for an absence so subtly effaced that it is never even mourned. It may be, as Phillips puts it, simply the prelude to horror.[34]

FAR FROM KITSCH

Midrashic texts elaborate unexpectedly on the implications of the flags:

> "He has brought me into the house of wine": When God revealed Himself upon Mount Sinai, twenty-two thousand

angels descended with Him, as it is said, "The chariots of God are two myriads, two thousands; God is among them at Sinai, in holiness" (Ps. 68:18), and they were all arrayed under separate banners, as it is said, "Marked out by banners from among myriads" (Songs 5:10). When Israel saw them arrayed under separate banners, they began to long for banners, and said, O that we also could be ranged under banners like them! Therefore, it is said, "He has brought me into the house of wine"—this refers to Sinai, upon which was given the Torah, which has been compared to wine: "And drink of the wine which I have mingled" (Prov. 9:5). So, "into the house of wine," is explained as referring to Sinai.

"And his banner over me was love": They said, "O that He would show great love for me!" And this is also expressed in, "We will shout for joy in thy salvation, and in the name of our God we will set up our banners." God said to them, "How you long to be ranged under standards! As you live, I shall fulfill your desire!"—as we read, "God shall fulfill all your petitions" (Ps. 20:6). God immediately informed Israel by telling Moses, "Go arrange them under banners as they have desired."[35]

These flags are the flags of desire. The tidal wave of love that sweeps through the people is aroused by the vista of angelic banners at Sinai. Inspired by angel-envy, they see these banners as the expression of a fine and selfless harmony. "If only we, too, could be ranged under banners like them!" Or, as the midrashic text literally reads, "If only we, too, could be *made of banners* like them!" Such unity of self and representation, such fierce clarity—if God would give them this, it would truly signify His great love of them. "His banner over me was love": God responds lovingly to their desire.

It is striking that the theme of desire (*ta'avah*) is generated by the word *otot* (signs, emblems) in the biblical text. "Each man by his flag [*b'otot*], under the banners of their ancestral house" (Num. 2:2). What is desired is the sign of full representation; to be significant, to belong, to fit harmoniously. God grants the human wish for an angelic transparency of meaning.

But this midrash raises troubling questions about such fantasies.

Or Ha-Chaim comments:[36] The people's desire is to surround God, to hold Him in their midst; "And I shall dwell among them" (Exod. 25:8) was God's assent to this desire. What reads in the biblical text as a commandment ("Let them make Me a sanctuary, and *I shall dwell in their midst*") becomes in the midrash an acknowledgment of an erotic desire, perhaps of an *unconscious* wish, that God should become a "sign in their midst."

The flags over the camp of Israel can be seen, then, as expressions of an intimate desire: to hold God at the center of one's being. After the Tabernacle is already in place, another emblem of this desire is instituted—the tribal formations, the flags—as though God's residence in the Tabernacle has not sufficed to banish a human ambivalence. The constant plenitude of God's presence cannot, it seems, be held by them. To preserve themselves from too much meaning, too much presence, the people need distance. And so they experience how the world withdraws from them. "The world," suggests Stanley Cavell, "must be regained every day, in repetition, regained as gone."[37] The yearning for more presence is every day recognized anew.

This desire for the flags, for a totally significant human world, then, cannot be satisfied by the simple presence of flags. For it carries a tragic dimension and, in that sense, evades the charge of kitsch. These flags are not emblems of ostentation; it is rather as emblems of desire that they rise in the air. What moves in the human heart is the knowledge of absence, death, sin, and forgiveness—the imminence of catastrophe.

The stakes are almost unbearably high:

"Each man by his flag": Thus it says, "We will shout for joy in Your salvation, and in the name of our God we will set up our banners" (Ps. 20:6). Israel said to God, "See, we are shouting with joy in *Your* salvation, for what you have done for us has been for *Your* name." So, "We will shout for joy in *Your* salvation"; as it is written, "God saved [*va-yosha*] Israel that day" (Exod. 14:30), where the text has *va-yivvasha*, "and God *was saved*": It was Israel that was being redeemed and, as it were, God Himself was being redeemed! ". . . and in the name of our

God we will set up banners"—for God has set His name into
our name and He has made us His flags," as it is said, "Each
man by his flag."[38]

To represent God is to celebrate His salvation—to celebrate being
saved by Him, as well as *saving Him*. To bear His name, to be His flag,
is not simply to be a container of holiness, but to be charged with the
future of His Being in the world. It is to live as a recurrent question,
acknowledging a lack.

The world of the wilderness gives time and space for that desire.
It involves long periods in which to "observe the mandate of God";
that is, to wait for God in a bad place—a place of "empty, howling
waste" (Deut. 32:10). Seforno[39] sees this capacity to "observe the mandate," to hold vigil, to remain responsive to the call of the future, as
the condition that Jeremiah describes so poignantly: "I remembered
in your favor the devotion of your youth, your love as a bride, how
you followed Me *in the wilderness, in an unsown land*" (Jer. 2:2). The
journey, with all its startlings, its many moments of recoil, when
God and His world withdraws from their grasp, is an act of trust.
The flags represent the imaginative life of a people who, in Maurice
Blanchot's phrase, keep watch over absent meaning.

This journey enacts the trajectory of a people who lose the world
repeatedly, and who therefore become frantic with questions. This
is not, then, a grand march, and its narratives take us to a place far
from kitsch. Perhaps we can say that Israel looks for a way to speak
its secret, for an idiom to express the complexity of its desires.

THE LEAP OF DESIRE

In this vein, Sefat Emet[40] revisits the midrashic sources we have
looked at, as well as the verse from Song of Songs: ". . . and His banner [*diglo*] over me was love." On this, the midrash[41] elaborates, playing with letters—*diglo/dilugo*—His banner, His *leaping*. Sefat Emet
invokes the *desire* to have flags like the angels, a desire that, we have
suggested, takes its cue from *otot*—signs, insignia. This desire is an
impossible yearning, which acknowledges its own impossibility.
Human beings clearly are not angels. But the yearning to be in an
"angelic" relation to God is itself what gains them those banners

(*degalim*), which constitute the "leap" (*dilug*) of desire. The angel fantasy is to be realized only in a momentary imaginative flash, desire closing that gap and love leaping toward its aim.

On one level, flags celebrate a world in which each person recognizes his own tribe and affiliates himself genetically with his past. On another level, we might understand this affiliation as an inner sense of connection with the fathers, going back to Abraham. "God said to Abraham, '*So* [*ko*] shall be your seed. . . . '" This should be read as a blessing: 'May your seed *resemble* you. . . . '" The flag, then, comes to celebrate not a simple and proper tribal grouping, but the spiritual act of identification with the father, the patriarch Abraham. To be "the seed of Abraham" is to remain connected, not to be alienated— to acknowledge one's inmost affiliation. It is a choice.

Sefat Emet quotes his grandfather, quoting R. Simcha Bunim of Psyshcha, who comments on the rabbinic aphorism: "One should always say, When will my deeds equal those of my fathers, Abraham, Isaac, and Jacob?" But who is so naive as to think that he can compare himself with the patriarchs? The aphorism means, however, that one should express a wish *not to be alienated* from the fathers, that one's life should have a *negi'a*—some *contact*—with their lives. In the same way, the signs, the insignia on the flags, express a yearning that one's life bear some intimation, some fleeting glimpse of affinity with their lives. This is the *leap,* the occasional (*lif'amim*) flash of desire that connects one with one's roots.

The flags with their emblems inhabit a universe of longing. In this universe, there is no given identification with the patriarchs or with the angels. Everything that is problematic in human existence is acknowledged at the outset: the distance between men and angels, between descendant and patriarch. Nevertheless, there comes the occasional throb of identification, some glimpse of connection. In this sense, the flags are made of desire, of questions, of absences. They are not folding screens to curtain off death, or doubt, or irony. The movement of desire is celebrated in all its ambiguity, by the flag, which is both *degel,* a visual manifestation of a presence, and *dilug,* a leap, an allusion to an absence. The whole Torah, writes Sefat Emet, is a complex of *hints,* allusions to the unattainable.

To leap is to leap *over,* to omit, to be suspended in midair. Unlike the grand march, the *dilug* expresses a short circuit, a kind of shock of contact. The image for longing is the flag, whose emblem flies, shifting shape, fluid in the wind.

In A. R. Ammons's poem *Sphere: The Form of a Motion*, the poet cannot find in nature an image for human longing, that is, "the image of myself." The image that he makes of mud finds no place in nature, which cannot answer its call. He must build a house for what only the human can recognize: that he is the scandal and the longing. His image for longing leaps free of "firm implication." It acknowledges death and finitude, uncertainty and failure, but transfigures them.

TRAUMA AND LONGING

The flags intimate, with their insignia, a realm "out of nature," where only longing can reach. These signs, the emblems on the flags, are called *otot*. Like letters—*otiyot*—they enigmatically evoke new worlds; they are the forms out of which meaning is composed.

The moment when a young child first learns his letters is a moment of true revelation. The Holocaust thinker and spiritual leader R. Kalonymus Kalman Shapira (known as the Esh Kodesh) addresses this moment.[42] The adult, too familiar with the shapes of the letters, will approach them with less imaginative excitement. Few adults are privileged to sense the wonder of the letters themselves; it is children who are inspired to reveal mysteries within their shapes. Indeed, says R. Shapira, only one who is learning something new can be said to be learning directly from God.[43] In the Talmud, Rebbe says, ". . . I have learned most of all from my students."[44] One's student is the source of the greatest revelations, simply because what he is learning is new to him, and therefore he is *being taught by God*. Similarly, when one relearns Torah that one has already learned, one should learn something new from it, so that God is again given the opportunity to be the teacher.

The real subject of this Book of the Wilderness, I suggest, is the longing of the people of Israel to learn directly from God, by learning something new about the Torah, about the world and themselves. What they are developing in their skeptical discourse is a language of imaginative truth, in which the fantasies of return to Egypt will be brought into connection with the miracles of Exodus. In them, traumatic suffering and traumatic revelation seek some subjective expression. The achievement of personal utterance, in a reality of *bewilderment,* is the contribution of Israel to the Torah. This book, unlike all other parts of the Torah, is made of the people's utterances, its longing to converse, however obliquely, with God.

ROUSING THE DORMANT ANGEL

In a time of catastrophe,[45] R. Kalonymus is preoccupied with the question of faith. In another passage,[46] he quotes the prophet Malachi: "The lips of the priest shall guard knowledge and Torah they shall seek from his mouth, for he is the angel of the Lord of Hosts" (Mal. 2:7). The Talmud[47] comments: "Only if the teacher resembles an angel of the Lord of Hosts should one seek Torah from his mouth." With this principle in mind, R. Kalonymus turns to another Talmudic anecdote:[48] "This was the custom of R. Yehuda b. Illai: On the eve of the Sabbath he would have a bowl of hot water brought to him and [after bathing] he looked like an angel of the Lord of Hosts."

Reading with apparent naïveté, R. Kalonymus finds a conflict between the two Talmudic sources: if R. Illai resembled an angel on the eve of Sabbath when he finished his ablutions, then how could his students learn from him on the other days of the week, when, presumably, he did not resemble an angel of the Lord of Hosts? From the immediacy of his own experience, R. Kalonymus provides a new understanding: If the teacher never resembles an angel, we should not learn Torah from him. However, if the teacher does not always resemble an angel, but only does so *lif'amim,* from time to time, we should still seek Torah from his mouth, even during the times he does not resemble an angel. In fact, precisely when he *does not* resemble an angel, we should seek Torah from him, so that the angel within him, which is dormant, will reveal itself. Without the demand of the student, the angelic potential of the teacher may fade away.

FROM TIME TO TIME

In this beautiful passage, R. Kalonymus confronts his own spiritual anguish, as his "angelic" potential disintegrates in a time of catastrophe. His anguish is about the survival of both his people and the Torah. What keeps Torah alive, he implies, is the desire of those who long for the angel of the Lord of Hosts to speak to them. The teacher needs the student's desire. His lips "guard [*yishmeru*] knowledge": that is, his lips wait and wish for knowledge to be revealed. This can happen only if the student draws out what seems to be gone. In the face of destruction, the teacher holds open a sense of a possible future, which the student, *from time to time,* recognizes in the teacher's face.

That flickering presence/absence of the angel face is the redemptive potential of *lif'amim*—from time to time. *From time to time* might seem to make a pitifully weak claim. But, like the leap, the *dilug,* of transcendence that the midrash discerns in the flag (*degel*), *from time to time*—*lif'amim*—represents a profound dimension of human experience. Evoking the human heartbeat (*p'imah*), *lif'amim* gestures at the sporadic nature of human desire-time. Sometimes, the pulse throbs faster, misses a beat, a syncope is experienced, and connections are made with the unattainable.

The story is told of R. Arye Levine who was once asked, "Are you one of the thirty-six hidden Righteous Men?" He answered, *"From time to time,"* thus avoiding both skepticism and kitsch and hoisting aloft, in the wilderness, the banner of desire.

TWO

Madness and Civilization

TWO NARRATIVES OF WOMEN

The first narrative of Sefer Bamidbar is the painful case of the Sotah. This is a legal narrative, describing the fate of the woman whose loyalty to her husband is in question. The Sotah has provoked distrust and doubt: she is subjected to a "trial" that is to resolve the suspicion that hangs over her.

At the end of Sefer Bamidbar, another legal narrative also tells of women, five sisters, who claim their right to inherit their father's land, in the absence of male heirs. One might say that the book is framed by the feminine; that women provide the armature for this Book of In-the-Wilderness.

The two stories are of course very different. The five sisters—the daughters of Tzelofchad—make their appearance against the background of a second census of the people. The Torah comments:

> Among these there was not one of those enrolled by Moses and Aaron the priest when they recorded the Israelites in the wilderness of Sinai. For God had said of them, "They shall die in the wilderness." *Not one of them survived,* except Caleb, son of Jephunneh, and Joshua son of Nun. (26:64–65)

"Not one survived": in the face of this absolute statement, Rashi cites a remarkable midrash:

> However, the decree against the Spies did not apply to women, because they loved the land. The men said, "Let us appoint a leader and return to Egypt" (Num. 14:4); while the women said, "Give us possession among our father's brothers" (Num.

27:4). This is why the episode of the Daughters of Tzelofchad is placed right after this.[1]

Rashi reads the word *ish*—"*no man* survived"—as applying only to men, as opposed to women. In this gendered reading, *ish*, twice used in two verses, becomes the basis for a large historical claim: women in the desert were distinguished by their love for the land and were therefore not punished; they survived the forty-year desert period. Only men sinned in the narrative of the Spies. Women are traced as a hidden population possessed of a separate life of desire, and a separate destiny. Invisible in the text, they represent a continuous presence within the narrated history of rupture.

This unperceived Other, the female population, enters the narrative by way of the midrash. Rashi credits women with being radically different from the male population: instead of hankering to return to Egypt, like the generation of the Spies, they "love the land [of Israel]." Immediately after this follows the narrative of the daughters of Tzelofchad: five sisters claim their right, in the absence of male heirs, to inherit their father's share in the land. In support of his claim about women's love of the Land, Rashi connects the two passages: the women in the latter narrative enact the very love of the land that Rashi has claimed for women in general.

These five sisters' claim is not only accepted: it is met with God's resounding words of praise: "The daughters of Tzelofchad speak *ken*—rightly, fairly, solidly, justly—*beautifully*."[2] For the first time in the book of Bamidbar, the Book of In-the-Wilderness—whose main issue has been the issue of *dibbur*, of speaking and misspeaking—for the first time in that forty-year chronicle of unhappy human forays into the realm of language, God congratulates human beings on the felicity, the aptness of their words. Rashi picks up on the celebratory tone of God's compliment:

"Rightly—*ken*—the daughters of Tzelofchad speak": As the Targum translates, "Fittingly, beautifully": Just so is this episode written before Me on high. This tells us that their eye saw what Moses' eye did not see. . . . *Fairly, beautifully* they have laid their claim. Happy the person whose words God acknowledges!

These sisters have a passion that inspires them to the first *happy*—blessed—use of language in the wilderness narrative. In the midrashic reading, this moment manifests a singularly *feminine* love. It brings to the surface an underlying history of women in the wilderness, which is linked to the hidden phenomenon of female survival, to the continuity of the generations that the midrash intuits, against the grain of the Torah's statement of rupture: "No man survived. . . ." The midrashic inflection allows us to hear what is at first inaudible: an absolute statement gives way to a nuanced, differentiated one. Suddenly, women emerge in the narrative.

Or perhaps women *reemerge*. The Sotah, the woman suspected of adultery, counterbalances the five sisters. If beauty and harmony is the subject of their narrative, here the narrative is a humiliating and repulsive one. The sin of which the Sotah is suspected, as well as the procedures that she undergoes, are demeaning. She is publicly shamed and, if guilty, divinely punished: her body dissolves, her reproductive organs fail her, she dies a death that manifests her guilt to all the world.

With all the obvious differences between these two narratives about women, I suggest that they provide a framing structure for the book. Both involve women who, by their very existence, raise a question, an uncertainty, that holds subversive implications. The five sisters articulate the injustice of their legal situation and are congratulated by God. The Sotah, on the other hand, representing an intolerable uncertainty that can be resolved in no other way, is brought to the Temple and subjected to the rituals that will determine her future fate. Except for one moment, when she gives verbal assent to the oath formulated by the priest—"Amen, Amen!"—she is silent throughout.

Her passivity and her muteness are highlighted by significant words that link the two narratives. Strikingly, the story of the five sisters begins with the verbs *Va-tikravna. . . . Va-ta'amodna* (Num. 27:1,2)—"They approached. . . . And they stood. . . ." In the unusual feminine plural form, these verbs describe a posture, an approach, even before we hear them speak. They imply courage, risk, exposure before the highest court of the people.

"They drew close," suggests a movement toward the sacred, which treads a fine line between approach and encroachment. Throughout Leviticus and Numbers, the verb is used for sacrifice, for the desire to approach the sacred, as well as for the dire consequences of inappropriate approach. Nadav and Avihu, Aaron's sons, die of that movement. Many of the laws at the beginning of the book of Numbers deal with the risks and penalties of *coming-too-close*. *Ha-zar ha-karev yumat*—"The encroacher shall be put to death" (Num. 1:51; 3:10,38; 18:7). The risks of heat exposure are great. But these sisters *stand*— they *stand in the face* of the male dignitaries of their people, they *stand* the pressure, they *stand for* a personal vision of justice that God then corroborates: "Their eye saw what Moses' eye did not see."

The Sotah, too, is described by means of the same verbs. The priest *brings her close,* and he *stands her* in the presence of God—in the courtyard of the Tabernacle. In the same site as the five sisters, the Sotah is, however, the passive *object* of the priest's action. Unlike the five sisters, she has no agency: it is the priest who sets her in her position of exposure and risk. Unlike them, too, she is silent. But these verbs are, in fact, repeated in her narrative (Num. 5:18,25) among other causative verbs that deepen the sense of her object status: twice, the priest is said to "make her swear" (5:19,21); twice, to "make her drink" the bitter waters (5:24,27). She is subject not only to the priest's actions but also to her husband's, who "brings" (5:15) her to the Tabernacle.

Until the moment of the oath, she says nothing and does nothing. Her one moment of action, which precipitates the actions of others, is the moment of disgrace: she *"goes astray"*—*tisteh* (Num. 5:12)—thus earning herself the name Sotah. But even this moment is set in the context of her husband's perspective and his uncertainty: *Ish ish,* the narrative begins—"If any man's wife goes astray . . ." This impression is deepened by the doubled expression: *Ish ish.*

Here, again, is a striking analogy with the narrative of the five sisters. In both cases, the female story is prefaced by a reference to the male. In the case of the daughters of Tzelofchad, an unexpectedly gendered reading yields a new focus: five women emerge from the shadows of a generalized *ish . . . ish* scene (Num. 26:64–65), in which the male is obliterated ("No man survived"). The Sotah, on the other hand, fails to emerge: she is absorbed in the agency of her husband and of the priest. It is as though the story is not, essentially, about her at all. She is a silent, manipulated figure—a kind of puppet, speech-less, uncertainly alive—in the narrative of others.

In this strange grouping—the Sotah and the five sisters—there is another link. The sisters protest a situation in which their father's name is endangered (Num. 27:4). They are grieved at the loss of meaning, of continuity, in the family's history: at the "diminishing" of their father's name. The procedure to which the Sotah is subjected climaxes in the ritual of drinking water in which is dissolved the Name of God (the ink of the written inscription of His Name). This essential element in the Sotah ritual also represents a loss of sacred meaning, a de-constitution or disintegration. Only in this way, it seems, can the truth of the Sotah's situation emerge.

ORDEALS

In this chapter, I want to discuss some of the implications of the Sotah narrative. Two female narratives, I suggest, structure cen-tral motifs in the book of Numbers. The movement from the first to the second registers the turbulent history of the people in the wilderness.[3]

Perhaps the most important feature of the Sotah episode is its ambiguity. The situation of the husband, the apparent subject of the passage, is one of *doubt:* either his wife is guilty or she is innocent. The two opposing scenarios are enacted in the opening verses: either she has, in fact, committed adultery—unwitnessed, undetected—and the husband's jealousy is justified, or else his jealousy is unjus-tified. Only in this situation, where her guilt or innocence can be decided in no other way, does the Sotah ordeal take place. In this case, divine aid is sought, and the general principle that issues are to be decided by due process, by witnesses and majority rulings, is, in this exceptional case, set aside.[4]

The husband's jealousy is clear, although its trigger is ambiguous. In the biblical passage, indeed, it seems that he need give no good reason for his jealousy. And yet, the text begins with the unambig-uous statement, "Any man whose wife has gone astray . . ." Why is she referred to as "gone astray," if that is yet to be ascertained? The Talmud reads this to imply that the wife must be in some way seri-ously compromised from the outset. Her relationship with another man has aroused her husband's concern, and he has warned her, in the presence of two witnesses, not to be alone with that man. In the presence of witnesses, she then meets him in private. This is the situation that, in rabbinic law, requires the husband to bring his wife to the trial by ordeal, which will resolve his doubt.

What cannot in this case be ascertained by testimony is what has transpired in that privacy. The Sotah ritual is an extralegal device instituted to put an end to a tormenting, in fact an untenable situation.[5] In rabbinic law, only if both husband and wife are interested in restoring the marriage is the ritual performed. Either partner may opt out and accept the option of divorce. The doubt that moves the husband concerns his intimate interests, and his jealousy is taken seriously by the Torah and society.

The Rabbis, in their complex elaboration of the Sotah ordeal, emphasize that the crime of adultery is a sin against God, as well as against the husband. Playing on the doubled *ish ish* of the opening, Rashi reads: "This teaches you that she betrays two 'men'—the 'man of war' on high, and her husband below."[6] The woman has broken faith with her husband and with her "other" *ish* above. The double betrayal reflects the fact that the expression *ma'al*—betrayal— usually refers to offenses *against God:* idolatry, violating oaths, and ritual sins.[7] Here, the two "men" she has betrayed bring her to the ordeal: her husband and the priest, who represents God.

It is interesting to notice the ways in which the Sotah ritual is similar to and dissimilar from judicial ordeals recorded in the ancient Near East. The water ordeal in Middle Assyrian texts provides the punishment as an integral part of the test, in which the victim was thrown into the water: if guilty, he sank; if innocent, he floated. The Sotah ordeal, too, provides that the punishment is built into the ordeal.

Ordeals of this kind, in which the verdict comes from God, are common in other cultures—in medieval Europe, for instance. They were practiced in England until 1818; and they are still practiced among the Bedouin and in West Africa, south of the Sahara.[8] Often, they involve suffering and injury—boiling water, scalding metal: if the injuries heal well, the victim is innocent. Sometimes, as with the Sotah, they involve harmless substances—like water. Here, guilt manifests in physical injury. In this case, the guilty verdict is a *mirac-*

ulous act, as injury is not inherent in the substance of the ordeal. The injury, moreover, is unequivocal, requiring no priestly interpretation.

Because the guilty verdict is miraculous, the innocent victim has no reason to fear the water. Only if she is guilty—and if she believes in the miracle—will she recoil from drinking and confess her guilt. If she is innocent, this reduces the factor of suggestion, or of sheer terror leading her to confess, or even inducing in her the symptoms of guilt.

PLAUSIBILITY STRUCTURES

This miraculous aspect of the ritual is at the heart of a striking discussion by Ramban (Num. 5:20). This ritual, he writes, is unique in the whole Torah precisely because it calls upon a miraculous sign from God, in place of juridical process. Uncertainty in the private life of the individual couple is to be clarified by an institutionalized miracle. This is to be understood, however, as answering to a national, public requirement: the safeguarding of the holiness of the nation. As such, it should be taken as a measure of the high moral stature of the people; it is a "sign of honor for Israel."

In support of his approach, Ramban cites the mishnah in Sotah that describes the end of the Sotah practice in an age when adultery became commonplace.[9] In Talmudic law, as Ramban goes on to describe, if the husband is guilty of similar adulterous relationships, the Sotah process is disabled. If this phenomenon becomes widespread, the deterioration in the moral climate of the people makes the Sotah ordeal meaningless.

On this reading, the effectiveness of the bitter waters is related to the *exceptional* nature of the situation, to a high baseline of spiritual health. In a cultural world where adultery is an unequivocal taboo, the practice of the ritual becomes a "sign of honor." Where the taboo has lost its force, an exquisite attunement to holiness has been lost and the ordeal's high import likewise becomes unappreciated.

At the center of his understanding, Ramban places the condition of the culture. The mishnah in Sotah implies that, in this case at least, religious belief and practice are linked to the social mores and practices of the group. As the philosopher Peter Berger puts it, in his far-ranging analysis in *A Rumor of Angels,*[10] it is the "plausibility structures," the "conversational fabric" of the group that ultimately determines its religious life.

In this important book, Berger discusses the significance of the sociology of knowledge for religious faith. He explores one of the basic suppositions of the sociologist Karl Mannheim's study of "the relationship between human thought and the social conditions under which it occurs. . . . The plausibility, in the sense of *what people actually find credible,* of views of reality depends upon the social support these receive. . . ." (emphasis mine). Social processes "manifest themselves as psychological pressures within our own consciousness. . . . It is in conversation, in the broadest sense of the word, that we build up and keep going our view of the world. It follows that this view will depend upon the continuity and consistency of such conversation, and that it will change as we change conversation partners."[11]

I suggest that in the mishnah, and in Ramban's use of the mishnah, such a view is implicit. In a social "conversation" in which adultery has become commonplace, the Sotah ritual is no longer practicable. A social process of desensitization has brought the individual to a point where the institutionalized miracle, the "sign of honor," has become meaningless—in the same way as, Ramban writes, it would always have been for other cultures.

The same principle is at work, even to the phrasing, in the following mishnah:

> When worldliness became commonplace, law became distorted and behavior corrupt. . . . When favoritism in court became commonplace, "Fear no man, for judgment is God's" (Deut. 1:17) ceased to apply, and "You shall not be partial in judgment" (ibid.) no longer held sway, and the yoke of Heaven was broken off, and the yoke of human beings replaced it.[12]

The mishnah describes a changed world of mores that affects the validity of biblical injunctions. If the bitter waters "cease" when taboos are no longer observed, if biblical verses likewise "cease" (*batel, passak*) when social behavior has deteriorated, then traditional values no longer subjectively exert pressure; the people no longer find them credible. As Ramban is at pains to emphasize, this does not in any way mitigate the gravity of the sin of adultery, or of corruption in the legal process. And yet, in the light of the latter passage about judicial corruption, one might say that the force of the biblical injunctions themselves has "ceased." God's word has become in some sense irrelevant. The subjective and the objective aspects of this change are not totally separable. These biblical words and rituals speak in a foreign tongue to a new breed of men. The law has lost both its deterrent and its persuasive power.

MAD OR WAYWARD?

What is the position of the Sotah herself in the traditional context in which, exclusively, the ritual applies? The very term "Sotah" reveals a peculiar ambiguity. It refers both to the woman who is under suspicion of adultery and specifically to the woman who has undergone the ordeal and been found guilty. As Rashi explains the word, it carries two quite different meanings:

> Our Rabbis have taught: "Adulterers never sin until a spirit of madness enters into them, as it is written of the Sotah, '*ki tisteh*—if she becomes mad [*shotah*]'"; and so, too, of him [the male adulterer] Scripture writes, "Whoever commits adultery with a woman has lost his wits" (Prov. 6:32). But the plain sense of the verse is that *ki tisteh* means: if she deviates from the path of modesty and becomes suspect in his eyes.[13]

In the first reading, derived from the midrash,[14] the Sotah is the bearer of a "spirit of madness." Otherwise, her act would be unthinkable. In order to read it this way, the Rabbis notice that the biblical word is, unexpectedly, spelled with a *shin*, from the root *sh-t-h*, which refers to madness, folly, craziness. In the second reading, *ki tisteh* is read in accordance with its sound, as derived from the root *s-t-h* with a *sin* or, more commonly, a *samech*—to deviate, be wayward, go astray. The woman has deviated from social norms of modesty; she is on a slippery slope that may already have brought her to full adultery.

Two different understandings of adultery are implied. In the first reading, the adulterous act is described as an act of madness, an incomprehensible loss of sanity; she is "out of her mind," she is "possessed." This is the *crime passionnel* that in French law traditionally constituted grounds for leniency. Such an offense is so unfathomable to the normal mind that it is to be situated in the *beyond* of madness.[15]

Such a diagnosis of the Sotah conveys the fear that such taboo acts arouse in normative society. One social strategy is to expel the transgressor to some barely human hinterland of insanity. The Rabbis here see an otherness that they define, perhaps in accordance with contemporary ideas about mental illness, as the invasion of "a spirit of madness." But if she is indeed possessed by such a demonic spirit, if she is, in modern terms, clinically insane, is she responsible for her own acts?

In the other reading, the "slippery slope" interpretation, the Sotah remains responsible; self-control is always possible. If she had not "deviated," she would not have reached this point. However, this rational perspective, although it preserves the sense of responsibility, loses an aspect of the situation that is clearly important to the Rabbis. Its very rationality obscures the madness of illicit passion, the otherness of what the Sotah represents—which opens up difficult questions about moral responsibility. Commonsense interpretations of the text and of the act are in tension with the mad truth of a reading that elides Sotah and *shotah*.[16]

If, at the moment of sin, the Sotah has become fundamentally irrational, then she has, in a sense, become a stranger to her daylight self. At that moment, she has been "entered" by a spirit of madness; she is invaded by external forces that are, strangely, now internal to her, acting through her. For society, she now represents the unthinkable, the terror of human permeability to momentary gusts of passion.

SEEING THE SOTAH

Immediately following the Sotah narrative, the law of the Nazirite is introduced. Rashi quotes the Talmud:

> Why is the section dealing with the Nazirite placed in juxtaposition to the section dealing with the Sotah? To tell you that he

who has once seen a Sotah in her disgrace should abstain from wine, because it may lead to adultery.[17]

The link between the two sections is a moment of *vision:* seeing the Sotah in her disgrace should bring one to swear off alcohol. The visual impact of her degradation is so unsettling that one should take preventive measures to ensure that one never comes to such a pass. Since drunkenness makes one lose control, we have here an eminently rational solution to the problem of prevention.

On the other hand, this advice may represent just that defensive approach that characterizes the "slippery slope" view of adultery. Perhaps there is something about the image of the Sotah's transformation that raises truly terrifying questions. What came over her? The disgrace that Rashi refers to—*kilkul* in Hebrew—implies damage, ruin, spoiling, disintegration. Revulsion at the sight of such degradation may lead one to deny that something more radical may be at stake than a concrete behavioral decision. If staying sober will prevent such transgressions, one can still live in a reassuringly simple moral universe. If, however, such "disintegration" is the effect of a "spirit of madness," then no preventive caution may suffice. In such a universe, the observer becomes as vulnerable as the woman he observes. The intoxication that brings a human being to such a pass may be of a less easily preventable kind.

What then lies at the heart of the peculiar tension that the Sotah inspires in those who witness her in her "ruin"? Beyond and through the shame of the public ritual—the disarrangement of her clothes and hair, the lowly barley offering—what is the inner experience, the particular "ruin," of the Sotah?

In the book of Proverbs, adultery is described in terms that intimate the uncanny core of the act, the blank at its heart. Her act is not only unknown to society but it is essentially unknowable, perhaps even to herself:

There are three things which are too wonderful for me,
Yes, four which I know not:
The way of an eagle in the air;
The way of a serpent upon a rock;
The way of a ship in the midst of the sea;

And the way of a man with a young woman.
So is the way of an adulterous woman;
She eats, and wipes her mouth,
And says, "I have done no wickedness." (Prov. 30:18–20)

The writer is baffled by "three or four" phenomena. Clearly it is the fourth enigma—the "way of a man with a young woman"—that most mystifies him. Adultery, it turns out, is the true subject of his meditation. The eagle, the snake, the ship may seem to move in unpredictable ways. But the adulteress arouses a larger sense of "wonder" about human sexuality, its strange separateness from the sane world of consequences. Suddenly, the writer gives us a vividly physical account of the insouciant gesture of the adulteress that wipes away any record of her act. The mouth that has eaten now becomes the mouth that denies the meal.

In illicit passion, something is staged that inhabits all human sexuality—a blurring of consciousness. With some plausibility, the adulterous woman may remove all traces of her act; in the daylight world of language, the acts of darkness can be effaced. Indeed, Ibn Ezra reads acutely: she wipes away the traces, so that *she will not know* that she has eaten.

For Ibn Ezra, it is unfathomable that adulterers have no "fear of God." How do they dispose of their own awareness of sin? Perhaps this sin can take place only if consciousness and memory are somehow obliterated. This is the sin of darkness, of essential secrecy, secret even to oneself. The main purpose of removing the traces is not to deceive others but to erase the act from body and mind.

DISSOCIATIONS

Several midrashic passages speak of the traumatic aspect of adultery:

"The eye of the adulterer waits for the twilight, saying: No eye shall see me" (Job 24:15). The adulterer says: No one knows about me. But God's eyes roam through the whole world and He says: "Can anyone hide himself in secret places that I shall not see him? says God. Do I not fill heaven and earth? says God" (Jer. 23:24). This is the way of sinners: they wait for the hour of darkness, the hour of twilight, so that no one will see them. And so it is said, "The eye of the adulterer waits for the twilight." Similarly, thieves wait for the hour of darkness, as it is said: "In the dark they dig through houses" (Job 24:16). So too it says, "Woe unto them that seek deep to hide their counsel from God, and their works are in the dark" (Isa. 29:15).

Hard is the case of the adulterer and the thief who remove God's presence as it were! For God fills the upper and the lower worlds, as it is said, "Do I not fill heaven and earth?" (Jer. 23:24). And in the place where they come to commit adultery or to steal, God's glory is there, as it is said, "The whole earth is full of His glory" (Isa. 6:3). *But the adulterer says, Remove Yourself and give me space for a moment! This thing is extremely hard, as it were. But He is long-suffering, and He gives them space for a moment. . . ."*

"Can anyone hide himself in secret places?" (Jer. 23:24). This can be compared to an architect who was also the tax collector of the realm. People began to hide their silver and gold in secret places. The architect said to them, I built the state and I made those secret places. Can you really hide from me? So God said to adulterers, Are you hiding yourselves from Me? "Can anyone hide himself in secret places?" I created you, and I made you full of secret cavities, as it is said, "You forgot the God who brought you forth" (Deut. 32:18). What is "the God who brought you forth—*me-cholelecha*"? It is the God who made you *mechilim mechilim*—full of cavities! You cannot hide yourselves from Me. Why? "I God search the heart, and I probe the kidneys, to give every man according to his ways, according to the fruit of his doings" (Jer. 17:10).[18]

At first, the midrash mocks the adulterer for imagining that he is invisible to God. Quoting biblical verses, the midrash proves triumphantly that it is impossible to hide from God. But the haunting refrain penetrates the mockery: the adulterer waits for darkness, secrecy is essential to his desire.

Then, there is an unexpected move: *Kasheh*—hard—"This is hard to deal with"? Or "serious"? Or "difficult to understand"? The emotional, or moral, or cognitive difficulty of the scene troubles the writer. The adulterer *removes* God from the scene—that same God who, on good authority, we know to be everywhere, consents to vanish at the request of the adulterer. In the urgency of his desire, he tells God: Remove Yourself! Give me space for a moment! This is extremely hard, repeats the midrash: "As it were, God does give him space for a moment."

Driven by his desire, a human being may solicit God's absence; he may achieve an enclave of privacy where God is not. The darkness that will allow him to go undetected in society must also shield him from God's eyes. Instead of mocking this as an infantile fantasy,[19] however, the midrash has God acceding to his demand.

The passage goes on to speak[20] of the eventual detection of the sin, by way of the child who is born of the act. Imprinted with the face of his father, the child exposes the secret. Indeed, the very existence of the child is God's way of making Himself inexorably present: the child represents the consequences of an act that was meant to leave no trace.

This kind of punitive satire is very much what one would expect from a didactic text. But the notion that God allows the human fantasy of invisibility is quite startling. Subjectively, of course, the adulterer requires relief from the sense of God's presence: how else can he satisfy his desire? But the midrash writes in objective language, as though God "really" evacuates Himself from that space and that time. He is slow to punish, says the midrash. He gives space and time for the adulterer to become free of Him.

Subjective and objective language blur here. The midrash has moved from easy mockery of the adulterous delusion to a kind of acceptance, it seems, of the idea of a Godless space. Perhaps this is similar to the passage from the mishnah that we noticed earlier about the Sotah waters *ceasing* when adultery became commonplace. Or about the biblical verses *ceasing* when legal corruption becomes commonplace. Something between the banal reading ("People are no longer paying attention to biblical injunctions or to the taboo of adultery") and the radical reading ("Biblical verses have become meaningless, the taboo itself has become void") is implied here. The midrash suggests an emotional and spiritual reality, a subjective state, where divine presence may indeed be voided.[21]

Adultery is then the quintessential act of darkness. This is the real problem: it is *extremely hard*—that God must vanish in such a moment. In a world where the sense of the divine and the sense of transgression are still active, the adulterer must enter a state of dissociation. He must fragment his reality. The secrecy that the couple desire goes deep; it becomes an inner discontinuity, as though one were keeping one's experience as a kind of secret from oneself.[22]

Perhaps in this sense we can understand why, in the Sotah ritual, God's name is *dissolved* in water (Num. 5:23). The Hebrew word is *u-machah*—to dissolve, disintegrate, de-constitute. Adultery dissolves God's presence as a meaningful reality. The "bitter waters" contain the inked words of the oath that are to become part of the Sotah's body when she drinks. In them are dissolved the terrible words of the oath, including the name of God. These words disintegrate, they lose their meaning; they enter her and react toxically with her secret being.

The question of secrecy in human experience becomes the subject of the passage that immediately follows in the midrash. God proclaims Himself the architect of underground caverns in the psyche. These secret enclaves are part of His design. Adulterers may try to hide their "silver and gold," but God challenges them in the most radical way: "From Me you hide yourselves? I created you full of cavities. . . ." The reference is to heart and kidneys, in their physical and their emotional functions.[23] As the designer of these cavities, God challenges the secrecy of what He has designed as secret. In the cleft of this dilemma, the adulterer is both mocked and, in a sense, affirmed.

Adultery thus becomes a site of trauma. Like the woman in Proverbs who wipes (*u-machtah*) her mouth and says, "I have done no wickedness," the Sotah lives in a dissociated world: as we have seen, it is only in a world where the taboo remains strong and God, consequently, must be evacuated from the room, that the Sotah ritual works. It is precisely in this disintegrated state that the Sotah waters tell of a radical repression. The transgression acquires an elusive, uncanny character. The transgressor can, perhaps must deny what, with another part of herself, she knows.

As we have noticed, God's effacement from the scene of adultery cannot be described simply as a fantasy. When the midrash describes God as acceding to his demand—"Absent Yourself!"—it hints at the powerful concept of *tzimtzum* in Lurianic kabbalah: in order to create the world, God retracts His light, leaving a *challal panui*,[24] a vacated space, from which the world and its divisions may emerge. In the dark scene of adultery, God gives the transgressors space, so that a different world of space and time may emerge. At this moment, He is perhaps creating the reality of *erech appayim*, of the long-suffering God, whose scrutiny is deflected, allowing the human reality of sin.

THE THIRD WHO IS BETWEEN THEM

Sexual transgression is, then, the clearest case of this evacuation of God from human experience. Precisely because it is a taboo and therefore cloaked in secrecy, adultery vividly raises the issue of God's absent presence. In the story of Joseph and Potiphar's wife, for instance, the midrash plays with the notion of secrecy.[25] In this elaboration, Joseph approves his mistress's gesture in covering the face of her idol; his God, however, is simply more visually competent than hers—His eyes roam the world, missing nothing.

It is characteristic of Joseph that, instead of emphasizing his God's difference, he appeals to a common religious instinct. He intimates the universal religious sensibility of *yir'ah*, fear of God. In the Torah text, Joseph says, "How should I . . . sin *against God*" (Gen. 39:9). It is this *yir'ah* sensibility that adulterers so strangely seem to lack, as we saw in the passage in Proverbs and in Ibn Ezra's comment. This is the enigma of adultery: it must be hidden, and it cannot be hidden from God's presence.

A similar theme emerges in Rashi's comment on Leviticus 5:21:

> "If a soul sin and break faith with God": R. Akiva said, What is the force of this expression [here, where it is not speaking of betraying "holy things of God" as in v. 15, but of betraying one's neighbor]? Because whoever lends or borrows money or does business with another does it as a rule only in the presence of witnesses or by a document; therefore when he denies the matter, he repudiates the witnesses or the document. But he who deposits something with his neighbor does not wish any living soul to know about it except the Third (God) who is between them; therefore when he denies this deposit, he is denying the Third who is between them (Sifre).

In denying that he has in fact received money, the receiver betrays[26] not only his friend but also God, the omnipresent Third. The striking expression, "the Third who is between them," suggests the larger truth of personal relationship. The French Jewish philosopher Emmanuel Levinas developed the idea of the Third (*le tiers*) as the concrete Other whose presence is implicit in the relationship of two faces:

> Language as the presence of the face does not invite complicity with the preferred being, the self-sufficient "I-Thou" forgetful of the universe; in its frankness it refuses the clandestinity of love, where it loses its frankness and meaning and turns into laughter or cooing. The third party looks at me in the eyes of the Other—language is justice. . . . The epiphany of the face opens humanity.[27]

This commanding presence creates society, responsibility, justice. Acknowledging the Third, who is both the human Other and the "On High," involves the "personal work of my moral initiative." Denying this Third, for Levinas, means the ruin, the disintegration of subjectivity.

Here, in the place of secrecy (in Levinas's words, "the clandestinity of love"), the question of "fear of God" gathers meaning. Where the sin is untraceable, the presence or absence of God becomes crucial. Repudiating the transcendental dimension of all relationships, the adulterer evacuates God from the scene.

"And you shall fear your God," declares the Torah in several places. For example, after exhorting the reader, "You shall not place a stumbling block before the blind," the Torah continues, "And you shall fear your God: I am God" (Lev. 19:14). Rashi interprets:

> Because it is not a matter of public knowledge whether this man meant it for good or ill when he (metaphorically) trips up a blind man through his advice, so that he can always claim, "I meant well"—this is why it is written, "You shall fear your God"—who knows your thoughts. And so in every issue having to do with the privacy of the heart where none can know his motives it is written, "You shall fear your God" (Lev. 19:14,32).

The test case of "fear of God" is one where no outsider can detect one's true intentions and therefore truth becomes a matter of God awareness.

THINKING MADNESS

We have seen, then, that although other situations open the question of "fear of God"—like denying a loan on oath, or placing obstacles before the blind, or giving bad advice—the illicit sexual relation is its most challenging arena. Here, the clandestine nature of the relationship means that the lovers may come to inhabit an enclave of dissociated experience.

For the husband, the unknowable nature of the event, the doubt in which he lives, may connect with a prevalent masculine myth about woman as troubling enigma: she is inscrutable, inward in her sexuality, covering her tracks. Even the paternity of the child she bears is always in doubt; even her sexual satisfaction cannot be ascertained. The most intimate aspect of his relation with her must be based on trust. In the worst case, her femininity constitutes a mockery of law and society. She may arouse in him anxiety, even terror.

In dealing with woman, therefore, the Talmud recommends, a man had best pray well:

"For this, every pious man should pray to You in a time when You may be found" (Ps. 32:6): one sage said this refers to woman, another said it refers to Torah, and another that it refers to death.[28]

This puzzling discussion becomes the subject of a meditation by Mei Ha-Shilo'ach. What all these triggers for prayer have in common, he suggests, is that they all generate *safek*—doubt, a sense of the unfathomable. In this situation, prayer becomes urgent. "Woman" is seen as a focus of male anxiety. The feminine is imagined as disrupting the orderliness of a masculine world. God's presence becomes a real need in the turmoil created by the encounter of man and woman.

Such a mythic view of the Other—of woman, in this case—also characterizes the social view of madness. "People do not commit adultery unless a spirit of madness has entered them." From the perspective of society, the mad represent an insoluble problem. In a classic study, the French philosopher Michel Foucault explores some of the complexities of the relation to madness in Western civilization. He discusses the medieval vision of human life as a Ship of Fools, which "embarks all men without distinction on its insane ship and binds them to the vocation of a common odyssey,"[29] and the later fifteenth-century development when the mockery of madness replaces the grinning imagery of Death in the medieval imagination. This is the absurd spectacle of humanity moving inanely toward death.

> Death's annihilation is no longer anything because it was already everything, because life itself was only futility, vain words, a squabble of cap and bells. The head that will become a skull is already empty. Madness is already the *déjà-la* of death.

Death is experienced from within: "the tide of madness, its secret invasion," embodies the futility of life.[30] The spectacle of the madman reminds others of the idiocy of animal existence, which fascinates and repels.

In a yet later development, known as the Great Internment, six thousand madmen were, in the mid-seventeenth century, confined in the General Hospital in Paris. This initiates the modern period, with its alienation and enclosure of madness, its medicalization, and its clear separation between the mad and the sane.

Literary scholar Shoshana Felman discusses this juncture as one in which the language of the mad, not just their bodies, is excluded from society. Their suffering becomes unutterable. Citing Foucault's desire to write "the archaeology of that silence," the history "of madness itself, before it has been captured by knowledge,"[31] Felman asks, How can madness be grasped without excluding it? Is the madman, as subject, *thinkable*? Is the Other thinkable? Is it possible to find a language "other than that of reason, which masters and represses madness" that may disclose the experience and the voice of madness in itself and for itself?[32]

She suggests that it is perhaps only in literature, in fiction, that a possible meeting place can be found "between madness and phi-

losophy, between delirium and thought."[33] The question underlying
madness, she writes, "cannot be asked," since the question is a form
of reason. But in the act of writing, "the question is *at work,* stirring,
changing place, and wandering away . . . it questions *somewhere else:*
somewhere at that point of silence where it is no longer we who
speak, but where, in our absence, we are *spoken.*"[34]

CONFOUNDING DISARRAY

The European history of madness and civilization and their increasing separation can be brought to bear on the case of the Sotah. As we
have seen, the Talmud identifies the act of illicit sexuality as madness:
"No one commits adultery unless moved by a spirit of madness."

Shtut—the mad state that "names" the Sotah—may be better
translated "folly." Or more precisely, by the French *la folie.* As Felman
points out, this "covers a vast range of meaning going from slight
eccentricity to clinical insanity . . . [also] appearing as an indication
of excess . . . Folie in French is feminine: its grammatical gender confers upon it a kind of elusive femininity."[35] Perhaps the French *folie,*
then, offers a more apt translation for the Talmudic "spirit of *shtut,*"
since it, too, covers a large range of meaning, from "slight eccentricity to clinical insanity." Both madness and folly are included in
shtut—sometimes sheer zaniness, sometimes a transgressiveness
that is defined as sickness.

The adulterous woman embodies the anxiety of unreason: the
normatively sane recoil from her "madness." Fear turns into scorn
and humiliation, for she carries with her a whole range of unfathomable experience, from insanity to folly. In her *kilkul,* her ruin,
her disintegration of recognizable being, she incarnates that "secret
invasion," which seems to indicate something terrifying about
humanity itself, "teaching men that they were no more than dead
men already." "The head that will become a skull is already empty.
Madness is the *déjà la of death.*"

This figure of *shtut* must be denounced in her difference.
Throughout the ritual, she remains mute. The only words she speaks
are *Amen, Amen,*[36] as she accepts the horror of her fate. The words
of the oath to which she gives such minimal assent are dissolved in
water and she drinks. Instead of speaking, expressing herself in lan-

guage, she imbibes: she incorporates into her body the words that, if she is guilty, will destroy her.

She is abject, ejected beyond the thinkable. In European philosopher Julia Kristeva's definition, the abject "is not an ob-ject facing me, which I name or imagine ... the jettisoned object is radically excluded and draws me toward the place where meaning collapses."[37]

The abjecting relation of society to the Sotah is deeply ambiguous. She arouses both disgust and fascination. She disturbs identity, system, order; she must be cast out; but she is, ineluctably, one's kin. "It is not by locking up one's neighbor," Dostoyevsky once said, "that one can convince oneself of one's own soundness of mind."[38] Locking up the neighbor is linked, in fantasy, with the need to convince oneself of one's own sanity. The need is to situate the madness outside—outside society, outside one's own precarious sanity. To know the truth about the Sotah's deeds means, on this level, to master her dangerous and elusive implications. At the same time, one cannot ignore the fascination that she arouses.

This ambiguity appears powerfully in one detail of the ritual. Before she drinks the "bitter waters," her hair is undone (*u-fara*) (Num. 5:18). This is a shaming act, which continues the motif of disarray in dress: she is stripped of ornaments and beautiful clothes. The underlying tenor of the ritual, then, is to undermine her beauty.

The Talmudic translation of the verb *u-fara* is *soter:* the priest loosens, unravels, tears down the structure of an elaborate hairstyle. In doing this, he undoes her previous beauty, which is expressed in another Talmudic passage,[39] where God is described as *plaiting* Eve's hair before bringing her to Adam. This is based on the word *va-yiven* (Gen. 2:22): God builds, constructs the rib He has removed from Adam into the figure of Eve—but also, God *constructs* (*plaits*) her bridal hairstyle.

Adornment involves the creation of harmonious structure, which includes some measure of artifice. The Sotah is stripped of these aesthetic qualities. She is placed in the posture of the unbeautiful, the deconstructed. She is undone, disintegrated; she embodies disorder in a way that viscerally affects both herself and those who see her. The memory of past beauty haunts those who are now both fascinated and repelled.

DISSOLVING GOD'S NAME

It is with attention to beauty as a construct that we turn to the "bitter waters" that the Sotah will drink at the critical moment of the ritual. This water contains the dissolved ink that once inscribed the name of God. The idea behind such an act—obliterating God's name—is deeply abhorrent. It is, in fact, the subject of a biblical prohibition.[40] To destroy God's name is to contribute to the deconstruction of the sacred in the world.[41] In dissolving God's name, then, the priest is transgressing a biblical command.

Indeed, the word *u-machah*—usually translated "dissolve"—like the word *u-fara*, implies an act of disintegration, deconstruction. The name of God, like other names, is, it seems, capable of being deconstructed. It is, for instance, quite within human power to ask God to absent Himself. Conversely, it becomes a positive act to "dissolve" Amalek's name, his *meaning;* God promises to dissolve Amalek's name from under the heavens.[42] And the Talmud comments, paradoxically, on the Sotah ritual: "This teaches that the text should be written in an ink that *can be dissolved.*"[43]

Central to the Sotah ritual, then, are acts that dismantle beauty: acts that withdraw meaning, coherence, harmony from the world. The Sotah is made an object of revulsion. The *ugliness* of the situation grips the onlooker who, horrified and fascinated, may well swear off wine, as a safeguard against such dissolution. She becomes the abject, cast out in order to preserve a world of harmony and beauty.

And yet, in the fascination she generates, she also reminds those who see her of their own madness. If she could dissolve God's presence, if she could demand that He absent Himself, that He give her space and time clear of Him, then so can every onlooker. The wish and the power to erase the sacred are not alien to human nature.

In sexuality, particularly, the sense of mastery dissolves. In asking God to leave the room, the adulterer expresses the ambivalence that often marks human sexuality. It is not surprising that bystanders try to ward off the terror of the Sotah's disarray by behavioral measures—by swearing off wine, for instance. If one remains sober, perhaps one will never lose mastery; one will never become *her.*

Neither is it surprising that the Sotah, in this situation of *safek,* doubt, is finally, in the interests of certainty, subjected to a clarifying test. Her body will demonstrate, with the desired precision, the simple, physical truth over which human language stammers. If she is guilty, her body will declare her guilt; if she is innocent, according to the Talmud, her body will achieve an unprecedented and triumphant fertility: she will give birth easily, to tall, beautiful, male children. This blissful outcome will act as a kind of advertisement for the aesthetics of virtue; it will match the dire consequences of guilt—the fatal collapse of her reproductive organs. All ambiguity will be resolved. In a silent and miraculous movement of the body, the secret will out.

But this silent compliance of the Sotah, like the muteness, the unutterability of madness, comes at a cost. The cost is, on one level, the erasure of God's name. Whatever the outcome, she will have drunk these waters of scattered presence. If she is innocent, the Talmud comments, it will be worth the cost in order to restore her marriage.[44] For marriage must be based on trust; suspicion must be resolved; extreme measures are justified to this end. And if she is guilty, clarity is equally necessary, since the marriage may not then continue.

However, it emerges that the desired clarity—which justifies even the undoing of God's name—is not, even in this laboratory situation, totally achievable. For, as we have seen, the Sotah ordeal will work only if the husband is innocent of similar sexual transgressions. Moreover, there is always the possibility that a guilty woman will know the law and will therefore be aware that certain virtuous behaviors have the power to protect her from the effect of the bitter waters. In both cases, she will emerge intact, although she is guilty, thus defeating the only justification for erasing God's name.

In other words, total certainty can never be achieved in human affairs. Meaning cannot be finally arrested, stopped in its tracks. It is affected by sociological conditions, even by the very fact of reading: the literate woman, who has read the Talmudic text, will be able to manipulate the outcome of such a test.

So, the erasure of God's name remains a real cost of the Sotah ritual. Moreover, in the face of the Sotah's mute madness, even the pious bystander may be poignantly reminded of her own ambiguities. She may be pierced by the human disarray that reduces the Sotah to silence. To attempt to extort the secret from the Sotah's body is "to *situate* madness—*outside,* to shut it out, to *locate* it—in the Other."[45] "One is *in* the madness," writes Felman. "To believe that one is on the outside, that one can be outside,"[46] is to be blind to one's own blindness, which is the very meaning of madness.

Les non-dupes errent, writes the French philosopher Jacques Lacan ("Non-dupes err").[47] The most suspicious and sophisticated onlookers and readers, those who are sure that they are not deluded and never will be deluded, are deluded by their own sophistication. For the blindness, the madness, the secret cavities are built into human life; unconscious desire is not totally mastered.

Recourse to the Sotah ordeal may seek to heal the world of its fractures, its lusts and jealousies. But it remains, nevertheless, an imperfect solution to the human need for certainty, for clear language. For if the ambiguities of sexuality and language are inherent, there is no safe spot outside them. Is there a way in which the Sotah may become thinkable, without excluding her? Or a way in which she may speak without killing her own deepest speechless knowledge?

THE THIRD POSSIBILITY

We have emphasized the problem of doubt, ambiguity, uncertainty, which is the context for the extreme measure of the Sotah ordeal. But it emerges from the Talmudic discussion that, beyond guilt and innocence, there is a third, hidden possibility: *she may confess.* In the Talmudic and midrashic literature, the priest in fact urges her to confess:

> "And the priest shall say to the woman: If no man has slept with you. . . ." (Num. 5:19): This teaches that he should open by offering a plea in her defense. He says to her: "Wine can be responsible for much, or frivolity can be responsible for much, or youth can be responsible for much. Many have been guilty before you and were swept away. Do not cause the great Name which is written in all holiness to be erased in the bitter waters!"
>
> He tells her stories from the Aggadah, and incidents that happened in ancient Scriptures, expounding a text like ". . . which wise men have told" (Job 15:18). And he tells her

things that neither she nor all the families of her father's house deserve to hear: for example, the affair of Reuben and Bilhah, and the affair of Judah and Tamar. Both of them, he tells her, confessed their deeds without shame. What happened to them in the end? They inherited life in the world to come.[48]

The very notion of confession is fraught with ambiguities. For the modern reader, it is shadowed by the literature of totalitarianism, by the Soviet show trials, by the Chinese culture of confession, and by accounts ranging from Koestler's *Darkness at Noon* to American philosopher Elaine Scarry's *The Body in Pain*. Confessions, we understand, serve political purposes; they may be extracted by torture, or by more subtle pressure. At the very least, in telling a stark story in clear language, they travesty life's complexity.

Our modern suspicion of confession is not entirely allayed by this midrashic narrative. Certainly, the priest is putting a kind of pressure on the Sotah, and certainly, as he tells her himself, he has theological ends in view in urging confession. ("Do not cause the great Name to be erased in the bitter waters!") And yet, it is hard to ignore a tone of tenderness in the priest's address to the woman.

In the midrash, the priest goes far in his efforts to find extenuating grounds—intoxication, youth, frivolity—for the Sotah, even in the case that she is guilty.[49] The priest is to speak *to the woman*: "in any language that she understands," says the Talmud.[50] He attempts to reach her by finding language that will open her to the very possibility of language. He speaks so as to make her speak. He speaks therefore with an acute sense of her singular position. She must understand him from her own place.

What is his argument? After listing possible mitigating factors, he refers briefly to the many transgressors who did not confess and were swept away. Then, he tells her confession stories from ancient texts, inscribed in holy books, like the narrative of Reuben or of Judah—both relating to sexual histories. "They confessed without shame—and they inherited the life of the world to come." His aim is to set her story in the epic context of those biblical heroes.

In this midrash, the priest's tone and intent are quite different from the didactic rigor and scorn with which the priest addresses the Sotah in the corresponding passage in the Talmud.[51] There, indeed,

one can sense the pressure that he is exerting to make her confess—
"and not cause God's name to be erased." In this midrash, by contrast, the priest cites ancient paradigms of the redemptive effect of
confession.

His concern, I suggest, is to reach her in the complexity of her
experience. By telling stories of biblical heroes and their ability to
acknowledge sexual misdeeds, he intimates the common reality
of passionate error, of what we might call *madness*, which human
beings, even "beautiful" human beings, are called on to acknowledge.
He evokes the spoken words of epic heroes to whom the ambiguities
of sexuality were not foreign. By the act of confession, they recon-
stituted, in some measure, the name of God that their transgression
had eroded.

In this midrash, the priest places the idea of confession in a different light. To confess is to tell a story of fragmentation. It is to
put on display that divided place where God is asked to absent Himself. The fragmented consciousness that has made God effectively
meaningless in the world now has two options before it: to speak
itself *without shame,* or to swallow the bitter waters, to suppress the
madness of that moment, so that it finds expression only in the toxic
language of the body.

ENGRAVED ON THE BONES

What confession might mean for the transgressor is the subject of a
radical passage by R. Nahman of Bratzlav:

> The sins of a human being are upon his bones, as it is writ-
> ten (Ezek. 32): "And their sin is [engraved] upon their bones."
> Every sin has a particular combination of letters which
> are then engraved, in malign combination, on the sinner's
> bones—thus bringing the particular language of that prohibi-
> tion into the realm of impurity, where it takes revenge upon
> him. . . . Through verbal confession these engraved letters
> leave his bones and compose the words of confession. For lan-
> guage issues from the bones, as it is written, "All my bones
> shall say. . . ." (Ps. 35). And confession destroys the structure of

the malign combination of letters, and reconstructs them into benign combination, creating the realm of holiness.

That is why our Sages said, When the Israelites were traveling in the wilderness, Judah's bones were rolling around in his coffin, till Moses said: "Hear O God the voice of Judah"— asking of God to remember in Judah's favor the confession he had made. That is why it is precisely his bones that are rattling around; because of his sin that is engraved on the bones. And that is why it is confession that brings them together again, so that they return to their proper place. So Judah represents mastery (*malchut*): since he rearticulated himself by way of verbal confession.[52]

R. Nahman's opening statement has a haunting ring, especially in the context of the adulterer's power to "absent" God from the arena of human action: *The sins of a human being are etched on his bones.* The adulterer may deny to others and to himself that anything is amiss in his history. He may even, apparently, expel the Third from the room, so that no witness, divine or human, can tell the tale. But his own bones are engraved with the text of his acts.

Repression goes only so far; imprinted in his body and his very being, a "malign combination of letters" skews his version of experience. Everything he says is affected by this inner distortion; language itself is twisted out of true; it is alienated from the fair, the just, the beautiful. With every word he speaks he destroys possible "benign combinations," meaningful versions of experience, and he constructs in their place toxic versions.

The transgression, then, has not vanished. It has left traces, etchings in the bones, traumatic residues. The direct expression of this bone-knowledge is *dibbur,* a language with its own fantasy structure, which issues from the bones, from the innermost self. The language of confession, on the other hand, has the power to exorcise the engraved sins and malign linguistic structures and to recombine the same letters into a different structure, one of holiness.

Confession is a form of language that has dynamic force—to destroy and to reconstruct. Speaking one's sins reorganizes the unconscious. Spoken words shift the inner structure of personality. Letters, the basic elements of language, move from disarray to coherence. Like the undone hair of the Sotah, like the voided world that God has evacuated, the letters have fallen apart into a gibberish that uncreates the world. The language of confession has equivalent power to rebuild structure out of chaos.

This miraculous movement, reconstituting meaning and beauty: How is it achieved? R. Nahman presents the cases of Judah and Reuben, the two exemplars of confession that the priest holds up before the Sotah. But R. Nahman, citing the Talmud,[53] emphasizes the abject, tragic dimension of the narrative. "Judah's bones were rattling around in his coffin"—a macabre postmortem history! R. Nahman comments: Judah's bones are dislocated to signify the radical effect of his transgression. Moses redeems Judah by recalling to God Judah's previous confession, in his confrontation with Tamar ("She is more righteous than I!" [Gen. 38:26][54]).

Moreover, according to the Talmud, it was Judah's confession that inspired Reuben to follow suit and confess his misdeed in relation to his father and Bilhah. This act reintegrated Reuben's inner world, so that his bones remained intact. But Judah's later impulsive words to his father, "I will be a sinner before you to all eternity" (Gen. 43:9), cut a deep groove in the structure of his personality.[55] *His bones rattle in the coffin.* Only when Moses reminds God of the powerful effect of Judah's confession on Reuben do these turbulent bones knit together again.[56]

What these midrashic narratives suggest is the *contagious* power of confession. Reuben is affected by Judah's ability to acknowledge his error. In the end, Moses articulates this connection in Judah's favor. Since his confession had a healing effect on the world, Judah's bones can be rearticulated.

In this way, adds R. Nahman, Judah becomes the paradigm of royalty, of mastery. The paradox is poignant: Judah's mastery is affirmed precisely when he acknowledges what it is to be in disarray. In his confession, he owns that place of madness: madness is not *outside.* He recognizes the Other—Tamar, abject, condemned, sexually shamed—who is "more righteous than I."

For R. Nahman, then, the fantasy life of human beings, their delusions, their sense of omnipotence—all can be re-spoken, in a different language, a better organization of letters. Like Freud's "talking cure," this confession transforms reality. It comes, strangely, *without shame*.[57] The authenticity of such speech carries an almost impersonal authority.

REARTICULATIONS

So we return to the Sotah. In speaking to her of confession, the priest is appealing to her to transcend the mute terror of her posture. In her dumb disarray, she appalls with the sense of the macabre quality of life itself. "The head that will become a skull is already empty. Madness is the *déjà-la* of death."[58] Like a puppet, she is sullenly alive, a "thing-soul."[59] The priest offers her paradigms of those who have uttered redemptive words and "inherited the life of eternity."

I suggest that in addressing her like this, the priest is assuming that deepest among her motivations is a real desire to achieve some "benign combination" of the fragments of her being. If his concern is that the name of God should not disintegrate in the bitter waters, this concern embraces a concern for the Sotah's humanity, which is compromised by her muteness. He therefore urges her to speak from the heart of her turbulence. She has the possibility of giving voice to the spirit of madness that has entered her, and thereby of exorcising it. This will mean relinquishing spurious masteries and surrendering to the truth of her experience.

If the Sotah confesses, of course, her husband and the priest will have their doubts resolved. But this certainty will be of a different kind from that offered by the toxic effect of the bitter waters. As we have seen, the Sotah ordeal offers a limited certainty. Confession, on the other hand, lacks the crystal clarity of bodily symptoms. Made of words, confession offers meanings that are in constant motion; dynamic, full of conflict and the pressure of desire. The demand for clear language—the language of the body, for instance—in which meaning is arrested, is a kind of terrorism; secrets are extracted under torture.[60] Confession, in its fullness, on the other hand, is suffused with the uncanny longings of imaginative life, now literally *put into words*.

To put it differently: no one can teach the Sotah what to say. Unlike the formula assent, *Amen! Amen!* of the ritual, the spontaneous inflections of her speech are hers alone; they are not the product of conscious control. In a sense, in her confession she is *spoken*. Her speech may even trouble as well as enlighten her husband, the priest, and others who hear her. There is something in a "true confession" that does not reassure. Only so, R. Nahman says, may the bones be resettled.

BEAUTY AND ERROR

The "secret cavities" of human experience—the world of sexuality, in particular—incubate error, waywardness, disfigurement of the structures of beauty. But God, the architect in the midrash, not only knows of their existence, He built them into those structures in the first place.

Elaine Scarry writes eloquently about the dialectic of beauty and error. The beautiful object

> ignites the desire for truth by giving us, with an electric brightness shared by almost no other uninvited, freely arriving perceptual event, the *experience of conviction* and the experience, as well, of error. . . . It creates, without itself fulfilling, the *aspiration for enduring certitude.* It comes to us, with no work of our own; then leaves us prepared to undergo a giant labor. [My emphasis.][61]

In this account, Scarry reimagines the Platonic notion of beauty and truth. At the heart of her vision is the organic connection of beauty and error. Beauty may be a "starting place for education." It offers the "experience of conviction," which generates the further "aspiration for enduring certitude." Our desire for beauty, she says, is inexhaustible, outliving its particular object and moving toward more enduring objects. This may involve disappointment, a sense of limitations, even of betrayal. But the longing for beauty persists, leading us to a more capacious regard for the world.

"The aspiration for enduring certitude" is another way of describing the force of *emunah*—at its simplest, of trust. The beauty—aesthetic, ethical, spiritual—of an integrated life, undivided loyalties, certainty, and trust, is the aspiration of husband and wife in marriage. But trust may hold within itself many uncertainties. Doubt, instead of being a destructive element in the relationship of man and woman, or of God and the human being, may become a force in the creation of a larger trust.

The Sotah waters can offer only a certainty of the last resort. Perhaps total certainty is ultimately not only unachievable but undesirable in human affairs. The apprehension of beauty, as Scarry suggests, may rather educate one to a lifetime struggle for truth, within a field of error—as though madness and error, questioning and conflict, were the unavoidable hazards of being human, and as though sin and confession were the unavoidable paradigm for life in the wilderness.

The philosopher Friedrich Nietzsche writes, "Error is the condition of life. . . . The knowledge that one errs does not *eliminate* the error."[62] *Acknowledging* that one has erred, putting the error into words, however, does indeed act on the error, not to eliminate it but to connect it with its root, with the desire for beauty that constantly aspires beyond its immediate limitations.

The Talmud puts it like this: "One never comes to master [lit., stand firmly, fully understand] the words of Torah unless one has stumbled over them."[63] Stumbling, erring is what, in a sense, authenticates the quest for truth. The secret cavities of human experience from which arise fantasies and madnesses are an essential part of human structure. The human being is ashamed and hides himself; and God claims that very self as His work.

THE SHIFTING WEIGHTS OF BEAUTIFUL THINGS

It is here, perhaps, that the narratives about women that frame the book of Numbers—the Sotah and the daughters of Tzelofchad—most dynamically address each other. The language of the five sisters, we remember, is praised by God as *ken*—which Rashi translates as "apt, *beautiful*": it has a fairness, a fitness, that is both aesthetic and ethical. But their language is not simply a masterful and immaculate artifact. Rather, it emerges from rupture, from the trauma of the loss of their father, who "died of his own sin," as they rather mysteriously put it. Fully human, his life and death yet involve losses beyond the usual.

"Why?" his daughters ask in pain and protest. "Why should our

father's name be diminished?" The name of the father is the meaning and survival of the family. Like the name of God, it is subject
to diminution, erosions, disintegrations. Asking the question, his
daughters dispute a certainty. But instead of bringing discord into
the arena, they bring beauty. And God acknowledges the *ken,* the creative force of their protest.

Theirs is a language that has its roots in the desire for beauty
and righteousness. In the accents of absolute demand, they cry out,
"Give us a holding among our father's kinsmen!" Perhaps only the
passionate experience of rupture and exclusion can break forth
with such eloquence and truth. But this truth is not a final truth.
Words speak partial, incomplete truths. This becomes clear when the
men of the tribe of Manasseh appear before Moses soon after this
with a counterargument—and are praised in the same terms: *ken . . .
dovrim*—"They too speak justly!" (Num. 36:1–5). The law is again
adjusted; but the resonant beauty of the women's original words,
from the place of rupture, is uncompromised.

By framing the book of Numbers with the two narratives of the
Sotah and the daughters of Tzelofchad, the Torah presents us with
some of the dilemmas of language, certainty, trust, and beauty. From
the Sotah, in her silent denial, and from the torment of doubt that
urges impossible certainties, we are brought eventually to a larger
sense of the possibilities and limitations of language.

Both narratives intimate the presence of God, within and beyond
social relationships, of an essential knowledge of beauty, to be struggled for, through vanishings and errors. "How one walks through
the world," writes Elaine Scarry, "the endless small adjustments of
balance, is affected by the *shifting weights* of beautiful things."[64] The
"shifting weights" animate language in all its forms. The Sotah may
confess; the daughters of Tzelofchad may author a passage in the
Torah; the presence of God may be invited to reenter.

THREE

Desire in the Wilderness

SAGA OF LOVE AND HATE

At the beginning of the book, all the signs indicate that the people are preparing for imminent arrival in the Land of Israel. For this purpose, a census is undertaken, clans and tribes are allocated battle positions, and the people move away from their camping place at Mount Sinai, in order to begin their trek to their destination. According to the midrash, indeed, this journey was to have been extremely brief: a three-day journey. Rashi reports this expectation in his comment on Moses' words to Jethro, "We are traveling to the place that God has promised us" (Num. 10:29). This is Rashi's comment:

> "Immediately. Within three days, we enter the [holy] land."
> Because at this first journey they traveled with the intention
> of entering the land, but then they sinned with the "complain-
> ers." And why did Moses include himself with them? Because
> the decree was not yet issued against him, and he thought he
> would enter [the land].

This journey was undertaken with the intention of immediate entry into the Land. It was only with the sin of the "complainers"—the following narrative—that this project was interrupted. Moses still thinks that he, too, will enter the Land, because the future has not yet happened—sins, failures, and decrees of exclusion.

Rashi catches the poignant moment of innocence, of full and immediate desire. At this moment, sin has not yet happened, so that Moses speaks unsuspectingly of desire and fulfillment. His sense of plenitude is reflected in the rest of his speech to Jethro:

Moses said to Chovav son of Reuel the Midianite, Moses'
father-in-law, "We are traveling to the place of which God
has said, 'I will give it to you.' Come with us and we will be
good to you; for God has promised *goodness* to Israel." And he
replied, "I will not go; but will return to my native land." He
said, "Please do not leave us, since you know where we should
camp in the wilderness and can be our guide. So if you come
with us, the goodness that God grants us we will extend to
you" [lit., "the *goodness* that God will do *good* to us, we will do
good to you"]. (Num. 10:29–32)

Five times, Moses utters the word *tov*—good. The source of good
is God, and that divine goodness will radiate out to Jethro as well.[1]
But all of Moses' blissful words of persuasion affect Jethro not at all.
As though deaf to Moses' blandishments, he simply says, "I'm not
going. I'm going home." And then he simply vanishes from the biblical record.

From this scene, we understand that the appeal to "goodness"
ultimately expresses a subjective sense of things. Moses may be
referring to concrete blessings that God has in store for the people,
but by repeating the word *tov* so often, he evokes an ecstatic sense of
God's bounty. This is Moses' perspective at this moment, but it is not
Jethro's, so that without feeling the need to argue with Moses, Jethro
acts on his own desire and goes home.

"Goodness," then, lies in the eyes of the beholder. It is striking that
in his early infancy Moses is described as "good." ("And his mother
saw that he was good. . . ." [Exod. 2:2].) And when God speaks to him
at the Burning Bush, He promises to redeem the people and bring
them to "a *good* and spacious land. . . ." (Exod. 3:8). The foundational
experiences of Moses' life are permeated by a sense of *tov*.

In the book of Numbers the words *tov* and *ra,* good and evil, are
used to express the subjective consciousness of "love" and "hate."
Moses' eyes are trained on that *good* destination that beckons so
alluringly. He is full of love. But since love is not always contagious,
Jethro remains unaffected by Moses' enthusiasm.

Here begins the saga of love and hate in the wilderness. Here
begins the subjective narrative of an ambivalent people who,
through a series of wilderness narratives, struggle with their own

volatile relations with God, with Moses, and, ultimately, with themselves. In the end, their loves and hates will postpone for an entire generation their entry into the land.

COMPLAINING AND DESIRING

These ambivalences particularly mark these early narratives. Even though it is ultimately the sin of the Spies that decides their fate, the earlier sins, which are recorded immediately after Moses' ecstatic speech to Jethro, have the immediate effect of disrupting the three-day fantasy of instant arrival. There are two such narratives: they "complain," or "bewail themselves" (Num. 11:1), and they are "filled with desire" (11:4). From this point (the twentieth of Iyar) until the narrative of the Spies and the loss of the generation (the ninth of Av)—that is, over ten weeks—the history of that catastrophe unfolds.[2]

The narrative of the Spies, I suggest, has its roots much earlier in the story. Where, exactly, does it begin? We might, of course, go all the way back to the earliest dissatisfactions and "testings" of God and Moses, starting immediately after the Exodus (or even earlier, in the process leading up to the Exodus), and culminating in the "great sin" of the Golden Calf (Exod. 32:30). But beginnings are always elusive; they recede as we pursue them. It is possible to conceive of many histories, many beginnings and endings. We are pursuing the particular history that is framed within the book of Numbers—a history that flares destructively with the narrative of the Spies but that neither begins nor ends there.

This narrative begins with the sins recorded in Numbers, chapter 11. Here is the core narrative:

> The people took to complaining bitterly [lit., evilly] before God. God heard and was angry: a fire of God broke out against them, ravaging the outskirts of the camp. The people cried out to Moses. Moses prayed to God, and the fire died down. That place was named Taverah, because a fire of God had broken out against them.
>
> The riffraff in their midst were overwhelmed with desire; and then the Israelites too wept and said, "Who will give us meat to eat? We remember the fish that we used to eat free in

Egypt, the cucumbers, the melons, the leeks, the onions, and the garlic. Now our gullets are shriveled. There is nothing at all! Nothing but this manna to look to!" ... Moses heard the people weeping, every clan apart, each person at the entrance of his tent. God was very angry, and in Moses' eyes it was evil. And Moses said to God, "Why have You done evil to Your servant . . . ?" (Num. 11:1–6,10–11)

Complaint and desire speak here. Indeed, it is striking that these sins are exclusively sins of *speech*. Nothing actually happens. But their complaints are "evil" (*ra*) in the ears of God, and their desire is "evil" in the eyes of Moses, who then complains to God about the "evil" that He has done to Moses (Num. 11:11). The atmosphere is full of words, and tears, and cries. A sense of evil pervades.

Even the opening sentence—"the people were *like those who bewail themselves*"—suggests a cloudy sense of resentment.[3] Their actual complaint is not recorded; it is evoked by the word *mit'onenim*, which suggests a posturing dissatisfaction, suffused with *ra*, a querulous, reflexive tonality that penetrates "God's ears."[4] They are instantly punished. Perhaps, suggests Ha'amek Davar, because of their so-recent encounter with God, they are still trailing clouds of glory from Sinai; God's presence is still palpable, with its attendant hazards. In this heightened state, every word, every whisper of *ra*, is instantly registered and exacts its immediate retribution.

In this reading, Ha'amek Davar is pursuing a theme that he sees as pervasive in the book of Numbers.[5] The intensified presence of God after Sinai makes demands that expose the people to the hazards of intimacy with the sacred. Not for nothing did God threaten the withdrawal of His presence after the Golden Calf: "I shall no longer go up among you ... lest I annihilate you" (Exod. 33:3,5). A world visited by Revelation creates a combustible atmosphere for human complexity. And indeed, fire breaks out, and subsides only after Moses prays.

In the next episode, the "riffraff"[6] *desired desire*. This cryptic expression is usually idiomatically translated, "were overwhelmed by desire." But the object of their desire is at first unexplained: they simply, reflexively, "desire desire." Only in the next verse do we hear the voice of the people, specifying their desire: "Who will give us meat? . . . We remember the fish. . . . The cucumbers, the melons, the leeks, the onions, the garlic!" The list is both specific and diffuse, particular objects of a restless desire that cannot find full gratification. But the unappeasable nature of desire is already implicit in the cognate verb and object: "They desired desire." A blank wishfulness haunts their cry: who will gratify this desire?

This episode leaves us with a sense of confusion. Why is their complaint so terribly punished? God first gratifies their lust and then kills them in their greed: why does He react so harshly to the sin of gluttony? And why has the pervasive sense of *ra* so suddenly replaced Moses' blissful language of *tov*?

THE REPRESSED FIRST SIN

Ramban sheds an unexpected ray of understanding on this text. Citing the Talmud,[7] he observes that the "complaining" is not, in fact, the first sin: before that, there was the sin of traveling "away from the mountain of God" (Num. 10:33). The Talmud detects a problematic element in that unexceptional statement: R. Chanina says: "This teaches us that they turned aside from following God" (*mei-acharei Ha-Shem*). Ramban cites another midrash: "They traveled away from Mount Sinai, gleefully, like a child who runs away from school, saying: 'Perhaps He will give us more commandments [if we stay]!'"

Ramban then comments:

This is the meaning of the expression, "And they traveled away from the mountain of God": their intention was to remove themselves from there *because* it was the mountain of God. This is the first [sin], and then the text breaks off [with the section on the Ark] in order that there should not be a sequence of three [sins] one after the other, which would create a *chazakah*—a new reality. . . . Possibly if it had not been for this sin He would have brought them into the Land immediately. . . .[8]

In this evocative passage, we are challenged by the notion of a repressed narrative. There were, it seems, not two but three sins, the first being almost invisible in the biblical text: "They traveled away from the mountain of God." Ramban, in the wake of his midrashic sources, intuits an original act of abandonment, of betrayal. Perhaps because the text emphasizes what they are traveling *from*—*the mountain of God*—the Talmud and the Yalkut detect a primal movement, hidden from the naked eye, which initiates a process of alienation. At first, the people have no words to express this subtle beginning. The fact that "the mountain of God," with the Tetragrammaton, is never otherwise used to refer to Mount Sinai,[9] lends the expression a metaphysical connotation. It is the godliness, rather than the mountain, that they are fleeing.

The Talmud interprets *mei-har Ha-Shem*—*mei-acharei Ha-Shem*; playing with the sound of the words, it offers the slightly awkward, "They traveled away from *after-God*." This carries the weight of association with texts that speak of the movement *after* the object, *following* the object. Ruth, for instance, begs Naomi not to press her to abandon her—"to turn back *from after you*" (Ruth 1:16). And Jeremiah recalls the Exodus as the time that God eternally remembers: "The love of your youth, when you *went after Me* in the wilderness . . ." (Jer. 2:2). To *go after* is to be enthralled—like the children who follow the Pied Piper, to death or to bliss.

R. Chanina in the Talmud thus describes the people as removing themselves from an entranced relation with God. Ramban sets this by the side of the Yalkut passage: the people ran away from God, like children playing truant to avoid the endless demands of school. This whimsical analogy yields a people who behave as children behave. Who does not understand such behavior? A natural resistance to the burden of the Law draws them away from God's mountain. The image carries its grave message: children must be schooled, the truant must return to his desk.

The effect of Ramban's commentary is to excavate a repressed "first sin," the beginning of a series of three. A set of three sins would create a *chazakah*, a changed reality, a presumption, in this case, of alienation from the God of Sinai. For this reason, as Rashi already suggests, vv. 35–36 of Numbers, chapter 10, are interposed, to break the set of three. In the text, they are even marked off with parentheses—(. . .). Paradoxically, by making this observation, Rashi is actually drawing attention to the set of three sins.

Almost imperceptibly, then, the process of withdrawal from God begins here. For Ramban, the flight is from the impositions of the Law. There is no apparent punishment for the original sin, he remarks, except for the fact that their entry into the Land is delayed by it.

In the view of Ramban, then, the catastrophe of the later story of the Spies is already implicit within this early cryptic moment. Like the butterfly's wing fluttering in India that eventually precipitates a hurricane in New York, an almost indecipherable movement away from God sets off a cataclysm of alienation.

EXCHANGE OF DELIGHTS

An intriguing alternative to this interpretation is offered by Ha'amek Davar. "Their intention," he writes, "was to turn aside from the delight [*oneg*] that was there [at Mount Sinai] with God. So they sought to indulge in delights of flesh."[10] On this view, the people exchange the spiritual ecstasy of Sinai for the physical pleasures of *bassar*—meat or flesh. Their desire for *bassar* begins immediately on leaving Sinai,[11] even though they never express it in words until after they "complain" over the forced marches. So that when they "return to weeping," in the desire episode, they are reverting to an *earlier* repressed desire. Turning aside from a fascination with God (*mei-acharei Ha-Shem*), they obey an impulse to flee from the intensity of Sinai to the simpler pleasures of the flesh.

This is a radically different view of the flight from Sinai. Instead of a flight from the burden of the Law, we have an exchange of delights. The same word, *oneg*, is used for both kinds of pleasure.[12] Desire for pleasure is the force that moves human beings. One pleasure is what we might call mystical, the other sensual. The latter he refers to as *bessarim*, in the plural, which means food in general—all the various kinds that the people list in their "desire" fantasy. It also, of course, refers to sexuality. In this narrative, the people revert from an experience of sublimation to a primal sensuality.

The Israelites begin to weep at the very mention of *bassar*.[13] As though a powerful chord has been struck, they fall back to an earlier sensuality that is associated with leaving God's mountain. This is not a choice between good and evil in the moral sense. It is a *turning aside,* an aversion from one source of bliss and its substitution by another.

But, as God diagnoses this movement a few verses later, its implications are grave. ". . . You have rejected God who is in your midst, by weeping before Him and saying, 'Why did we ever leave Egypt?'" (Num. 11:20). God describes their desire for "flesh" as a rejection of Him and, indeed, of the whole Exodus project. Of course, the people did not utter these precise words ("Why did we ever leave Egypt?"). What they said was, "Who will give us meat to eat?" But God provides an unexpected elaboration for that apparently banal craving: ". . . you have wept in the ears of God saying, 'Who will give us meat to eat?'—*It was good for us in Egypt!*" (11:18). This is God's summary of their fantasy memory of Egyptian foods. Here, the word *tov—good—* emerges as a definitive and outrageous utterance. In the context of Moses' uses of the word *tov*—in connection with redemption and entry into the land—the Israelites' use of the word suggests a different world of subjective meaning. Essentially, they are saying, "We love Egypt, the place of *bassar.*"

Of course, again, the people never actually say these words. This is God's elaboration of "Who will give us meat to eat?" God understands their *bassar* fantasy as a profound shift in loyalties, in loves, as though He hears the intimate implications of their craving for meat. It is their words that God interprets so radically. Their speech betrays a repressed passion of which they themselves may not be fully conscious. As in a sounding chamber, their words are returned to them, amplified, fraught with meaning.

JOUISSANCE AND PLEASURE

To understand more closely the *oneg* experience of Mount Sinai, I suggest that we invoke Jacques Lacan's term *jouissance*—bliss, joy, ecstasy. Lacan writes of *jouissance* as primordial, infinite desire. Particular desires, on the other hand, act as paths, filters, bindings for *jouissance,* but also as defenses against it: "Desire is a defense, a prohibition against going beyond a certain level in *jouissance.*"[14] Unbounded *jouissance* is annihilating, a fire that threatens to obliterate the self. Desires are bounded by Law; the dialectical tension between Law and Desire thus makes it possible for us to live with some openness to the *jouissance* that is our deepest wish.

The psychoanalyst Michael Eigen creatively misreads Lacan to identify *jouissance* with God. Every self contains a "spark" of that originary, boundless fire. At the same time, the self is bounded, combustible, needing limits, which are set by our particular desires. "In delight's extremity," he writes, "desire gets in the way. . . . It is helpful to think of desire not simply as a pointer towards infinity, but as a defense against it."[15] Desires, that is, are a defense against the delight that is God.

Lacan calls these particular desires *pleasure:* "For it is pleasure that sets the limit on *jouissance.*" Pleasure "binds incoherent life together."[16] It is linked with prohibition, bonding, regulating psychic life: "Pleasure, desire, is a filter or opening for *Jouissance,* a necessary dampening, toning down. . . . It gives us a rest from *Jouissance,* at the same time that it lets us taste the latter. What is really pleasurable about pleasure is the *Jouissance* that shines through it." At the same time, "to mistake pleasure for *Jouissance* is to seriously downgrade our nature."[17]

INCESTUOUS DESIRE

The complex field of pleasure, desire, *jouissance* is also, I suggest, the subject of Ha'amek Davar's commentary on the early narratives of the book of Numbers. Turning aside from Sinai means abandoning the *jouissance,* the *oneg,* of being with God. Sensual pleasures offer themselves as substitutes, filters, defenses against that bliss. This may be a necessary regression. But it nevertheless represents a loss: the true wine of existence, the love of God, has been replaced by sensual pleasure, the bread and meat of life. Love of God, or *oneg* with God, cannot be reduced to what usually passes for love. As the English psychoanalyst W. R. Bion puts it,

> For that there has to be a language of infra-sensuous and ultra-sensuous, something that lies outside the spectrum of sensuous experience and articulate language. . . . The artist who paints a little street in Delft can see and communicate a reality

to the observer who then sees something that is quite different from any brick wall or little house that he has ever known or seen in his life.[18]

Bion attempts to convey psychic experience by referring to a painting of a brick wall, which refers to a reality unknown to the senses. The senses remain as vehicles for something they cannot contain. The imaginative freight they bear all but effaces them.

Similarly, by using the word *oneg,* Ha'amek Davar suggests both the complex links between the two worlds of pleasure—love of God and love of flesh—and the absolute difference between them. The craving for *bassar* represents a visceral defense against that other mystical delight.

Rashi foreshadows this understanding of the wilderness period that begins with the journey away from Sinai: he cites midrashic interpretations that highlight significant *bassar* moments—desire, pleasure, weeping:

> "Like complainers": *mit'onenim* refers to a pretext. They seek a pretext in order to turn away from [following] after God. Similarly, it says about Samson, "for he seeks a pretext" (Judg. 14:4).[19]

Rashi reads *mit'onenim* as *seeking a pretext,* a cover story, a subterfuge to enable their flight from God. Bewailing themselves, weeping, they camouflage a repressed desire.

Again:

> "Who will give us meat to eat?" Did they not have meat? Did it not say previously, "A motley crowd also went up with them with sheep and cattle, etc."? Perhaps you will say that they had eaten them. But does it not say, when they entered the Land, "Much cattle belonged to the sons of Reuven, etc." Evidently, they sought a pretext.[20]

The word *bassar,* which seems so concrete, so self-explanatory, is exposed as a pretext—again, a cover story, a word that covers for the inexpressible.

". . . fish which we ate in Egypt freely . . .": Perhaps you will say that the Egyptians gave them fish freely? But did it not already say, "Straw will not be given to you"? If they did not give them straw freely, would they have given them fish freely? Then what is meant by "freely"? Free of commandments.[21]

Here, "fish for free" is decoded to open a world of desire—for a life free of responsibility. What is the nature of that desire?

"Weeping in their families": Every family gathered together and wept, to publicize their complaints openly. The Rabbis remark that *le-mishpechotav* means "concerning family matters"— concerning incestuous relations forbidden to them.[22]

Here, finally, Rashi expresses the inexpressible. The tears that accompany the word *bassar* flow from bodies traumatized by Sinai, by God's demands, specifically by His restrictions on incestuous desire. This, it emerges, is the hub of their desire, the repressed meaning of *bassar*. They are weeping about "family matters."

What they have lost is the primal fantasy of sexual union in the family, a fantasy of free and unfettered sexual gratification in the context where it can be found most easily.[23] The traditional view is that what has been forbidden at Sinai is *secondary* incest. First-degree incest, between the closest family relations, is universally forbidden in the seven Noachide laws. At Sinai further stringencies are imposed: six more distant family relationships are now included in the taboo.[24]

Incestuous desire is, essentially, a desire for a *desire-free* life. In fantasy, family love is a resource that can be exploited without effort. One need never yearn for *jouissance,* for that dangerous and intoxicating fire. But once incest is forbidden, sexuality becomes a force bound by prohibitions.[25] In that moment, desire is born. A partner has to be sought from beyond the family group. As the midrash puts it, a man has to engage a matchmaker to speak for him, so that he may marry his friend's daughter.[26] Gaps must be bridged, language shaped to frame laws, conventions, a network, a fretting, through which the fire of *jouissance* may shine.

If the people cannot tolerate the incest taboo, that is because they cannot tolerate *desire*. The meat, the flesh they yearn for is the flesh that requires no yearning. It is free—gratuitous, momentary pleasure, requiring neither frustration nor language.

CONTINUAL DESIRE

In a similar vein, Ha'amek Davar reads the people's outbreak of desire. He reads the expression *hit-avu ta'avah*, "They were consumed with desire"—"they desired and *resented their desire*." For instance, they complain about the manna that falls every day—precisely because they receive only one day's ration at a time, which forces them into a position of continual desire. Ramban already expresses the idea: "They said, Even the manna that we live on is not truly in our hands, so that we may have the pleasure of seeing it available to us. Instead, we yearn for it and lift up our eyes to God to pray for it, that it may appear again today" (Num. 11:6).

The manna becomes an object of desire and a reminder of their vulnerability. They resent their dependency, the posture of prayer, the sense of *not-to-have*, which, as the poet Wallace Stevens has it, is the beginning of desire.

But, Ha'amek Davar adds, they are also embarrassed by their own repudiation of desire and of prayer. For that reason, they adopt a cover story—lust for meat, as though constant sensual gratification will secure them against the agitation of yearning.

"*Ein kol!*—There is nothing at all! Nothing but this manna to look to!" (Num. 11:6). Their own gaze turned heavenward makes them profoundly uneasy. "There is nothing," they cry. Or—more literally—"There is not everything!" The only thing that could allay their anxiety would be *kol*—everything, a plenitude of gratification that leaves no gaps of frustration.

In this complex reading, Ha'amek Davar explores some of the subtleties of desire. The manna, which is in general celebrated precisely for its plenitude (enough for each person) and for its regularity (it falls every day), is at the same time a figure for continual suspense: will it fall again tomorrow? It is the very opposite of the gratification called *pat be-sallo*: lit., bread in the basket—the confidence that one has all one needs for the future. The manna is a constant reminder that desire can never be finally appeased, so that the object of desire carries with it intimations of dependency, possible frustration, endless yearning—and resentment. The other face of the gift of manna is the prohibition against hoarding. Like the gift of love, desire must be encountered anew each day.

THRESHOLD OF AN EMPTINESS

The English psychoanalyst Adam Phillips tells of a child patient who is referred to him for being "excessively greedy and always bored." The boy says, "If I eat everything, I won't have to eat anymore." And Phillips comments:

> For this boy, greed was, among other things, an attack on the desiring part of the self, a wish to get to the end of his appetite and finish with it once and for all. Part of the total fantasy of greed is always the attempt to eat up one's own appetite. But for this desolate child greed was a form of self-cure for a malign boredom that continually placed him on the threshold of an emptiness, a lack, that he couldn't bear.[27]

The "total fantasy of greed," for the Israelites, too, includes an "attack on the desiring part of the self." For them, too, greed becomes a kind of self-cure for the recurrent emptiness, boredom, and yearning that can never be totally allayed. The immensity of desire has become too frightening to bear.

In another context, Phillips reports on another patient, who has become phobic about going to the university library. She says it is "too much for her . . . she couldn't take it all in." And Phillips suggests that this is like being faced with a huge meal and being told she has to finish her plateful. She replies, "Perhaps I should blow up the library." He comments: "It was as if her primary task was managing her greed. In a sense, she wanted it so much she couldn't take it in. She said to me at one point, as a joke: 'I really envy the library, it knows everything already.'"[28]

What Phillips conveys in these stories about greed is the sense of

too much desire, of flinching before the beauty and goodness of the
world, and with this, the rage, the destructiveness. When the Israelites say, "There is nothing!" they are really saying, "There is a lack of
everything!" The *jouissance* that they desire they also fear and repudiate. It is too much and too desirable; they must *blow up* the library
and their own desire for it.

When, therefore, they hanker for meat ("Who will give us meat to
eat?"), God interprets this as a rejection of the Exodus history and,
indeed, of God Himself ("'It is good for us in Egypt. . . .' You have
rejected God who is in your midst!") In fantasy, they are choosing the
banal pleasures of Egypt over "God-who-is-in-your-midst."

This is, in fact, a much more visceral statement than it appears
in English translation. "You have rejected"—*m'astem*—indicates revulsion, abjection, the vomiting reflex. Something that has been
eaten with appetite suddenly nauseates one; it is expelled from
one's innards. This is the bizarre physical imagery of God's speech.
It is God—or, as Ha'amek Davar rephrases it, the delight with the
God of Sinai—that is now being violently expelled. "That exalted
delight," the *jouissance* of Sinai, has visited them with a sense of
larger life. The uncanny, indwelling presence of the Other has now
become unbearable. If the people say, "It is good for us in Egypt,"
they are imagining a pre-Sinai state in which that *jouissance* was
unknown to them. Saying these words, they violently put it outside
themselves.

"Why ever did we leave Egypt?"—With these words, they destroy
the past, the Exodus story, with its blissful intimations. But those
who refuse to leave Egypt are fated to die. This remains true, even
after the historical fact of the Exodus. Retroactively, one has the
power either to affirm or to repudiate that originary *jouissance*. It
may be as simple a matter, it seems, as saying the words *tov* or *ra—*
good or *evil:* "I love it" or "I hate it." Or even as asking an incredulous rhetorical question: "Who will give us meat to eat?" (Num.
1:4)—which God elaborates: "For it was *good* for us in Egypt!" (11:18).
With such words, adds the Ha'amek Davar, they actively undermine
the goodness of the Exodus narrative. The Talmudic expression for
such swerves of consciousness is *toheh al ha-rishonot*—devaluing the
virtuous decisions of the past.[29] If one comes to regret one's earlier
good deeds, the regret, in a sense, obliterates the deeds.

THE AESTHETIC CONFLICT

This movement of the soul, the oscillation between the experience of Revelation and the wish to destroy that experience, has its origins in the very beginnings of human life. This is the claim of several psychoanalytic thinkers, among them Jean Laplanche, Donald Meltzer, W. R. Bion, and Melanie Klein.

For Laplanche, the infant is the recipient of "messages" from the parents (at first from the mother) that are beyond his comprehension. These messages are unconscious and therefore *enigmatic;* neither the mother herself nor the infant fully understands them. The sexuality of the mother, for instance, specifically of her breast, is opaquely communicated to the child along with the obvious comforts of her milk. Without any conscious intention, the mother transmits messages that baffle the child, so that throughout life the child will translate and retranslate these messages. But the mysterious and traumatic impact of the other person will remain, implanted within him.

As Adam Phillips puts it: "The infant, in narcissistic closure is, so to speak, in recovery from having been too open, too confoundingly receptive to the mother's messages.... Laplanche's essence of the human soul is a traumatic but unavoidable—and therefore constitutive—receptivity to the other."[30]

Caught in the orbit of the other, the infant is radically decentered. This leads to an attempt to close off from desire, to "translate" the experience into comprehensible or bearable terms. A kind of inevitable captivation thus is part of the formation of the human soul; it is punctuated by a recurrent flight into language—an attempt to repossess oneself in coherent narratives—that Laplanche calls narcissistic closure.

Another version of the primal human drama is told by Donald Meltzer.[31] He writes of the impact of the beauty of the mother and of the conflict this creates in the child. This "aesthetic conflict" begins very early in the life of mother and baby. The "ordinary beautiful mother holds her ordinary beautiful baby and they are lost in the aesthetic impact of one another." The conflict that follows this rapture can result in the baby's "closing down his perceptual apertures against the dazzle of the sunrise."

Meltzer writes of the "afterimage of pain," of the conflict that is evoked by overwhelming beauty and the wild recoil from the pain of that pleasure: "The tragic element in the aesthetic experience resides, not in [its] transience, but in the enigmatic quality of the object." He quotes Keats's "Ode on Melancholy":

She dwells with Beauty—Beauty that must die;
And Joy, whose hand is ever at his lips
Bidding adieu . . .

It is the enigmatic quality of joy and beauty that tantalizes the soul. This central experience of pain rises from an "uncertainty tending towards distrust, verging on suspicion." "The impact of the beauty of the world, and of passionate intimacy with another human being" must then be avoided. Who can know for sure what is within that beautiful exterior, that face, that breast? She is not always there when I want her; worse, when she is there, shadows cross her face, her thoughts shift, leaving me abandoned. What does she truly want?

For Beauty's nothing
but the beginning of Terror we're still just able to bear
and why we adore it so is because it secretly disdains
to destroy us.

—Rilke, *Duino Elegies* I

Placing the "aesthetic conflict" at the beginning of human experience, Meltzer connects with Melanie Klein in her insistence that "a certain level of mental pain . . . is essential for development of the personality."[32] Meltzer also refers to W. R. Bion, who wrote of "the 'new idea' which impinges on the mind as a catastrophe, for, in order to be assimilated, this sets in flux the entire cognitive structure." This "new idea" presents itself in Bion's thought as an "emotional experience" of the beauty of the world and its wondrous organization. Since "at the passionate level . . . pleasure and pain are inextricably bound together,"[33] one has to develop the ability to tolerate the conflict. This tolerance Bion, quoting Keats, calls "negative capability":

"When a man is capable of being in uncertainties, mysteries, doubt, without any irritable reaching after fact and reason."[34]

Faith in the interior world of the beautiful mother is, then, something that the baby must develop, if she is to survive the anguish of *not-knowing*. Otherwise, the baby will tend to "clos[e] down . . . [her] perceptual apertures against the dazzle of the sunrise."[35] The infant may then withdraw into the narcissistic closure that is the reverse side of that rapture.

THE OUTRAGEOUS METAPHOR: MOSES SUCKLES THE PEOPLE

The psychoanalytic thinkers we have glanced at all focus on the mother-baby relation, particularly in the passionate experience of nursing. From this phase of human development emerge many of the momentous issues of the embodied soul, conscious and unconscious: thirst, hunger, desire, fear, hatred, loss, trust, distrust. The self and its conflicted relations with the world are folded up in this originary moment. The infant at the breast is both enraptured and resentful. The mother's breast is essential but tragically unreliable, or excessive, or enigmatic. The mother appears and disappears. The baby "never has uninterrupted possession of the breast . . . he is in a constant state of being weaned."[36]

This central, blissful, and perilous experience of nursing is also the central moment of Moses' poetic understanding of his own relation with his people:

And Moses said to God, "Why have You dealt ill [*ra*] with Your servant, and why have I not enjoyed Your favor, that You have laid the burden of this people upon me? Did I conceive this entire people, did I bear them, that You should say to me, 'Carry them in your bosom as a wet nurse carries an infant,' to the land that You have promised on oath to their fathers?" (Num. 11:11–12).

In reaction to the burden of the people's desires and resentments (Num. 11:10), Moses cries out his own protest at the *ra* of God's treatment. Suddenly, *ra* inhabits the center of his imagination, infiltrates his own voice.[37] His recent litany of *tov* expressions, celebrating God's goodness (10:29–32), has abruptly modulated into another sense of things. Seamlessly, the "burden" of the people becomes the burden of the unborn child in the womb and the burden of the suckling child in the bosom. And Moses unfolds from being God's "servant" to being that womb, that bosom. His words paint himself as the nursing father, the *omen:* masculine figure with feminine womb and breast.

This is a moment of great imaginative power, in which, almost despite himself, Moses reaches beyond the conventional limits of language. He cries out from a transitional place; tantalized by a feminine image of total nurturance, he protests that this is inconceivable for him. Yet in one movement of imaginative genius, he frames his relation to his people as that of an *omen:* a fantasy figure of infinite constancy and compassion, merging self and other. In such a relation, he would indeed be an *omen,* a source of unbounded nurturance, of *emunah,* of trustworthiness. As such, he could not fail to elicit a responsive trust from them. But the very words in which he articulates this image undermine its force. Framed in rhetorical questions—"Did I conceive this people, did I bear them . . . ?"—his fantasy of himself is deflected from the outset. Even as a fantasy, it is not viable.

It is worth noticing that, in Hebrew, his questions are more physically focused and pungent than in English translation. Literally, he asks, "Was I *impregnated* with this people, did I *give birth* to them?" A note of scorn disturbs his questions; even his repeated reference to "*this* people" betrays a tonal change from his earlier rhetoric of solidarity with them. (In the Golden Calf narrative, he repeatedly referred to them as "*Your* people" and identified his fate with theirs [Exod. 32:32].) Immediately, the force of his metaphor begins to disperse: the concrete situation takes over—the people's craving for meat, his inability to provide it (Num. 11:13), the *weight* of the administrative burden. Nursing father and suckling child vanish from his speech. But, of course, once spoken, the fantasy rides the air. Somewhere in the universe there exists a Moses who, flowing with milk, can inspire faith in his people.

Moses as pregnant and nursing mother wrenches our concepts, our logical differentiations, our usual uses of language. For T. S. Eliot, it is precisely such unexpectedness that measures the success of poetic metaphor.[38] "No one is a poet," says essayist Octavio Paz, "unless he has felt the temptation to destroy language and create another one, unless he has experienced the fascination of non-meaning and the no less terrifying fascination of meaning that is inexpressible."[39]

What begins in Moses' metaphor, as in all-powerful metaphor, is a process in which unconnected images—Moses and the pregnant mother, or Moses and his people—fail to quite connect with each other. An abyss yawns between words, between Moses and his people, between Moses and God. What makes that abyss palpable is the very force of Moses' yearning. But a metaphor blossoms from this fissure. His language has never been so alive, as at this moment of complex love.

For Moses and the people both know that he is, in fact, the assigned *omen,* the wet nurse. One of the most beautiful descriptions of this relationship is found in the midrash on Song of Songs, which inscribes the image of suckling maternal breasts on Moses' identity:

> "Your breasts are like two fawns" (Songs 4:5): These are Moses and Aaron. Just as these breasts are the beauty and glory, the harmony, honor, and praise of a woman, so Moses and Aaron were the beauty and glory, the harmony, honor, and praise of Israel. And just as these breasts are full of milk, so Moses and Aaron filled Israel with Torah.[40]

Here, two different roles are assigned to the breasts of a woman: they are the source of nourishment, and they are the sign of her beauty. In the Song of Songs, the erotic beauty of the beloved's breasts is the plain meaning of the text. But Rashi, in his reading, selects the feeding function of the breasts: *"Your two breasts—that suckle you."*[41] In a startling move, the woman's breasts in erotic love become the breasts of *her* mother who once suckled her—a strange act of dissociation that shifts the breasts from one site to another. They are "your breasts" only in the sense that they nurtured the beloved in infancy: in fantasy, they remain ever hers.

But in the first part of the midrash, it is the *beauty* of Moses and Aaron that is held in focus—a representative beauty that draws admiration upon the entire people. The feeding function follows, but only once the aesthetic value is established. The midrashic metaphor works to express the organic connection between the obvious "beauty" of Moses and a hidden dimension of his people. He represents them, he is the most dazzling part of them. Without them, his beauty is unrealized; he is dazzling precisely *as* their "breast."

What is his effect on the people? On the obvious level, he is their source of spiritual sustenance. But on the aesthetic/erotic level, he evokes Meltzer's and Laplanche's accounts of the dazzling impact of the mother on the infant, and the conflict of uncertainty that results from that impact. For the breasts serve a double function: their maternal use is always haunted by enigmatic messages of erotic life. Moses becomes a figure of erotic power who is also the nurturer, the transmitter of the words of Torah. For the people, he is the source of life, at the same time as he intimates a transcendent and dangerous beauty—which is a reflection of *their* beauty.

In other words, the breast imagery in the midrash both dazzles and intimidates. It confers on Moses—and, through him, on the people—the comforting and constant nourishment of Torah. At the same time, Moses tantalizes the people by evoking that *jouissance,* the overwhelming bliss of Sinai. The people *turn away* precisely from that brilliant light; they close their apertures against the dazzle of the sunrise.

"HE WOULD NOT NURSE"

In considering this complex moment of Moses' desire to be an *omen,* we remember his own early experience of the breast. It is striking that the Torah pays so much attention to the question of a wet nurse for the infant Moses. In the end, his own mother is hired by the Egyptian princess to nurse the baby. So, in a sense, all ends well and Moses returns "home." But his mother's breast comes to him constrained by her slave role; it returns to him, also, after a deathly interim when he is abandoned to the waters of the Nile.

The midrash takes up the basic question of the attention paid—three verses of dialogue between Miriam and the princess—to the nursing requirements of the infant Moses. Would the princess not have had Egyptian wet nurses at her disposal?

"A wet nurse from the Hebrews": Why is this specified? To teach that she tried out many Egyptian wet nurses, but he would not nurse. God said, "The mouth that is destined to speak with God should suckle impure milk!!"[42]

Among other things, this passage conveys a sense of the spiritual precociousness of the infant Moses. *"He would not nurse"*: Some unthinking trust in the breast has already been ruptured. It is scarcely surprising, then, that he finds it hard to achieve that kind of instinctual faith in the connections that link self and world.

"LET ME NOT SEE MY EVIL"

This faith, this trust, and its failures, constitute the history of the people in the wilderness. Lack of faith (*emunah*) is a recurrent problem in their early history with God and with Moses. The issue is at root one of *trust,* and the story of its oscillations is connected with the *omen* metaphor. A foundational experience of trust—which the English psychoanalyst Donald Winnicott calls *basic trust*—is incarnated in the happy relation with the breast.[43]

From the beginning of his mission, Moses expresses doubt about the people's capacity to trust. "They will not *believe* me" (Exod. 4:1), he says at the Burning Bush; implicitly, he conveys his skepticism about his own capacity as an *omen,* as a source of reliable nurturance. But soon after, we read, "And the people did *believe* him" (4:31); and at the Red Sea: "They *believed* in God and in Moses His servant" (14:31). Moses is praised by God as *"trusted [ne'eman]* throughout My household" (Num. 12:7); but in the end God will accuse him of "not *believing* in Me to sanctify Me before the eyes of the Israelites" (20:12).

In all these cases, it is not belief that is at stake, but trust. And in each case, one might say that trust is largely a function of the trustworthiness of the other. If some failure has occurred, it may be the *omen,* the source of the milk that has proved insufficiently reliable. However, the issue is complicated by the fact that whatever in fact happened at the beginning of life is filtered through the fantasy life of the infant. It is this inner world that ultimately shapes and colors reality.

In this sense, the question of trust is set in a complex field of meaning. If Moses cannot trust himself to provide for the people, then this may well be symbolically connected with his own early history. His origins as the endangered child of a persecuted nation create the canvas on which his deepest knowledge of the world is painted. And when he turns to "bearing" that people, his trust in their capacity to trust reflects this precarious reality.

The moment when this complex sense of things comes to the surface is when he cries out to God: "If this is how You deal with me, then kill me rather, I beg You, and *let me not see my evil!*" (Num. 11:15). This literal translation conveys the mystery of Moses' prayer. He asks for death, to avoid further witnessing of *his* evil. He asks to die, so as not to endure further experience of disappointment.

But *"my* evil" raises questions: does he mean "the evil done to me"? Or "the evil that I do"? In a fascinating comment, Sefat Emet notes that Rashi refers to a repressed meaning: "*my* evil" is a cover for "*their* evil." In other words, he is implicitly blaming the people for his distress. Exploring further, Sefat Emet retrieves a still more repressed level of meaning: "*their* evil" covers for "*Your* evil."[44] In this startling reading, Moses is creating a field of fraught meanings. On the one hand, he is expressing his profound connection with both the people and God. But, more darkly, he evokes a diffuse sense of "evil," without clear linear causality. Ultimately, his distress and that of the people, as well as the harm that he and they do—the distrust that they bring to the world and bequeath to others—has a metaphysical dimension. God as *omen* has somehow failed to create sufficient trust in His human creatures.

REJECTING THE BREAST

This distrust makes the people turn away from the dazzling vision of Sinai. Instead they look to a world of objects, of appetites and limits. They want to grasp these objects: meat, fish, onions, garlic, leeks, and readily available sexual objects. In this world, which the French philosopher Maurice Blanchot calls the world of *turning away,*

> objects reign, along with the concern for results, the desire to have, the greed that links us to possession, the need for security and stability, the tendency to know in order to be sure, the tendency to "take account" which necessarily becomes an inclination to count and to reduce everything to account.[45]

In a sense, the people are gripped by an *aversion*. Blanchot continues, "Whenever we turn away, there is death."[46] What is at stake is an intimate way of seeing the world, which also sees through the world and its limits. He quotes Rilke on the life of the artist:

A being with no shell, open to pain,
Tormented by light, shaken by every sound.

And again Rilke: "He who creates cannot turn away from any existence."[47]

When the Israelites express revulsion from the manna, they are enacting their flight from the traumatic exposure of Sinai. When they say, "Who will give us meat to eat?" they are taking shelter in the graspable certainties of the world. And, as God paraphrases their words, they are indicating their *love* for Egypt, their recoil from the revelations of the Exodus. Emotionally, they are *expelling* the God who is within them; they are vomiting forth their own inmost parts.

Such a strong image is apparently necessary to convey the people's visceral anxiety and hatred. Their actual words have been simple, concrete, flat: "Who will give us meat to eat?" But God creates a metaphoric language to convey the force of their envy. What they have taken into themselves, like mother's milk, is now abjected by them.[48] "You have repudiated God who is in your midst," means, effectively, "You have repudiated your own deepest intimacy, your own desire, which challenges you with its immensity." The implicit metaphor is carried over from the description of their punishment: the meat, apparently so graspable and containable, will be vomited out of all body apertures (Num. 11:20).

Images of the child at the breast express primal, unconscious levels of human experience. Here is the original site of trust, faith, *emunah*—in the relation of mother-father-*omen* and child. But here, too, images of *ra*, of explosive fragmentation, replace the ideal images of reliable nurturance. The happy incorporation of the world—where mother and child, Moses and his people, are revealed as intimately connected, mirroring each other—shatters in the bodily imagination of both partners.

A further midrashic analogy associates breast milk with the manna that the people reject. The Torah describes its taste rather mysteriously as "like the taste of *le-shad ha-shamen*"—usually translated as "like rich cream" (Num. 11:8). Playing on the word *le-shad*, R. Abbahu comments:

> Just as this breast tastes to the infant of many tastes, depending on what the mother has eaten, so the manna tasted to the Israelites of many tastes. This is based on the word *le-shad*—literally, the taste of the breast. [49]

The subjectivity of the people, their *taste,* is at the center of this reading. Like the baby at the breast, they experience in the manna an oceanic bliss that transcends that of any particular food. This is *jouissance* food, like mother's milk. Moreover, this experience is attuned to the subjective taste of each individual. The Talmud discusses the three main flavors of the manna—bread, oil, or honey—which are adapted to the age and needs of each individual.[50]

In entering into the taste requirements of the individual, the midrash focuses on the interior of the body, on purely subjective experience. Taking its cue from the biblical text—"its taste was like the taste . . ."—the Talmud moves our attention to the inside of the mouth, the taste buds and their experience of mother's milk. A primal sensuality is evoked, through the image of manna as ideal gratification.[51]

In spite of all this, the people respond to the manna with distrust and anxiety. In Psalm 78, the Psalmist expansively revisits this wilderness condition:

> A generation whose heart was inconstant, whose spirit was
> 　　not true [*lo ne'emna*] to God. (v. 8)
> They forgot His deeds and the wonders that He showed them.
> 　　(v. 11)
> They spoke against God saying, "Can God spread a feast in
> 　　the wilderness?" (v. 19)
> They did not put their trust in God, did not rely on His
> 　　deliverance. (v. 22)
> They had no faith in His wonders. (v. 32)
> They seduced Him with their words; their hearts were

inconstant toward Him; they were untrue [*lo ne'emnu*] to
His covenant. (vv. 36–37)

The root *a-m-n* is used repeatedly, with its meanings of constancy, consistency, truth, faith, belief—and, most centrally, trust.
Witnessing the wonders of God, the people would have no difficulty
believing that these things are happening to them, nor that God is at
work in them. Their chronic crisis is one of *trust*—the conviction
that God will fulfill His promises, that His past wonders express His
reliable intention to see them through to their destination. What is
at stake is not so much God's *power* as His love. It is this basic distrust
that marks the stories of the wilderness—especially the early stories
that lead up to the Sin of the Spies. It is distrust that disrupts the
momentum of the redemption narrative.

ANXIETY AND COURAGE

The breast imagery we have looked at in the midrash gives us two
models. In one, the perfect integration of food and palate evokes a
fantasy of total bliss. In the other, the *beautiful* breast may have a disturbing impact on the infant, may arouse conflict and anxiety. Enigmatic messages implant themselves in that newly embodied soul. The
open heart closes up. The fragile integrity of the self is threatened.
And a pattern establishes itself, in which at crucial phases of life one
is challenged to new self-integrations, with the disintegration—the
anxiety—that accompanies such crises.

The existentialist philosopher Paul Tillich calls this experience the
"anxiety of nonbeing" and contrasts neurotic reactions with what he
calls "courage":

> Courage does not remove anxiety. Since anxiety is existential,
> it cannot be removed. But courage takes the anxiety of non-
> being into itself.... He who does not succeed in taking his
> anxiety courageously upon himself can succeed in avoiding
> the extreme situation of despair by escaping into neurosis. He
> still affirms himself but on a limited scale. *Neurosis is the way of
> avoiding nonbeing by avoiding being.*[52]

To avoid despair is to diminish the possibilities of the self. Courage is the name Tillich gives to the ability to struggle with the reality of nonbeing, to take it into oneself rather than to abject it. The opposite of courage is a habitual avoidance of passionate and troubling experience.

The wilderness experience, with Sinai at its heart, represents both death and life. This is the place of passionate love, of the *jouissance* that floods the gates of perception. It is also a terrible and inconceivable place, where being-with-God—or containing God-within-them—endangers their being. The Revelation at Sinai is *instantly* followed by its backlash, the Golden Calf. And even after the Tabernacle has been built in their midst, with God at its heart, a profound ambivalence makes them *turn away* from Sinai—from the unfathomable "heart of the mystery" that might forever change them.

What they flee is what they unbearably desire: "One cannot master [lit., stand upon] the words of Torah, unless one has stumbled over them."[53] The stumbling block is the words of Torah, which make one falter, incapable of mastering them. In the moment of stumbling, of loss of familiar being, something is taken in: the anxiety of nonbeing of which Tillich speaks. Only in this way can one come to *stand,* in a new place.

From this point of view, the wilderness is the stark theater in which human courage is to be practiced. In this vein, Mei Ha-Shilo'ach[54] writes a kind of meta-narrative of the wilderness. The book of Bamidbar, he says, is about an essential darkness in the human being, even the greatest human being. The *midbar,* the wilderness, is the scene of aggression and annihilation. As Moses reminds the people at the end of his life, "Remember, do not forget how you angered God *in the wilderness*" (Deut. 9:7).

This *midbar* is an inner condition, which challenges the individual to become human. The most sublime experiences contain that "wilderness energy," the primal forces out of which one generates a larger humanity. The theater of that struggle is called *midbar.*

The Hasidic master is acknowledging the libidinal and aggressive forces that inform the spiritual aspirations of even the greatest people. Life and death wishes create a force field within every individual.

On this rough ground, standing, understanding, speaking become significant human acts.

SPEAKING THE WILDERNESS

"The superiority [*motar*] of the human over the animal is naught," dolefully declares Ecclesiastes (Eccles. 3:19). In a profound misreading, R. Yosef Albo interprets: "The very excellence of the human being is *ayin*—the awareness of nonbeing." A human excess (*motar*) organizes itself around that *ayin*. Here, subjectivity may begin to form around a primordial and foundational lack. This brave subjectivity forms itself through language. "Remember, do not forget, how you angered God, your God, in the wilderness" (Deut. 9:7). To remember, says the midrash,[55] is to *speak* of it, to tell the story, so that the past with all its losses intermeshes with present and future.

Moses, in the name of God, urges the people to *remember*, to keep alive in their imagination the anxieties and rages of the past. To be in a *midbar* means to acknowledge the heart of the mystery—the posture of a nation of individuals faced with the *oneg*, the *jouissance* of God's presence. If their brief standing at Sinai turns immediately into a *turning away*, that, too, is a human posture.

Emerson would write of his contemporaries: "Man is timid and apologetic; he is no longer upright; he dares not say 'I think, I am,' but quotes some saint or sage. He is ashamed before the blade of grass or the blowing rose. . . . they are for what they are, they exist with God today."[56] But the bad posture, the recoil from God, the conformity, the self-conscious shame that precludes responsibility—it is not Emerson's contemporaries alone who can find themselves in his critique. Through Emerson's text, we can also sense the range of postures—standing, stumbling, fleeing—of the Israelite wilderness narrative.

SINAI—THE REPRESSED RESIDUE

If the flight from Sinai is like the truancy of a child from the burdens of schoolwork, the moral issue is readily understandable. But if, as Ha'amek Davar more opaquely suggests, this is a flight from the *oneg*, the *jouissance,* of being with God, more disturbing questions arise. Revelation is met with a self-conscious anxiety, an entirely human faltering in courage. Perhaps, as T. S. Eliot says, "Humankind cannot bear very much reality."[57] The human being turns away; the apertures of perception narrow.

In this narrative, it is from beauty that the people recoil—an enigmatic beauty that both enraptures and sows terror. Their flight will be continuously reenacted in the wilderness, as they try to dislodge God who is in their midst. But Sinai is now inescapable: its impact is already lodged within them. In Laplanche's language, the Other has left a "repressed residue" of troubling beauty.[58] God at Sinai, deeply unfathomable, leaves the people *decentered,* captivated.

Hosea and Jeremiah will speak of the experience of Revelation as an act of seduction: "Therefore I will seduce her to the wilderness [*midbar*] and I will speak [*ve-dibbarti*] to her heart" (Hosea 2:16). "You have seduced me and I yielded to Your seduction . . ." (Jer. 20:7). Enigmatic messages are the very stuff of seduction, "leading astray," disturbing given structures. God has allowed the people to see something that they cannot understand. The matter of Sinai is not dogma, which can be grasped, or even Law, which apparently needs no commentary, but *messages,* which remain for them to translate. The force of this "translation drive," as Laplanche calls it, lies in the compelling nature of the to-be-translated message. The "repeated attempt at translation, justification, delimitation and mastery" is, essentially, a struggle to recenter the decentered self, to create closure, to achieve some stability. What remains untranslated, the residue, reopens the self, exposes it again to the originary relation to the Other.

These narratives in the wilderness tell of the people's first attempts to deal with the "traumatic" impact of Sinai. Destabilized, filled with to-be-translated messages, they recoil from the very beauty of the encounter. They suffer, not from lack of *belief,* but from lack of *faith,* or *trust.* Anxiety, impatience, inattention will not allow them to be seduced by God.

A VISCERAL TONGUE

Where does Ha'amek Davar draw his license to use erotic language, the language of *oneg,* to describe the Revelation at Sinai? He is, of course, drawing on a rich literature of kabbalistic and midrashic imagery. But the original source of such language is found in the Song of Songs.

In the erotic dialogues of the Song, lover and beloved enact the hidden drama of redemption and revelation. Traditionally, the Song has been read precisely as a dialogue between God and Israel. More specifically, it has been read as the passionate history of the Exodus, the Revelation at Sinai, and the wilderness period. But what characterizes the Song so poignantly is that, in all their modes—loving, fleeing, calling, answering, preceding, following—the lovers never unite. There is great yearning, great sensuality, and great absence. The lovers speak their love; they speak its *impossibility*, which Julia Kristeva describes as "an impossibility set up as amatory law."

The woman, particularly, hears and sees, but, especially, *imagines* her beloved. For the first time ever, Kristeva claims, the amorous wife "begins to speak before her king, husband, or God. . . . The amorous Shulamite is the first woman to be sovereign before her loved one."[59] And, in speaking, she constitutes herself *as lover*. She sings, "I am black but beautiful, daughters of Jerusalem, like the tents of Kedar. . . . He has taken me to his banquet hall, and his banner over me is love. Feed me with raisin cakes, restore me with apples, for I am *sick with love*."

Here is the nation after Sinai, identifying with the Shulamite— "Divided. Sick and yet sovereign." "She is sovereign through her love and the discourse that causes it to be."[60] In Bamidbar, she contains in herself God and Moses; her desire and her fear, her despair, her flight, her aversions and her conversions, all seek a passage into a different language. Here in the wilderness, she learns to speak a visceral tongue, rooted in the body in its innermost parts. From these obscure places, strange metaphors blossom—wilderness fruit, bewilderments of love.

FOUR

"Sing—Now!—to God": Miriam and Moses

SPEAKING AGAINST MOSES

Emerging from the general chorus of lament and desire in the previous narratives, Miriam and Aaron initiate a mysterious episode, in which the two siblings attack the singular status of Moses' prophecy.

In the end, Miriam alone is punished—stricken with leprosy[1] and quarantined outside the camp. Her fate mobilizes the dramatic action in the narrative: Aaron pleads with Moses to intercede for her; Moses prays to God for her healing; God declares final sentence. She is the true protagonist of the story: the verbal attack on Moses is initiated by her—*Va-tidabber Miriam v'Aharon* (lit., "And she spoke— Miriam and Aaron") (Num. 12:1). Both Miriam and Aaron speak against Moses; but the verb is singular and feminine, and Miriam is mentioned first—all eloquent hints that the driving spirit is hers,[2] even as a certain ambiguity is maintained.

Miriam and Aaron speak in the plural voice: "Is it only through Moses that God has spoken? Has he not spoken through *us* too?" (Num. 12:2). God summons all three siblings, who enter the Tent of Assembly as a group; Miriam and Aaron are then separated from Moses, leave the Tent, and listen to God's magisterial response to their complaint. Miriam is left "leprous as snow," half her flesh consumed like a stillborn child, in Aaron's poignant description. She is quarantined for seven days, while the people wait for her to be "gathered in" once more into the camp.

However, this general summary of the narrative is complicated from the beginning. Miriam expresses envy of Moses' dominance: God spoke with us, too, not only with him! But the narrator describes the siblings' complaint differently: "She spoke against Moses, because of the Cushite woman he had married: 'He married a Cushite woman!'" Who is this Cushite (Ethiopian? dark-skinned?)

woman?[3] She is first mentioned by the narrator, and then immediately in quoted speech by Miriam and Aaron. How does this exotic reference connect with the rest of their speech? No sooner is the Cushite mentioned in this double way—by both indirect and direct speech—than she drops out of the story. God addresses only the substance of Miriam's speech: the question of Moses' prophetic prestige.

In the wake of a strong midrashic tradition, Rashi gives us an unexpected version of the story. The Cushite woman is not some other woman but Moses' own wife, Zippora. He has separated from her because of the demands of his prophetic mission. And Miriam is exercised by what seems to her Moses' hubris in repudiating married sexuality:

1. "And Miriam and Aaron spoke": She opened the conversation, therefore Scripture mentions her first. And whence did Miriam know that Moses had separated himself from his wife? R. Nathan answered: Miriam was beside Zippora when Moses was told, "Eldad and Medad are prophesying in the camp!" (Num. 11:17). When Zippora heard this, she exclaimed, "Woe to the wives of these men if they have anything to do with prophecy, for they will separate from their wives just as my husband has separated from me!" It was from this that Miriam knew about it, and told Aaron. Now Miriam who had no intention to disparage Moses was so severely punished—How much more so is one who intentionally disparages his fellow! (Sifre).

    "The Cushite woman": This tells us that all agreed as to her beauty, just as all agree as to the blackness of an Ethiopian.

    "Cushite": The numerical value of this word is the same as that of "a beautiful woman."

    "Because of the Cushite woman": Because of the fact that Moses had divorced her.

    "For he had married a Cushite woman": What is the force of this statement? (It appears redundant.) But sometimes a woman is pleasant on account of her beauty but unpleasant because of her deeds; or sometimes a woman is pleasant because of her deeds but not because of her beauty. This woman, however, was pleasant in every respect.

"The Cushite woman": Because of her beauty she was called "the Ethiopian," just as a man calls his handsome son "the Moor," in order to ward off the evil eye.

"He married a Cushite woman": And had now divorced her.

2. "Has God spoken with him alone? Has He not also spoken with us?"—and we have not separated from our spouses![4]

Why is Zippora called the Cushite woman? Rashi offers three explanations: because her undeniable beauty is indicated in the undeniable blackness of an Ethiopian; because of the numerological value of the word "Cushite," which is equivalent to the word for beauty; and because referring to her as black, instead of its opposite, beautiful, wards off the evil eye. She is, moreover, referred to twice as the Cushite woman because her beauty is both moral and physical. Miriam conveys a certain tension around her beauty, a sense of being immaculate but endangered, of exotic otherness.

It is striking that the midrashic narrative centers on Moses' *separation* from his beautiful, virtuous wife. This secret meaning inverts the obvious meaning of the story. It is not Moses' marriage but his abandonment of it that agitates his siblings. This private matter becomes known to Miriam alone, because she overhears Zippora's reaction when, in the previous narrative, Eldad and Medad break into ecstatic prophecy. Zippora expresses sympathy for their wives, who now will share her fate as grass widows.

A subversive world of meanings is intimated—the world of female sexuality, in its most private relation to the esoteric but publicly expressed world of prophetic spirituality. Miriam now knows what no one else knows: Zippora is abandoned by her husband, despite the fact that he married her, and that she is beautiful in every possible way. What Miriam actually says about Moses barely indicates the complexity of her concerns: why should Moses separate from his wife? She and Aaron, too, have had their prophetic moments without requiring separation from their spouses! In fact, words are used to imply their opposites: "black" means "beautiful"; "he married her" implies "he separated from her."

The effect of this covert sexual narrative is to deepen the resonance of Miriam's complaint. Rashi in fact emphasizes that she did not intend to disparage Moses; she is punished for merely remarking on, questioning, Moses' celibacy. But the text itself describes her as speaking *"be-Mosheh"*—normally translated "against Moses"; and God then explicitly charges Miriam and Aaron with speaking *"be-avdi be-Mosheh*—against My servant Moses" (Num. 12:8). Their antagonism seems clear; Rashi, however, indicates that Miriam's question is not as hostile as it appears.

And indeed, this prefix *be-* is richly complicated by the different use that Miriam and Aaron themselves immediately make of it: "Is it only *through* Moses [*be-Mosheh*] that God has spoken? Has He not also spoken *through* us [*banu*]?" Apparently, the prefix has two meanings: speaking *against,* or speaking *through* (or more literally, *in*). These two meanings are sustained in tension throughout the narrative. (See Num. 12:6–8.) God tells of revealing Himself from *inside* something—*in* a vision, *in* a dream, of speaking *inside* Moses, who is *inside* God's house; as well as to Miriam and Aaron's speaking *against* Moses, and to God's anger *against* (but literally *inside—bam*) them. Perhaps these meanings inform one another, modulating and enlarging the power of language? Perhaps Miriam's misspeaking is registered on an arc that embraces the experience of prophecy, of being *spoken through*?

SEXUALITY AND PROPHECY

We will return to this question. For now, we note that Miriam alone knows of Moses' celibacy. The rumor emerges from the women's enclave, from whispered words, scarcely meant to be heard at all. This knowledge represents a woman's interpretation of a public fact: Eldad and Medad are prophesying in the camp. The men's understanding of this fact is quite different. According to the Talmud, Eldad and Medad are prophesying: "Moses is about to die, and Joshua will lead the people into the Land!"[5] This occurs against the background of a mass outbreak of prophecy among the seventy elders. This outbreak, however, is described as an "emanation" of Moses' power (Num. 11:25). Eldad and Medad, on the other hand, prophesy independently, declaring Moses' impending death and replacement.

The timing is significant, since the people are preparing to enter the Land, perhaps within a very short time. Suddenly, in the words of the two freelance prophets, Moses is to be supplanted by Joshua. Joshua, Moses' "attendant from his youth," cries out in great anxiety, "My lord Moses, restrain them!" (Num. 11:28). This prophecy borders on blasphemy: Joshua's beloved master is being scandalously removed from the stage of history. Moses reassures his younger companion: "Are you wrought up on my account? Would that all God's people were prophets, that God put His spirit upon them!" (11:29).

In an acute psychological reading, Or Ha-Chaim suggests that Joshua perhaps protests too much. His urgent expression of loyalty to Moses, his peremptory demand to restrain the delinquents, may cover for his own ambivalence about coming to power. What we may call an oedipal anxiety drives him to an almost imperious tone, which the midrash identifies as inappropriate: he was "issuing legal instruction, in the presence of his teacher."[6] This reading sheds light on some of the spiritual and emotional implications of a prophetic outbreak of this kind. Suddenly Moses' mortality enters public discourse and provokes oedipal overreactions like that of Joshua. The end of an epoch approaches. Prophecy is spreading like wildfire. And Moses himself acquiesces in such an expansion of the ecstatic experience to "the whole people."

These questions and anxieties about ecstatic prophecy arise on one plane of the narrative of Eldad and Medad. But, in the women's world, quite different meanings emerge. "Woe to their wives!" says Zippora. And Miriam understands something about Moses' private life that deeply troubles her. What she says, then, may have different meanings for herself and for Aaron. For him, the question of Moses' singular prophecy may be a relatively simple question. He, too, has played the prophetic role, during the Egyptian slavery, before Moses returned to Egypt from Midian and from the Burning Bush.[7] There may be some envy in his words, as well as genuine puzzlement. What, after all, is the difference between his prophecy and that of his younger brother?

But for Miriam, I suggest, the same words resonate with intimate questions about sexuality and prophecy. For Moses, evidently, the two states of being cannot coexist, while Miriam's experience of prophecy brought no interruption to her sexual life. Her difference from Aaron lies in her womanhood, in the fact of her particular relationship with her brother.

She speaks *be-Mosheh*—against Moses, but also in intense identification with him. In speaking of him, she projects her own experience onto him, to the point where his difference from her becomes unthinkable. For she, too, knows what it is to have God speak in and through her. A kind of transference takes place. Moses has become so deeply interfused with the significant movements of her own life that she cannot conceive of him in other terms. A fantasy of Miriam/Moses is played out, so that his celibacy strikes her as anomalous, out of place.

THE LOGIC OF CELIBACY

What then is Miriam's experience of sexuality and prophecy and of the space they share? Why is she so reluctant to accept Moses' ascetic behavior? In the Talmudic account,[8] Moses' decision to separate from his wife was inspired by God's command to the people, three days before the Giving of the Torah at Mount Sinai: "Do not go near a woman" (Exod. 19:15). Moses understands the implication for himself of God's words: if, in the larger community, sexual relations are to be suspended when God reveals Himself, then in his case total celibacy is required. Since Moses' life is always to be subject to divine communication, he must always be in a state of receptivity.

The logic of Moses' celibacy is, however, a result of his own thought process. It is not a direct command from God. It is true that later, in Deuteronomy, Moses remembers that God commanded the people, "Return to your tents!" while telling Moses, "You stay here with Me!" (Deut. 5:27–28). From this, the Talmud concludes: "Moses had separated from his wife, and here God *agrees with his decision*."[9] The people at large return to their sexual lives "in their tents," while Moses is to *stay with God*, in the posture of "standing at Sinai," of prophetic celibacy. God here obliquely ratifies Moses' intuition. But his original separation from his wife was not at God's command. Moses acted on his own interpretation of God's words.

Perhaps for this reason, Moses' separation from his wife appears to Miriam a kind of spiritual hubris. Moses apparently senses that this is God's will, and Miriam cannot tolerate what seems to her not only presumption on his part but, in some profound way, misapprehension of God's will.

SEPARATIONS

For, after all, the issue of sexuality and spirituality plays a significant role in Miriam's history. In the classic midrashic reading, Miriam's parents first enter the biblical narrative in a state of separation from each other: "And a man of the house of Levi went and married a Levite woman" (Exod. 2:1). "He *remarried* her," Rashi comments, after he had separated from her in despair over Pharaoh's decree that male children be thrown in the river. This inspired the Israelites to follow suit and separate from their wives. It is at Miriam's instigation that her father is reunited with his wife, and, as a result, all the other separated couples are also reunited. We notice here the same pattern as we have seen in the narrative in Numbers, chapter 12—a reference to marriage is read as a covert reference to separation. And in both narratives, Miriam wishes to undo the separation.

In one midrashic narrative, Miriam's rhetoric of persuasion is surprising: "Your decree is harsher than Pharaoh's," she tells her father; "he decreed only against male children, while you decree against all children!"[10] She describes her father as resembling Pharaoh, engaged in decrees of destruction. He is, in effect, collaborating with Pharaoh by preventing the continued life of his people. Such is the effect of the *gezerah,* the edict—that Pharaonic mode of speech that cuts apart, isolates the elements of a complex situation, and imposes rigid and sterile divisions. In a sense, she claims, her father's decision is even more rigid than Pharaoh's—precisely because of her father's righteousness. Miriam gains her point. Through her provocative speech, which constitutes a specific attack on the *gezerah* mentality, she restores the Israelite marriages with their fertile possibilities.

In a significant midrashic move, she is identified with Puah, one of the midwives who defy Pharaoh's baby-killing decree. "And they gave life—preserved, nurtured—the children" (Exod. 1:17). This relates to the time before the public decree to throw male infants into the river. Rashi associates the name Puah with the cooing sounds of the caregiver who soothes the crying child.[11] That is, before Miriam becomes involved in the drama of remarriage in her own family, she is already characterized as the source of preverbal, hypnotic sounds that help an infant make passage into the world. Earlier still, she is also associated with the labor gasps of the birthing woman.[12] Primal sounds issue from her—the pain and comfort of life itself.

It is also striking that this version of the midrash introduces an unexpected detail: when her parents separate, her mother is already three months pregnant with Moses! In most other versions, the purpose of her prophecy is to reunite her parents and make it possible for Moses to be born. Here, the meaning suddenly shifts. Reuniting her parents becomes not simply a means of enabling birth, this particular birth; it expresses the intrinsic significance of sexual union as the ground of life. Miriam speaks against the *gezerah* that disrupts the vital force of the family and the people.

This moment of vital defiance is Miriam's moment of prophecy. Her father is identified as the Head of the Israelite Court—in other words, a judicial authority whose word is law. But it is Miriam's words that sway him to a different decision. Later, at the Red Sea, she will be called "Miriam the prophetess, sister of Aaron" (Exod. 15:20). Her hour of prophecy, comments Rashi, came when she was sister only to Aaron, before Moses' birth. Her prophecy enabled his birth.

But we hear nothing of this prophetic activity in the biblical text; there, we hear only retroactively that she has already prophesied— "Miriam the prophetess"—at some moment in the past. That is, her confrontation with her father remains private. It is, after all, not a trivial matter to intervene in one's father's marriage and in his public authoritative role. Eighty years later, when she sings at the Red Sea, her prophetic status will be powerfully and publicly confirmed.

By speaking of birth and salvation and against patriarchal decrees, Miriam has reopened the channels of life. But her prophecy, like many prophecies, arouses antagonism as well as compliance:

"And his sister stood afar off" (Exod. 2:4): Why did Miriam stand far off? R. Amram in the name of Rav said: Because Miriam prophesied, "My mother is destined to give birth to a son who will save Israel." And when the house was flooded with light at the birth of Moses, her father rose up and kissed her head and said, "My daughter, your prophecy has been fulfilled." This is the meaning of, "And Miriam the prophetess, the sister of Aaron, took a timbrel" (Exod. 15:20); "the sister of Aaron," but not of Moses?—She is so called because in fact she said this prophecy when she was only the sister of Aaron, Moses not yet having been born. Now that she was casting him into the river, her mother struck her on the head and said, "My daughter, where is your prophecy now?" This is why it says, "And his sister stood afar off, to know what would be the outcome of her prophecy."[13]

Her prophecy is at first confirmed: the birth of the radiant baby brings her father to kiss her head, in a gesture of paternal approval. But then the clouds gather, and the baby is cast into the river: now, her mother strikes her on the head in a gesture of maternal rebuke. In some versions of the midrash, it is her father who both kisses her and strikes her. The impact of this family ambivalence about Miriam's prophecy becomes visible in the eloquent description of Miriam, "stationing herself at a distance by the river, to learn what would befall Moses" (Exod. 2:4). Firmly, attentively, she holds vigil over her infant brother; but the midrash positions her *at a distance— from her family*. As a prophetess whose prophecy, apparently, has failed, she is ostracized by her family. But she bears that prophecy within her staunchly like a pregnancy, waiting to know its outcome.

In the biblical text, this fraught moment is her moment as *Moses' sister* (Exod. 2:4). Her role as a prophet is obscured at this point of the biblical narrative, as it is obscured in the minds of her parents. In most midrashic narratives, however, it is her prophecy that brings Moses into the world; and it is her prophecy, too, that isolates her from her family. Shamed, excluded, she *stands*[14] in a posture of affirmation, in the flux of unresolved present reality, waiting for the future to emerge.

This moment as Moses' sister is, I suggest, deeply implanted within her. It will emerge later, when God declares judgment over her: "If her father spat in her face, would she not bear her shame for seven days? Let her be shut out of the camp for seven days, and then let her be readmitted" (Num. 12:15). Strangely, her early history of prophecy is reenacted when God quarantines her; again, her Father puts her at a distance. The Talmud notices another link between the two episodes: "As she waited for Moses [in his basket in the river], so Israel waited for her in the wilderness."[15]

Alienation and solitude, a father who kisses and strikes, a people that gathers her in—at the heart of Miriam's drama is her intense relation with her brother Moses, which continues throughout her life. Her prophetic role in bringing him into the world endangers her position in her family; as Moses' sister, she risks her identity as her father's daughter. Then, her little brother grows bigger and eclipses her. Her prophecy ceases; his begins and flourishes. But her prophetic personality reappears, transfigured, at the Red Sea.

IT SINGS

At the Red Sea, both Moses and Miriam lead the people in song. The timing of the song is significant and apparently clear: "Moses sang *then—az*" (Exod. 15:1)—*after* the Israelites had been saved from the Egyptians, now visibly dead on the seashore (14:30–15:1). However, there is another possibility: that he sang *"while* the Israelites were still walking on dry land in the midst of the Sea" (15:19).[16] Such a reading transforms the nature of the song—no longer a paean of triumph but an expression of the terror and faith of those who are still "in the midst of the Sea." While they are still walking the precarious passage between massed walls of water, *then,* at this uncanny moment, Moses has the idea of singing a song. *Az yashir Mosheh*—"Then, at that moment, he *would* sing"—he conceived the notion of singing.[17] Singing in celebration *after* victory would be understandable. But if this happened "in the midst of the Sea," what kind of singing did Moses have in mind?

Not a song of victory but, extensive midrashic passages suggest, a cry from the depths of anguish. The German composer Wagner thought that the origin of singing is in the *scream,* the primal cry of loss, separation. And in fact, such a scream is audible in the cry of the Israelites, as they see the Egyptians bearing down on them at the Red Sea: "And the Israelites cried out to God" (Exod. 14:10).[18] These midrashic passages cite the Song of Songs (2:14): "Let me hear your voice, for your voice is sweet." God desires, He finds "sweet," precisely that true voice produced by authentic passion in the face of death—by helplessness and isolation, as well as faith. This authentic scream modulates into the song "in the midst of the Sea." Vulnerable, in medias res, the song resounds in the presence of death.

In a powerful meditation, the nineteenth-century Hasidic commentary *Shem Mi-Shmuel* asks how Moses and the Israelites managed spontaneously and simultaneously to sing the same words and melody.[19] All sing *Zeh Keli*—"This is my God"—though the words are, in a sense, Moses' singular idiom. In general, *zeh—this*—is considered his personal idiom, expressing the clarity of vision that characterizes him: "God's presence speaks from out of his [Moses'] throat." But at this moment, all Israel shared his immediacy of vision—God within their vocal chords; even embryos in their mothers' womb, says the Talmud, sing in the Sea[20]—although, *Shem Mi-Shmuel* notes, their vocal chords were not yet developed! That is, the experience was of the song arising from deep within them, from some internal otherness. Essentially, it is the Shechinah—God's presence—that sings. The song is theirs only in the sense that they *intend,* like Moses, to sing. But their song is not theirs, in the sense that some voice beyond the personal sings through them: *It sings.*

This Hasidic teaching conveys a sense of the personal-impersonal sources of song. Unconscious desires and fears vibrate within the singing voice. A whole people here open themselves to the deep experience of an *elsewhere.* In a sense, they are not responsible for their own song. In that sense, *it* sings.

The psychoanalyst Donnel B. Stern writes: "The more fully an experience is our own—the more it comes from what we like to call 'deep down within us'—the more it usually feels, oddly enough, as if it comes from elsewhere."[21] Many poets and composers have described the experience of inspiration in similar terms: Coleridge, Blake, Mozart ("Where and how they come I know not"), Keats ("The poet does not know what he has to say till he has said it"), Rilke ("Let each impression and each germ of feeling come to completion quite in itself . . . beyond reach of one's own understanding"), Valéry ("A poem is a discourse that requires and sustains continuous connection between the voice that is and the voice that is coming and must come"), Tsvetaeva ("The poet's hand does not belong to her but to that which waits to exist through her").[22]

"And He placed in my mouth a new song," the Psalmist writes (Ps. 40:4); and the midrash adds, "This refers to the Song of the Sea."[23]

Between the miry clay of Egypt and the firm foothold in the midst of the Sea, a new song is formed. Something unpredictable sings from Moses' throat. What then can we say about Miriam's song?

RECOGNITION AT THE SEA

A classic midrash intimates the singular quality of the women's song. This arises from the women's history as child bearers in Egypt. They conceive their babies in the Egyptian fields:

> . . . And when the time for birth came, they would go and give birth in the field under the apple tree (where they had conceived), as it is said, "Under the apple tree I aroused you. . . ." And God would send from the highest heavens one who would cleanse them and make them beautiful, like this midwife who cleanses the newborn. . . . And when the Egyptians noticed them, they would come to kill them; a miracle would be done for them, so that they were swallowed into the soil, and the Egyptians would bring oxen that would plow over them. . . . After they left, the babies would sprout forth like the grass of the field. . . . And when they would grow, they would come in flocks to their homes. . . . And when God revealed Himself at the Sea—they recognized Him first, as it is said, "This is my God!"[24]

The story tells of desire—seduction, conception, and birth—in the fields of slavery. The Israelite women give birth under conditions of double danger—the normal hazards of childbirth and the Egyptian terror. Even after they are born, their babies survive only by extreme miracle—transfigured as grass of the field or as flocks of sheep. Using a mosaic of quotations from the Song of Songs, Ezekiel, and other biblical texts, the midrash introduces God as a midwife[25] who, in the throes of perilous birth, cleanses and prepares mother and child for entry into the world. The end point of this birthing process is the cry of recognition as mothers and babies break into song at the Sea: *"This* is my God!" God is revealed to them for the *second* time: they already know Him as the One who so intimately eased their passage between death and life in the killing fields of Egypt.

"This is my God":—they point their fingers in profound recognition, signaling the reconnection with their most intimate
experience.[26] The babies, too, rear their heads away from their
mothers' breast and sing in recognition of that God.[27] God is
ultimately the *zeh* (the *this*) in human experience—the still
point of the turning world.[28]

PREPARED FOR MIRACLES

An invisible thread links mothers and babies with the divine. From
this place, they sing. In the midst of uncertainty and danger, women
sing a different song. And Miriam leads them with "timbrels and
dancing." Where did these timbrels come from? "These righteous
women were so confident that God would do miracles for them that
they brought timbrels with them from Egypt."[29] Miriam, the ring-
leader, is for the first time named "the prophetess," as though her
early experience with her parents around Moses' birth is now suddenly reactivated. It inspires her to "take the timbrel in her hand."
And the women who thought to pack timbrels, at a time when there
was no time for bread to rise, act as those who are well schooled in
the paradoxes of terror. They are confident, says Rashi, that God *does*
miracles; the thread that connects them with the divine vibrates particularly in time of danger. They leave without leavened bread—but
prepared for miracles, provided for song and dance.

The song of Miriam, then, is expressive of a sensibility that knows
the bitterness of the place between death and life. In fact, Miriam,
according to one midrash,[30] is named for the bitterness that the
Egyptians inflicted on the Israelites: *Va-yimareru*—"They embittered
their lives" (1:14). A child of terror, she knows from birth how God
can sing from her throat.

"SING—NOW!—TO GOD"

The French feminist thinker Catherine Clément provocatively
declares, "She who sings must die," as she meditates on the fate of
heroines in opera.[31] Stanley Cavell picks up on her claim and elaborates it. Woman's singing exposes an unbearable secret: the power of

her desire. It exposes her to a pitch of passion that may be impossible to domesticate: her aria causes her to

> leap, as it were, from a judgment of the world as unreal, or alien, to an encompassing sense of another realm flush with this one. . . . Such a view will take singing, I guess above all the aria, to express the sense of being pressed or stretched between worlds—one in which to be seen, the roughly familiar world of the philosophers, and one from which to be heard, one to which one releases or abandons one's spirit . . . and which recedes when the breath of the song ends.

Expressing the inexpressible, the operatic heroine is in a state of abandonment, "as if opera is naturally pitched at this brink."[32] "Women's singing exposes them to death, the use of the voice to the stopping of the voice."[33] "Whatever causes happiness does not occur in the absence of pain."[34]

"Our beyond," writes Cavell, "is not eventual but always."[35] The "beyond" of Miriam and her singing women is expressed not in operatic arias, but with timbrels and dancing. They sing, but they do not die. However, in a number of midrashic passages, Miriam and the Israelite women are pitched on the brink between this world and another, on a traumatic verge that brings their song to life.

One important midrash, for instance, depicts the righteous in the world to come circling around God in a ring dance. Here, Miriam and her dancing, drumming women have an uncanny place of honor:

> R. Berachia and R. Helbo and Ulla Bira'a and R. Eleazar said in the name of R. Chanina: In the world to come, God will lead the chorus [*cholah*] of the righteous—as it is written, "Mark well her ramparts—*chelah*" (Ps. 48:14)—but it is written *cholah* [i.e., a circle dance]. They will dance around Him with youthfulness and point to Him, as it were, with a finger, saying: *This is God, our God, for ever and ever; He will lead us* almut (48:15)—i.e., with youthfulness, with liveliness. *Almut* means "like young girls" [*alamot*], of whom it is written, *In the midst of young girls playing upon timbrels* (Ps. 68:26). Aquila translated the word *almut, athanasia* [i.e., *deathlessness, immortality;* that

is, He will lead us to] a world where there is no death. Or, *almut* means two *olamot*—worlds: He will lead us in this world, and He will lead us in the world to come.[36]

In an ultimate choreography, the righteous dance a *machol*—a circle dance—around God in the world to come. Pointing their fingers to the center of the dancing circle, they acclaim God: "*Zeh—This* is God, our God, forever—He will lead us *almut.*" This strange word evokes Miriam: it associates to the *almah,* the young girl who ran to bring her mother to act as wet nurse for Pharaoh's daughter (Exod. 2:8). The other proof text refers to young girls drumming and thus again to Miriam and her dancing, drumming women.

Two more meanings are suggested for *almut:* "beyond death," and "through both worlds, this one and the one beyond." The dancers in the world to come evoke a world beyond death, as well as youth and love—Eros and Thanatos both. Through elaborate wordplays, the midrash conjures the singular quality of Miriam with her light-footed quality, dancing and singing her awareness of a *beyond* that draws her between worlds, beyond death itself. The writers of the midrash evoke the anarchic power of words, how they lead in different directions and suggest unimagined connections between worlds: death and life, Miriam's circle dance at the Sea and the ultimate ring dance around God in the world to come.

This ultimate "dance of the righteous" takes Miriam's dance as its paradigm. In the teaching of R. Kalonymus Kalman Epstein (the Maor va-Shemesh), the circular form of the *machol* provides a kabbalistic image for the feminine, the mode in which all points on the circumference have an equal relationship with the center. At the end of days, all the hierarchies of this world, which is run on principles of masculine linearity, will be superseded: the circle will replace the straight line as the modality of the world to come. All the dancers will relate in equal intimacy to God's presence.

The paradigm is Miriam's ring dance, which prefigures the "new covenant" in Jeremiah 31:22: "Then the woman shall circle the man—*nekevah te-sovev gever.*" This mysterious prophecy serves in Hasidic thought to indicate the transformation of sensibility at the end of days. "No longer will they need to teach one another and say to one another, 'Heed God'; for all of them, from the least of them to the greatest, shall heed Me, says God" (Jer. 31:33). Transcending all categories, Miriam and her dancing women enact the highest possible spiritual consciousness, as their ring dance *draws* God down into their center.

They thus create an unprecedented reality, in which they transform Moses' song by changing one word. Instead of singing *Ashirah* ("I shall sing to God"), they sing *Shiru* ("Sing now to God!"). For R. Epstein, at this moment Miriam displays a more sublime consciousness than Moses himself: where he can sing only of some future ideal reality, she brings the divine into the very midst of the turning circle. The language of her song solicits a new dance.

"At the still point, there the dance is."[37] Drawn to the other realm, the world beyond death, Miriam in her dance *draws* God down into the space between worlds. Her passion does not end in death, but there is a brink on which she perilously wheels: "the women's singing exposes them to death, the use of the voice to the stopping of the voice." Erotic, knowing mortality, and leaping beyond, Miriam's song makes a claim on eternity between worlds.

Drawing on these midrashic and Hasidic meditations, we find a Miriam who knows that this moment of the song-dance was created through rather than by her. God's presence sang and danced through her. Whereas Moses could sing only of some future revelation, Miriam and her women know that God descends and dwells in their midst. Such a possibility is a "secret," accessible only in the moment of enactment—"Sing—now!—to God." Moses is not privy to this secret: he lives within the hierarchies and separations of higher and lower, teacher and student, giver and receiver, male and female. Miriam and her women have allowed two worlds to interpenetrate.

SPEAKING AGAINST AND THROUGH MOSES

When, therefore, Miriam speaks *be-Mosheh*, she speaks both against and through him. Her life circles around him from the start; even her prophetic life is focused on him. He grows beyond her; but she has known the full force of God's voice within her. Her original moment of prophecy was the moment when she reunited her parents and

brought Moses into the world. Protecting him and advocating for
him in his infancy, she has lived through the meanings of that
prophecy, and paid the price of ostracism and isolation. And then,
he grew beyond her, assuming leadership over the people. But, at the
Sea, a deep residue of Miriam's prophetic power sings within her,
transcending perhaps that of her brother. The hierarchy of distance
and difference that he represents has, at least for the duration of the
song, been superseded. He has become part of the ultimate circle of
the righteous.

Her prophecy is always concerned with life in the face of death,
with survival, and with continuity. The mere rumor of Moses' separation from his wife troubles her: she *knows* that in order to have
God singing out of one's midst, one does not need to abandon sexuality. When she speaks about Moses, she seeks an intense involvement with his experience, a way of seeing herself through him. She
is, in a sense, embedded within her radical relation with him. Imaginatively, she lives within him; she seeks a way of being continuous
with him.

STANDING IN THE SPACES

Identification, projection, and envy make a potent mixture: ". . . and
God heard it" (Num. 12:2). God enters the story suddenly, immediately after Miriam and Aaron's speech, at the end of the same verse.
God alone truly hears what lies behind and within Miriam's speech.
Moses is not present; moreover, since he is "a very humble man,
more so than any other man on earth" (12:3), he is perhaps incapable
of fully hearing Miriam's words. In the drama of envy, he is simply
not a player; the issues of superiority and competition do not touch
him. So God responds in his place—"*Suddenly,*" God speaks.

Rashi comments on the startling suddenness of God's appearance:
"God revealed Himself to them *suddenly,* while they were in a state
of sexual impurity and were crying out, 'Water! Water!' This was to
tell them that Moses had acted rightly when he separated from his
wife, since God revealed Himself to Moses constantly, without fixed
arrangements."

Again, the theme of sexuality and revelation is forced to the surface. Miriam and Aaron are given an experience of God's appearing while they are in the midst of a heightened sexual state. There is no interval, no gap between the two states. "Water! Water!" they cry. Water purifies the impure. But this "impurity" has nothing to do with sin; it is the intense, sometimes compulsive state that does not allow any other state to intervene. Immersion in water is the passage of rebirth into a new state. Suddenly, Miriam and Aaron are confronted with the genuine need for transition between one human state and another.

What is impressed on them is a notion that challenges Miriam's lifelong prophetic sensibility. Human beings live in different states. Experience is not all of a piece, although a common ground of being interfuses it. The tension between states needs to be negotiated. The alternative may be a kind of dissociation of one or the other state.

Miriam and Aaron come to know the *suddenness* of being precipitated from a sexual to a prophetic condition. Crying out for water, they know shame. Shame is precisely the sense of sudden self-consciousness, of losing the experience of immersion in a particular state. Suddenly, one is in a void, between states. There is no time to adjust one's posture. In this sense, Miriam and Aaron understand Moses' intuition about giving himself entirely to the unremitting demands of his prophecy.

"THE TIME IS OUT OF JOINT"

The issue of shame first comes up in Genesis 2:23: "And the two of them, the man and his wife [Adam and Eve], were naked and unashamed." This is the last moment of primal shamelessness: all is about to change. Soon, shame will become constitutive of human consciousness. As Ha'amek Davar points out in his provocative discussion, the word *yit-boshashu* bears two meanings: to be ashamed and to be delayed.[38] This is the poetic quality of the Hebrew language, he notes—opening up differences, channels of complication that make reading no simple matter. Adam and Eve are not yet subject to the delays that will later complicate both spiritual and sexual life. They are naked, in a double sense: physically without clothes; also, metaphorically, without barriers, inhibitions—accessible to states of altered consciousness, like the state of passionate union with each other, or the state of passionate communion with God.

What begins after they have eaten of the Tree of Knowledge is a new kind of self-consciousness, which Ha'amek Davar calls *da'at enoshi*—human consciousness—and which, I suggest, includes the workings of the unconscious. In this new phase, delays, impediments, inhibitions mark the transition into the moment of desire. In a sense, it is this experience of delay that now constitutes desire. Now, *arousal* becomes necessary, which implies a *time lag* between first impulse and fulfillment. We are haunted by time—by memory, expectation, dreams, and disillusionment—in short by imaginative life. Sexuality, as well as spirituality, seems often to rule out simplicity. The time is out of joint.

In this fraught interval of "delay," shame becomes real. To ignore this reality would be, in the Talmudic expression, *chutzpah*—insolence. Ha'amek Davar quotes from the Talmudic tractate *Berachot* (34b), where one who presumes to pray in the open field is characterized in this way; he denies the spaces, the differences that separate the human from God. These spaces also separate the human from himself or herself. The poet Emily Dickinson writes that she has "to wonder what myself will say."

If Miriam and Aaron are surprised by God's appearance in the midst of a sexual state, this intimates the need for *arousal*, for a space and time of transformation. Here is the *slowness* of the interval of *boshesh*; and here, too, is the shame of *bushah*. "I am not myself today," we say, unwilling to acknowledge that this, too, is a self.

Prufrock, master of delays, says:

This is not what I meant at all
That is not it, at all.

And

In a minute there is time
For decisions and revisions which a moment will reverse.[39]

In this liquid state, the firmness of identity is lost. Privacy, a modest interval, is needed to initiate oneself into the new state.

"NOT SO MY SERVANT MOSES"

God summons Miriam and Aaron, separates them from Moses, and speaks to them about prophecy, their prophecy and his.

> "Hear these My words: When a prophet of God arises among you, I make Myself known to him in a vision, I speak with him in a dream. Not so with my servant Moses; he is trusted throughout My household. With him I speak mouth to mouth, plainly and not in riddles, and he beholds the likeness of God. How then did you not fear to speak against my servant Moses?" (Num. 12:6–8)

"Hear these My words": what God is about to reveal is in itself a form of prophecy: it refers to their own immediate experience. Like all other prophets, they see only through visions and dreams— *ba-mar'ah, ba-chalom.* They are human beings who need to be immersed in a particular state in order to know God. Moses is the singular exception: he is "My servant, trusted throughout My household." There is a daylight clarity in God's communications with Moses. Unlike other prophets who require altered states—dreams, hallucinations—in order to experience God, Moses knows God with a simple and lucid intimacy: mouth to mouth. God speaks *bo*—from within him.

What are the implications of this gap that sets Moses apart from his own siblings, as well as from the human norm? One implication of the expression "mouth to mouth" is that God corroborates Moses' ascetic intuition: he is right to separate from his wife.[40] The lucidity and pervasiveness of his prophetic gift leaves no space for other states. His intuition was finely attuned to God's will.

Moreover, the dream state, which is a strategy of "arousal" to prophecy, may easily give rise to a sense that God is speaking *in* and *through* one: within the dream, God may *be felt* to speak through one.[41] In dream, boundaries disappear, identities merge; all is possible. Miriam's wish is to know God from within herself, in the midst of the dancing circle of her life. Perhaps, suggests the Maor va-Shemesh, Miriam indeed created such a possibility in her dance at the Sea. Certainly, in the midrashic tradition, she played a crucial role in speaking for God in the death culture of Egypt. But now she is faced with the challenge of distances and differences. Only in a dream can she find again that interfusion of the erotic and the divine.

"Not so my servant Moses," God declares. Moses is other; God speaks from within him, not in a dream but in lucid wakefulness. Moses is *ne'eman*, "trustworthy throughout My household," says God. What is the quality of *ne'eman*? Are other prophets lacking in trustworthiness? Sefat Emet[42] makes a striking suggestion: *ne'eman* means stable, unchanging. Moses, of all prophets, is the one who is *unchanged* by his prophetic revelations. All other prophets experience transfiguration: "their faces would flame like torches." Moses alone remains constantly attuned to God in the very core of his being. His face, his mouth is infused with God's presence: "mouth to mouth" expresses an intimacy without gaps, without ebbs and flows. Other prophets are called to receive revelation; sometimes, their name is called twice—"Abraham! Abraham!" "Samuel! Samuel!"—as though to bridge the gap between two separate states. Moses alone is not summoned twice, since the "higher" and the "lower" Moses are identical.

In this view, then, Moses is a highly specialized being, his sexuality sublimated in *devekut*—passionate intimacy with God. Perhaps for this reason, he wears a veil[43] in order to mute the constant radiance of his face when he speaks to the people. When he has a question, he has the confidence to tell the people: "Stay here, while I hear what God will command you!" (Num. 9:8).

Other prophets, however, represent the human norm, moving between different self-states, allowing time to elapse between states so as to re-attune themselves. Moses is anomalous—he is *lo chen*, not so, not "regular," not normally sporadic, but *ne'eman*, extraordinarily constant in His relation to God. He has no need for arousal or for shame. Organized differently, Moses cannot be a role model for others. He is the theoretical exception that sheds light on the norm.

ALTERNATING CURRENT

What then is Miriam's relation with Moses? We can speculate that she envies not simply his status as primary channel of prophecy, but his intimacy with God. She desires to have God speak within her once more. In her dream, she, like him, is a vessel for divine inspiration. And her dream comes authorized by experience that has changed the world.

God responds first by isolating the three siblings in the Tent of Assembly, then by further isolating Miriam and Aaron. He tells them of differences, of the gap that separates Moses' life from theirs. Miriam, alone, is afflicted with *tzora'at,* usually translated as leprosy.[44] Aaron appeals to Moses to intercede for her; and Moses cries out to God: "God, please heal her, please!" (Num. 12:13).

Mei Ha-Shilo'ach suggests that when God speaks to Miriam and Aaron of Moses' difference, they apprehend God's words dynamically, along a spectrum of prophetic lucidity. They oscillate between two poles: at some moments, they receive illumination that is as clear as Moses'; at others, meanings dim for them, so that they realize something of Moses' difference. Unable to master the ebb and tide of revelation, they realize that it is not truly *theirs;* it comes to them through Moses. The flickering light tells them that "there exists spiritual power beyond their own."[45]

An alternating current allows Miriam and Aaron to achieve an uncanny experience: to benefit from Moses' spiritual energy as, in a sense, their own energy, and yet to become aware that their perception is, properly speaking, derived from him. This strange idea conveys something of the complexity of inspiration. The light that seems to emerge unbidden from one's own depths flickers, and one has a sudden apprehension of limits, of margins unilluminated. One realizes how what belongs to the other can irradiate one's mind so that it seems innate. In this reading, Miriam and Aaron are suddenly assailed by a new depth perception. Instead of merely observing their brother's prophecy, they are given a profound intimation of his spiritual apprehension—only to have it recede from their minds.

For Miriam, this might mean a dual awareness: of being "mixed up" with Moses, totally identified with his experience of prophecy, and then of being separated out, knowing that *his* prophecy is not *hers.* She had spoken *be-mosheh,* in and through and *against* Moses: merged with him, mirrored in him, ultimately denying him his singularity. Envy begins here, in the family, between siblings who are and are not alike. Miriam, who came before Moses, in order of birth and in order of prophecy, witnesses the brother in whose birth she was so enmeshed grow beyond her. What bond could be deeper than the bond between this sister-mother and this brother-child? Miriam of the waters—fluid, drawing God down among the dancing women—is Miriam of reunited couples, of the flow of possibilities. But Moses is *drawn out* of the water; he is *ne'eman*—centered, focused steadily in a world of flux. He knows that for him separation from his wife is God's will; and God, in calling him *ne'eman,* acknowledges his intuition. How can we understand the relation between two who are so unlike?

ONE FLESH

God's words to Miriam and Aaron delineate a world of differences: *lo chen avdi Mosheh*—"Not so my servant Moses!" Distinguishing between kinds and intensities of prophecy, God is really telling Miriam and Aaron about the ways of "normal" revelation. What Miriam has experienced is that transitional space that is apprehended in visions and in dreams; in ecstasy, where one is *beside oneself,* and yet feels inspired by the breath of all life. This means that she experiences Moses as, in a sense, part of her. And, indeed, Aaron hints at this when he appeals to Moses: "Let her not be as one dead, who emerges from his mother's womb with half his flesh eaten away!" (Num. 12:12). If Moses' sister, who has come forth from the womb of his mother, is afflicted with leprosy, then it is as though half his flesh, too, is consumed.

The macabre image conveys Aaron's understanding of the intimate connection between Miriam and Moses. All three siblings emerged from the same womb—and siblings are one flesh.[46] But Aaron speaks of *his* (Moses') mother's womb, and of *his* flesh alone. Moses has the power to intercede for his sister, precisely because of the primal connection between them. They emerged from their mother's womb in a unique sense: for Miriam had brought that womb back into the world of possibilities by reuniting her parents.

Miriam half-consumed is Moses half-consumed.[47] Or, as one midrash puts it, one who has felt the chain around his neck will identify uniquely with another who is similarly enchained. Moses cries out to God, the midrash implies, with vicarious pain. Both Moses and Miriam have known the living death of leprosy; in fact, the same simile is used in both cases—"leprous as snow" (Exod. 4:6; Num. 12:10).

Aaron's appeal is expressed in clogged language, as though he cannot quite articulate what he means. But this clogged language becomes uniquely expressive of the charged world of meanings that is shared by Miriam and Moses—perhaps including the zone of unregulated language that is signified in the Torah by leprosy.[48] Brother and sister are indeed profoundly involved with each other. Then Moses prays a short, convulsive prayer: from his own flesh, a cry stronger than empathy.

SHAME, AROUSAL

It is striking that Miriam's leprosy is mentioned twice: in one breath, as it were, the Torah records: "And behold *Miriam was leprous* as snow; and when Aaron turned to Miriam behold *she was leprous!*"[49] Ha'amek Davar translates the second *me-tzora'at* as "shocked and dumbfounded with grief." This interesting translation probes the psychic implications of *tzora'at*: it refers to a clinical, physical condition, but also to the traumatic state—she is "struck dumb"—that results from it. She is, one might say, shocked out of her dream of oceanic revelation.

She is—in the Aramaic translation of *me-tzora'at*—*segiru:* locked up, enclosed, isolated. The legal penalty of *tzora'at* may include a period that is called *hesger:* seclusion, quarantine—pending the priest's further observation. This is a kind of probationary period of seven days, until a conclusive diagnosis can be made. This seven-day period is a time when things are undecided; the opposite condition is *muchlat*—decided, irreversible. But the Aramaic translation of *tzora'at* itself as *segiru* implies that Miriam is already in a state of suspended animation, struck dumb, isolated. God, in a sense, formalizes this state when He excludes Miriam from the camp for seven days: "She shall be shut out of camp for seven days—and then she shall be gathered in" (Num. 12:14).

The experience of *tzora'at* itself is, essentially, an experience of being closed in on oneself. It is a kind of limbo, of not yet knowing what to think or what to say; of being engrossed, bewildered.[50]

The double reference to Miriam's *tzora'at,* then, suggests her shock in realizing her limbo situation. Once a prophetess whose words were clearly God's words speaking through her, she suddenly experiences the situation of delay, of speechlessness, that Ha'amek Davar associates with the *shame* of a human being emerged from the idyll of Eden. *Lo yit-boshashu*—in Eden, they were not ashamed; they lived in the oceanic moment, without memory or expectation. Then came the vibrations of self-consciousness, the crosscurrents of past and future.

This, perhaps, is the shame of which God speaks to Miriam: the sharp rebuke of the father who has the power to shatter the dream. Miriam has known alienation and isolation at the hands of her father; it was a hazard of her prophetic singularity. Now, God reminds her of this early experience. Then, she remained staunch even as she was distanced from her family; she waited for the truth of her prophecy to emerge. Now, too, God has her enact a limbo period of silence, of *bewilderment,* of not knowing what to say. Something must shift in her inner world; some arousal must happen; she is engrossed in the paradoxes of sameness and difference, sexuality and revelation, inside and outside.

An ordinary case of *tzora'at* lasts at least fourteen days.[51] It is possible that Moses' prayer was answered and Miriam was phys- ically cured right away. But there remains the problem of shame, which is represented by the quarantine period: for seven days she is alone, engrossed in the shifting boundaries of self and other. *Then,* she is "gathered in" to the camp, as God had declared: "And then [*afterward*—*achar*] she shall be gathered in." The word *achar,* though apparently redundant, suggests that, when Miriam is brought back inside, to her proper place in the world, a process has been com- pleted. This can happen only *after* a time of renewed consciousness.

For Miriam, who begins and ends the story, the last note is that "the people did not travel until Miriam was gathered in." She knows, in her isolation, that some thread holds her in connection with the people. Shamed, she is also *honored* by God and by her people, so that they wait for her as she lives through the gap—just as she waited for her baby brother in the river for one hour, so Israel waits for her for seven days.[52] The connection with her past moment of limbo in a sense redeems her present situation. In her absence, there is a kind of standstill. Respectfully, the people wait to absorb her again.

MIRIAM IN THE *MIDBAR*

The book of Numbers recounts complaint after complaint, episodes of disordered speech, of resentment and envy of Moses. In this dark web of language, Miriam's case stands out, in the intense focus it brings to bear on a particular history, a particular relationship of sister and brother who are prophets. But singular as the story is, it resonates with more general human bewilderments.

Separations and unions, fusions and diffractions mark the narrative. And a new world of poetic language—double meanings that enact tensions of inside and outside, of beauty and ugliness, of marriage and divorce, of the dangerous and fertile space in the midst of the Sea, with God in the midst of the dancing circle—is spoken and sung by Miriam and Moses. God, too, speaks in this newly imaginative mode, picking up the ambiguity of Miriam's use of *be*—both *within* and *against*—even as His anger burns against her. And Aaron, praying for his sister, touches off depths as he speaks of the shared, half-consumed flesh of his siblings. Even as she angers God, Miriam's words are suffused with imaginative fire. Struck dumb, she undergoes the essential catastrophe of the wilderness world: her genius is pent up, closed in, excluded, but ultimately gathered in.

Mei Ha-Shilo'ach[53] makes a large observation about the book of Numbers. The book as a whole, he says, tells of the failings of great people. All the protagonists—even the rebels who complain and desire and hate—are of heroic stature. The list of tragic heroes includes Moses and Aaron and their sin at the rock of Merivah. One understands that, as Ecclesiastes puts it, "There is no righteous person on earth who does good and does not sin" (Eccles. 7:20). Or, as the medieval Spanish-Jewish philosopher Yosef Albo reads the verse: "There is no righteous person on earth who, *in doing good,* does not sin!"

Good and evil are mixed together. And the *midbar,* the wilderness, represents the elements of destructiveness in each individual. "Remember, do not forget, how you angered God, your God, *in the wilderness!"* (Deut. 9:7). These aggressive elements need to be worked through so that they inform and enrich the force of human life. In this sense, the life of the individual is fundamentally a *midbar,* awaiting the evolutions and integrations of human work.

Miriam is not specifically mentioned in this teaching. But her story, as we have gleaned it from midrashic fragments and Hasidic meditations, is a particularly eloquent example of its theme. Here emerges the sense of a woman's life in time, evolving in sometimes startling movements and regressions; inspired, and subject to baffling intensities of feeling. Bitterness and song, death and desire, are the motifs of her life; but more than anything, yearning—yearning for that other world so close to this one—that one step of the dance, one note of the song, will bring her there, even while she is still here.

FIVE

Bewilderments

THE CHANGE OF HEART

The narrative of the Spies, with its tragic aftermaths, lies at the very heart of Sefer Bamidbar—at the very heart, we might say, of the *midbar,* the wilderness, itself. This is the critical point, the great failure, that radically changes the future history of the people. As a result of this moment, the whole adult generation is condemned to sink into the sands; a new generation will fulfill the prophecies of redemption so that, in a sense, not only the future but the past, too, is reconfigured: the promises of the Exodus will have to be reinterpreted.

A delegation of princes is sent to spy out the Land. The Spies bring back a report that reduces the people to terror and tears and the cry, "Is it not better for us to return to Egypt? . . . Let us appoint a leader and return to Egypt!" (Num. 14:3–4). Beginning as a wish, the idea of returning to Egypt becomes, for the first time, a concrete proposition. Rashi connects this moment with the very beginning of the Exodus from Egypt:

> And it was when Pharaoh let the people go, God did not lead them by way of the land of the Philistines, although it was nearer; for God said, "The people may have a change of heart when they see war and return to Egypt" (Exod. 13:17).
>
> Rashi: If they had traveled by the direct route they would have returned [immediately]. Even so, in spite of the fact that God took them by the circuitous route, they said, "Let us appoint a leader and return to Egypt!"—If He had taken them by the direct route, how much more so!

In an unusual narrative move, the Torah informs us of what God said to Himself; He communicates His thoughts to no one. In soliloquy, He articulates a reality in which the desire to return to Egypt is bound, at some point, to erupt. Returning to Egypt is, in effect, a core fantasy of the people; from the outset, it secretly organizes their inner world. Sooner or later, in reaction to the fear of war, it will inevitably disrupt the project of the Exodus. And indeed when the people cry, "Let us appoint a leader and return to Egypt!" they give a newly political expression to an old desire, till now never so fully articulated.[1] Something has been waiting to crystallize. Even God's strategy, the roundabout route out of Egypt, has been able only to *delay* an inevitable crisis. The change of heart that God foresaw is realized in the Spies story.

The roots of the narrative therefore reach back into the past. Its impact is felt, moreover, far into the future. According to a classic mishnah,[2] this narrative is dated the ninth of Av, which is to become a fatal date in Jewish history. Time after time, catastrophes will fall on this day, so that it will be institutionalized as a national fast day, accumulating its own complex history of cataclysmic loss.[3] Far from being an isolated incident, then, this story gives expression to profound movements in the Israelite soul. It becomes the rootstock of many future national sorrows.

ENIGMATIC PASSIONS

On the face of it, this is a story about fear. The people recoil from the prospect of defeat in war. The Spies bring them an ambiguous report, acknowledging the fertility of the Land, even carrying a sample branch of its bounteous fruit: "We came to the Land you sent us to; it does indeed flow with milk and honey; and this is its fruit" (Num. 13:27). "*However [Efes]*," they continue, "the people who inhabit the country are powerful, and cities are fortified and very large; moreover, we saw the Anakites [giants] there. Amalekites dwell in the Negev region; Hittites, Jebusites, and Amorites inhabit the hill country; and Canaanites dwell by the Sea and along the Jordan" (13:28–29).

As Ramban points out, the pivot of their speech is the unusual word *efes*: literally, *nothing, zero*[4]—here translated "however." They undercut their own beatific report, in which they essentially confirmed God's original description of the Land, at the Burning Bush.[5]

What the Spies seem to be saying is, "That may be true, but *we can't*. . . . The inhabitants are too strong, too terrifying." *Efes* carries the sense of the "Delete!" key on a computer keyboard. "All the goodness of the Land is ultimately irrelevant: we are powerless." Responding to their fear, Caleb protests: "We *can indeed* go up and possess it, for *indeed we can prevail* over it." Their fellow Spies reply: "But *we cannot* go up against them."

Fear in a situation of war is a rational emotion. Indeed, as we have seen, it was precisely foreseen by God from the outset. But the reaction that the Spies arouse in the people is not entirely rational. The people weep all night, they wish they had died in Egypt, "or else in this wilderness" (Num. 14:2). Evidently, they would prefer to be dead than to face the danger of death. They both fear death and wish for it, deciding to return to Egypt, the very site of death.

The theme of the giants, too, plays a remarkable role in the Spies' report, creating an unexpected frisson in a sober account of military challenges. At first, indeed, the Spies tell of a fearsome population and well-fortified cities. But immediately, they modulate to a different key: "Moreover, *we saw* the Anakites there—the offspring of the giants." "Moreover" (*ve-gam*) sounds like an afterthought; or is it perhaps an intensification, intimating a secret terror? What intimidates them is not the strategic difficulties of this war, but the sheer mythic size of these giants, their mythic stock. This is what they really *saw*. They return to this theme twice more: first, in their description of the Land as "eating its inhabitants—and all the people *we saw* in it were immense" (Num. 13:32). What began as a narrative of a terrifying race of giants has become a general description of the population—"*all the people*." And then, again, reverting to the gigantesque: "And there *we saw* the Nefilim [giants[6]], the Anakites are part of the Nefilim—and we looked like grasshoppers in our own eyes, and so we looked in theirs" (13:33).

Clearly, *we saw* organizes the uncanny experience of the giants, in whose shadow the Spies *see themselves* as grasshoppers and assume that the giants also see them as such. So far from registering an empirical view of the Land, *seeing* and *seeing oneself* precipitate the narrative into a dynamic of madness, of images, fantasies, and projections.

In Midrash Tanchuma God frames a critique of the Spies' inner world:

They said, "We looked like grasshoppers in our own eyes." God said, "This I can overlook. But, 'And so we looked in their eyes'—here I am angry! Did you know how I made you look in their eyes? Who told you that you didn't look like angels in their eyes?"[7]

God analyzes the Spies' words: apparently, it is legitimate to imagine oneself as a grasshopper in the presence of a giant. This is how human beings begin life, small and powerless in the presence of immense powers. And this is how, perhaps, we always in fantasy remain. To see a world of giants is to remind oneself of a primal sense of things. But to project one's own fantasy onto the giant is to limit the possibilities of fantasy and of otherness.[8]

The midrash allows for the power of fantasy, of imaginative ways of seeing reality, even for the terrified fantasy of the helpless self. To limit the equivalent freedom of imagination of the other, however, is to presume too far. What God is particular about is preserving the sense of difference and therefore of the "possibility of possibility."[9]

What the Spies see, therefore, convulses them not simply with fear, but with a sense of intimate *efes:* they are annihilated. The word *aliyah—going up* to the Land—is suffused with the sense of *looking upward* at the contemptuous eyes of the gigantic inhabitants of that Land. To see, for them, is to allow the world to mirror their deepest life. The Spies evoke in the people that same sense of *efes,* of annihilation. They fear to die, because they are, in imagination, already dead: "If only we had died in the land of Egypt, or in this wilderness if only we had died!" (Num. 14:2). The perfect chiasmus (a-b-b-a) expresses a closed and fatal condition, succinctly encased in mirroring words. The wish to return to Egypt is the wish to be in the death place, at the end of imagination.

Such fantasies of self and other seek confirmation from the outside world. Here, in the Tanchuma passage, God is angered at their fatal constriction of imaginative possibility. Perhaps it is this that makes Moses and Aaron "fall on their faces before the assembled congregation of the Israelites" (Num. 14:5). In the face of a mass panic that admits no alternative vision, Moses and Aaron are themselves struck with despair. In the words of Seforno,[10] they saw the "crooked that cannot be straightened" (Eccles. 1:15); they resembled the Talmudic Sages who "pressed their faces into the ground," too intimidated by King Yannai's power to deliver their judgment.[11] Moses and Aaron are dumbfounded by the people's nihilism; a core fantasy has them in its grip, as God had predicted at the moment of the Exodus.

So powerful is this state that Moses and Aaron can offer no resistance. It remains for Joshua and Caleb to attempt a different rhetoric. They try to reassure the people, to no avail (Num. 14:7–10). In response, the people attempt (lit., *they said*) to stone them, their intention thwarted by the sudden appearance of God's glory.

In this mysterious passage, Joshua and Caleb affirm and reaffirm the goodness of the Land, which, after all, had never really been in question.[12] Their exhortations about fear, too, are strangely framed: The phrase, "They are *our bread*" evokes the Spies' fantasy of *being eaten* by the natives ("a land that eats its inhabitants" [Num. 14:32]), as though the only way to allay the infant fantasy of being eaten by the giants is to eat the eaters, impotence shuttling with omnipotence. In the same way, "Their shadow has left them" (14:9): the protective shadow that gives the other his giant force can only be countered by the equivalent totality of ". . . And God is with us."

This is not the language of strategic security concerns; and the people's reaction is violent, an attempted lynching. A vision of God's glory halts them. What they see is ineffable; no words help us understand what it is that prevents them from acting out their destructive passion. But that passion, too, is enigmatic, as is the counter-passion of Joshua and Caleb.

God's glory will in fact appear several times in the book of Numbers—always ineffable, a wordless event that blocks the people from going beyond words in their rebellions.[13] Strikingly, this rebellion is *all words:* the Spies see, show, and tell. The people cry, rebel— all in words. The one action they contemplate—stoning Caleb and Joshua—is described in terms of a speech act: "they *said* to stone them" (Num. 14:10). It is this narrative of sounds ("And they gave forth their voice and they wept") and words that precipitates God's decree—the disappearance of a generation.

To the vociferations of the people, Moses and Aaron have nothing, apparently, to say. Their faces to the ground, they enact a wordless despair—the counterpart, perhaps, of Caleb and Joshua tearing their garments (Num. 14:6). This despairing gesture will be repeated four times in the course of the book of Numbers.[14] Like the epiphany of God's glory—and almost always in conjunction with it—this gesture becomes a leitmotif in the desert saga.

A remarkable midrash subversively connects the two sentences in the verse: "They intended to stone them with stones. And the glory of God appeared to all the Israelites."—"*They took stones and hurled them upward.*"[15] As the Maharsha comments, if we read this as one run-on sentence, the stoning has two objects, Caleb/Joshua and the glory of God. (The usual phrasing would place the verb "appeared" before the subject, God's glory—*va-yera kevod Ha-Shem*—marking the second sentence off from the first.[16]) Perhaps because there is no break between the two sentences, it becomes possible to suggest a secretive intention behind the stoning. Caleb and Joshua have become the screen target of the people's hatred, which is essentially directed against God. The would-be lynching represents a radical human animus that generates a radical divine response.

DIFFICULT FREEDOM

How can we understand the people's animus in this critical narrative? We have suggested that fear—of the rigors of war, of defeat—does not sufficiently account for the emotional depth charges that erupt from the people's words. Could the core issue be, after all, a doubt about the basic *goodness* of the Land? The Spies' mission was framed by Moses, who asked not only about the strength of the population and their strategic force but—more insistently—"What is the Land in which they live—Is it *good* or *bad?*. . . . Is it fertile or infertile?" (Num. 13:19–20). The question of good and evil seems so primary that the reader assumes that the Spies' failure must be a failure in answering this. And yet, as we have seen, the Spies report faithfully, "It is a land flowing with milk and honey." They not only acknowledge the Land as fertile but they speak faith-full words that acknowledge God's promise at the Burning Bush. They even bear back with them the laden branches of fruit to confirm that faith. And strikingly, when Moses narrates the story to the people forty years later, he remembers the Spies as reporting simply, "The Land is *good*" (Deut. 1:25).

So, on the face of it, *goodness* is not the point at issue. Why, then, do Caleb and Joshua revert so fervently to this issue of *goodness*, when they respond to the people's death wish? *Tovah ha-aretz me'od me'od*, they say—"The Land is a very, very good one!" (Num. 14:7). Perhaps the question of goodness is, after all, at the heart of the narrative?

We remember how the question of good and evil haunted previous narratives: Jethro resisting Moses' persuasions, with all their repetitions of the word *tov* (good)—five times in a brief narrative; the people complaining about "*Ra* [evil] in the ears of God" (Num. 11:1); the people "desiring desire," which is "*evil* in Moses' eyes" (11:10); Moses complaining to God, "Why have you done *evil* to Your servant?" (11:11). We suggested[17] that *tov* and *ra* hold a distinctly subjective meaning in this text; that they represent a personal experience that could be called *love* and *hate*. This book is concerned with the emotional and imaginative lives of its protagonists rather than the teaching of an absolute ethical system.

In the Spies' narrative, this subject is ruthlessly exposed. From the first words of the narrative, the emphasis is on the subjective lives of Moses, the Spies, and the people. *Shlach lecha*—"Send *for yourself* people to spy out the Land," says God to Moses. The whole notion of a spy mission comes from God, with the force of a command. What, then, is the effect of *lecha—for yourself?*

In his comment, Rashi strikingly integrates this story with the later story Moses will tell about the Spies, at the end of the forty-year desert trek:

> Send for yourself (Num. 13:2): On your own judgment; I do not command you; if you wish, send them. God said this because the Israelites came to Moses and said, "Let us send men before us. . . ." As it is said (Deut. 1:22): "And you approached me, all of you, saying, 'Let us send men. . . .'" And Moses took counsel with God, who said, "I told them that it is a good land, as it is said (Exod. 3:17), 'I will bring them up out of the affliction of Egypt . . . into a land flowing with milk and honey, a good and spacious land. . . .' As they live, I swear that I will give them now an opportunity to fall into error through the words of the Spies, so that they should not come into possession of it."

In Rashi's account, the word *lecha* intimates God's reservations about the Spies' mission, as if to say, "I command but I do not com-

mand"; as if to defer—ironically?—to Moses' judgment. Here, God
emerges as offended by the people's doubts as to the *goodness* of
the Land: "I told them that it is a good land!" Here, this is the central issue. The goodness of the Land is the issue that the people are
driven, essentially, to resolve. To this end, they demand the Spy mission. God reacts with subtle displeasure at their skepticism, but at
the same time, He allows space for human desire, human judgment,
human choice—and human error: "I will give them room for error."
Like a parent of an adolescent child who is set on a course of action
his father deplores, God uses a language of free choice—if you *wish*,
on your *judgment*, I do *not tell* you to do this—in order to convey a
complex message. Ultimately, the child must make a free choice that
includes knowledge of the parent's disapproval. Rashi's synonyms
for *lecha* basically register the *tone* in which God speaks.

God gives Moses the "difficult freedom"[18] of an adult decision. He
opens for Moses a transitional space, in which to navigate between
God's desire and the people's. In the Deuteronomy narrative, Rashi
elaborates on the unconscious dimensions of the moment:

> And the matter was good in my eyes: In my eyes but not in
> God's eyes. But if it was good in Moses' eyes, why did he men-
> tion it in rebuking them? A parable: A man says to his friend,
> Sell me your donkey! He replies, Yes. The buyer asks, Will you
> give it to me on trial? He answers, Yes. May I try it on hills and
> mountains?—Yes. When the buyer sees that the seller puts no
> obstacles in his path, the buyer thinks, This man is quite con-
> fident that I shall not find any defect in it—So he immediately
> tells him, Take your money, I don't need to try it! I too con-
> sented to your words, thinking that you would perhaps think
> better of the Spy idea when you saw that I put no obstacles in
> your path. *But you did not think better of it.*[19]

In place of a direct command, we have the psychology of a situation of desire—in this case, a commercial transaction. The buyer
who asks for a *nissayon*, a trial run, is reassured when the seller
accedes to all of his demands. Unspoken, the issues of desire and
doubt, the wish for assurance about the quality of the object of
desire, make eminent sense, as does the seller's genial manifestation

of confidence. This is a story of justified anxiety and the tactics that
facilitate the transaction.

But within the commercial parable, the buyer ought at some point
to back off from his anxious wish for a test run. In Rashi's parable,
this is Moses' view of the situation: the rational anxiety of the people
about the Land should be allayed by Moses' willingness to send the
Spy mission. But the poker game goes strangely wrong. The people
do not back off from their desire to send the mission. And Moses
is faced with the unexpected depth and complexity of the people's
anxiety. Perhaps, after all, the donkey analogy is not as satisfactory a
metaphor for this situation as Moses imagines?

In Rashi's midrashic source,[20] the commercial model for the anxiety of desire is itself tested and found wanting. Moses comes to realize that his earlier understanding of the situation was not adequate.
An ironic note enters Moses' narrative: "The matter was good in my
eyes but not in His eyes." Vision is subjective and subject to error.

The sixteenth-century commentary Maharal subtly elaborates on
this midrash.[21] God's use of the word *lecha*—it's up to you—suggests
to Moses that God is not in favor of the Spy mission, that the issues
here are more radical than may appear: *Is it a good land or a bad one?*
He therefore explicitly raises this question in his instructions to the
Spies. By articulating the people's deepest anxiety, he hopes to allay
it. But—again—Moses' idea does not work. Both Rashi and Maharal
imply that the people are driven by inexplicable anxiety about the
goodness of the Land. All of Moses' pragmatic tactics, his very willingness to engage with their repressed doubt—all prove inadequate.
Under cover of a reconnaissance mission, the people are tormented
by inexpressible doubts.

This confrontation, then, stages the uncanny nature of the core
question: is it a good land or a bad one? Moses underestimates the
complexity of the question for them, and so brings their bad faith to
light. Words cannot engage with their terror. Only by acting it out
can their secret life unfold.

It is interesting to compare this reading with that of Ramban. In
his reading, Moses is quite happy to send the Spies, not only because
this constitutes legitimate preparation for war, but also because it
will establish beyond doubt how *good* the Land is. He himself has no
doubts on this score, since God's praise at the Burning Bush: it is "a

good and spacious land." But he wants to engage the full desire and willing cooperation of the people. He therefore instructs the Spies to notice its *goodness*—"so that they will know it and convey it to the people, who will rejoice and be filled with new strength to go up there."[22]

For Ramban, *goodness* is a concrete matter of soil and fruit and economic prosperity, easily determined by empirical testimony. For Rashi, on the other hand, the anxiety about *goodness* and *badness* is not so easily resolved. In the end, it proves to be a subjective matter, and it engages the indirections of unconscious life. The issue of *ratzon*—wish, desire, motivation—is staged here. Moses attempts to meet the people's anxieties by manipulating the field of social desires and fears. He fails, since he cannot recognize the depth of the *goodness* question in its intensely subjective reach. Here, the question becomes one of *love* and *hate*—*tov li* and *ra li*—*What is good or bad to/ for me?* On this level, there may be more than one right answer.

In a sense, all the questions that Moses lists for the Spies are, in the end, about *goodness* and *badness*. Perhaps even the questions about the strength of the inhabitants and of the fortifications are not simply about the difficulty of conquest but also act as indications of the goodness of the Land.[23] The Spies, however, interpret these indications as deterrents. Ultimately, interpretation is subjective; one man's love is another man's fear and hatred. Does this mean, as Sefat Emet claims, that the Spies sinned *by interpreting:* they were asked simply to report, not to interpret?

THE SKEPTICAL BRIDEGROOM

The core idea of the Spy mission is refracted through a different parable in the following midrash:

> R. Joshua says: To what might they be compared? To the case of a king who secured for his son a wife who was beautiful, of good parentage, and rich. The king said to him, "I have secured for you a wife who is beautiful, of good parentage, and rich." The son answered, "Let me go and see her!" *For he did not believe his father.* His father was sorely vexed and said to himself,

"What shall I do? If I tell him, 'I will not show her to you,' he will think, 'She is ugly; that is why he does not want to show her to me.'" At last, he said to him, "See her and you will know whether I have lied to you! But because *you did not have faith in me,* I swear that you will never see her in your own home, and that I will give her to your son!"

Similarly, God assured Israel, "The land is good," but *they had no faith,* and said, "Let us send men before us that they may spy out the land for us." Said God, "If I prevent them they will say, 'He does not show it to us because it is not good.' Better let them see it. But I swear that not one of them will enter the land"; as it says, "Surely they shall not see the land which I swore to their fathers, nor shall any of them that despised Me see it!" (Num. 14:23).[24]

The prince wants to see his bride for himself—on the face of it a legitimate desire. But the midrash explains: "because he did not believe his father." The king is faced with the same problem as the seller in the buying-a-donkey midrash: if he is not to lose his son's trust altogether, he cannot simply forbid him to see her. What the prince needs to ascertain is the bride's *beauty;* for her other qualifications his father's word, apparently, suffices. But the king is indeed insulted by his son's *lack of faith in him* (lo he'emanta bi). Subtly, the midrash changes its wording from its original description, "he did not *believe* his father" (lo haya ma'amin le-aviv). The father is aggrieved by a failure of relationship. It is not simply the bride's beauty that is at issue, but more radically, the son's *trust* in his father. For this reason, the father lets him see the bride but defers the full *seeing* of marriage to the next generation—"I will give her to your son!"

The skeptical bridegroom in the parable subtly deflects the meaning of the Spy narrative. If the bride's beauty represents the goodness of the Land, this is conveyed at first as an objective matter—she either is or is not beautiful—and the prince's insistence on seeing her indeed constitutes doubt of his father's word; it insinuates that his father is lying. But in the case of a marriage, it would seem, at least to the modern reader, quite legitimate for the bridegroom to see the bride, since beauty is, in this context, a subjective matter.

In fact, Jewish law forbids marriage to take place unless bride and groom have met. What the bridegroom wants to ascertain is whether he loves his bride. The father seems to understand this and speaks of *trust in me*—as though his son's doubt violates the depth of their relationship, the trust that the father knows his son's heart.

Assigning the bride to the prince's son creates an uneasily oedipal solution, which casts an uncanny light on its analogy in the narrative of the Spies. Through the prism of this midrash, the project of sending spies is tainted from the outset. And yet God's perspective stands in an uncanny relation to the human world of love. Ideally, perhaps, what God declares to be loveable should indeed be loved. But this narrative deals with the axis of human vision that cannot always be totally aligned with God's axis.

The marriage parable is thus more fraught with meanings than the donkey-sale parable. In this context, beauty is inevitably subjective: Is the bride beautiful *to him*? Might trust in his father cover this question? Perhaps indeed God the Father wants to be trusted to understand the personal desires of the son? Or perhaps the son's desire to know not only the bride but his own desire is a sign of a kind of maturity, a necessary basis for marriage? Or again, perhaps the desire to *see*, to ascertain, itself compromises the possibility of trust? The canny "consumer" glance, by its very nature, perhaps erodes the growth of relationship, the full *seeing* of marriage?

The marriage model thus stages the Spies' mission as ambiguous, requiring interpretation. To question the *goodness* of the Land may represent the legitimate human need to experience one's own desire, as Ramban suggests. Or it may suggest that one is deficient in that basic trust that is the very liquor of life. This trust or faith is the ability to *see the other in one's home*—to see the possibilities of connection.

Moreover, the king's strange decree—"I will give her to your son"—makes visible the grotesque aspect of God's decree to the people, "Your children of whom you said, They will be carried off—these will I allow to enter, they shall know the land that you have rejected" (Num. 14:31). Suddenly, the biblical decree displays its uncanniness. This becomes a narrative about the deeper losses entailed in skeptical rejections.

THE SKEPTIC AS NIHILIST

In this crisis of trust, there is a bleakness, an experience of "world-consuming doubt," as the philosopher Stanley Cavell character-izes the condition of skepticism. This condition, Cavell writes, is a "standing threat to ... human existence."[25] At root, the people's doubt is not about the Land, or even about God's goodness, but about what Cavell calls "natality." Hamlet's question, "To be or not to be," emphasizes not "whether to die but ... whether to be born ... whether to affirm or deny the fact of natality, as a way of enact-ing, or not, one's existence." Hamlet's condition, says Cavell, is that of the adolescent who, in preparation for becoming an adult, faces decisions about accepting or rejecting rebirth into the world. Suf-fering from the "incurable malady" of skepticism, one may yet come to accept "that the existence of the world and others in it is not a matter to be known, but one to be acknowledged. . . . *The world must be regained every day*" (my emphasis).[26]

The mission of the Spies, I suggest, raises similarly radical issues. The skeptical question—How can you tell what exists, whether lan-guage applies to anything?—represents not simply a failure of *knowl-edge* but a failure of *acknowledgment;* its result, as Cavell forcefully puts it, "is not an ignorance, but an ignoring ... an unappeasable denial, a willful uncertainty that constitutes an annihilation."[27]

Cavell discusses Shakespeare's portrait of Leontes in *The Winter's Tale* as the portrait of the "skeptic as fanatic." Leontes repudiates his own son, for lack of certain knowledge. The people who insist on sending eyewitnesses to validate the good Land, like the prince who questions the beauty of his bride, are apparently engaged in a legit-imate concern for personal desire. The more radical truth, however, is that both, in some sense, wish for there to be nothing. Doubt of this kind wishes not to love; not to participate in *being born;* not to marry; not to acknowledge one's son—a portrait, in Cavell's words, of "the skeptic as nihilist."[28]

We remember the Spies' report: it is a good land, it flows with milk and honey; here is a sample of its bounty. But then the nihil-ism breaks through: *efes* ... Usually translated "however," *efes* acts, at the least, to qualify the positive report just uttered. The root of the word denotes "the end," the extremity, nonexistence. *Afsei aretz*—the edges of the earth—focuses on a vanishing point of meaning, a horizon beyond one's visual grasp.[29] Used as a conjunction, as it is here, it signifies not simply "on the other hand," but a total negation of the Spies' own praise of the Land. *Efes* annihilates: "All that goodness is meaningless." The Spies thus both affirm and deny the goodness of the Land. In other words, they bring back empirical knowledge of a goodness they have no ability to acknowledge. They can take no account of it. They can neither enter into it nor see themselves as part of it.

Efes annihilates personal meaning. The Spies, and, through them, the people, attack not only their own potency, or God's power, but their own minds, their ability to make meaning. This is not simply a matter of a conflict between desire and fear. *Efes* erodes the idyll of fertility they themselves have evoked. Desire is shot through with the horror of giants. The Land flowing with milk and honey—the mother flowing with sweet milk to feed her children—becomes a "land that consumes its inhabitants," a monstrous mother who eats her young.

This catastrophic Land is an object of fascination and revulsion. Even its fruit is gigantic—a cluster of grapes requires two bearers. The visual impact of this Land is both wondrous and horrifying; ungraspable; in a sense, *unseeable*.

The biblical account of the Spies' first response to the Land is revisited in the letters and journals of the early European explorers in the New World. This is the subject of Stephen Greenblatt's study, *Marvelous Possessions,* which documents the prevailing sense of the "marvelous" in these testimonies; the prodigious, the literally *amazing.* The explorers experienced neither pleasure nor pain but a *bewildering* loss of identity. Longing and horror both characterize their response to the inhuman scale and beauty of the place. Indirectly, Greenblatt shines a spotlight on the uncanny dimension of the original encounter of the Spies with the Promised Land. The biblical text and its midrashic elaborations play on the Spies' anguished wonder. Will the Land eat us, or will they be our bread? Are we grasshoppers or angels? In an equivalent of the infant's "startle reflex"—eyes widened, arms thrust up—they are flooded by an excess that annihilates them.[30]

So the impeccable first account of the Land immediately erupts in riotous fantasies beyond human measure. Projections and introjections break through, a fear of the radical difference of this Land. "Who told you that I did not make you seem as angels in their eyes?" God is aggrieved at the Spies' *knowingness*, at the way they foreclose possibilities in their rush to already understand. As we have seen, Beit Yaacov reads this as a kind of skepticism: a denial of the other as bearing an equivalent imaginative freedom.

THE TRANSPARENT EYEBALL

Efes obliterates the personal value of objective goodness: fertility, prodigious increase. *Efes* declares that this Land is not good *for us*; it cannot be loved *by us*. As Freud put it, "In the world of the neuroses it is psychical reality which is the decisive kind." For the Spies, external reality—the goodness of the Land—becomes a representation of their inner reality. In this narrative particularly, the Spies set aside the metaphysical meaning of words—*good* now means "I love it, I want it." In place of the philosophical and the ethical *good* and *evil*, there now arise the passionate, idiosyncratic associations that constitute their psychic reality.

Is this, then, the "sin"[31] of the Spies, as it is colloquially known? We have seen that Sefat Emet takes this position: they were not asked to make interpretations of the goodness of the Land. In allowing themselves to be drawn into their private obsessions, they distort the objective reality they are to report.

I suggest that the problem here is rather different. An impersonal report is not, in fact, possible; it may not even be desirable. All language is shot through with the hues of fantasy, of love and hatred, wonder and fear. Worlds are created rather than replicated. In the intensity of experience, would it have been possible for the Spies to strip their vision of its personal, idiosyncratic elements? Perhaps, on the contrary, the Spies and, in their wake, the people are not sufficiently conscious of the power of unconscious fantasy in themselves and in others. Their account of the giants emphasizes subjective vision: "*We saw* the giants, *we seemed to ourselves* like grasshoppers." But they report this in a tone of clinical objectivity, as though *efes* had not created a rift between public and private reality, as though *efes* had not already negated the publicly shared reality, in favor of a private symbolic world.

Perhaps, then, the work of the negative is inevitable. The world cannot be seen without "interference." According to a classic Talmudic description, Moses alone of human beings "saw *b'aspaklariah meirah*—through a clear lens." All others, including prophets and seers, saw through an unclear glass, a distorted lens of subjectivity.[32] The problem arises when one is not aware of one's own deflections of vision. Imagining oneself clear-eyed, one may become the greatest fantasist of all. *"Les non-dupes errent"*—"The undeceived err"— claimed the French analyst Jacques Lacan; the greatest illusion may be the pretension to total lucidity.[33]

The "clear lens" of undistorted vision is evoked by Emerson in his essay "Nature":

> Crossing a bare common, in snow puddles, at twilight, under a clouded sky, without having in my thoughts any occurrence of special good fortune, I have enjoyed a perfect exhilaration. I am glad to the brink of fear. In the woods too, a man casts off his years, as the snake his slough, and at what period soever of life, is always a child. In the woods is perpetual youth. . . . In the woods, we return to reason and faith. There I feel that nothing can befall me in life,—no disgrace, no calamity, (leaving me my eyes,) which nature cannot repair. Standing on the bare ground,—my head bathed by the blithe air, and uplifted into infinite space,—all mean egotism vanishes. I become a transparent eye-ball; I am nothing; I see all; the currents of the Universal Being circulate through me; I am part or particle of God.[34]

Emerson's ecstatic experience in the woods transports him beyond the accidents of life to a purity of vision that strips him (or *sloughs* him—evoking the serpent in paradise?) of egotism and of the densities of a self accreted through the years. Dropping all the accoutrements of ego, he becomes a *transparent eyeball:* almost a translation of the *aspaklariah meirah,* the clear lens of the Talmud. He is nothing but a walking I/Eye—pure perception, subject of revelation. Paradoxically, even as he proclaims his American visionary dislocation from the English traditions of vision and poetry—he finds in the New World a "perpetual youth"—his language is deeply informed by Romantic lyrical traditions. The literary critic Mark Edmundson[35] points out that the "perfect exhilaration" of the self become transparent eyeball is an "appealingly grotesque modification" of Wordsworth's vision: "While with an eye made quiet by the power / Of harmony . . . / We see into the life of things."[36]

In Edmundson's view, Emerson retreats from the encounter with the "opposition," or the "antagonist," with whom his metaphysical vision contends. Genuine transformation is believable only if the "possibility of irreparable harm" is confronted. The grief of the world, the experiences of loss and mourning, the passing of time, are eluded here in a willful movement of ecstasy—by the eyeball that renders all things transparent: "I am part or particle of God." This form of transcendence is achieved by negation: "All mean egotism vanishes. . . . I am nothing; I see all. . . ."—all and nothing: but fear of the losses that the world may yet inflict still haunts the passage.

Emerson's grotesque image of the transparent eyeball with its ecstatic lucidity brings us back to the drama of the Spies. The Spies return with a mythically framed "good" report of the good Land ("a land flowing with milk and honey"). This represents the physical reality of nature and the metaphysical promise of God's love. But instantly their worst fears flood back, the possibilities of "irreparable harm." The visionary mode proves precarious; the objective *goodness* of the Land cracks under the force of the lava that erupts in their words.

Efes signals an imagination enthralled by the menacing figures of catastrophe. The good report can be achieved only by neutralizing these terrors, but then it is easily neutralized in turn. Here is the skepticism that Cavell describes as a kind of fanaticism. In a sense, the skeptic "wants the annihilation that he is punished by . . . [he] wants for there to be . . . nothing . . . nothing but plenitude."[37] The human condition of partial knowledge enrages him. All or nothing; better not to have been born, to be neither natal nor mortal. The possibility of acknowledging his (limited, not fully understood) part in the world would involve the repeated grief of mourning for the losses intrinsic to such a world.

THE CORE FANTASY

The people resort to a nightlong paroxysm of weeping, wishing to be dead. This moment of apocalyptic despair is, at heart, a wish never to have been born. "If only we had died" leads them to only one thought—the wish to return to Egypt, to the place of primal non-being. To be a *no-thing*[38] is, in effect, to annihilate one's beginning, one's birth. This is the extremity of the *efes* state. Here, thought itself becomes intolerable.

I suggest that what is breaking through in the Spies' words is what the philosopher and psychoanalyst Jonathan Lear calls a core fantasy. Such fantasies have great imaginative power to organize the self, in fact to answer the question, "Who am I?"[39] The core unconscious fantasy that erupts in the Spies' report represents a collective identity quite at odds with the conscious sense of practical identity. "It is a mark of the human," he writes, "that we do not quite fit into our own skins." Moreover, the "remainders," the "flotsam and jetsam" of what does not fit into one's social identity constitute "organized attempts to form an identity around the solution to a primordial human problem. . . . The fantasy thus serves as a source of unity of the self."[40]

The Spies express their unconscious ambivalence about being and nonbeing—"To be or not to be." The people respond in tumult and hysteria ("And Caleb hushed the people. . . ." [Num. 13:30]). They seek to avoid death in war by returning to the place where they may cease before being born. A core fantasy emerges that annihilates goodness and the possibility of love. The world is intolerable, but even that fact cannot be acknowledged. The distorting lens carries the illusion of clarity.

Moses, on the other hand, is that unique human being who may be described as seeing through a clear lens; he lives as close to the "transparent eye-ball" condition as is humanly possible. His perception may lay claim to an objectivity that, the Talmud says, is beyond the reach of all other human beings. In other words, the Talmud is defining what constitutes the human—an excess of fantasy that colors and shapes reality. Not quite fitting into their skins, human beings create their own realities.

"Is the Land a good land or a bad one?" Unconsciously, this translates for the Spies and for the people as, "Do I love it or hate it?" Or, more starkly, "Do I love or hate?" Asking the question, the self is suddenly aware of its own mystery. All the workable illusions become questionable. "I come to know that I do not know."[41] Paralyzed, the people "gave forth their voices and they wept on that night" (Num. 14:1). All that is heard in the darkness is the *voice* of the people, the wordless weeping of an enigmatic sorrow. Only in the next verse, their keening resolves into words of complaint.

The lament constitutes a moment of "self-disruption,"[42] in Jonathan Lear's terms. He uses the expression to analyze Freud's description of a "disturbing habit" that his infant grandson developed whenever his mother left him for a few hours. He would throw a wooden reel with a piece of string attached into his cot so that it disappeared. At the same time, he would utter a loud *o-o-o-o* sound, which all agreed represented the German word *fort* (gone). He would then pull the reel out of the cot again by the string with a joyful *da* (there). Freud comments that this represented the child's "compensation to himself for his mother's absence, by himself staging the disappearance and return of objects within his reach."[43]

As Lear puts it, "This is a moment of self-disruption in an already disrupted life." Lear adds: "What the disruption is *for* really depends on what happens next." He then speculates what would happen if the child could never get to *da:*

> He would then get stuck repeating "o-o-o-o" over and over again. We would then see something that looked like a traumatic neurosis. Indeed, the child might begin to use these outbursts to attack his own mind. For the child would never be able to get a thought together if each attempt to do so was interrupted by an outburst of "o-o-o-o." Rather than face the loss, the child might opt to attack his own ability to understand what has happened to him. This would be the beginning of a massively self-destructive, self-annihilating character.[44]

The *fort-da* game enables the child to bring "experience together rather than blow it apart. The invention of the game converts this rip in the fabric of experience into an experience of loss."[45] The mother's absence becomes something the child can play with, think through and around. The mother becomes someone "who can be present, go away, and come back again, all the while maintaining . . . her distinct identity."

Lear strikingly calls this game "courage-in-the-making . . . the development of protocourage."[46] The child is impelled to develop the capacity to tolerate absence, for only in the absence of the object does *thinking* begin. Giving a name to his pain seems to transform the pain. But "the name of loss requires the game of loss." In playing his game, the child develops ways of living with his loss.

At the same time, Lear acknowledges, the "disruption in the fabric of life" to which the game is a response has been in some degree covered over. Life has been creatively reinvented—but something has been left out; there is a "remainder," which is precisely the disruption that generated the process in the first place. This is "Freud's deepest insight . . . that . . . life can never be lived without remainder."[47]

During their night of weeping, I suggest, the people are crying "o-o-o-o," mourning a nameless loss. The core fantasy of *efes* has made it impossible to think; they inhabit the "rip in the fabric of life." The question Lear raises is, "What is this disruption *for*?" If it fails to generate the game of loss, a name for loss, it remains a wail of "gone." The world is gone away and cannot be recalled.

This is what the Talmud calls *bechiyah shel chinam*—literally, crying for nothing. This is the meaningless weeping, a failure in that courage that Freud and Lear describe. But this crisis raises bewildering questions about the nature of courage, of faith, of goodness and badness in the wilderness. Joshua and Caleb, the "courageous" Spies, respond to the disruption by enacting a mourning scene—"They tore their garments." They declare: "The Land that we passed through to explore it is a very, very good land!" (Num. 14:6–7). What is the force of this response to the weeping nation! After all, on the level of public reality, the Spies had freely acknowledged the goodness of the Land. What, then, are Joshua and Caleb adding, by intensifying their description of goodness—"very, very good"? If anything, the intensifiers only weaken the force of God's original description: "a land flowing with milk and honey"—which Joshua and Caleb, in any case, reiterate in the next verse.

In a remarkable reading, Ha'amek Davar connects "very, very good" with God's final vision of His created world: "And God saw all that He had made, and behold it was *very good*" (Gen. 1:31). On each previous day, God has seen the world as simply *good*. Is it the sheer fact of completing His work that intensifies God's sense of *tov*? Or is it, perhaps, the final object of Creation—the human being—that is *tov me'od, very good*? One midrash points out that *adam*, the human being, is an anagram for *me'od—very* (good).[48] It is the human presence in the world that is *tov me'od*.

But Ha'amek Davar cites another, more challenging midrash: "*Me'od—zeh malach ha-mavet—Very good* refers to the Angel of Death!"[49] Human mortality sharpens, intensifies the goodness of life. Unalloyed pleasure becomes cloying; the experience of limits, of loss, allows one to experience delight more acutely. Similarly, Joshua and Caleb are not describing the objective fertility of the Land but the subjective human experience of pleasure and satisfaction. They acknowledge life and death as inextricably interwoven. They speak with a keen understanding of what Mark Edmundson calls the "antagonist"—the Angel of Death, their own worst fears, the possibility of irreparable harm. They affirm the paradox of the game of loss through which courage can be developed. *Very, very good* signals a human mourning process that salvages the possibility of desire.

For the people, Joshua and Caleb's acknowledgment of the paradoxical beauty of the world is enraging; their impulse is to hurl stones "upward," at God's glory.[50] What they are attacking is the notion of what the poet Gerard Manley Hopkins calls "Pied Beauty":

Glory be to God for dappled things—
. . . .
All things counter, original, spare, strange;
  Whatever is fickle, freckled (who knows how?)
    With swift, slow; sweet, sour; adazzle, dim;
He fathers-forth whose beauty is past change:
            Praise him.

Constantly losing the world, Joshua and Caleb acknowledge that it must be regained every day; absence and presence become the essential game. But the people live in the place of loss, in a malady of skepticism to which, apparently, there is no alternative. They inhabit a world in which love and hate, goodness and badness, are radically split.

It is only their children, says God, who "will know the Land which you have *reviled*" (Num. 14:31). The Hebrew word for "reviled"— *m'astem*—suggests a visceral rejection, physically the vomiting reflex. The same expression occurs in Psalms 106:24: "And they *reviled* the desirable land; they did not believe His word." The key terms are concentrated, as though welded together—hatred, desire, belief. The Land is *desirable,* but not to them; they have no ability to regain the world that has gone from them. And again, "Because you have *reviled* God who is in your midst" (Num. 11:20). Their hatred is directed against God, who is in a sense *within them.* In this sense, it is self-hatred that marks their experience of God Himself.

The most explicit expression of this split is in Moses' narrative, forty years later, of the night of weeping: "You sulked in your tents and said, It is because God hates us that He brought us out of the land of Egypt, to hand us over to the Amorites to wipe us out" (Deut. 1:27). By this time, the core fantasy is fully recognized: the people experience God's *hatred* as informing the epic narrative of the Exodus. It is as though the people cannot figure themselves as lovable to God. Rashi strikingly catches the projection implicit in their fantasy: "Really, He loved you, but *you hated Him*—as the proverb has it, What you have in your heart about your friend you imagine he has in his heart about you!"

This shocking diagnosis has taken forty years for Moses to articulate. Perhaps this is the time it has taken for the people to be capable of hearing such truths about themselves. What erupted during the night of weeping annihilated the very possibility of love, whether God's love for them, or, more disturbingly, their own love for God. It is only after the forty-year wilderness trek and the death of a generation that Moses can confront them with their own destructiveness.

"WITH ALL YOUR HEART"

The English psychoanalyst Donald Winnicott discusses the difficulty of acknowledging the "destructiveness that is personal, and that inherently belongs to a relationship to an object that is felt to be good—in other words, that is related to loving."[51] The primitive aspects of emotional development are often experienced as intolerable. The destructive aims of early life, in which the infant in effect consumes the mother without compunction, are felt in later development to be too ruthless even to acknowledge. The notion of "health," Winnicott suggests, requires the capacity to take "full responsibility for *all* feelings and ideas that belong to being alive."

The patient in analysis, therefore, needs to reach first to the destruction in himself, before he can meaningfully experience constructive and creative work. Conversely, a "platform of generosity can be reached and used so that from it a glimpse might be gained of . . . that which underlies the generosity, and which belongs to primitive loving."[52] "Toleration of one's destructive impulses results in a new thing: the capacity to enjoy ideas, even with destruction in them. . . . This development gives elbow room for the experience of concern, which is the basis for everything constructive."[53] The clinical cases that Winnicott cites illustrate this slow movement toward toleration of destructiveness; otherwise, the result is "either depression or else a search for relief by the discovery of destructiveness elsewhere—that is to say, by the mechanism of projection."[54]

The people in the wilderness manifest some of the dilemmas of love and hatred. They live through the destructive urges that accompany the experience of loving. To love God, or the Land, or themselves, is a project that becomes possible only when they can begin to tolerate the full extent of their hatred.

The God who performed many miracles for them, who freed them from slavery and promised them a good and fertile land, elicits from them both love and hate. For He is also uncanny, both familiar and strange, making inscrutable demands of them, massacring them by the thousand. And His land is inhabited by giants who consume those who live in it. Their revulsion against God and Land is, on Winnicott's model, an aspect of their love that they must come to acknowledge and, to some extent, integrate. They need to live all parts of themselves, if faith is to gain ground within them. For the catastrophe of otherness, of a world gone away, is part of the process of becoming a self.

Michael Eigen discusses what he calls "the area of faith" in the work of the great British psychoanalyst Wilfred Bion:

If, for example, one's emotional reality or truth is despair, what is most important is not *that* one may be in despair, but one's attitudes *toward* one's despair. Through one's basic attentiveness one's despair can declare itself and tell its story. One enters profound dialogue with it.[55]

In a similar way, acknowledging the otherness of God, or of other people, means entering into profound dialogue with it—and ultimately, with one's own otherness. One's destructiveness plays a role in the vitality of love. Perhaps this is what the Talmud intimates when it comments on the biblical command "You shall love God, your God, with *all your heart*" (Deut. 6:5). Since the Hebrew for "your heart" is spelled here with a double letter *beit* (*levav,* where *lev* is generally used), the Talmud comments that one should love God with both one's hearts, "with both one's inclinations, good and evil."[56] *Tov* and *ra,* good and evil, are expressed in love and hate, closeness and distance, continuity and rupture, constructive and destructive impulses. Both must be acknowledged if the reality of love is to be experienced.

It is striking that only after Moses, at the beginning of Deuteronomy, has confronted the people with the full extent of their hatred can he begin to explore a new vocabulary of emotional connection between his people and God. Loving, yearning, desiring (*ahavah, chefetz, cheshek*) appear for the first time in the language of relationship—a movement of feeling flowing both ways. For instance, God asks for their love, because "it was only your fathers that God desired in His love for them, so that He chose you, their seed, from among all peoples this very day" (Deut. 10:15). Rashi comments: "[He chose you:] As you *see yourselves desired* from among all the idolaters this very day." God's desire becomes an existential reality for the Israelites; they become capable of seeing themselves as desirable and desired. On this basis, they can be asked to love God "*le-tov lach*—for your good" (10:13).

I suggest that it is only after the people have acknowledged the full extent of their hatred that they can register love flowing from them and to them. Their original acceptance of the Torah and its commandments gave them what Winnicott calls a platform of generosity from which a glimpse might be gained of their own destructiveness. Perhaps only after the sin of the Spies can they begin to mourn for the losses they have incurred. With mourning comes concern, and the playfulness that allows one every day to regain the lost world. This process of acknowledgment, mourning, and play reaches a new pitch when Moses can speak to them, at the end of the forty years in the desert, of their own hatred.

DRAWN IN DESIRE

To love God with "both one's hearts" involves the violence intrinsic to hatching processes;[57] it is part of the human developmental struggle. It involves disruptions and deeper forms of integration; and the discovery of what Lear calls uncanny longing.[58] As though longing strangely arises at moments when given reality comes into question. Joshua and Caleb say to the people in the moment of their greatest crisis, "If God *desires* us, He will bring us to this Land and give it to us, the land flowing with milk and honey" (Num. 14:8). It is all a matter of desire; God's for them, theirs for God. But the people are enraged; they are in a state of hatred, as Moses will remind them forty years later—God's for them, theirs for God. The root of their trouble, Moses will tell them quite matter-of-factly, was that "you did not *want* to go up" (Deut. 1:26).

Moses records this as a failure in faith, basically in *trust*: "In this matter, you did not believe in God, your God" (Deut. 1:32). *"In this matter,"*: says Rashi, "He promises to bring you into the Land and you do not trust him." And, in real time, God expresses the failure to Moses: "How long will this people not trust Me, despite all the signs I have performed in their midst?" (Num. 14:11), again the paradox of an inscription in their very being—which they cannot trust. The kind of faith God waits for is not a dogmatic belief in His power but rather faith in His love for them. A people who think themselves hated by God cannot trust the signs of His benevolence, however deeply experienced. To trust means to acknowledge the enigmatic messages of the other who is truly unknowable, who is absent in His very presence. God's enigmatic "signs" ask to be translated by human desire.

In the final analysis, to trust is, as Sefat Emet puts it, to be "drawn in desire" after the other.[59] Human desire arouses divine desire that overwhelms all the limitations of time and space. In this way, Sefat Emet repeatedly translates Joshua and Caleb's words, "If God desires us . . ." as, "All depends on Israel's desire."[60] On the realistic view, the people in fact have not yet developed that true self that is capable of such a desire and such a trust. In this sense, the moment is indeed not yet ripe for going up into the Land. Yet, from a different perspective, as Sefat Emet suggests, if the people had been really impassioned—drawn after God—the surge of miracles that redeemed them from Egypt would have borne them into the Land. In this sense, the people make a kind of unconscious choice. They choose to live within the natural human world of love and hate, trust and distrust, connection and separation. It will then take them forty years, and the concentrated tidal rhythm of death and birth, to begin to integrate their "two hearts" and find the love that will only then become utterable.

IN TRANSIT

The wilderness time is a journey toward fuller experiencing of the possibilities of love and trust. It is a time of movement, spent in transit toward a way of living with all that, in Winnicott's terms, is experienced as *not-me*. The developing child learns to "play" with the experience of absence, of the mother who has gone away. This is a journey through time, from a sometimes obliterating sense of *efes*, in which "All I have got is what I have not got."[61] The people travel back and forth between here and there, between subjective and objective reality. The great dread is of being pulled apart by their own aggression, of being lost in some wilderness. For coming to know this, there is nothing like being, in fact, in a wilderness. In transit, viable symbolic objects, representing loss and recovery, can be created. Time and again, these objects will fall apart and be re-created. God, the Land, their very selves, will tend to disappear, like the grasshoppers of their fantasy.

Their journey can already be glimpsed within the frame of the narrative of the Spies itself. For even in the maelstrom of weeping on that fateful night, an utterance emerges, an act of *dibbur* (language) about the people's reality. Sheer *voice* ("They gave forth their voice. . . .") settles into an expression of the *nothing* that they inhabit: "If only we had died in the land of Egypt, or in this wilderness if only we had died . . ." (Num. 14:2). The wish never to have been born modulates gradually into the full fantasy of return: "Let us appoint a leader and return to Egypt" (Num. 14:4). In this speech, the people become for a moment consciously expressive of their unconscious condition. Something has broken through into speech that is suffused by the fantasy it describes. This is a moment of "uncanny disruption," in Lear's words; an official self gaps open and another identity becomes visible: "The aim of unity," he writes, "should not be to overcome these disruptions, but to find ways to live well with them. Ironically, the unity that is available to us is a peculiar form of disunity."[62]

Even a concept like *efes*—nothingness, negation—marks a stage on a journey, a moment when a guiding fantasy comes into view. Putting their imaginative life *into* words, so that the fantasy "suffuses the words,"[63] does not—surprisingly—destroy the world: the world survives, as does God, and their own selves. More than that, through such moments of rupture, something new is hatched.[64]

Reading the wilderness narrative in this "therapeutic" way depends on a radical assumption: that the people can, in a sense, *hear themselves* as they speak. Their angriest outbursts act not least *on themselves*. A truth has been uttered that they themselves may find bewildering. Such eruptions of fantasy life may constitute a journey through a "great and terrible wilderness" (Deut. 1:19). In transit, possibilities of love and desire and faith may become visible.

In this wilderness journey, the question of *goodness* will unfold its complexity. For Moses, there never was a question about the goodness of God's guidance. Seeing through a clear lens, Moses speaks, to the end, of the *good Land* that he yearns for. When, in the last months of his life, he cries to God, "Please let me cross over and see the good Land . . ." (Deut. 3:25), perhaps he wishes to demonstrate the truth of its goodness to his people. His dearest wish is to confront his people with this manifest goodness; after this, he is willing to die. But God interrupts his plea: "Enough! Do not speak to Me anymore of this thing!" Moses is not to go on harping on this question of the Land's goodness.[65]

Perhaps the reason that God interrupts Moses is that just here, in "this thing," the rift between Moses and his people opens wide. Moses' state approximates to the "transparent eye-ball" evoked by

Emerson. For him, goodness is an objective matter; he and all reality are "part and parcel of God." But the people are driven by fantasies and anxieties that make goodness an issue of love and hate; the Land represents other questions about themselves, the world, and God. No demonstration of lush fruit can ever lay to rest the *efes* coiled within them. Moses' dream of vindication cannot address their need. For them, a journey will have proved necessary, if they are to find a way of speaking of the good Land with all their heart.

SIX

Black Sun: Moses and Job

ASCENT OR DESCENT?

The problem of God's anger, His periodic destruction of His people—
what is known as His *middat ha-din*, His attribute of severe justice—is
central to the narrative of the wilderness. From a human point of
view, at such moments God is perceived as *cruel*. At the heart of
the wilderness, the narrative of the Spies—and, perhaps even more
painfully, the sequel to that narrative—embodies the anguish of this
perception.

At the end of the narrative of the Spies, God declares the fate of
the people: "All these people who have seen My glory and My signs
which I have performed in Egypt and in the wilderness and yet have
tested Me ten times now, and refused to listen to My voice—I swear
that they shall not see the Land which I have sworn to their fathers"
(Num. 14:22–23). Those who have tested God shall not see the Promised Land. Over the course of forty years—matching the forty days
of the Spies narrative—this "evil community" will meet its end in the
wilderness.

Moses reports God's words to the people and they "mourn exceedingly." What follows is unexpected:

And they rose up early next morning and set out toward the
crest of the hill country, saying, "We are prepared to go up to
the place that God has spoken of, for we have sinned." But
Moses said, "Why do you transgress God's command? This will
not succeed. Do not go up, lest you be routed by your enemies, for God is not in your midst. For the Amalekites and the
Canaanites will be there to face you, and you will fall by the
sword, since you have turned away from following God and
God will not be with you."

Yet defiantly they marched [*va-ya'apilu*] toward the crest of the hill country, though neither God's Ark of the Covenant nor Moses stirred from the camp. And the Amalekites and the Canaanites who dwelt in that hill country came down and dealt them a shattering blow at Hormah. (Num. 14:40–45)

Instead of accepting the death sentence that they have just mourned, the people demonstratively stage what seems like a mass act of repentance. Where previously they had said, "We cannot go up" (Num. 13:31), they now *go up* toward the hill crest, which symbolizes their intention to *go up* to the Land of God's promise. Full of ardor ("They rose up early"), they declare *Hinenu*—in the classic expression of dedicated readiness to do God's will; and they confess their sin ("We have sinned"). They disregard Moses' warnings, persisting in their plan, and they are totally massacred.

Why is such a well-intentioned act of repentance, of *teshuvah* (turning), met by words of such grim repudiation—"you have turned back [*shavtem*] from following God"? Why is their movement of return to God impugned as a kind of counter-*teshuvah*? And why is their ardent insistence on *going up* (expressed in words of the most positive resonance) met by a barrage of negatives—"You are transgressing . . . will not prosper . . . do not go up. . . . God is not in your midst . . . He will not be with you . . ."—and, ultimately, by a shattering blow in battle? "They persisted—*va-ya'apilu*—in going up . . . and the Amalekites and the Canaanites *came down* upon them."

Why is God not with them in their act of manifest penitence? Like Abraham before the Binding of Isaac, they declare *Hinenu!*— "Here we are!" In the face of God's sentence, "They shall not see the Land," they declare themselves prepared to ascend to the place from which just yesterday they recoiled. Today, their movement *upward* is spurned as a transgressive act: *Al ta'alu*—"Do not go up!"

Forty years later, Moses will retell the story; then, he will repeat God's warning with a slight difference: "*Lo ta'alu*—You will not go up!" (Deut. 1:42). Rashi comments: "This will not be an ascent for you but a descent!"[1] The negative *Lo* is not simply a command but also an evaluation of their act and its consequences: what looks like an upward move will prove to be a downward one. Apparently, even the expression *aliyah,* with its unequivocally positive connotations, can prove unreliable.

In the course of his retelling of the story, Moses uses the strange expression *va-tahinu*—"You persisted in going up the mountain." Rashi comments: "This derives from the expression, *hinenu*—which you said—at root, *Hen* (Yes!)" The purest expression of the positive (*Yes!*)—"You *yessed*"—is repudiated by God (*lo ta'alu*).

Attended with ambiguities and paradoxes, the protagonists of this story are traditionally referred to as the *ma'apilim*—from the verb *va-ya'apilu,* used in the narrative (Num. 14:44) to describe their persistence. Does this rare word connote daring or defiance, courage or arrogance? From within this field of possible meanings, their act is to be understood and judged.

The classic commentaries have understood this cryptic event in a number of different ways. The mainstream understanding is that this is not, in fact, an authentic act of *teshuvah* (turning). It ignores God's verdict against the people. What might yesterday have been a genuine act of *teshuvah* has come too late; reality has irrevocably changed since the Spies' narrative, and *teshuvah* itself has taken on a transgressive coloring. As Seforno puts it, the people indeed repent of their lack of faith, they come in prayer to God ("You turned around and wept before God" [Deut. 1:45]); but God's Name has been profaned and only death can atone for this.[2] What has been said cannot be unsaid. Since God is no longer in their midst, they are unprotected against the Amalekites.

Their act is, therefore, condemned as presumptuous, self-willed, perverse, heedless. All these are translations of *va-ya'apilu.* Literally, the root refers to a protuberance, a tumor; therefore, to climbing a mountain. But as it is used in this context, the term clearly has moral connotations. In Arabic, the root signifies turning one's mind away from danger—a heroic act. Strikingly, in modern times, it denotes a daring and heroic Zionist movement of *aliyah.*[3]

In our text, it suggests a seriously wrongheaded act that is terribly punished. Nevertheless, some commentaries have seen this episode as, at worst, magnificently quixotic; as in itself heroic, if badly timed.[4] In one fascinating account,[5] this narrative becomes a test case for the virtue of persistence: a virtuous, high-minded act disregards essential elements of reality. "*This* will not succeed," Moses warns them: in this particular context, such acts will have fatal consequences.

How are we to understand a situation in which the desire to undo yesterday's sin can lead to massacre? Yesterday, they recoiled from God who was in their midst (Num. 11:20); today, Moses tells them, God is not in your midst.

THE CRUELEST MOMENT

Perhaps the cruelest moment in this strange episode emerges in Moses' account forty years later. After the massacre, the people "again wept before God; but God would not listen to your voice, He would not give ear to you" (Deut. 1:45). The people's despair is repudiated by God—as though their weeping is another in the series of hysterical outbreaks that precipitates upon them harsh judgments.

Rashi comments on God's refusal to listen to their cries: "As it were, you have made His attribute of compassion as though it were cruel." Rashi points to the *cruelty* of God's refusal to listen. In the world of human relationships, turning a deaf ear to the cry of the sufferer is the quintessentially callous act. Similarly, Rashi reads God's repudiation of the Israelites' cry as cruelty, even as he hedges such irreverence with triple qualifications—*as it were, you have made, as though it were.* If God's behavior seems cruel, it is the people's fault. Their perversity has distorted God's compassion. In any case, anthropomorphic descriptions of God are to be read with proper caution.

And yet, with all his qualifications, Rashi has made a pointed comment on the human experience of not being heard by God. Poignantly, Moses himself will undergo a similar experience when, at the end of his life, God will refuse to listen to his prayer. At that juncture, God "would not listen to me . . . 'That's quite enough! Never speak to Me again about this matter!'" (Deut. 3:26). In that extreme moment of not listening, God effectively closes Moses' mouth on "this matter" of his desire to enter the Land. Rashi comments: "So that people should not say, How harsh the teacher! And how obtuse the student!" Again, the sense of cruelty is framed in "what people will say," as though to play down the outsider's judgment, while at the same time presenting it as plausible. In both cases, God's cruelty becomes a function of a relationship in which the human partner bears some responsibility for the way God presents Himself in the world.

MOURNING AS TURNING POINT?

If the people weep after the massacre, they have already "mourned exceedingly"(Num. 14:39) at the beginning of the narrative. Then, they were responding to Moses' report of their fate. This *exceeding* (excessive?) *mourning* both marks the end of the Spies story and initiates the *ma'apilim* episode. A wave of mourning sweeps over the nation, perhaps a mourning for their own (future) death.

We remember a previous moment of national mourning, after the sin of the Golden Calf. Then, God had declared, "I shall not *go up in your midst.*" He had withdrawn His presence from among them. "And the people heard this evil thing and they mourned; and no one put on his finery" (Exod. 33:3–4). In that parallel crisis of loss and mourning, the people recognized the *evil* in God's absence, just as in our narrative, the people mourn God's description of them as "this evil community" (Num. 14:26,35). An evil is to be mourned, a fantasy of immaculate innocence to be relinquished.

What is such mourning for? What follows mourning? As Julia Kristeva writes in her poignant discussion of melancholy, *Black Sun*, the dynamic of mourning is crucial to human development. She describes how the child relinquishes its primary object, the mother; they become separate; in place of symbiotic union arises language, a system of symbolic substitutes that allow the child to think about her absence: "If I did not agree to lose mother, I could neither imagine nor name her."[6]

One who refuses to acknowledge primal loss may find herself assailed in later life by inexplicable melancholy. "My depression points to my not knowing how to lose—I have perhaps been unable to find a valid compensation for the loss? It follows that any loss entails the loss of my being—and of Being itself. The depressed person is a radical, sullen atheist."[7] And again: "The child king becomes irredeemably sad before uttering his first words; this is because he has been irrevocably, desperately separated from the mother, a loss that causes him to try to find her again, along with other objects of love, first in the imagination, then in words."[8]

If this mourning process is thwarted, the vital flow of language and desire is stalled. Even if language is formally learned, it has an artificial quality: "the speech of the depressed is to them like an alien skin; melancholy persons are foreigners in their maternal tongue. They have lost the meaning—the value—of their mother tongue for want of losing the mother."[9] In a sense, the depressed remain painfully riveted to the gates of Eden, unable either to enter or to detach themselves.

In her Freudian portrayal of human development and its casualties, Kristeva places the mourning process at the center. The primal loss must be absorbed and accepted; only then can the child begin to replace the mother with the "substitutes" of imagination and language.

It is striking that in the narrative of the Golden Calf, the people's mourning signifies a turning point. God accepts and reinforces their mourning practice: "'And now, strip your finery from off you. . . .' And the Israelites stripped their finery from Mount Horev" (Exod. 33:5–6). They strip themselves of a certain grandiosity. They "agree to lose" Moses who takes himself off to his Tent of Meeting outside the camp. An uncanny yearning animates them as they stand gazing after him, watching him recede from their grasp. God gives them a second set of Tablets to replace the shattered originals.

If this first act of mourning was so successful, why is the fate of the *ma'apilim* so different? They, after all, mourn *exceedingly*. . . . In this episode, too, they suffer the loss of God's presence and of Moses in their midst. Both narratives are marked by the experience of cruelty, of *ra*. Yet here, there is no compensation for their loss; rather, it is violently reenacted on their bodies. Here, their mourning does not constitute a turning point. Instead, it precipitates them into the tragic sequel to an already tragic narrative.

THE SPIES AND JOB: DIVINE CRUELTY

The people's original night of weeping becomes the subject of a midrashic meditation on the historical resonances of the moment:

Israel had wept on the night of the ninth of Av, and God had said to them: You have wept a causeless weeping before Me.

I shall therefore arrange for you a permanent weeping for future generations. At that hour it was decreed that the Temple should be destroyed and that Israel should be exiled among the nations; for so Scripture says, Therefore He lifted up His hand and swore concerning them, that He would overthrow them in the wilderness; and that He would cast out their seed among the nations, and scatter them in the lands (Ps. 106:26ff). The "lifted hand" was retribution for the "lifted voice."[10]

God responds to one paroxysm of tears with a history of tears. Crying *for nothing* becomes the rootstock for the future catastrophes of destruction and exile. That original night was the ninth of Av, which is then marked as the date of multiple disasters—"I'll give you something to cry over!" The link between the uncanny weeping over the Spies' report and the justified weeping over the destruction of the Temples is traced through a play on words: the people "lifted up their voices and wept" (Num. 14:1), so God "lifts up His hand" (Ps. 106:26) to vow their scattering among the nations. Such links establish a formal meaning, while at the same time evoking more troubled reactions in the reader. A *meaningless* cruelty seems to cry out from such linkages.

The notion that cruelty is an aspect of the human experience of God is a recurrent theme in biblical and rabbinic writings. The expression *middat achzariut*—the attribute of cruelty—is sometimes used in midrashic sources as a synonym for God's attribute of *middat ha-din*—severe and inscrutable divine justice in the human world.

The core text for such a sense of things is the book of Job. Job in fact uses the word *achzar* (cruel) in describing the unfathomable change in God's behavior toward him: "You have become cruel to me; with Your powerful hand you harass me" (Job 30:21). Rashi indirectly interprets the word in his commentary on a different verse: "He alienated [*ach zaru*] my kin from me; my acquaintances disown me" (19:13). Rashi reads *ach zaru* (alienated) as *achzar* (cruel), as though the unusual four-letter root *a-ch-z-r* were an amalgam of two words— *ach zar*. Cruelty in Rashi's view is essentially alienation, indifference toward one's friends.

God's cruelty can be understood as treating Job as though he were of no special importance, as though there were no connection between them. The human experience of this kind of cruelty is of being diminished, belittled, held of no account. Like a child, one senses oneself as *invisible*. A fantasy of self-sufficiency is punctured. One searches the face of the other, trying in vain to penetrate the enigma.

It is striking that the Rabbis specifically trace connections between the book of Job and the narrative of the Spies. For example, the Talmud[11] connects Moses' question to the Spies: "Are there trees [*etz*] [in the Land]?" (Num. 13:20) with the fact that Job dwells in the land of *Utz*. The Spies experience the Holy Land as a place of death—a land that eats its inhabitants—because Job has just died and the impression of his funeral colors the Spies' view of the country.

Cruelty makes a complex appearance in another midrash on the Spies narrative, where Moses pleads for his people on the grounds of what "people will say" about God's punitiveness: "Let the nations not say, Because God was unable to bring the people into the Land He had promised them, he slaughtered them in the wilderness" (Num. 14:16). In the course of elaborating on this, the midrash adds:

> Let the nations not regard You as a cruel being: There came the generation of the Flood, and He destroyed them; then came the generation of Babel, then the Sodomites and the Egyptians, and He destroyed them. Now, even those He called "My firstborn son" He consumes, like that Lilith who when she finds nothing else turns upon her own children![12]

As in other midrashic descriptions of God as cruel, the notion is projected outward upon the nations or other misguided perceivers. Moses' argument is that God should give others no loophole for such demonic misreadings. And yet, by elaborating on a cruel narrative of indiscriminate mass killings, and through their macabre reference to Lilith, the Rabbis conjure up the monstrous possibility they are officially denying.

In this case, they project a Moses who in the biblical text articulates the heretical thought of God's *powerlessness* to complete His people's redemption, but who in the midrash is profoundly exercised by a different possibility: not that God is *unable* to redeem but that He actively destroys and wishes to destroy even His own children. This is *cruelty*, a moment of grotesque alienation. Moses pleads with God to act in such a way as to make this scenario unthinkable.

The Moses who emerges from the midrash is, like Job, troubled by the very possibility of divine cruelty. The Rabbis take the Moses-Job connection even further when they attribute the book of Job to Moses' authorship.[13] This startling idea shifts the boundaries of the "fictional" and the historical. If a character in one book is described as the author of another, he is endowed with a three-dimensional reality that is capable of generating a creation of its own.[14] We now have a Moses who is more than a biblical character, completely transparent to the author. He is given the opaque stature of one who, in his own imaginative "fiction," works through one of the fundamental dilemmas of being human.[15] We will return later to this intriguing suggestion.

HATRED, BLASPHEMY, VIOLENCE

First, however, I'd like to address moments in the biblical narrative when the theme of cruelty and hatred between man and God comes to the surface. One version of the theme appears in Moses' retelling of the Spies narrative. Describing the night of weeping, Moses will, forty years later, remind the people: "You murmured in your tents and said, It is *because God hates us* that He brought us out of the land of Egypt, to hand us over to the Amorites to wipe us out" (Deut. 1:27).

In Moses' narrative, their furious weeping expresses a persecutory sense of being hated by God. Seforno explains this by referring to their own sense of guilt from the time before the Exodus, possibly because of their idolatry, or "for some other sin."[16] Rashi goes further, responding to the bizarre nature of their complaint by treating it as a projection of their own hatred for God. Unable to recognize their own aggressiveness, the people yield to projection and depression.

In human affairs, hatred is recognizable as a plausible reaction to cruelty. Rashbam, for instance, points out that when kings and judges issue oppressive judgments that affect life and property, "people are accustomed to curse them." This is his explanation for the commandment not to curse judges (*elohim*).[17] The Torah declares a taboo on an all-too-natural response to persecution.

To curse is to express hatred verbally. Elizabethan swearwords

are vivid examples of such verbal acts of aggression against authority, specifically against divine authority. Since kings and courts deal
in vital existential matters, a harsh verdict will naturally elicit such
expressions of aggression. This verbal violence is directed against
elohim—both human judges and the divine Judge.

The cruel power of kings, of the law, and of God in His dimension
of *middat ha-din*—the attribute of strict and inscrutable justice—
arouses powerful resentments in human beings. The curse, or the
blasphemy, is, in effect, a cruel response to what is sensed as cruelty. In the grip of a passionate hatred, the blasphemer strikes to kill,
the words of the curse doing the work of the *makkah,* the blow that
physically destroys.[18]

The biblical case of the *mekallel,* the blasphemer, therefore, is of
special interest.[19] This anonymous man, son of an Israelite woman
and an Egyptian man, blasphemes in the heat of a brawl with an
Israelite man. A sentence of death is divinely imposed on him, and
a general law of blasphemy is framed; interestingly, this is set in
the context of other acts of violence—*makkot*—killing or wounding
human beings and animals.

As the Rabbis read the story, however, the blasphemer's situation has its own undeniable pathos. The brawl breaks out against a
background history in which the blasphemer's Israelite mother was
raped by an Egyptian taskmaster. The blasphemer's identity is thus
tragically confused. He is driven to his blasphemy when his claim to
a place in the Israelite camp is denied in court. He thus emerges as
the very type of one who finds himself entangled in a legal thicket, a
victim of the law's imbricated stringencies.

What is striking is the way that Ramban,[20] for instance, constructs the pathos and outrage of the blasphemer's situation. His
complicated parentage places him in a contested legal situation—
whichever way we read it, he suffers—so that he is provided with
maximum motivation for his act of hatred. Like the *mamzer*—the
illegitimate child of an adulterous union[21]—his life's possibilities are
diminished because of his parents' act.

One provocative midrash[22] refers to the Great Sanhedrin, the
Supreme Court, which issues such judgments, as "oppressors." Quoting Ecclesiastes 4:1, the midrash refers to "the tears of the oppressed
who have no comforter": in this world they have no consolation, for

they do not fit into the norms of society; but, God declares, "It is for Me to comfort them!" The power of the Law, of the Torah itself, finds a test case in the blasphemer, whose helpless outrage God acknowledges. God takes up the slack, the compassion for the individual and his subjective pain that the Law ignores.

At the same time, the sin of blasphemy is judged as a capital offense. So grave is the utterance of such violent words against God that all who hear it tear their clothes in mourning. This applies even to the officers of the court who have necessarily heard testimony to the blasphemy in court.

Daringly, Or Ha-Chaim suggests that Moses himself is implicated in the slanders against God that he puts in the mouth of "the nations." His rhetoric of appeal to God, we remember, cast the other nations in the role of commentators on God's impotence or even cruelty.[23] Within that framework, he appealed to God not to give them any ground for such slurs. Now, Or Ha-Chaim suggests, he must express contrition for speaking such words, even if he was only "testifying" to a potential blasphemy. For this reason, he reaffirms God's power: "*And now*,[24] may God's strength be magnified" (Num. 14:17). An attack on God has taken place; a healing countermovement is called for.

The idea that Moses is implicated in even imagining the blasphemy suggests that its violence on some level belongs to him. He is, after all, the author of the words: he speaks them; they are, in a sense, his words. Some restitution is called for; some recognition of his own aggression.

From the beginning of his history to the end, Moses, that most humble of all men, is portrayed as prone to episodes of anger, verbally or even physically expressed.[25] He is God's faithful messenger whose love for God and his people can be in no doubt. At the same time, his sensitivity to issues of injustice and cruelty repeatedly moves him to harsh indictments.

"WITHOUT CONTRARIES IS NO PROGRESSION" (WILLIAM BLAKE)

In this context, the Talmud's claim that he is the author of the book of Job takes on unexpected life. The subject of that difficult book is, most obviously, the suffering of the innocent at the hands of an inscrutable God. From Job's viewpoint, all his attempts to "justify" God fail. Even though he refuses to yield to his wife's insistence that he "blaspheme and die" (Job 2:9), he struggles obsessively with the issue of God's justice, both in direct address to God and in debate with his friends. In the end, God vindicates his reproaches and restores his lost family and wealth.

However, from a different perspective, not God but Job himself is the subject of the book. The British psychoanalyst Marion Milner creates a challenging psychological portrait of the man Job, who represents the internal struggle to evolve toward a position of integration and creativity.

She reads the Job story through the prism of Blake's twenty-one engravings, *Illustrations to the Book of Job*. In the first of these engravings, Job is shown praying with his family. But strangely, God above has the same face as Job, and musical instruments hang unused on the tree. Imagining himself as godlike, she argues, Job begins by denying his own destructiveness and therefore his creative powers. His sin is implied in his praise: he is "a perfect and upright man" (Job 1:1). His sense of perfect innocence disowns the Satan who leaps into him and demands expression. Consciously virtuous—he "fears God and avoids evil"—he cannot acknowledge his own unconscious rage.

Milner quotes Blake's aphorism, "Without contraries is no progression."[26] In her Freudian reading, Job needs to accept his dual nature, the male and female aspects of the soul, as well as its conscious and unconscious dimensions. He needs to be disillusioned of his infantile belief in his own omnipotence; to accept his dependence and relinquish the fantasy of wholeness. Where he had worshipped a God who was his own "wrought image,"[27] where he had cultivated a sterile self-righteousness, he comes to recognize his own imaginative power to create symbols that may represent the contrary forces of his being.

In the end, Blake portrays Job with pictures of destruction on his walls, and with marginal drawings of musical instruments and the leaves and fruit and delicate tendrils of the vine, as well as a palette and brushes, and ripe ears of corn. Imagined acts of violence, not real ones, allow him to encompass all the manifestations of primitive energy, which can now be channeled for creative ends.[28] In the final engraving, he is together with his wife and daughters—representing the recovered feminine—now restored to life and all playing upon their instruments.

For Milner, the meaning of Blake's work on Job is that primitive rage, pain, frustration need to be *known* and, in a deep sense, accepted. Symbol formation is the offshoot of a process of mourning. Most powerfully, she intimates the "fundamental paradox":

> true change of heart, growth to maturity of feeling, only comes about through facing the psychic pain of the recognition of opposites in ourselves. . . . Change of heart seems to come only when we *give up trying to change*. . . . [These are] moments in which *hopelessness about oneself is accepted;* and it is this which seems to enable the redeeming force to come into play . . . [then] the ideal and the actuality seem to *enter into relation with each other and produce something new.* [My emphasis.][29]

At the heart of this "fundamental paradox" is the experience of *mourning.* Milner strikingly portrays this as the ability to live with *hopelessness,* without resorting to manic denials and resolutions for change. Here, she intimates the moment of faith: that something new will indeed emerge from "just looking" at the pain of loss. In some measure, this recalls the classic rabbinic description of the process of *teshuvah* (repentance), where the stage of "recognition of the sin" precedes the abandonment of the sin. This encompasses precisely Milner's notion of contemplating the gap between the ideal and the actual in "one moment of vision," without rushing to close it.

VIOLENT INNOCENCE

Mourning over gaps and losses marks important moments of experience. We have seen the subtle interpretation of Or Ha-Chaim, in which Moses recognizes that his projected "blasphemy" has destroyed something of divinity in the world; for this he mourns, and finds words to bridge the gap. Like the court officers who necessarily hear the witnesses' blasphemy, he at least metaphorically "tears his clothes" over the rupture in the wholeness of the world.

With this, we can return to the mourning of the Israelites after

the Golden Calf. Stripping themselves of their finery, of their fantasies of omnipotence, the people expose themselves to a new way
of having God live in their midst. Rejecting perfect mirrorings of
themselves, they acknowledge a void, an absence. They make no
heroic attempt to *change;* rather, they surrender to the truth of their
stripped condition. Then, God mysteriously says, "My face shall,
after all, go [with you]" (Exod. 33:14). The state of mourning brings
them to a delicate balance between self-righteous bustle and inert
melancholy.

The mourning of the *ma'apilim* has very different results. Perhaps this is because, unlike the Golden Calf narrative, this episode
describes its protagonists as mourning *exceedingly.* The problem with
this mourning is that it is excessive, willful, full of conscious virtue—
and spiritually sterile. "God is not with you," says Moses. "*This* ascent
will not succeed." Manically self-sufficient, the *ma'apilim* have not
internalized the meanings of their sin. They confess, "We have
sinned" (Num. 14:40), but they link their confession with the words,
"*God said* [that we have sinned]"—as though the good child within
them cannot fully own the knowledge of sin.[30] Their turn toward the
Land holds arrogance at its heart; their upward movement is really
a kind of forced entry into a Land that will not yield to such violent
innocence.

UNCIRCUMCISED LIPS

"Moses wrote the book of Job," states the Talmud. One implication
of this may be that Moses, *Moshe rabbenu*—Moses our Teacher—is
profoundly implicated in the live issues of the book of Job. In writing a book, the author works through the dilemmas and paradoxes
of his life, which are also the dilemmas and paradoxes of the lives of
his readers. If the book of Job is concerned with the experience of
cruelty and injustice, as well as with the internal struggle with primitive responses of anger and frustration, its large resonance attests to
the universality of these dilemmas. The life of Moses, "the *man* who
brought us up out of Egypt," holds at its heart a deep concern with
these issues.

Moses' history begins with his mother's vision of him as *good:*
"His mother saw him that he was *good*" (Exod. 2:2). His mother sees

him as luminously beautiful; at his birth, the whole house fills with light.[31] God then calls on him at the Burning Bush to lead his people into a *good* and spacious land.

Countering this motif of goodness and beauty, however, there is the violence of his deathblow against the Egyptian. Chronically, too, there is the foreign body that blocks his mouth: he describes himself as *aral sefatayim*—of uncircumcised lips (Exod. 6:12); an excess demands to be removed. His body edges (*sefatayim*—lips, also edges) leave no space for that physical-spiritual activity called language. He is sealed against the world by a burden of tongue and mouth. Only gradually does he come at this formulation of this block; only when God calls on him does he begin to articulate his own impediment, describing himself as "not a man of words," "heavy of mouth and heavy of tongue" (4:10).

When he finally describes himself as having uncircumcised lips, he has undergone the uncanny violence of an encounter with God at a "hotel." God seeks to kill him, and his wife takes a flint and circumcises her infant son. The foreskin falls at Moses' feet; she then addresses the baby: "You are a bridegroom of blood to me!" Later, after God has relented, she says, "A bridegroom of blood because of the circumcision!" (Exod. 4:24–26).

Circumcision obviously plays a central role in this episode. Apparently, Moses has neglected to circumcise his son. Perhaps, however, another circumcision is being required of him. The impediment on his lips needs to be removed. He needs to surrender to God's call, to speak in His name. He needs to open his mouth to the embarrassments of language.

It is striking that when he complained about his speech problem at the Burning Bush, God made no move to heal him; He did not even promise him that his situation would change, for this problem is expressive of a radical resistance on Moses' part, which arouses God's anger and almost brings about his death at the hotel (*malon*).

R. Yosef Kimchi suggests that God's threatening message to Pharaoh may hold a secret address to Moses himself: "Israel is My firstborn son. I have said to you, 'Let My son go, that he may worship Me,' yet you refuse to let him go. Now I will slay your firstborn son" (Exod. 4:22–23).[32] In this imaginative reading, God's attack on Moses (or on his son) expresses His anger at Moses' posture of refusal.

Some unconscious aggression in Moses will not enable his people's redemption.[33]

In a similar vein, we may understand the "sign" of his hand turning leprous at the Burning Bush. Here, too, is a "sign" addressed to Moses himself: at the edges of his flesh, at the place where his body meets the world, his skin goes dead. Both the leprosy and the attack at the hotel intimate a divine anger at Moses' refusal to speak.

In the end Zippora acts by circumcising her baby, and saves the life of Moses (or of his son). For *milah*—circumcision—is what the whole story has been about. Rashi cites a macabre midrash about closed-off body surfaces: God's attack on Moses takes the form of a serpent that swallows him head downward, then feet upward, till the place of circumcision. From this, Zippora concludes that the heart of the matter is precisely sited there—"it was all about the *milah!*"

But the word *milah* also refers to the *word*;[34] the whole strange narrative has pivoted on the need for language. Both sexuality and speech are forms of communication with the world and both are constituted by a kind of limitation, a reduction of power. Moses resists entering the symbolic world that requires relinquishing an uncompromised inwardness. He is required to be born into the powerful but vulnerable world of language.

Milah as circumcision, as the word: this brief narrative engages in wordplay to make its point. Even the strange reference to the hotel—*malon*—can be read as part of Moses' "dream text." A narrative medium is woven in which God's intention is played out.

BIRTH INTO LANGUAGE

In relation to Moses' resistance to language, mystical traditions support the idea that Moses is in this matter different from other human beings. His "speechlessness" represents an *excess,* not a defect. In this sense, too, circumcision of the lips is an apt metaphor. Unlike others, he is not born into the language process; he will need to undergo a late rebirth, which will involve a late circumcision.

One expression of this idea is found in Maharal's *Gevurot Ha-Shem.*[35] Maharal's text is the Talmudic passage in which the Neoplatonic myth of human birth is recast: "When the newborn emerges into the air of the world, an angel comes and strikes it on the mouth and makes it forget the whole Torah [that he had fully known in the womb]."[36]

In Maharal's reading, the mouth is the site where the human being becomes human, a *speaking* being. The moment when the angel strikes the infant on the mouth is also the moment when the totality of Torah is forgotten. Soul becomes welded to body, so that pure and total intellectual knowledge is no longer possible. As a *nefesh chayah* (Gen. 2:7), a living being in the fullest sense, the infant at this moment becomes a complex "speaking" (i.e., embodied) spirit.[37] At this moment the child is completed as a human creature; the angel's tap on the mouth, like the sculptor's final tap with the chisel, signifies completion.[38]

As a speaking being, then, the child is embodied spirit—both amplified and reduced. At this moment of loss and gain, a "violent" act, a *makkah*, a blow opens the mouth to the negotiations and embarrassments of language.

At the close of his discussion, Maharal characterizes Moses as one who never experienced this moment of humanization. In some sense, he retains the oceanic awareness ("knowing the whole Torah in its entirety"[39]) of the unborn infant. His mouth and tongue and lips have never moved with the complex human desire to compensate for the loss that constitutes one as human.

In Maharal's dramatic reading, a trauma of loss and mourning initiates speaking life. Moses is the exceptional person who continues to trail "clouds of glory"[40] well into adulthood. For him, the entry into language represents an acceptance of structures and conventions that will narrow his inner world. It requires a choice to join the human world, a conscious act of "circumcision." Indeed, from the moment he speaks of his "uncircumcised lips," he has already made that choice.

LOSING GOD'S GAZE

Moses' movement "downward" into the human world mirrors the trajectory of his identification with his people. Born *good* (Exod. 2:2), he discovers evil when his people suffer: "Why have You done evil to Your people?" (5:22), he cries to God when redemption is delayed. He is outraged at the human suffering and death that mark this delay.[41]

Later, he describes the Land as *good*—five times in his short dialogue with Jethro (Num. 9:29–32). But when his relationship with his people becomes more baffling, he cries out, "Why have You done evil to Your servant?" (11:11).

When, at Mount Sinai, Moses asks God for his heart's desire, what he asks is, essentially, to comprehend the most baffling enigma of all—the meaning of human suffering. The way the Talmud puts it is less dramatic: "Why do some of the righteous prosper and others suffer? Why do some of the wicked prosper and others suffer?"[42] In other words, the bewilderments of God's dealings with human beings preoccupy him; he wants to understand the crosscurrents of good and evil in the world. "Let me know Your ways! . . . Let me see Your glory!" (Exod. 33:13,18). What he desires is to know and to see the hidden face of God.

In the Talmud, God answers: in this world, the *incompletely* righteous person suffers, while the *incompletely* wicked person prospers. Since in this world perfection is rarely to be found, there can be no master key to God's ways. Moses must be frustrated in his desire to understand, because he yearns for a total mirroring of his desire, a world that is readable by the urgency of its beam. In the Torah, God's answer translates his desire: "You cannot see My face, for no human being can see it and live" (Exod. 33:20). God's *glory* becomes God's *face:* what Moses desired was to see that face, to see himself perfectly mirrored in God's gaze.

God's answer allows for a fragmentary and displaced glimpse of such vision. Placed in a "crevice in the rock," Moses will see God's "back"—*achorai*—not His face, *after* He has passed by. Even the crack of light in the cave will be covered by God's hand in the moment of His passage. Moses' desire is infinite, untamed by early angel taps on the mouth. But God places him in a hole, a void, a blind knowledge of God's presence. Only *afterward,* he may see God's back, which is also God's *past-ness.*[43] He will know that precisely God's mirroring face is what he does not see. He will profoundly experience the absence of that gaze that he so desired. He will understand only retroactively the hidden structures of history. He will know that God *was* here; that only through the crack of loss and mourning can He be glimpsed in the world.

The Talmud describes Moses' experience of God's trace by saying that Moses is shown the *knot* of God's *tefillin* (phylacteries). God places Moses firmly in the world of the *kesher*—the knot or link that separates and connects: the world of language, of translation and interpretation, where the complexity of knots, rather than the endless mirroring gaze, links him with the unknowable.

If we imagine Job as Moses' creation, we can conceive of the complex depth of Moses' struggle. Repeatedly, Job speaks of his loss of God's gaze.[44] This yearning is never requited, even in the idyllic ending. Moses as the author of the book of Job brings into view a version of his inner struggle to translate inordinate desire into the stammerings of language.

In his darkest moment, Moses, like Job, asks to die: "Kill me, I beg You, out of hand, if I have found favor in Your eyes, and let me not see my own evil" (Num. 11:15). To know himself, to accept his own "evil," his lack, limitation, disunity, Moses writes a book in which he portrays in poetic language the voids and indirections of desire. Speaking, writing his book of Job, Moses turns to a language informed by lack.

The knot of God's tefillin represents all that can be known of God and His meanings. Speaking, writing of Job's God in the past tense, the author glimpses an oblique presence. The knot of obscure meanings appears only *after* He has passed—binding him to his yearning.

PIOUS RESENTMENTS

Forty years later, at the end of the wilderness time, Moses, author of the book of Job, will speak in his own voice of God's cruelty to his people: "God would not listen to your cries" (Deut. 1: 45). He will later return to the theme of God's cruelty, this time in relation to himself: "And He would not listen to me . . ." (Deut. 3:26), God, yet again, turns away His face from Moses' desire. Here, Moses expresses a profound solidarity with his people's pathos: like them, he knows what it is to be baffled by God's inattention.

But he also speaks of this solidarity in rather different terms: "Because of you, God was incensed with me, too, and He said: You shall not enter it either" (Deut. 1:37). His fate is intertwined with theirs—strangely, even contingent on theirs. Through these utterances, he stages the problem of cruelty, of the unfathomable rule of law—*middat ha-din*—in a world of human desire. In a world where God's face is hidden, Moses tells his story of love and hate, faith and resentment.

The problem of cruelty is the subject of a teaching by Mei Ha-Shilo'ach. He speaks of the resentment that is felt particularly by those who serve God—resentment at alienation from a world in which God acts harshly and inscrutably. God's *middat ha-din* most painfully wounds those who believe in His providential goodness. God says to such sufferers: "Let him [the priest] not defile himself for any dead person among his kin" (Lev. 21:1). Mei Ha-Shilo'ach interprets: Let the pious sufferer not nurse resentments of this kind against God—because they *defile the soul.* "Tell [*emor*] them"— *Whisper*[45] to such sufferers that even in the grip of *middat ha-din*, of experiences of loss and lack, they should avoid resentment, for God's intentions, even when He behaves inscrutably, are profoundly (*ba'omek*) benevolent.[46]

In this passage, the problem of religious existential resentment appears in all its complexity. Serving God does not cushion one against the whips and scorns of time. On the contrary: the pious sufferer reacts to tragic experience with a peculiarly personal resentment against the personal God. As Job angrily expresses it: "It is all one; therefore I say, He destroys the blameless and the guilty" (Job 9:22). But to allow oneself to welter in such resentments is bad for the soul. For this reason—rather than because of theological dogma—this state should be avoided.

However, the therapeutic point of this teaching is in its final emphasis on the *whisper.* The only possible address to the sufferer is through the medium of a whisper; the muted voice that may penetrate all resistances. To preach God's hidden benevolence to the victim of His destruction is to risk exacerbating the victim's anger. Too strident an address turns such a message into dogma. The whisper, that the listener can hear only by coming close, by bending his ear to shy meanings, allows the sufferer the authority of his own experience, even while it offers an intimate deflection of that experience.

In describing the peculiar collision of the religious sensibility with the harsher exasperations of experience, the Hasidic master engages with the conflict of love and hate in the soul. When our desire is fulfilled, the world becomes transparent, its meanings yield to our desire. When we are thwarted, our desire for complete understanding is also thwarted.

BECOMING REAL

However, such exasperations can also have the effect of making otherness real to us. The philosopher Alexander Nehamas[47] discusses the experience of *incompleteness* in art, which generates a sense of verisimilitude. Socrates, in Plato's early work, is "both predictable and incomprehensible. . . . That is why he appears more real than fictional." Plato implicitly admits that he does not understand Socrates, but his very opaqueness, the sense that he seems to hold a secret, "creates an unparalleled sense of verisimilitude and realism. . . . Incompleteness is essential to verisimilitude." Since a crucial feature of subjectivity is precisely not being totally knowable to the other, an imperfectly known Socrates acquires for the reader an aura of inscrutable subjectivity.

Moses, too, we have suggested, becomes unknowable and therefore more real to us when he is imagined as the author of the book of Job—that most opaque of characters and texts. Seen in this way, Moses is withdrawn from our grasp as a mere character in the biblical text. As the art historian Ernest Gombrich puts it, when Rembrandt leaves the eyes of his most moving portraits in shadow, or when Leonardo "blur[s] precisely the features in which the expression resides, thus compelling us to complete the act of creation," we are reminded of that human otherness that resists our knowing.

Perhaps when God—in sacred texts—behaves in ways we do not understand, one effect is to make Him real in His very opacity. The portrait is incomplete; we must complete the act of creation. Something of this notion holds when God acts in *middat ha-din* in real life; suddenly, our vision is incomplete, and God becomes patently real.

THE CRUEL HATRED OF CRUELTY

The political philosopher Judith Shklar adds an unexpected perspective to our discussion. In the course of discussing the paradoxical situation of those who "put cruelty first" in their list of vices, she focuses on Montaigne and his "cruel hatred of cruelty." Such a position, Shklar suggests, embodies "a radical spirit of denial." An over-concern with cruelty involves "a loss of the habitual acceptance of one's own world." Montaigne adopts a position of "isolating aloof-ness" that allows him to reject "both misanthropy and . . . a world whose fantasies and aspirations sooner or later leads us to cruelty."[48] But for those who "put cruelty first," misanthropy, or moral cruelty, remains a real hazard.

The paradoxes and puzzles that Montaigne encounters in his thinking about the hatred of cruelty create a moral minefield. Like the rage at an imperfect world, hatred of cruelty may dehumanize us. Paradoxically, it represents a belief in the justice of the world that places compassion and solidarity out of reach.

This is the posture of Job's friends, who, like Job, base their arguments on what Adam Phillips calls a "furtive utopianism."[49] In Job's case, this leads to self-righteous protest, while in theirs, it emerges as moral cruelty that withholds compassion from Job. In this state, one merges God's face with one's own. God, for his part, refuses, as it were, to play God. He appears *incompletely* in the world, whether in the unfathomable role of *middat ha-din*, or, equally, in the role of compassion—*rachamim*, that most human virtue, that womblike[50] contains all the incompleteness of the world.

MOSES WRITES JOB?

After God's harsh verdict in the narrative of the Spies, the people respond to the hopelessness of their situation by mourning *exceedingly*. Where they might have stripped themselves of their grandiosity, they instead gird themselves with weapons of war. Manically denying loss and incompleteness, they launch their strike—their forced entry into the Holy Land. They bind themselves to the rhetoric of heroism, even while they transgress God's word. They aim themselves upward and shatter against reality.

The moment of the *ma'apilim* is, in the view of Mei Ha-Shilo'ach,[51] the moment of deepest melancholy for the people in the wilderness. It represents the reverse face of the Spies' narrative. Between the two episodes, the people "mourn exceedingly." They sense an irreparable fault line in themselves—perhaps they are radically unredeemable? *Yatza libam*, says one midrash;[52] their heart fails them, they are *dis-*

heartened. Perhaps they will never be capable of loving the Land—or, perhaps, of loving at all? Something is terribly amiss with their heart. Out of this dejection arises the blind venture of the *ma'apilim*.

Moses' history vitally connects him with their dilemma. It brings him moments of critical awareness of all that is incomplete in the world. Seeing God only in the traces remaining after He has departed, Moses' lips are opened to language. He may be, as the Talmud claims, the only human being to "see God through a clear lens."[53] But this means, for Rashi, that "He alone knows that he cannot see His face." Yearning binds him to God. After the fact, he prays for compassion, and, perhaps, he writes the story of Job.

SEVEN

"From Another Shore": Moses and Korach

BRUTE APOCALYPSE

On the face of it, the Korach rebellion is a struggle over questions of power and ambition. Korach and his followers suddenly appear as a faction within the Israelite community, confronting Moses with their manifesto of resentment: "*Rav lachem*—you have gone too far! For the whole community are entirely holy, and in their midst is God. Why then do you exalt yourselves over God's congregation?" (Num. 16:3). "*Rav lachem*—you overreach yourselves!" These words are twice picked up by Moses in his response: "You have gone too far, sons of Levi!" (16:7). And, in paraphrase: "Is it not enough for you?" (16:9). The same rhetoric of *too much* and *too little* appears again in the riposte of Dathan and Aviram: "Is it not enough . . ." (16:13). Implicit in this language is the issue of desire and greed, of legitimate and illegitimate ambition.

On the rebels' lips, the words are sarcastic jibes at the power hunger of the leaders. When Moses speaks them, however, they are less rhetorical; they frame a genuine questioning of the rebels' dissatisfaction with the roles assigned them by God:

> "Hear me, sons of Levi. Is it not enough for you that the God of Israel has set you apart from the community of Israel and given you access to Him, to perform the duties of God's Tabernacle and to minister to the community and serve them? Now that He has advanced you and all your fellow Levites with you, do you seek the priesthood too? Truly, it is against God that you and all your company have banded together." (Num. 16:8–11)

In this chapter, I would like to discuss the relation between two attitudes to the oral, two uses of the mouth, as embodied in the relation between two men, Moses and Korach, who are first cousins and whose differences arise out of a shared history. Beyond the power struggle between them, the narrative raises profound questions about the nature of language itself. Metaphors of rising and falling, up and down, haunt the text—haunt, particularly, the language of both Moses and the rebels. At issue between them, in the end, is the world-creating, fictive character of language. We will look at the exegetical traditions that run from the Midrash to Hasidic teachings, where the central issue of *machloket,* of schism, turns out to hold surprising and conflicting meanings.

From the beginning of the narrative, the Korach rebellion sounds a strangely mixed note of resentment and envy, on the one hand, and, on the other, a certain idealized beauty: "the whole community are entirely holy, and in their midst is God." Moses' response echoes their rhetoric but to different effect: he speaks of God's will as the source of the power hierarchies and of the rebels' ambition as a conspiracy against God. By placing their worldly relation to God at the center of the discussion, Moses attempts to move the discourse from the rhetorical to the pragmatic/theological plane.

At this juncture, the rebels divide into two groups. Korach and all his followers place incense in their fire pans and gather mockingly at the entrance to the Tabernacle. God's glory appears, and God instructs Moses and Aaron to separate from this group. Moses and Aaron then move to the other site of rebellion, around the tents of the rebels. He tells the people to distance themselves from the rebel tents and the terrible narrative of apocalypse is played out:

> Now Dathan and Aviram had come out and they stood at the entrance of their tents, with their wives, their children, and their little ones. And Moses said, "By this you shall know that it was God who sent me to do all these things; that they are not of my own devising [lit., not from my heart]: if these men die as all men do, if their lot be the common fate of all mankind, it was not God who sent me. But if God brings about something unheard-of [lit., if God creates a new creation], so that the ground opens its mouth and swallows them up with all that belongs to them, and they go down alive into Sheol, you shall know that these men have spurned God." Scarcely

had he finished speaking all these words when the ground
under them burst asunder, and the earth opened its mouth
and swallowed them up with their households, all Korach's
people and all their possessions. They went down alive into
Sheol, with all that belonged to them; the earth closed over
them and they vanished from the midst of the congregation.
All Israel around them fled at their shrieks, for they said, "The
earth might swallow us!" And a fire had gone forth from God
and consumed the two hundred and fifty men offering the
incense. (Num. 16:27–35)

Two kinds of death befall the two groups of rebels: those bearing
incense pans, challenging the priestly prerogatives, are burned by
divine fire, while those around the rebel tents are swallowed up in
the earth.[1] The fire receives short shrift at the end of the passage; it
happens at the same time as the other scene of punishment.[2] The
latter scene, however, is both longer and more fraught with tension.
Moses announces the showdown to come, dramatically expressing
his view of the whole narrative: "By this *you shall know* that it was *God
who sent me* to do all these things, that they are *not of my own devising*:
if these men die as all men do . . . it was *not God who sent me*. But if
God brings about something unheard-of . . . *you shall know* that these
men have *spurned God*" (Num. 16:28–30).

It is *knowledge* that is to be achieved, knowledge that Moses' role in
"all these things"—the whole history of the Exodus, Mount Sinai, the
desert journey—is an expression of God's will. "For it was not from
my heart": here, it seems, is the crux of the matter. Moses exposes
the nub of the argument: did God send him, or is the whole story a
fabrication, in conscious or unconscious pursuit of power? Moses
is willing to set the stakes high. The truth of his claim is to pivot on
the exceptional, the prodigious nature of what is to befall the rebels.
There is to be an opening of the mouth of the earth, a swallowing,
a descent into the underworld—or else, "it was not God who sent
me."[3] The fact that Moses is willing to articulate such words, annihilating in retrospect his whole mission, indicates the seriousness
of the moment. He is willing to risk his credibility on the event of
an apocalyptic moment. In this way, the truth of the matter will be
clarified for all time.

And indeed, "The ground under them burst asunder, and the earth opened its mouth and swallowed them up." The text insists on the grotesque oral imagery of Moses' scenario. That the ground bursts asunder and the rebels go down to the underworld is apparently not sufficient to convey the scene. The earth must become a maw yawning wide, swallowing up its victims. When does this moment of oral horror arrive? With great precision, the narrative presents the timing: "Scarcely had he finished speaking all these words . . ." (Num. 16:31).

Moses finishes speaking all these words. He comes to the end of words—and the earth opens its mouth and swallows. . . . Implicitly, a tension is set up between speaking and eating, the two oral functions. As long as Moses speaks, the mouth of the earth remains closed. When it opens, it is not to speak but to consume.[4] The terrible alternative to spoken words is the cataclysm of final and irrefutable revelations. Moses had, as it were, *exhausted* (*k'chaloto . . . et kol ha-devarim*) all the resources of language, so that nothing remained but the brute apocalypse. The limitation of human language, indeed, is that words can never achieve that finality, the *last word*, of the consuming earth. Moses speaks to the very last moment, in order, in a sense, to hold an option open. Strangely, he speaks of the destruction of language—the hungry earth's mouth, the site of death—as *beriyah, creation* (Num. 16:30), as though in this moment of destruction, something, some world, might still be created.

The horror of the scene comes to its climax in the last detail: "All Israel around them fled at their shrieks, for they said, 'The earth might swallow us!'" The shrieks of the doomed cause a stampede of the survivors, fleeing with words of torment on their lips. They are left with one wish: to avoid the fate of their companions. The physical terror of the survivors is matched by their imaginative repulsion from *this* death, *this* engulfing mouth.

A ZONE OF VULNERABILITY

When words come to an end, the mouth consumes. The tension between eating and speaking, two uses of the mouth, is enacted through the relation between Moses and Korach. Each comes to represent a different way of living that tension. From the beginning of the story, the two cousins manifest this difference.

The rebels' opening statement, their slogan, is "The whole community are entirely holy and God is in their midst" (Num. 16:3). They proclaim a totality of holiness—a world of all, of wholeness, of perfect circles, with God at the center. Malbim reads this: "The whole people, *without exception,* are holy, from the tops of their heads to the soles of their feet." Without difference, without more or less, without excellence, without gaps, the people are *wholly holy.*[5]

Such a political platform allows for no debate—like the image that the midrash introduces here: the rebels appear before Moses wearing *tallitot she-kulan techelet*[6]—prayer shawls entirely woven of blue-dyed wool. Instead of one statutory blue thread, these shawls—all two hundred and fifty of them—flaunt a total blue; a sea of blue confronts Moses, as Korach provocatively demands: "Do *these tallitot* still require a single blue thread?" Clearly this theatrical moment represents in visual form the central issue of the rebellion—of holiness and sacred roles as concentrated in a particular man, or a particular family, rather than democratically shared by all. The image speaks louder than a thousand words, ridiculing and silencing Moses.

Moses responds to this demonstration with silent despair: "And Moses heard, and he fell on his face" (Num. 16:4). His face on the ground, his body expresses speechlessness. What can be said in reply to the theatrics of totality? As Rashi puts it: *his hands fell limp.* But, surprisingly, in the next verse, he is speaking—at some length—to the rebels. First, he addresses Korach and his group, then Korach alone, and finally Dathan and Aviram. Transcending his despair, he attempts to engage with the rebel leaders. But Korach has no reply, so that Moses' words fall on deaf ears:

> With all these arguments, Moses tried to win Korach over, yet you do not find that the latter returned him any answer. This was because he was clever in his wickedness and thought: If I answer him, I know quite well that he is a very wise man and will presently overwhelm me with his arguments, so that I shall be reconciled to him against my will. It is better that I should not engage with him. When Moses saw that there was no good to be got of him he took leave of him. . . .
>
> "And Moses sent to call Dathan and Aviram" (Num. 16:12). They too persisted in their wickedness and did not deign to

answer him. "And they said: We will not come up." These wicked men were tripped up by their own mouth; there is a covenant made with the lips, for they died and *went down* into the bottomless abyss, after they had *"gone down* alive into the underworld" (v. 33). . . . . "And Moses was very angry" (v. 15). Why? Because when a man argues with his companion and the other answers him in argument, he has satisfaction, but if he does not answer he feels grieved.[7]

In the view of the midrash, Moses attempts to make peace with Korach, who is too canny to respond. Korach considers Moses' power with words to be dangerous, seductive. Perhaps it is language itself that he senses as treacherous: better to avoid any relationship in which communication is given free play. Observing that there is "no good [lit., no benefit] to be got of him," Moses turns to Dathan and Aviram. What had Moses hoped for in addressing Korach? At best, presumably, to win him over, convince him to abandon his rebellion. But perhaps Moses had hoped at least, simply, for dialogue, for words in reply to his words.

Compelled to abandon this project, he turns to the other rebels, where he fares just as poorly. Dathan and Aviram do in fact technically reply to Moses' overture, but the gist of their reply is *Lo na'aleh—We will not come up!* In other words, they use words to refuse dialogue, ending their scathing speech by repeating *Lo na'aleh!* Their reply is a verbal sneer.

Here, the midrash makes a startling interpretation: "they were tripped up by their own mouth, and there is a covenant made with the lips." Dathan and Aviram find themselves speaking words whose sinister meaning they cannot even begin to fathom. The midrashic idiom here is a way of referring to the Freudian slip: refusing to *come up*, they will very shortly find themselves on the way *down* to the underworld. Unwittingly foretelling their own macabre fate, they speak unawares.

Perhaps, indeed, they are not so much foretelling as *testifying* to the course they are already set upon. Rejecting language, refusing to treat with Moses, they are already turned toward death. The biblical motif of "the silence of the grave" is implicit here. "The dead shall not praise God, nor any that go down into silence," says the Psalmist.[8] The dead cannot speak, praise, communicate. Silence becomes in many biblical passages a synonym for death. In choosing not to respond to Moses' call, the rebels have refused language; they have chosen death over life. If they will not *come up*, they are already on the way down into the silent shades.

Moses' angry reaction to their repudiation becomes in the midrash a deep *grief*.[9] In the midrash, this is presented as a normal human reaction to being ignored by another. But, we may remember, Moses has particular reason to be pained by such an experience. In terms of his personal history, when his overtures fall on deaf ears his worst fears are fulfilled. At the Burning Bush, at the very beginning of his mission, he had shied away from God's call with the words: "But they will not believe me, they *will not listen to my voice,* they will say: God never appeared to you!" (Exod. 4:1). Pleading his inability to make the people listen to him, he went on to use idioms and metaphors to convey his rejection of God's mission: "Please, O God, I have never been a man of words, neither yesterday nor the day before, nor now that You have spoken to Your servant; I am heavy of speech and heavy of tongue" (v. 10). "Moses spoke to God, saying, 'The Israelites would not listen to me; how then should Pharaoh listen to me, a man of uncircumcised lips!'" (6:12).

When he complains of being unable to speak, he means he is unable to make people listen to him. If the other refuses to respond, clearly communication has failed. To *speak* in the fullest sense is to make the other speak, to elicit a response.[10] It is this nexus of communication that from the outset arouses dread in Moses. Now, in his scene with the rebels, it seems that his dread is realized in the most painful way. Reaching out to them, his gesture meeting with no response, an old wound reopens: he has failed to *speak*.

God responds in an unexpected way to Moses' complaint at the Burning Bush. Instead of reassuring him, promising him fluency, communicative power, God asks a question: "What is that in your hand?" This is the scene that follows:

And he replied, "A rod." He said, "Cast it on the ground." He cast it on the ground and it became a snake; and Moses fled from it. Then God said to Moses, "Put out your hand and grasp it by the tail"—he put out his hand and seized it, and it became

a rod in his hand—"so that they may believe that God, the God
of their father, the God of Abraham, the God of Isaac, and the
God of Jacob, did appear to you."

   God said to him further, "Put your hand into your bosom."
He put his hand into his bosom; and when he took it out, his
hand was encrusted with snowy scales! And He said, "Put your
hand back into your bosom."—He put his hand back into his
bosom; and when he took it out of his bosom, there it was
again like his own flesh. (Exod. 4:2–7)

Instead of healing Moses of his oral dread, God enacts with him
the very experience, in the flesh, of his dread. The rod in his hand
is no sooner named as such than it becomes a snake—"And Moses
fled from it." An object that has just emerged from his own body, a
safe, definable object, which was, in a sense, a symbolic extension of
the power of his hand, now arouses in him an uncontrollable, visceral fear. In an instant, as it leaves his hand, it becomes unrecogniz-
able, terrifying. Then, at God's command, he overcomes his fear, and
grasps the snake, which retransforms in his hand into a rod. "This is
the first sign," designed to create belief in the Israelites (Exod. 4:8),
but a sign, as well, to himself, a staging of his own fear of that which
emerges from his body and can no longer be mastered.

   The second sign is even closer to the bone: his hand emerges from
his bosom covered with snowy scales; when he puts it back in his
bosom and again withdraws it, it has been restored *kivsaro*—to be
part of his flesh again. Here, Moses' very flesh goes dead as it goes
forth toward the world—a kind of ghastly birth; the very same movement of *in-out* then brings his hand back to life, to be again his own
flesh.

   I suggest that in addition to the public role of these signs—to
convince the people of the truth of Moses' claim that God indeed
appeared to him—they have another purpose: Moses is being
brought face-to-face with the dynamic of his own fear. Both signs
reenact the trauma of the act of speech: the movement from an interior to an exterior world, and the dread of what cannot be controlled
in that movement of communication. In speaking, in meeting the
other, there is sacrifice, there is transformation, even a fantasy of
losing himself. Taken through a flesh parable of fear, death, and res-

urrection, Moses must think of the edges of his body, his hand, his skin—and of that quintessential edge that is the mouth.[11] Here, the self touches the outer world; here, volatile changes and exchanges take place. This is the site of desire and fear, the boundary that creates longing and recoil. Between the lips rises the erotic space, the wish to transmit messages, to dissolve boundaries.

This erotic reach constitutes the very nature of language, flouting the edges of things, enhancing meaning, inspired by an impossible desire. It begins with the first oral experience of the infant at the mother's breast.

It is striking that the Torah devotes considerable space to a description of Moses' infant nursing history. Clearly, if the baby Moses is to be saved from the fate of Israelite male infants, some provision will have to be made for feeding him. But the fact that the Torah gives prominence to this technical issue (the wet nurse is a common resource in ancient aristocracies) signals a site of tension.

It is Miriam, Moses' sister, who volunteers to bring Moses' mother to act as a surrogate for the Egyptian princess. But several verses (Exod. 2:7–10) then recount, in slow motion, the process of her hiring and feeding of the child, as though to allow the reader to dwell on the paradox of the situation. Moses is to be nurtured by the princess's hired surrogate—who happens to be his birth mother.

Rashi quotes from the Talmud: "The princess tried out many Egyptian wet nurses, but he refused to nurse, because he was destined to speak with the Shechinah" (*B.Sotah* 12b). Here, the double sense of orality is explicit: the mouth that will engage with God cannot feed from foreign breasts. The basic oral impulse—to feed—is in this child inhibited at the earliest stage. Fraught with his future, he cannot inhabit his body, reach beyond its edges with full spontaneity. Even when he is reunited with his mother, she nurses him in a double role—as his mother, and as the princess's surrogate.[12]

Could there be a connection between this element of alienation in his infant oral experience and his later description of his relation to his people?—"Did I conceive this entire people, did I bear them, that You should say to me, 'Carry them in your bosom as a wet nurse carries an infant,' to the land that You have promised on oath to their fathers?" (Num. 11:12). The bizarre image of Moses as failed male wet nurse suggests a deep frustration, a yearning for a simpler, more organic world of connection. Wishing and fearing to feed, to be fed, to speak, to evoke response, Moses knows the traumatic gap that makes *dibbur*, the human speech function, a zone of vulnerability.

THE WORLD OF *AS-IF*

Returning now to the Korach narrative, we may appreciate the history of Moses' despair. When the rebels make their stand, with their dazzling and unanswerable assertion of total holiness, "Moses heard, and he fell on his face" (Num. 16:4). However, after this moment of speechlessness, he gets to his feet and attempts to speak, to Korach and to Dathan and Aviram. Both overtures are rejected, one in silence and the other in words of repudiation. But the fact that he tries again after Korach has rebuffed him becomes the trigger for an important Talmudic teaching: "From here we learn that one should not persist in a dispute, for Moses sought them out [lit., courted them] in order to come to terms with them through a peaceful dialogue."[13]

The lesson is phrased in the negative: one *should not persist* in a *machloket,* in a dispute. This is learned from the fact that Moses *courts* the rebels, trying by every means to win them over. The imagery of courtship, with its erotic implication, evokes Moses as willing to sacrifice his dignity in his desire for connection with the rebels. A tension is set up between the static hold of *machloket* and the dynamic, even seductive project of speech. To persist (lit., hold on tight) in *machloket* is to create a rigid, unchangeable situation. Moses overcomes his own resistance to language in order to reach out to Korach, and then again to Dathan and Aviram.

The sarcastic reply of the latter raises further questions about language:

And they said, "We will not come up! Is it not enough that you brought us out from a land flowing with milk and honey to have us die in the wilderness, that you would also lord it over us? You have not even brought us to a land flowing with milk and honey, and given us possession of fields and vineyards— will you gouge out these men's eyes? We will not come up!" (Num. 16:12–14)

Beginning and ending their speech with refusal, Dathan and Avi-ram repeat, "We will not come up!"[14] As we have noticed, the mid-rash reads this as referring ominously to their final descent into the earth. We suggested that this descent reflects the movement away from language, downward into silence. In addition, on a conscious level, the rebels mock Moses' pretensions: he claims to be bringing them up, to life and the inheritance of the Land, when the reality is that they will all die in the wilderness. *Lo na'aleh* means then, "Your use of idioms of *aliyah* is mere propaganda. The truth behind your rhetoric is *yeridah,* loss, the final descent to death."[15]

Seforno makes a fascinating suggestion. The problem he addresses is that "You have not even . . . given us possession of fields" reads in Hebrew as though it is a positive statement (lit., "you *have given* us"—the word *not* must be carried forward from the previous phrase). He reads: "Is it not enough that you have brought us out of a land flow-ing with milk and honey to this wilderness, but *you are also mock-ing us: your rhetoric pretends* that you are giving us an inheritance of fields and vineyards. Every time you speak about the command-ments to be fulfilled in the Land, it is *as though* the Land is really to be ours, with its fields and vineyards."

In this reading, the rebels are exposing the propaganda language of a ruler who is trying to pull the wool over their eyes—in the text, to gouge out their eyes. Unmasking his rhetoric, the rebels accuse Moses of demagoguery. Perhaps we can even say that they here express a deep distrust of language itself. Twice, Seforno uses the word *k'eelu*—as if—about Moses' way of using language. "You are mocking us, playing with us," they claim. What they cannot tolerate is the very nature of language—metaphorical to the core. *Your words are "as if,"* they say. Perhaps all significant language is *as if,* refer-ring only partly to a demonstrable reality, but otherwise expanding the edges of plain meaning, in the effort to encompass the not-yet-known.

Or Ha-Chaim, for instance, notices the same phenomenon that the rebels resent and satirize (in Seforno's reading). When Moses tells the people, "When you enter the Land that I am giving you to settle in" (Num. 15:2), he seems to be projecting a future that this generation will, in a literal sense, never see. Or Ha-Chaim reads this as a subtle reframing of the people's hope: they are being asked to imagine their children's prosperity as their own. "You" can mean the concrete individuals who stand before him, or it can refer to the enlarged "you" of the self connected with others. "You" need not be hollow rhetoric but an expression of the fictive nature of language itself.

Dathan and Aviram are the "unmaskers." They will not be fooled by Moses' language. Of course, they themselves use language in order to unmask Moses, but their language, they would claim, hews to the "plain meaning" of words. "A land flowing with milk and honey," for instance: this simply means a fertile land, and anyone with eyes in his head can see that Egypt, and not the unachieved Land of Israel, is the fertile land. This literal understanding of language, however, is a travesty of the meaning of the iconic phrase, "a land flowing with milk and honey." This is always used to refer to the Land of Israel;[16] when the rebels use it to refer to Egypt, it is they who are dislocating meaning.

Their disenchanted sneer is itself unmasked. The world of *dibbur*, of language, is a world of *as if,* which acknowledges imagination, desire, the role of *eros*. The fiction of the future, the ongoing invention of the self, the attempt to dissolve boundaries, are all part of the project of language. As Jacques Lacan puts it, *Les non-dupes errent*—"Those who will not be duped are themselves in error."[17] Compulsively suspicious, the rebels attack Moses' language, ignoring their own implication in the world of *dibbur*. They may, in fact, be the most duped of all, since their own fantasy world remains unacknowledged.

In his struggle for integrity in language, Moses is now faced with the silence of Korach, on the one hand, and with the verbal sneer of Dathan and Aviram, on the other. Both represent a radical rejection of the world of *dibbur*. Indeed, the drama of this confrontation rises partly from Moses' own history of refusal to speak. But Moses' history indicates a struggle with that refusal. Perhaps from the moment when he describes himself as "of uncircumcised lips," there is born in him an awareness of an *impediment,* a block to be overcome.[18]

EVOCATIVE SPACES

Maharal, the great sixteenth-century philosopher and commentator on the Torah, offers a striking insight into the nature of *machloket*.[19]

Usually translated "dispute" or "dissension," this is the vice that is associated in midrashic sources with Korach. Maharal character- izes the personality type, *ba'alei machloket,* "masters of dissension," "schismatics," as those who, in the words of the Talmud, "set all their words upon *din* [strict law]." The paradigm for this is the generation of the Destruction of the Second Temple, whose pathology is defined in this way. Like that generation, Korach's discourse is one of total rightness, of uncompromising and transparent righteousness. Such people bring ruin upon the world: inflexible, unyielding, they are incapable of "going beyond the strict line of law." This type is *kulo din,* unequivocal, all of a piece, and inevitably he brings destruction on himself and others. His proper place is Gehinnom, the under- world, where all language is silenced.

What is striking about this passage is the implication that the "master of dissension" is precisely not one who cultivates argument: he is one who is so "right" that there is no possibility of discussion. He knows nothing of the yearning, the inner lack, that reaches out to know, to court, to love—to the utterance that is informed by *Eros*—*l'amour de loin,* as the troubadours called it. The "master of dis- sension," then, suffers from a kind of manic rationality. His words avoid metaphor, questions, any indication of the incompleteness that inspires language. In this sense, he represents a *resistance* to lan- guage, to *dibbur.*

One might say that such a person refuses to mourn: to acknowl- edge the gaps, the differences that beset human experience. Perhaps harking back to a lost paradise of oceanic wholeness, but unwilling to admit the loss, he is aware neither of his own edges nor of his desire to transcend them.

This is Korach: compulsively sane, he knows nothing of the dynamic inner void, the question that lives at the heart of creative language. The French philosopher Maurice Blanchot writes:

> The question is movement ... there is the request for some- thing else; incomplete, the word that questions recognizes that it is only a part. Thus the question is essentially partial; is the setting where speech offers itself as ever incomplete.... The question puts the sufficient assertion back into the void; it enriches it with this preexisting void.[20]

Speech of this kind is a form of desire: declaring itself incomplete, it achieves itself. Paradoxically, it is the sense of the void that moves language to its erotic quest.

Maharal's reading of Korach brings to mind G. K. Chesterton's provocative statement: "The madman is not the man who has lost his reason. The madman is the man who has lost everything except his reason . . . his mind moves in a perfect but narrow circle."[21] The perfect circle of the mad mind may take the form of a world of wholly holy people, undifferentiated from one another and from themselves, defined by their rightness.

The paradox, of course, is that this mentality is described by Maharal as the *machloket* mind, while, in a sense, it is precisely argument, discourse, that this mind avoids. There are two kinds of *machloket,* then: one expressing itself in open and passionate discourse, the other closed within its own perfect but narrow circle. The positive model is the subject of one of the most important teachings of R. Nahman of Bratzlav.[22]

Basing himself on the cosmological model of Lurianic kabbalah, R. Nahman focuses on the moment of Creation. Before that moment, God, the Infinite One, encompassed all reality. Desiring the existence of a world, He retracted His light, drawing it in so as to leave a *challal panui,* a Vacated Space, in which, through language, to project a world: such a world as ours, with boundaries, separations, objects, space, and time. In the same way, suggests R. Nahman, if all thinkers thought alike, there would be no place, no *space,* for the creation of worlds. Drawing in their own light, scholars allow that space between themselves where language can create *something else.* The very purpose of the discourse of scholars, of their mode of debate, is, in *imitatio dei,* to create the world.

The creative discourse of scholars is based on the separations, the edges that characterize difference, and that lend movement and passion to communication. What is *between* the scholars, that evocative space, makes it possible for new scholars and new scholarship to come to the world. Between any two who speak or argue, it is the void allowed by each, the willingness to suspend prejudices, that opens to unpredictable insight.

The philosopher Walter Benjamin writes: "Friendship does not abolish the distance between human beings, but brings that distance to life."[23] This, too, for R. Nahman, is the role of *machloket*: to bring to life worlds not yet seen. This gestation requires a space—the irreducible distance between human beings.

Similarly, D. W. Winnicott writes of the "potential space" that is the young child's first experience of separation from the mother. The child moves from an imagined omnipotence, a magical control of the world, into an intermediate area that belongs to both inner and outer reality. Here, she is lost in play; objects are caught up in a private game with the materials of the world. Winnicott calls these "transitional objects," and the play space, "transitional space." This will become the location for cultural experience, the space in which worlds of philosophy and religion, art and music and poetry, may emerge—all versions of *dibbur*, in which human beings struggle to use the materials of external reality in their quest to give form to their inner reality.

Korach, averse to spaces, suspicious of speech, is declared in the Zohar to have "repudiated the creation of the world."[24] This mystifying statement may be related to R. Nahman's description of worldmaking,[25] which is itself based on kabbalistic thought. If the creation of the world involves the acceptance, or even the creation of a containing space, then Korach is seen as allergic to such spaces from which *something else* may emerge. Intelligent, sane, like Chesterton's madman, he is *all din,* incapable of the movement of desire.

FANTASIES OF WHOLENESS

A similar reading of Korach is to be found in Mei Ha-Shilo'ach. He characterizes Korach as apparently impeccable. What is missing in him is precisely any sense of his *incompleteness* (*chissaron*). He lacks all awareness of his own lack, of the void within him. Most pitiable of all human beings, he cannot access his own void. Engulfed in an illusion of self-possession, he is entirely "lost." (The word *oved* [lost] is the one used to describe the disappearance of the rebels into the earth: "*va-yovdu*—they vanished from the midst of the community.") Korach emerges as a nonperson even in his life: the apparently successful man with an internal void that is unrecognized by himself. This hollowness is a constitutive aspect of being human; ignorant of this, Korach has no access to his life's spiritual project, which relates precisely to that potential space.[26]

The Korach syndrome, then, consists both of a blindness to difference, to gaps, between people and of a similar blindness to internal gaps, places of difference with one's conscious self. These inner blind spots make growth impossible. The philosopher Jacques Maritain speaks of "some abiding despair in every great poet, a certain wound in him that has set free the creativeness."[27] Korach, averse to gaps, wounds, spaces, cannot struggle with his limitations; by the same measure, he cannot access his subjective creativeness. Yet here Mei Ha-Shilo'ach reverses himself, imagining possible reversal for Korach. In the future, he writes, God will reveal to him the truth of his inner world and in one instant he will become conscious of his own *chissaron* and move from darkness to light.

He bases his redemptive narrative on Isaiah 27:13: "And it shall be on that day that there shall be a blast of the great shofar and the *ovdim*, those lost in the land of Assyria and those dispersed in the land of Egypt, shall come and bow down to God on the holy mountain in Jerusalem." On the one hand, before the moment of revelation, Korach is a lost soul, his true self not yet born to consciousness; on the other, after the moment of revelation, he is transformed by a critical new awareness—of the *chissaron*, the incompleteness in himself. Till then, Korach is seen as living an almost-life, essentially disabled by a blindness.

This blindness is finally described thus: he cannot experience "the difference between himself and Moses." Mei Ha-Shilo'ach is clearly referring to Korach's original slogan: "The whole community are entirely holy. . . ." Envious of Moses' claims to difference, to privileged status, Korach is blind to a significant otherness in Moses. But perhaps Mei Ha-Shilo'ach also means to imply that Moses' difference lies precisely in the fact that he is aware of his own *chissaron*.

Korach and Moses are, after all, first cousins. The question of sameness and difference is particularly significant to their relationship and to the struggle between them. Perhaps similar in talent and ability, they are differentiated in their attitude to language. For Moses, too, the world of language is fraught with tension. The desire for totality, the oceanic sensibility, impeded his creation of the necessary internal space through which language might emerge. But acknowledging himself as *aral sefatayim*—"of uncircumcised lips/ edges" (Exod. 6:12)—he recognizes the "foreskin," the impediment, that needs to be removed. When he becomes aware of this as an impediment, a project is born: the opening of his body and mind to a sense of its own incompleteness—a circumcision of sorts.

With this movement comes a sense of his difference *from himself*. No longer all of a piece with himself or with the world, aware of his edges, internal and external, Moses is reborn as a *speaking* being capable of symbolic thinking and therefore of creating his own specific world. A fantasy of wholeness is relinquished. This consciousness is what distinguishes him from his cousin Korach. For Korach to understand this would be for him to understand his own difference from himself.

UNATTAINED BUT ATTAINABLE SELF

Ralph Waldo Emerson reflects on the encounter with one's own unrealized self: "In every work of genius we recognize our own rejected thoughts; they come back to us with a certain alienated majesty."[28] The bittersweet experience of finding one's own repressed thoughts expressed in the words of another confronts one with the ghostly shadow of a self both known and unknown.[29] One's own potential but ignored majesty comes to remind and reproach.

Stanley Cavell responds to this passage by wondering about the value of reading the work of others:

> Think of it this way: If the thoughts of a text such as Emerson's (say the brief text on rejected thoughts) are yours, then you do not need them. If its thoughts are *not* yours, they will not do you any good. The problem is that the text's thoughts are neither exactly mine nor not mine. In their sublimity as my rejected—say repressed—thoughts, they represent my *further, next, unattained but attainable, self.* To think otherwise, to attribute the origin of my thoughts simply to the other, thoughts which are then, as it were, implanted in me—some would say caused—by let us say some Emerson, is idolatry. [My emphasis.][30]

Cavell sharpens the implications of Emerson's remark. To read the work of another is to encounter not merely oneself or merely the other; the alchemy created in the encounter acts to make more real one's own not yet realized self. To commit idolatry, then, would be to discount the always present activity of the mind and imagination in reading—or in any moment of encounter. Texts do not implant the thoughts of the other in my mind; these thoughts live in the potential space of interpretation, of loss and yearning and desire. "They represent my further, next, unattained but attainable, self." The self is not hewed in stone, it is not all of a piece. One reads, or speaks, in order to arouse potential selves, pregnant voids.

For Korach, redemption might mean to become aware of the difference between himself and Moshe, between himself and himself. Such awareness would mean a desire to *further* himself, a new sense of a *beyond*. In a sense, it would mean allowing the world of fantasy to open in his mind, as well as allowing for it *as* fantasy. It would no longer be possible to proclaim: "The whole community are totally holy and in their midst is God," as a realistic statement in the political world.

On the other hand, these same words might well become a poetic affirmation of a fantasy image, expressing an aspiration. In fact, in another passage, Mei Ha-Shilo'ach credits Korach with great sincerity in speaking these words.[31] Korach sees his people in the mythic light of a dynamic centering structure, without gradations or hierarchies.[32] This present world, however, is marked by differences, separations, gaps. In order to construct such a world, the mind requires symbolic procedures, essential discriminations that include a fine awareness of the human *chissaron*, the hairline crack of imperfection that divides the real and the ideal.

Korach's fantasy of omnipotence leads him down to silence, to the destruction of the world. And yet, Mei Ha-Shilo'ach suggests, Korach's blindness may be of a different order from that of popular imagination. Possibly, he is not, after all, a figure of gross ambition, but rather a worthy counterpart to Moses; their struggle may convey a sense of the complexity of the self and the subtlety of its movements and refusals: its spectrum of unattained but attainable potential selves.

FROM ANOTHER SHORE

These issues of language and otherness, of totality and infinity, are closely related, then, to the question of *machloket*. If, as R. Nahman will have it, *machloket* is the exchange that maintains the vital gap between two who speak to each other, then the refusal to speak holds large implications.

This vital gap, writes the French Jewish philosopher Emmanuel Levinas, involves a basic "calling into question of the I," in the presence of the Other: "This voice coming from another shore teaches transcendence itself."[33] There is an irreducible distance between self and other that is of the very nature of relationship: it introduces the experience of transcendence into the basic fabric of human life.

In a similar vein, Maurice Blanchot writes: "The relationship with the other . . . is a transcendent relationship, which means that there is an . . . insurmountable distance between me and the other who belongs to the other shore."[34] This gap between two people who talk to each other has the effect of suspending easy assumptions about the other.

For Levinas, this gap is also the site of Revelation, which enters through the "fracture" that opens up in a narcissistic view of the world. Indeed, God can reveal Himself to human beings only because of this human ability to allow the shock of otherness, in the encounter with another human being. The face of the other creates a "traumatic upheaval in experience," which ruptures the complacencies of one's own prejudices. The human *face-to-face* relation is thus the theater in which revelation may be realized.

This is the vital rupture that makes it possible to experience revelation or inspiration. Ever conscious of the traumatic dimension of such encounters, Levinas disarmingly speaks of the *worry*, the uncontainable impact of God's Infinity, which in itself makes man human. When one welcomes one's neighbor, when one greets him with *Hineni*—"Here I am"—one opens oneself to this divine worry, which is divine inspiration.[35]

In this model of relationship, Korach's downfall is created by his refusal of the *worry* of uncontainable otherness; he closes himself against that human fracture that allows man to welcome his neighbor and to open himself to the inspiration of God's Infinity. One effect of his refusal is his repudiation of Moses' transcendent experience of Revelation.

For Levinas, Revelation, then, is an awakening from a stultifying self-possession: "Are there not grounds," he hauntingly asks, "for imagining a relation with an Other that would be 'better' than self-possession?"[36]

The figure of Moses, moreover, is for Levinas necessarily one who is "not a man of words": "The language of the Old Testament is so suspicious of any rhetoric which never stammers that it has as its chief prophet a man 'slow of speech and of tongue.'"[37] Revelation creates a rupture in him, interrupting his repose, creating the "worry," the inspiration of response. His is to be language that never forgets its stammer, the difference between inner and outer worlds, between self and other.

THE CRACK IN THE VESSEL

The relation between Moses and Korach, then, can be read as a confrontation between two attitudes to language: response and repose. In the cluster of midrashic and Hasidic sources that we have cited, we can detect a kinship with the work of Levinas and Blanchot on otherness.

At this point, I would like to introduce into the conversation a passage from Sefat Emet that weaves together some of the strands we have been tracing.[38] He "creates a world" in language, a metaphysical world in which there is creation and repose, turbulence and rest, rupture and wholeness. Quoting the midrash,[39] he declares that the world cannot exist on *din* alone: that is why God created it ultimately through two projections of his Being, two different divine Names, *din* and *chesed*, signifying law and grace. But Sefat Emet takes this in a different direction: total rightness (*din*) is unworkable in this world because of the essential *incompleteness* of this world. In the language of Levinas, we might say that there is a rupture, a crack in the cup, which does not allow for total self-possession. In human experience, there is a great *chissaron*, an unappeased yearning for wholeness.

Since this world is not a closed system, this yearning will always build toward a transcendent source of grace (*chesed*)—such as the Sabbath. Quoting from the Zohar, Sefat Emet remarks on the last-minute creations of the twilight moment "between the suns"—the *mazikin,* the demons of chaos. These demons are a kind of inevitable explosion of the forces of *chissaron,* of lack, which are endemic to this world. At the very moment when God has completed His creation, these demons threaten to overwhelm the apparently ordered world, exposing its inherent turbulence. And at that moment, Shabbat comes to close the fissure, to lay the demons to rest. The world is for the instant of the Sabbath reconnected with a primal wholeness.

That liminal hour, between the apparent order of the world and the transcendent peace of Sabbath, draws out an essential restlessness and raises it to fever pitch. Only in the full experience of the yearning for wholeness—that is, in the experience of its lack—can the Sabbath flow in and transfigure reality. At this moment, *between the suns,* the crack, the fracture in self-possession, becomes a radical opening to the light of infinity.[40] The broken vessel becomes whole, containing blessing. Or, in a different register, as the Kotzker Rebbe put it: "There is nothing as whole as a broken heart."

At this point, Sefat Emet turns to the Korach narrative. The "mouth of the earth," the gap in the surface into which the rebels vanish—it, too, was created in that primal twilight. Like the demons, the hungry mouth represents the fracture in the nature of this world, which Korach sets himself to deny. In its place, he holds to a world of unyielding *din,* of total coherence. Manically rational, he is precipitated into the madness that he has denied: "there leaps upon him the fury of the underworld." Demonic forces take their revenge and engulf him. The *chesed* that he has repudiated encompasses the dynamic of longing, the erotic reach that informs language. Rigid with selfhood, Korach has lost the sense of the gaps and edges of human experience; and with it the ability to be permeated by infinity. Like a stone, he sinks into silence.

REOPENINGS

In the biblical narrative, this is the conclusive end of the Korach narrative. And yet, in the Talmud (the *Oral* Torah), a question is raised that comes to disturb the dark repose of the ending. *Are the Korach conspirators destined to reascend from the underworld?*[41] R. Eliezer declares that they will be redeemed; other Sages declare that Moses and Hannah will pray for them.[42]

In the biblical text, the reopening of the question is focused on Numbers 26:11: in the course of a census of the people, the Korach story is retold and a full verse[43] is devoted to the statement: "And the children of Korach did not die." This seems to be in contradiction with our narrative: "And the ground under them burst asunder, and the earth opened its mouth and swallowed them up with their households, *all Korach's people . . .*" (v. 32)—which seems to indicate that his sons did die. On the other hand, his children could not have died, since they later are recorded as the singers in the Temple; several of the Psalms are attributed to the sons of Korach.[44] Yet the Torah creates a sense of tension around the apparently unequivocal moment of engulfment. Is it possible that they are swallowed up, but they do not die?

One resolution is offered in the Talmud: "A place was reserved for them in the underworld and they sat there and *sang*."[45] That is, they go down with all the other conspirators, but at the last moment they repent; or, more precisely, they experience *pangs (hirhurim)* of repentance—qualms, pangs of *worry*. Some revelation comes to them, brings them, at the last moment, their humanity. In a time out of time, those who were sealed in their stupor are cracked open, disrupted, and their mouths finally open—in song?

What the Talmud may be suggesting is that at this place at the edge of up and down, of life and death, an uncontainable awareness comes to them, and they burst forth in the song that their descendants will sing in the Temple.

Here is one of the Psalms later attributed to them (Ps. 88):

A Song, a Psalm of the sons of Korach . . .
O Lord, God of my salvation,
By day I cried, in the night before You.
Let my prayer come before You
Incline your ear to my cry.
For my soul is sated with troubles,
And my life comes close to the grave.
I am counted with those that go down into the pit;

I have become as a man that has no help;
Set apart among the dead,
Like the slain that lie in the grave,
Whom You remember no more;
And they are cut off from Your hand.
You have laid me in the nethermost pit,
In dark places, in the deeps. . . .

Shall Your mercy be declared in the grave?
Or Your faithfulness in destruction? (Ps. 88:2–7,12)

The whole Psalm is imaginable as the explosion of a spirit threat-ened with extinction. If this is the song of Korach's sons, it comes to teach, in the most rigorous way, the truth of Levinas's perception: "The 'less' is forever bursting open, unable to contain the 'more' that it contains."[46] Even the conclusive ending of the Korach story, which Moses has invoked to prove the truth of his narrative, even the resealed face of the earth cannot fully absorb the otherness of those who have been swallowed. As long as there is life, there is always a mouth that will open; language will make a crack in things—worry, questioning, seeking, desire—intimations of a relation with an Other.

This is the Talmudic scenario of repentance and of song as forces that may reopen the most closed of narratives. One more way of tell-ing the story is hinted at in a beautiful teaching of Sefat Emet. Here, the issue is: what happens, in this world of *dibbur,* where gaps and differences and shortfalls must be confronted, to that other world of fantasy that can never be fully spoken? In the world to come, the righteous may wheel endlessly around God, all equal, dancing their praise. But in this world, does the heart's desire survive its repre-sentation in words, or steps, or strings plucked? Does the fantasy of wholeness and holiness, the vision of the lover, of the new parent, of the composer whose melody lives its primal life within her—are these fantasy worlds entirely subsumed in the forms and structures of reality?

Contemplating another song, Sefat Emet quotes the beginning of Moses' Song of the Sea: "*Az yashir Moshe—Then Moses sang/would sing . . .*" Rashi reads the unusual future-tense narrative form: "Then there came up in his mind the intention to sing a song." He also quotes the midrashic reading: "This is a biblical indication of the resurrection of the dead." What Moses actually sings is that part of his internal song that lends itself to the words of this world. But an ineffable residue remains within, the fantasy of praise that cannot pass the barrier of consciousness. This unconscious life is what the midrash refers to when it says that the text hints at the resurrection of the dead. *Then*, in that unspeakable time, the heart's song will be consummated in a shared space.[47] The infinite desire of a human being, which she struggles to express in fragmentary ways in this world, will have its future.[48] It is vindicated, then, even in its unknowable presence.

Perhaps the Talmudic notion of the song that Korach's sons sing at the very verge of the underworld also suggests that the fantasy world of Korach does after all receive some recognition. What is revealed to his sons is a space between the ideal and the real, which is the world of song, with its infinite desire and its formal expressions of that desire, as well as its residue held over for another time and place.

In this Hasidic teaching, nothing is wasted, even the untimely and destructive fantasy of Korach's band. From the edge of the pit, living voices find their true desire. Somehow, from that liminal space, live children emerge, whose choirs fill the Temple with song.

EIGHT

Heart of Stone, Heart of Flesh

1. THE MYSTERY OF THE ROCK

FAILURE TO SANCTIFY?

The saga of the Israelites' wilderness journey is beset with complaints, resistance, regressive longings, satirical witticisms, and a sense of world-weariness. These form a kind of sonic barrier filled with cries and laments that divide the people from Moses, from God, and from the Holy Land. Inevitably, they are followed by God's words of judgment; punishment pursues sin, as divine justice takes its toll.

On only one occasion do the people's complaints go unpunished. This is the enigmatic episode that takes place in Kadesh, toward the end of the journey. Here, surprisingly, God speaks gently of the disgruntled people who have just lashed out yet again at Moses. Moses then hits the rock twice to produce water for them. And God, even more unexpectedly, turns on Moses and Aaron and bars them from leading the people into the Land.

Here, then, is a double surprise—God's unusual tenderness toward the children of Israel and His shocking harshness toward Moses and Aaron; the sin that goes unpunished and the punishment without—apparently—a sin create a palpable disjunction between the narrative at the rock and God's judgment that follows it.

This enigmatic narrative has been the subject of multiple interpretations. But no interpretation stands for long without being attacked by a later commentary, which in turn is criticized by yet another commentary. Or Ha-Chaim counts ten such theories, only to conclude that none is satisfactory. In spite of this—or perhaps because of this—he declares that the reader is still obliged to make sense of this most resistant narrative.[1] This pattern of criticizing previous theories and suggesting new ones has its absurd side. Or Ha-Chaim quotes the Italian-Jewish scholar Samuel David Luzzatto: Moses commits only one sin and the commentaries pile on more than thirteen! Critical ingenuity ends up riddling Moses' character with endless flaws—surely a perverse exercise!

But the exegetic history of this narrative demonstrates at least one thing: that the Torah has not provided a clear answer to the question of Moses' culpability. Too many versions of Moses' failure hover over a gap in narrative meaning.

The narrative in Numbers 20:1–12 is rich with detail and nuance. Let us look at it in its entirety:

> The Israelites arrived, the whole community, at the wilderness of Zin on the first new moon, and the people stayed at Kadesh. Miriam died there and was buried there. The community was without water, and joined against Moses and Aaron. The people quarreled with Moses, saying, "If only we had perished when our brothers perished in the presence of God. Why have you brought God's congregation into this wilderness for us and our beasts to die there? Why did you bring us up out of Egypt to bring us to this evil place, a place with no grain or figs or vines or pomegranates? And there is no water to drink!"
>
> Moses and Aaron came away from the congregation to the entrance of the Tent of Meeting, and fell on their faces. The presence of God appeared to them, and God spoke to Moses, saying, "You and your brother Aaron take the rod and gather the community, and before their very eyes speak to the rock so that it gives forth of its water. So you shall produce water for them from the rock and you shall provide drink for the congregation and their beasts."
>
> And Moses took the rod from before the presence of God, as He had commanded him. Moses and Aaron assembled the congregation in front of the rock; and he said to them, "Listen, you rebels, shall we produce water for you from this rock?" And Moses raised his hand and struck the rock twice with his rod. And copious water emerged, and the community and their beasts drank.

And God said to Moses and Aaron, "Because you did not trust Me enough to affirm My sanctity before the eyes of the Israelite people, therefore you shall not lead this congregation into the land that I have given them." Those are the Waters of Merivah—meaning that the Israelites quarreled with God—through which He affirmed His sanctity.

The story begins with the death of Miriam, her burial, and the urgent need for water. The people attack Moses and Aaron who seem to flee from their presence[2] to the presence of God. God's glory then appears to them. Every other occasion where this happens in the book of Numbers is followed by words of judgment.[3] Here, however, God speaks tenderly about providing water to nurture the people: Moses is personally and intentionally to produce the water *for them* and to bring it to their lips. When Moses strikes the rock twice, the water simply "emerges"—he does not directly produce it, nor does he personally tend to the people's needs: "the community drank."

It is at this point—when the narrative seems to have achieved a happy conclusion—that God declares His inscrutable decree, couched in language that rings with strange lucidity: "*Because* you did not trust Me enough to affirm My sanctity before the eyes of the Israelite people, *therefore* you shall not lead this congregation into the land . . ." (Num. 20:12). In this logical form, the death sentence is even more shocking. For the explanation itself needs explaining: Moses and Aaron did not trust in God? They failed to sanctify Him? But the self-evident tone of the decree is carried over to the last sentence, where the waters are named for the people's "quarrel" with God, Who is "sanctified by them." Again, the apparent coherence of a closure that justifies the original name of the place—Kadesh (v. 1)—without, in fact, clarifying anything: how is God sanctified in this place where Moses and Aaron have failed to sanctify Him?

SCENARIOS OF SANCTIFICATION

The classic explanation of Moses' sin is Rashi's: Moses was commanded to speak to the rock, not to strike it. "If you had spoken to the rock and it had produced water, I should have been sanctified before the eyes of the community: they would have said, If this rock, which does not speak or hear, and has no need for sustenance, fulfills God's word, how much more should we!"[4]

Rashi emphasizes the *public* nature of the scene: it is enacted before the eyes of the mass of Israelites—the same mass from whom Moses and Aaron have just fled. God finds them fallen on their faces and urges them to return to face the people. Publicly, before their faces and their eyes, Moses and Aaron are to speak to the rock. But how would this have generated faith, or trust, or sanctification? What, after all, is the difference between striking a rock and speaking to it? One might say that striking the rock is precisely what is meant by "speaking" to it.[5] How else does one communicate with a *thing* that is impervious to words? A blow with a stick is just the language that the rock understands. . . .

But Rashi's scenario of sanctification is intriguing. The rock's obedience to God's words would have produced a thoughtful response in the people, who would have seen themselves in the place of the rock. By an imaginative act of projective identification, they would have come to recognize the power of God's word in their own vulnerable and dependent lives. Their own human situation would have been illuminated by the miracle of the rock. The purpose of the exercise was the impact it would have on *the people's eyes*. Failing to speak, hitting the rock, Moses misses the point; the imaginative process is short-circuited; the double blow of the rod induces no self-reflection in the people.

Many commentaries are unsatisfied by Rashi's reading. In the narrative, after all, God tells Moses to "take the rod" (Num. 20:8): for what purpose is he to take it, if not to strike with it? And striking the rock does produce the water that God had promised. There is no indication in the narrative that God is displeased with this act—until the shocking coda that immediately follows.

Rambam[6] takes a different tack. Moses' sin lay in his address to the people and not in his striking the rock. "Listen now, you rebels." An inappropriate anger informs his words. He is punished, however, not for the anger itself but because God at this moment is not Himself angry with the people: Moses is misrepresenting God, Who has just spoken solicitously of them. It is the public context of Moses' angry outburst that leads to God's judgment: he has failed to create in them the trust that a conviction of God's love would have generated; he has not sanctified God by conveying a sense of His nurturing concern for them. The gravity of such a moment of misrepresentation, Rambam implies, justifies God's decree.

THE TURNING POINT

Instead of criticizing the people for their complaints, God turns His attention to the leaders. God's glory appears, on this occasion, not to the people but to Moses and Aaron. This is a portentous moment for the leaders rather than the people. For the first time, the focus of God's scrutiny shifts; it is Moses who is held accountable for God's sanctity in the people's eyes. As a result of this judgment, Aaron will die in the near future (Num. 20:23–29); Moses will lead his people through the battles of Transjordan and the final months of the fortieth year. Miriam has already died, just before our narrative (20:1). Moreover, midrashic tradition connects her death with our narrative, suggesting that the miraculous well that had accompanied the people on their journeys vanished when she died. The people thirst for water when this vital resource—Miriam's presence and her well—disappears.

This pivotal narrative, then, crystallizes an important motif in the history of the wilderness. It is the turning point: an ending and a beginning. The three leaders fade from the scene, and the people reach a moment of transition.

The historical context of this moment is signaled in the first verse: "The Israelites arrived, the whole community, at the wilderness of Zin." Rashi, citing Midrash Tanchuma, comments on the unusual harmonics of the expression: "The Israelites . . . the whole community . . .": "those who were to die in the wilderness had already died, and these were set apart for life." Suddenly, a dramatic crisis comes to light. This is the moment when all the dying is done. The death of a generation has been completed; God's original decree after the sin of the Spies has been fulfilled. Those who survive are now set on a different journey, to life and not to death. Perhaps that is why the law of the Red Heifer—offering purification from death pollution—is now promulgated (Numbers, chapter 19).

The poignant moment between death and life, however, carries its own mystery, for we suddenly become aware that thirty-eight

years have passed without our noticing. Behind the scenes, a generation has vanished into the sands. There is something uncanny about
this hidden passage of time, with its harvest of so many deaths. A
new generation is suddenly identified in the midrash, but in the
Torah the intervening thirty-eight years go unrecorded. Suddenly,
the people arrive at Kadesh, at the border of Edom, at the threshold
of the Promised Land. In the blink of an eye, we find ourselves looking back at the unrecorded wilderness trauma. Like a traveler whose
sense of continuous time and space is disrupted by a sudden sight
of the Grand Canyon, the reader moves from the story of Korach,[7]
for whom the earth opened and closed, to our narrative of the rock.
What had seemed continuous is revealed as an abyss.

The "complete community," which has achieved the form in
which it will enter the Land, now loses its original leaders, one after
the other. There is, I suggest, a similarly uncanny character to these
individual death narratives. Miriam dies—just the stark fact—and
suddenly there is no water. Abruptly, Moses and Aaron are sentenced
to death; we are compelled to *reread* the preceding narrative, which,
on a first reading, gave no hint of a sin that might merit such punishment. Aaron dies at the top of Mount Hor, where Moses divests him
of his priestly robes and dresses his son in those very robes. Moses,
too, dies at the top of a mountain, but he dies alone, overlooking
the Land. He dies "by the mouth of God"—by a kiss?[8] He is buried—
Va-yikbor otto—but who buried him? God? He buries himself?[9] "And
no man knows his burial place till this very day"—even Moses, the
quintessential *man* (the "man of God"—*ish ha-elokim*[10]), did not know
where he was buried?[11] These narratives cry out for interpretation.
They are haunted by untold histories; couched in silences, they represent the fraught nature of moments of transition.

These narratives of transition are preceded by the mysterious law
of the Red Heifer. This law becomes the epitome of the unfathomable in midrashic thinking:[12] a hair of the quasi-mythical Red Heifer
both purifies those polluted by contact with death and, also, in a
different context, pollutes the pure. *Yalkut Shimoni* quotes Ecclesiastes 7:23: "All this I tested with wisdom. I thought I could fathom it,
but it eludes me"; and comments: "Solomon said: I understood the
whole Torah; but when I arrived at the passage of the Red Heifer I
would search it, investigate it, interrogate it."[13]

About this law of the Red Heifer, fraught with existential issues—life and death, purity and impurity—even Solomon the wise is baffled. Similarly, as generations of commentators have testified, no key has yet been found to unlock the mystery of the rock episode at Merivah.

The rock and the rod—these are the objects that mark this transitional moment between the wilderness and the Land. As we remember their history, these objects begin to vibrate before our eyes; they are *things* that are charged with narratives, with laws—ultimately, with *words*. They gleam secretly with hope and fear, with past and future, with the intense experience of those who live with them.

2. ARCHAEOLOGIES: ROCKS, RODS, WATER, BLOOD, SNAKES, PLAGUES, PRAYERS

TWO ROD-ROCK STORIES

God tells Moses to "take the rod." This rod was last seen in Moses' hand in that original water-from-the-rock episode at Refidim. Then, too, God had told Moses:

> ". . . And the rod with which you struck the river—take it in your hand . . . and strike the rock; and water will issue from it and the people will drink." And Moses did so before the eyes of the Israelite elders. (Exod. 17:5–6)

Here, Moses does exactly what is expected of him, striking the rock *before the eyes* of the Israelite elders. The rod has done its work. And it is Moses who names the place in such a way as to register his criticism of the people: that rock, too, strangely, is called Merivah.

What follows that early rock-water episode is the battle with Amalek: "Moses then told Joshua, 'Go forth to fight the Amalekites. Tomorrow I shall stand on the hilltop *with the rod of God in my hand.*'" The battle is waged, with the Israelites in the field and Moses on the hilltop, the position of his hands somehow governing the vicissitudes of the battle:

And it was when Moses would raise up his hand, Israel would prevail; and when he would rest his hand, Amalek would prevail. And Moses' hands were heavy; and they took a stone and placed it under him and he sat upon it. And Aaron and Hur supported his hands from either side, so that his hands were stable [*emunah*] until the sun set. (Num. 17:11–12)

Here, again, the rod seems to be in use, at least in the sense that Moses plans to hold it in his hand. Surprisingly, though, there is no further reference to the rod, although Moses' hands remain at the focus of the narrative, determining the fortunes of war. They rise and fall; they are heavy and must be supported. But no mention is made of the rod in those hands. Trying to visualize the battle, the reader's imagination falters: is there a rod in his hands, as they rise and fall? At any rate, we have seen this rod for the last time until the moment of our narrative forty years later, when Moses is again commanded "Take the rod."

In comparing the two events, we are struck by the fact that both rock-water sites are named Merivah ("dispute"), although they are clearly situated in different places[14] and times. Aside from God's instruction in the first narrative to strike the rock, we also notice the impersonal, factual tone of His words. In the second narrative, God addresses Moses and Aaron by name, emphasizing their relationship; they are to address the rock "before the eyes of the people"; and with an awareness of the people's perspective; the rock is personified—"it will give forth its waters"—while Moses will be animated by the intention of providing water *for them*; he will personally give them (and their cattle) to drink. Subtly, God's language animates the inanimate—the rock and the water—setting it in relation with both Moses and the people.

As for the rod, it is once again in Moses' hand in this different place and time. Where has it been in the interim? "And Moses took it *from before the presence of God*"—*milifnei Ha-Shem*—referring to the Ark in the Holy of Holies (Num. 20:9).[15] In effect, this suggests that in the intervening thirty-eight years between the two rock-water episodes, the rod was lodged "in the presence of God." Like the jar of manna, which was stored "in the presence of God, as a memento for

your generations" (Exod. 16:33), the rod is also described as stored "as
a memento in the presence of God" (Num. 17:25)—as laid up far from
active use, as a significant memento of the people's history.

Meshech Chochmah[16] suggests that "as a memento" implies that
the object is suspended from its normal usage within time and space,
in order to sacralize its miraculous status. As soon as the Tabernacle was erected in the second year in the wilderness, both the jar of
manna and the rod were laid in storage "before God's presence"—
although the manna would continue to sustain the people till the end
of the wilderness time. The act of conserving a specimen for future
generations demonstrates the miraculous status of the manna; framing it as a memento would mark it as godsent.[17]

The manna is thus represented as occupying a paradoxical space
in the lives of the people. It is to be a part of life in nature and in
time—collected and consumed daily—and yet, by being conserved
for the future, the manna "in the presence of God" becomes a symbol of the starkly miraculous. Poised between nature and miracle, it
is already absent, a keepsake for the generations, even as it falls daily
upon the camp.

Like the manna, the rod is laid away as a symbol of the miracles
of the Exodus.[18] The rod comes to represent an early period of powerful and miraculous interventions into the natural order. Till God
tells Moses to "take" it in the second rock-water narrative, it has been
retired from active service; it has become a museum piece. What
were its original characteristics? In what situations was it used? And
how do the associations of these historical moments impact on one
another in memory?

THE POSTURE OF TRUST

In the first rock-water story, God instructs Moses: "Pass in front of
the people. . . ." Rashi subtly deflects our first reading of God's words:

> "Pass before the people": ". . . and see whether they stone you!
> Why have you spoken slander against My children?" . . .
> 　　"And your rod with which you struck the river": What is
> the force of the words, "with which you struck the river"?—
> They are apparently superfluous. But they were added because

the Israelites had said of the rod that it was intended only for punishment. By the rod Pharaoh and the Egyptians had been stricken with many plagues in Egypt and at the Red Sea. Therefore, it is said here: Take the rod, with which you struck the river—they shall see now that it is effective also for the good.[19]

As Rashi tells the story, a drama of fear and suspicion is being enacted between Moses and the people. Moses has, in fact, just expressed his fear of being stoned by them. To this God replies, "Pass before them! You are slandering them by speaking of them as a lynch mob!" What will happen if Moses passes unprotected in front of them? They will witness a benevolent use of that rod, which before had been used only to "strike"—that is, to plague the Egyptians. This rod, in other words, is fraught with punitive, destructive meaning, bringing death and suffering to the Egyptians. As soon as the Israelites see that the rod can be an instrument of benevolent—and not only destructive—power, their aggression will abate.

In this midrashic reading, God reproaches Moses for "slandering his people." At first, he is paralyzed in a posture of fearful antagonism, facing a people for whom the rod has only one set of associations. These obvious punitive associations are now to be inverted; the rod will act beneficently, giving water rather than turning water into blood. The familiar rod of the plagues suddenly becomes uncanny. Imbued with memories of the past, its meaning is now destabilized. Apparently, a rod is not always a rod. Implicitly, Moses' relation to the people is affected by this old-new usage of the rod. In effect, God is teaching Moses how to shift the people's traumatic associations; how to evoke in them a measure of trust.

When then Moses goes up to the hilltop to oversee the battle against Amalek, he announces that "the rod of God will be in my hand." And yet, as we have noticed, the rod seems to disappear from the narrative. Like the conductor of an orchestra, Moses seems to conduct the progress of battle. But where is the conductor's baton? He conducts with bare hands? His hands are heavy; he is seated on a stone and his brother and nephew support his hands. "And his hands were *emunah* until the sun set."

The description is dense with physical detail, haunted by hands, so that we feel the strain involved in holding the position that will bring his people victory. "His hands were *emunah*": his hands held steady, so that the people prevailed. But Rashi shifts the drama to the spiritual plane: "Moses held up his hands outspread toward the heavens in *faithful* and constant prayer." The steadiness of his hands becomes an expression of a difficult posture of the soul, the posture called *emunah*—faith, trust, stability—which is the characteristic of prayer.

A tableau is enacted in which Moses prays with his hands outstretched to the heavens. But if we are to visualize the scene in this way, where is the rod? Ramban treats the question in all seriousness. Moses goes up the mountain so that he may *see* the people in battle and "look upon them in benevolence." They, too, will see him, spreading his hands heavenward and praying; they will trust him and will be filled with courage. But in this case, at the moment of prayer, with hands outstretched, he cannot be holding anything in his hands.

The very nature of prayer, of *emunah*, precludes the use of the rod. Ramban suggests that the rod was raised to bring down destruction upon the Amalekites—in the same way that it had been raised to bring plagues upon the Egyptians. In spite of its recent benign conversion in the Merivah story, the rod is clearly an instrument of violence, and violence is endemic in battle. But the essential role of Moses in this narrative is to discard the rod and spread his hands in prayer. The vulnerable open hand held high brings victory to the people.

What is the connection between Moses' hands and the people's triumph? Do his hands hold magical power to determine the fortunes of war? The question is raised in a well-known Talmudic passage:

> Did Moses' hands make the fortunes of war? Or break the fortunes of war? But to teach you that as long as Israel were looking upward and submitting their hearts to their Father in heaven, they would prevail; but if not, they would fail.[20]

If Moses' hands do not have magic power, what role do they play? According to this midrash, victory in battle depends on the spiritual attitude of the people, of their hearts' connection with God. But where do Moses' hands feature in this connection? Another midrashic passage shifts the emphasis: "As long as Moses held his hands high, Israel would gaze at him and *trust* the One who commanded Moses to do this. And because of this, God did miracles and prodigies for them."[21]

Here, the people's hearts are affected by the position of Moses' hands. By gazing at him as he prays, they are led to their own place of *emunah*. Moses' hands are the visual link between the people and God.

Who, then, is Moses for the people? In the moment of *emunah*, seeing him evokes from them their own spiritual possibilities. What this moment costs is implied in the human heaviness of his hands, in his need for support, in the discarding of the rod, with its well-practiced gestures of authority and confidence. When they look at him, the people instinctively replicate his posture: "When he kneels, so do they; when he prostrates himself, so do they; when he stretches his hands to heaven, so do they. Just as the prayer leader prays, so the whole people pray after him."[22]

This is a radical description of the mimetic relation of Moses and his people. Moses is to pray from a position where he can be seen; the spiritual life of his people is attuned, in some sense, to his. *Before their eyes,* he goes through the gestures of humility and trust in the presence of God. An intimate prayer experience becomes a visual and spiritual focus for others. In the context of the battle, Moses and the people are engaged in two incompatible processes: the people's eyes and hands are involved in waging war, while at the same time they are fixed on Moses and imitating his prayer gestures. Moses holds the rod of power and violence, while at the same time his hands are outstretched in the posture of one who grasps at nothing[23]—the open-handed posture of the caress, tender and tentative, attentive.

Such a tableau, the midrash concludes with astonishing aplomb, is the model for every prayer community. The work of souls who attach themselves to a leader and, like children, repeat prayers after him, is done in the very midst of the cut and thrust, the ambitions and drives of life—as though, in prayer, all one's competence is disarmed, and one allows oneself the dangerous vulnerability of trust.

In this narrative, Moses' hands, with or without the rod, come to represent a dynamic epiphany of connection with God; hands high or low, Moses' figure becomes an object of intense suggestiveness

for those who see him. Their position brings power—*gevurah*—to
his people, or to their enemies. Their final stable position becomes
an icon of faith—that will conserve for the future an early moment
of private and collective experience.

When, therefore, forty years later, God tells Moses, "Take the rod,"
the earlier moment of *emunah,* encompassing the first rock-water
episode, flickers into potent life. This time, however, the staff fails
to ignite *emunah.* Moses fails to find the posture that will make sense
of this later moment. The space between himself and his people and
the rock remains unsanctified. "Because you did not trust in Me to
sanctify Me before the eyes of the Israelites, therefore you shall not
lead this congregation into the Land."

The remembered moment when, as Ramban puts it, Moses looked
in love at the people looking at him, is later suffused with a kind of
aura. The biblical scholar Robert Alter writes about Walter Benjamin's use of the term: "an object imagined is felt to have numinous
value, an effect of the sacred, because it is steeped in memory."[24] A
form of personal revelation, the moment holds a "potency of the
truth" that has to be recuperated in the later time. For Benjamin,
the aura is associated with "involuntary memory," originating in
the unconscious and capable of endless epiphanies: "For an experienced event is finite," Benjamin writes in his essay on Proust, "at
any rate, confined to one sphere of experience; a remembered event
is infinite, because it is *only a key to everything that happened before it
and after it*" (emphasis added).[25]

THE PLAGUES—BLOWS TO THE HEART

Suffused with associations, the early rock-water episode is remembered by Moses when rod and rock again come together. We are not,
I suggest, thinking only about two texts, two narratives separated by
time and space, and marked by similarities and differences. We are
thinking about the way the earlier narrative becomes fraught with
memory in the later moment. The Torah itself gently reminds us of
this linkage between moments by introducing a flashback into a yet
earlier narrative: God's reference to the rod, "with which you struck
the river." In a regressive series, each appearance of the rod evokes
the associations of an already extinct past.

The Plagues, for instance, begin with a literal *makkah*—a blow of the rod that turns the Egyptian river into blood. This most concrete act of violence resonates with unconscious meanings. Fish die and stink in the river. If here, by means of the rod, water becomes blood, a later rock will become water. If here blood seeps uncannily through the trees and the stones in all the land of Egypt, later the water will spill straight into the thirsty mouths of the people. Death, life, liquid, solid, soft, hard, desire, disgust, voluntary, involuntary— sensory images of the first plague are mirrored and transformed in the miracle at Refidim.

On another level, unconscious meanings cluster around the issues of power and authority: Moses strikes and "kills" the sacred river, which is Pharaoh, who is his "father," who holds the power of life and death. Such aggression is bound up with terror. When God refers to it at Refidim, He initiates a process of transformation, generating life instead of death.

The primal horror of the bloody river in the end achieves nothing: "And Pharaoh's heart was hardened, and he did not listen to them. . . . He paid no heed even to this [lit., He did not take it to heart]" (Exod. 7:22–23). Pharaoh's heart remains unaffected by the blow of Moses' rod. Ultimately, all the plagues—all the "blows" of Moses' hand and rod, whether physical or gestural—are aimed at Pharaoh's resistant heart. *Kaved, chazak, kasheh* are the adjectives that repeatedly convey a sense of the stiffness, hardness, density of this heart. Impenetrable, unimpressible, this heart is to be battered into submission.

One might say that this heart, imagined as a tactile organ, looms over the Exodus text, as though contemplating this powerful, perverse organ provides the Israelites with ways of thinking about other things—their own hearts, for instance.

Time and again, Pharaoh's heart clenches and closes against the impact of God's hand, often represented by Moses' hand. Before the seventh plague, the hail, God has Moses tell Pharaoh: "This time, I am sending all My plagues against your heart" (Exod. 9:14). In Rashi's reading, God is here referring to the final plague, the ultimate blow— the death of the firstborn. In this last plague will be concentrated all the cumulative terror of "all My blows." Will the Egyptians acknowledge the terrifying impact of God's words upon their hearts? Will they "take to heart" Moses' warning and protect their servants and livestock from the hail by bringing them indoors (9:21)?

What is clear, however, is that all these blows—up to and possibly even including[26] the final concentrated blow—fail to penetrate Pharaoh's heart. Ramban suggests that the bombardment of plagues has a perverse effect: Pharaoh is afraid and clenches his heart all the tighter.[27] In other words, these *makkot,* these blows of hand and rod, are not simply a series of events. They act dynamically within Pharaoh's memory, altering the field at every stage. Pharaoh's history is one of trauma breeding increasing intransigence. Such histories, too, lie within the human repertoire.

SEEING AND BELIEVING

At the same time, Moses, too, lives with the clusters of memories aroused by his rod. His attack on the river takes its license from a still earlier narrative, his first encounter with God at the Burning Bush. Here, God announces His scenario of redemption, which includes the condensed narrative of the plagues: "I will stretch out My hand and smite Egypt with all My wonders which I will work in their midst; after that, he will let you go" (Exod. 3:20). In this projected future, Moses is to play an essential role. As God's emissary, he will effectively[28] liberate his people from Egypt: "Go, I will send you to Pharaoh, and you shall free My people, the Israelites, from Egypt" (3:10).

In a real sense, he is to be the redeemer. Moses protests: "Who am I? Who shall I say sent me?" God answers, and Moses listens in silence to God's scenario of redemption—nine verses in the Torah text. At the end of God's speech, Moses protests with considerable force: "Then Moses spoke up and said, 'But they will not believe me; they will not listen to my voice. They will say: God did not appear to you'" (Exod. 4:1). God then responds with two signs: Moses' rod is transformed into a snake and reverts to its original form; and his hand becomes leprous and also reverts:

God said to him, "What is that in your hand?" And he replied, "A rod." He said, "Cast it on the ground." He cast it on the ground and it became a snake; and Moses fled from it. Then God said to Moses, "Put out your hand and grasp it by the tail"—he put out his hand and seized it, and it became a rod in his hand—"that they may believe that God, the God of their fathers, the God of Abraham, the God of Isaac, and the God of Jacob, did appear to you." (Exod. 4:2–5)

The rod is introduced as the first of the "signs" that God offers in response to Moses' protest. At this crucial point of the scene, Moses' doubts surge from the depths of his being. This time, they cannot be resolved by God's words alone. Moses' body—the rod that is an extension of his hand, and then his actual hand—has to deliver a sign that will affect the people's belief in him and in his narrative.

Perhaps we can add that the sign will affect *his* belief in the people's belief in him and in his narrative. The reflexive nature of Moses' protest implicates him in his skeptical description of the people: "They will not believe me!" The nexus between him and the people will fail: they will not trust him, and he will be incapable of arousing trust. In the face of God's assurance: "They will listen to your voice" (Exod. 3:18), he cries out. "They will not listen to my voice!" His complaint implies that he will be incapable of conveying, by voice and words, a credible narrative of revelation.

Indeed, a passage in the Talmud diagnoses the leprosy that afflicts his hand in the second sign as a punishment for "suspecting the innocent": God praises the Israelites as "believers, children of believers."[29] Apparently, it is their faith, or trust, that is at issue here, but it is Moses who requires *signs,* indications that will allow him to trust them! As the Talmud puts it, the people's faith is amply proved since the Torah vouches for them: "He performed the signs before the eyes of the people. And the people believed . . ." (Exod. 4:31). So God gives the people credit for *emunah.* Moses, on the other hand, must undergo experiences in which his body becomes an instrument of *emunah*—capable of eliciting *emunah* in the people.

The scene of the signs at the Burning Bush begins with God asking Moses, "What is that in your hand?" The reader is thus led to visualize the rod in Moses' hand. Perhaps, as Rashi suggests, God is drawing Moses' attention to the *thing* in his hand: "You acknowledge it is a rod?" Moses names it, only to have it transformed into a snake. In other words, Moses is being made aware that his own understanding of things is limited: his names turn out to be inadequate or provisional. Forms will change; new names will have to be found. The rod—the extension of the power of his own hand, more potent, more effective—is transformed into a sinuous, uncanny creature that turns against him: "And Moses fled from it."

After the snake reverts to a rod in his hand, God turns to that hand: "Put your hand into your bosom" (Exod. 4:6). In and out, and his hand is "encrusted with snowy scales."³⁰ In and out again, and it reverts *ki-vesaro*—into the vulnerable, soft flesh that signifies life.

After each of the signs, God speaks of *emunah*—the effect of the sign on the people's belief. They will believe the first sign, God says. If they don't believe the first sign, they will believe the second. And if they believe neither, if they don't listen to Moses' voice, then he should pour water from the river—it will turn to blood. Strangely, God shifts His ground in relation to the people's belief: the first sign will produce belief—but if it fails, the second will succeed—but if they both fail, he should perform the water-blood transformation, which is not called a sign, nor does God promise that it will affect the people's belief. Assurances turn into contingency plans, which turn into acknowledged failure.

Perhaps this indicates that the underlying issue is *Moses' faith in his people's faith.* The first two signs offer an opportunity of moving Moses to that faith. In both cases, his bodily integrity and his confidence in his own names for things are shaken. Transformations rapidly affect him: life and death switch places and back again. There is fear, recoil from his own alienated body. In the end, there is just his flesh—vulnerable, impressible, volatile, a reminder of the existence of others and of the mutuality of flesh. The messages that are the "voice of the sign"—*kol ha-ot* (Exod. 4:8)—are not magical effects, but human meanings transmitted by a messenger who is himself the instrument of *emunah*.

SUCKLING MOSES

If it is indeed Moses who is, in part at least, the target of the signs, the experience of transformation is charged with a sense of isolation that is part of his narrative from its earliest days. His life begins in a world that wants him dead. Set adrift by his mother in the Egyptian river, he is taken into the bosom of the Egyptian princess, who is persuaded by his sister to hire a wet nurse from among the Hebrews—his own mother in fact—to nurse the baby "for her." The fact—Moses is nursed by his mother—reflects a deceptively "normal" situation. But this situation is fraught with history, its meanings complicated by power relationships: his mother has been hired by the princess to nurse the baby *for her*.[31]

The Torah pays great attention to the arrangements for Moses' nursing, as though to convey the deep structure of Moses' formation, the ways in which the earliest experience of nurturing may be registered and enriched in memory by unconscious fantasy. To suckle a child is to be an *omenet*, to offer a first encounter with a loving, trustworthy world. *Omenet* shares a root with *emunah*: the notion of trust, faith, stability, is embodied in the primal human connection with the nursing mother.

However, the word is never used in this narrative. If *emunah* is a recurring theme in the early narratives we have looked at, it is significantly absent in this explicit description of the nursing relation. Here, the physical facts may be secondary to the emotional grounding that is signified by them. Moses is born into a world of genocide and then nurtured in an equivocal situation, between two worlds. The confirmation of being, so simply achieved by others, does not quite happen for him.

In this vein, when the infant Moses cries in his box in the river, one midrash hears in his sobs a kind of unconscious solidarity with his suffering people: "She opened the basket and saw that it was a child; and behold! a boy [*na'ar*] crying" (Exod. 2:6). Since *na'ar* is an unusual term to apply to an infant—it usually designates a youth—the Midrash collection *Tzror Ha-Mor* relates the word to another verse: "Israel is a *na'ar* and I love him" (Hosea 11:1).[32] Uncannily, the baby's voice is prematurely aged, thickened by the pain of his people.

A better-known midrash speaks of Moses' nursing history. Only after many Egyptian wet nurses have tried—and failed—to nurse the infant Moses is his own mother hired. *Lo yanak*: this baby refused to nurse, detached himself from these breasts—because his mouth is destined to speak with God.[33] Such a precocious awareness of destiny complicates intimate connections. In this history, weaning precedes nursing. Communication with the world will never be straightforward; an incommunicado element will be part of Moses' relation with all that is not God.

THE FIELD OF VIOLENCE

Such layerings of self-experience, extending back in time, create clusters of meaning around voice and mouth, hand and rod. "This rod," God tells Moses at the Burning Bush, after he has tried in every way to resist his mission, "you shall take in your hand and perform the signs" (Exod. 4:17). Even as it is flesh, this hand is empowered. "And Moses took the rod of God in his hand" (4:20). "See," says God, "all the wonders I have placed in your hand" (4:21). Moses will return to Egypt; the people will believe him when he performs the signs "before their eyes" (4:30).

But rod and hand are by now already saturated with meanings. How unexpected these meanings may be is suggested by Rashi in his comment on Moses' leprous hand:

> "They will believe the voice of the latter sign": As soon as you say to them, "On your account I have been smitten with leprosy—because I uttered slander about you," they will believe you, for they are already familiar with this—that those who collaborate to harm them are smitten by plague—like Pharaoh and Avimelech, who were punished on Sarah's account.[34]

By performing this sign with his hand, Moses will paradoxically be confirming the people's sense of being loved by God. Moses will be offering his own painful experience as evidence that those who slander Israel are made to suffer. Rashi converts a simple magical manifestation of power into a message—at Moses' own cost—of validation to his people. For this elaborate message to work, however, it is Moses who will have to find words to frame it. These words—of slander, punishment, affliction—are born in the darkness of Egypt. In order to create trust in his people, Moses will have to speak about his body in the language of violence and revenge.

The violence begins early in his history. In the first memorable event of his life, Moses "goes out" to his brothers, "And he saw their suffering; and he saw an Egyptian man striking a Hebrew, one of his brothers" (Exod. 2:11). In one swift, complex vision of his world, Moses witnesses suffering and violence—the blow (*makkah*) inflicted by one man upon another. "And he turned this way and that, and he saw that there was no man; and he struck down the Egyptian and buried him in the sand" (2:12). Immediately, there is the circumspect glance, and the blow that kills the Egyptian in retaliation.

His response is given with the same word used of the Egyptian's violence, *makkeh*. Like the Egyptian, he strikes to kill; in effect, to save his brother. In Rashi's reading, his circumspect glance takes in the systemic persecution that lies behind this moment; it is a glance, too, that perceives that the persecutor has no redeeming potential.[35] The time gap between Moses' first glance and his act represents a judicious inquiry into the justice of his own act of violence. Perhaps Rashi, in the wake of the midrashic traditions he cites, is sensitive to the fact that Moses' first recorded act is a *makkah*, an act of violence, which mirrors the violent world into which he emerges.

The second act follows, on the "second day" of his life. This time he protests against the violence among his own brothers: "Why do you strike your fellow?" (Exod. 2:13). From the Hebrew's response, he realizes that his killing of the Egyptian is now public knowledge. He fears for his life and flees. The two episodes are clearly linked; both address the issue of *makkeh*, inflicting fatal bodily harm. The aggressive Hebrew slave sarcastically questions his role as a self-appointed "chief and ruler over us"—terms that imply the power to inflict punishment. Moses did kill the Egyptian in the name of justice; and yet the fact that he uses the same word, *makkeh*, when he protests against his brother's violence, suggests a more troubling awareness.

In a remarkable Talmudic comment, Resh Lakish learns from this narrative:

One who raises his hand against his friend, even without hitting him, is called wicked, as it is said, "And he said to the offender [*ha-rasha*—lit., the wicked one], Why do you strike your fellow?"—it does not say, "Why *did* you strike," but, "Why will you strike?"—even though he had not struck him, he is called wicked.[36]

The Torah describes as "wicked" one who is merely *about* to strike another. This becomes a legal principle: the menacing act of *raising one's hand* disqualifies one from giving testimony in court.[37] Such a remark reflects a critical awareness of the nature of human destructiveness. While, on one level, Moses is justified in killing the Egyptian to prevent him from killing the Hebrew, the very same impulse of *makkeh* is, at least in Moses' mind, at work in the fight between the two Hebrews: an impulse that is tainted at its source.

Beyond the world of law, with its nuanced and contextualized licenses to kill, there remains the sense that *makkeh* characterizes the field of violence that is Egypt. It implicates all who are born into it—including the Hebrews, and Moses himself, from the moment he "goes out" into it.

The language of redemption is shot through with destructiveness. In order to liberate them, to "bring them out" of Egypt, God inflicts ten "blows" on the oppressors. He engages Moses as His emissary, which means that, in addition to *speaking* in His name, Moses is also to *raise his hand* repeatedly throughout the plagues and on the Red Sea. At the Red Sea, two different verbs are used (*natah* as well as *ramah*), but the power of the hand that cleaves the ocean remains palpable. The upraised hand has become a weapon. In the end, Moses records the marches of the Exodus: "the Israelites started out defiantly [with raised hand—*b'yad ramah*] before the eyes of all the Egyptians" (Num. 33:3). The meanings of the gesture—swearing an oath, defiance, aggressiveness, destructiveness, even blasphemy[38]—vary according to context, but Resh Lakish's remark lingers in the mind.

When this characteristic gesture of the Exodus story appears again at Refidim, in the scene of the battle against Amalek, it undergoes transformation. Here, Moses wages war by other means; his upraised hand is outstretched in prayer, transformed into *emunah* ("And his hands were *emunah*" [Exod. 17:12]). The rod is nowhere to be seen. If defiance has become prayer by an extension of the fingers, does this imply that primal impulses are being sublimated? By such small adjustments, the body moves into new worlds.

But if the *makkah* is Moses' first significant gesture, it is also to be his last. In the second rock-water episode at Merivah, he raises his hand and he strikes: "And Moses raised his hand and he struck the rock twice" (Num. 20:11). The concentrated violence of the moment differentiates it from the first episode at Refidim. There, it is God who, in the context of a continuous future-tense narrative, commands Moses to strike. Moses' act, on the other hand, is summarized as a simple act of obedience: "and Moses did so" (Exod. 17:6). At Merivah, by contrast, Moses obeys only until the moment that he "takes" the rod, "as He had commanded him" (Num. 20:9). After that, even in his assembling of the people, he speaks and acts with an aggressiveness that is not "as God had commanded." He raises his hand and strikes with all the pent-up power that once split the sea and rained down deathblows on the killers of his people. Now, the violent power of this hand surges one last time. His life from Egypt onward has come to a dark fruition.

3. POTENTIAL SPACE

BY THE HAND OF MOSES

But the history of Moses' hand is complex and layered. Shaped as an instrument of divine anger, Moses' hand gathers memories of past selves, conserving the experience of particular moments of being. Each memory is itself saturated by previous moments. Revelations from the past cluster around these memories, which flash back like lightning to the beginning. We remember Walter Benjamin on Proust: "For an experienced event is finite . . . a remembered event is infinite, because it is only a key to everything that happened before it and after it."[39]

The body that holds these memories becomes an instrument of both anger and *emunah*. The Torah itself was given, in the language of Scripture, "by the hand of Moses." This metaphor refuses to die; Moses' real hand gives it heft.[40] In a particularly telling moment, when Moses resists all of God's blandishments to become His messenger, he ultimately cries out, "Please, O God, make someone else Your agent!" (Exod. 4:13)—lit., "Send by the hand of the one You will send." Rashi glosses this: "Send by the hand of another whom You will choose as Your messenger! I am not destined to bring them into the Land and to be their future redeemer. You have many messengers."

From his first encounter with God, Moses apparently senses that he will not, in any case, complete the mission. God wants him, his hand, his agency—but only for the first part of the journey. This knowledge will be officially revealed to him at the end of the story, after the rock-water narrative at Merivah. But the issues of anger and trust have already crystallized; Moses' hand will not be the hand that will move the people out of the wilderness. From the beginning, Moses *knows* this, as he already knows the power and powerlessness of his hand—as though God's decree will have been long in place. What will be enacted forty years later at Merivah will flash back to an original moment of revelation at the Burning Bush.

WITH THEIR OWN EYES

By the time Moses has traveled from the Bush to the rock, his rod has been long out of use—lodged "in the presence of God," as a memento for future generations. Fraught with associations that gather up the inner history of Moses and his people, this rod has been retired from active service. Now, God tells Moses, "Take the rod; and you shall speak to the rock. . . ." Does taking the rod mean striking with it? Or does the rod now gleam with its clustering associations, with the aura that plays around it, a thing become words?

Moses is told to take it, to hold it, and to speak before the eyes of the Israelites. This is to be a strictly *visual* project: Moses and Aaron will speak, and the people will watch them speak. What they say will not enter the people's ears but their eyes. A scene is to be played out in which rod and words affect the people like a new epiphany.

For the people's eyes, too, carry memories going back to the beginning of the story. Precisely this expression, "before the eyes of the people," accompanies Moses' original performance of the signs—"And the people believed . . ." (Exod. 4:30–31). Very simply, miraculous signs create belief in those who witness them. But theatrical performances may involve illusion. Public testimony to miracles may generate faith; seeing is believing; "I saw it with my own eyes." But as conjurers and faith healers know, the eye sees what it wishes to see.

When, for instance, Joseph imprisons Simeon *before the eyes* of his brothers, this may mean that an illusion is being practiced upon them; behind the scenes, Joseph releases Simeon.[41] When God appears and acts before the eyes of the people ("And God came down on Mount Sinai before the eyes of the whole people" [Exod. 19:11]), the truth of the Revelation is attested by its eyewitnesses. But, at the same time, "before the eyes of the people" also suggests limited perspectives, subjective meanings triggered by visual impressions.

"Take utmost care ... so that you do not forget the things that you saw with your own eyes, and so that they do not fade from your mind as long as you live" (Deut. 4:9). Referring to the Revelation at Mount Sinai, Moses here addresses the new generation who, in fact, *did not see* that Revelation. All those whose eyes had literally seen have vanished into the sands. How can this new generation be urged to remember things seen only by others?

Perhaps it is precisely in the absence of that visual experience that a deepened inner vision, clusters of memories that reach through the generations, can be evoked. "One who internalizes his learning—*sover*, works it into his mind—will not quickly forget."[42] The movement away from concrete vision into the world of thought and memory offers alternative ways of conserving the potency of the past.

STRANGE MASTERPIECE

From this point of view, the last words of the Torah open up radical possibilities:

> Never again did there arise in Israel a prophet like Moses— whom God singled out, face-to-face, for the various signs and wonders that God sent him to perform in the land of Egypt, against Pharaoh and all his courtiers and his whole country, and for all the great might [lit., hand] and awesome power that Moses performed *before the eyes of all Israel*. (Deut. 34:10–12)

The Torah summarizes Moses' career of manifest prodigies and miracles—awesome, visible by all. Rashi quotes the Talmud and other sources:

> *For all the great might [hand]:* that he received the Torah in the form of tablets *in his hands. Before the eyes of all Israel:* that he

was inspired [lit., his heart lifted him up] to break the tablets
before their eyes, as it is said, "I smashed them *before your
eyes. . . ."* (Deut. 9:17)

Breaking down the categories of power manifested by Moses,
Rashi focuses on Moses' hands, which received the stone tablets.
These are also the hands that performed fearsome miracles in "that
great and fearsome wilderness" (Deut. 8:15). But finally these hands
manifested their supreme strength "before the eyes of all Israel,"
when they smashed the stone tablets that they themselves had
received.

The power of the act is represented by the power—the shock—
inflicted by this midrashic narrative. It closes with God acknowledging Moses' act: *Yishar kochacha she-shibarta*—"Congratulations that
you smashed them!"[43] God affirms and blesses Moses' iconoclastic
act. This is the true climax of Moses' prodigious life, as he himself
records it, "I smashed them before your eyes." And God, in this
provocative midrash, validates and blesses this act.

This, Rashi suggests, is the crowning moment of his life, as well as
the last word of the Torah. Rashi seems to point to the extraordinary
courage that Moses displayed in such a public way. "His heart lifted
him up": he has no official imprimatur for doing what he does; he
shatters his own conscious expectations of himself and of God. He
braves the gaze of all those eyes to shatter the concrete, "permanent"
representations of God's word. Some extraordinary inspiration
raises him above normal considerations to commit this most violent
deed; and God celebrates the moment.

Moses' heart and hands have here achieved a strange masterpiece.
Another midrashic version of the story, however, shifts our impression of the scene. On Moses' narrative in Deuteronomy 9:17: "I seized
the two tablets and I cast them *out of my two hands,* and I *smashed
them before your eye,"* the Jerusalem Talmud reads: "The tablets sought
to fly off and Moses seized hold of them."[44] Moses tries with the
force of his hands to restrain the tablets as they fly out of his hands;
but then he apparently yields to their impulse and lets them fly out
of his control.

Here, Moses' hands surrender their power in the moment of shattering. Counterintuitively, we are to imagine the force of his hands

exerted in preventing the tablets from flying. In smashing the tablets, he paradoxically surrenders control, allows the tablets to fly! Some unconscious force subverts his hands' mastery. The tablets "wish" to fly. . . . What unrecognized longing does the midrash intimate? The imagery sets heaviness, hardness, the will to preserve God's words engraved forever on a thing of stone, against lightness, movement, the thrust of life—the fluidities of oral memory.

For by smashing the tablets Moses undoes the act of engraving, inscribing, preserving. Moses' hand is, among its other functions, a hand that writes. At the end of his life, he writes the Torah; he writes—engraves—the second set of stone tablets, as well as partic-ular segments of the Torah. Writing to God's dictation, his hand acts as pen and incisor. Accepting the divinely inscribed tablets into his hands, he embraces the act of writing.

The art historian Michael Fried has written about the work of writers, painters, and surgeons, who represent and remake the world, dissecting, describing, sometimes disfiguring and causing suffering, even in the interest of recovery. He focuses his discussion on the contrast between the "spaces" of reality and of literary representa-tion, which requires "that a human character, ordinarily upright and so to speak forward-looking, be rendered horizontal and upward-facing so as to match the horizontality and upward-facingness of the blank page on which the action of inscription was taking place."[45]

The power relations of the writer's hand, eye, and subject do, in a real sense, *subject*—throw the subject down onto the blank page. When Moses raises his hand in Egypt and at the Red Sea, he subjects the world to physical pain and terror; bodies are cast down on the ground, laid low. But Moses' hands are also implicated in the pro-duction of the Torah itself. We read these narratives as writing on the page: words that have passed through Moses' hands, represent-ing God's voice. And these hands hold conflicted experience: they are flesh; they have been lifted in prayer, palms spread to heaven. This, too, has happened before the eyes of the people, moving their bodies and hearts to imitation.

Inscribing, describing, dominating, praying—are Moses' hands open or closed? What happened to the rod? Is it exchanged for the pen or the chisel? What is it that the people see that affects their hearts? Perhaps Moses' greatest moment is when his hands surrender

their power, as the people allow Moses' hands to lead them upward
to the source of their gesture; as the narrative surrenders its claim to
reduce the moment to the *writeable*—to set it down.

LETTERS FLY OFF

The tension inherent in such moments comes to a climax, I suggest,
when Moses undoes God's writing in the stone tablets. Moses' hands
open and let the tablets fly. This is done before the eyes of all Israel;
it responds to and challenges their human desire to confirm the evidence of their senses: to be redeemed from the terrors of time by an
object hard as stone, eternally present, inscribed by God Himself.

"If the tablets had not been smashed," says the Talmud, "the Torah
would never have been forgotten from Israel."[46] Two different readings suggest themselves: "If only the tablets had not been smashed,
the Torah would never have been forgotten." Or else: "Smashing the
tablets made forgetting possible—which has generated the dynamic
world of the Oral Law."

Rabbi Yitzhak Hutner reads in this second way, elaborating on the
virtues of forgetting.[47] The life of the Oral Torah begins here. When
conscious memory ends, the mind begins to reconstruct. Because
of forgetting, a world of interpretation and vital argument springs
up. What the people have once *seen* is immediately forgotten on
the death of Moses:[48] three hundred laws vanish from the national
memory—until the judge Otniel ben Kenaz retrieves them through
his *pilpul*, his brilliantly creative interpretations. "Sometimes, the
unmaking [*bitul*] of Torah is its fulfillment."[49]

In remembering, one holds on to what one knows; in forgetting,
one smashes the icons of the past, makes it possible to know differently, to access by a different route what was once simply present. Here is both loss and gain: stability, continuity, things hard as
stone are fragmented, fly off into the air, and draw the human eye
upward after them. The sense of the body responding in time turns
the eyes and heart upward, participating in the movement of the
object, anticipating its trajectory. The eye moves through possible
viewpoints, establishing a relationship with what is seen and what
is no longer seen.

"Meet it is I set it down," says Hamlet as he seizes his tablets, "that one may smile and smile and be a villain."[50] To "set it down" is to control, on the horizontal, on the blank page, the overwhelming impact of human treachery. It is also to remember it forever in this reduced form. To *forget* it might be to release it to unconscious transformations, elaborating it in a world of diffuse impressions. To set it down, to master it in writing, is to preserve it, to become the curator of experience; to smash it is to restore it to its elements, to pure potential; it is to practice a different—internalized, free—kind of learning. Unmaking things, as the philosopher Susan Stewart argues,[51] perhaps gives value to our making.

So if the survival of the Torah has depended on the organic *forgettings* of history, this, Rav Hutner suggests, has given the Oral Torah its particular dynamism. If Moses' greatest moment was when he smashed the tablets before the eyes of all the people, then eyewitness report is being invoked to complex ends. The visible, graspable Torah, written by the finger of God, becomes, in an instant, invisible; its letters fly off. The people see the *thing* unmade, liberated into its elements.

IN THE PRESENCE OF THE ROCK

At the end, at Merivah, God tells Moses and Aaron: "You shall *speak* to the rock *before their eyes*." Once before they had seen sounds: at Mount Sinai, they had "seen the voices" (Exod. 20:15).[52] Something of the power of God's word had affected them with the primal, traumatic impact of vision. Perhaps, suggests Meshech Chochmah, now, at the end of the wilderness time, as they are about to reenact the Sinai Covenant, God wishes them to reexperience the visionary impact of the word. At Sinai, they had been confronted with its demand. Now, each individual will envisage Moses delivering that impact to unimpressible rock. They will bring themselves to bear on the scene; their eyes will be sanctified by *seeing* the holy word.

However, Moses, because of his anger with the people, calls only on their sense of *hearing:* "*Listen* now, you rebels, shall we bring water forth for you from this rock?" *Seeing* God's message would have generated faith, trust, intimate connection. But he fails to engage their depth perception of the moment. To see God's words is to bring one's personal presence—conscious and unconscious—to the scene;

to be affected to the roots of one's being by something staged before one's eyes.

But for this to happen, one must have eyes that can see. Such an intensity of vision is evoked in the midrash: "Each person saw himself standing in the presence of the rock."[53] This is a scene of presences: the people are gathered *el pnei ha-sela—face-to-face* with the rock. Each person sees his/her own presence in the presence of the rock. Looking at the *thing,* one endows it with a face; a space is created between two faces. One enhances the rock with one's own life.

The English psychoanalyst Donald Winnicott calls the space between mother and baby *potential space;* it is electric with fantasy and dream. In this space, mother and baby create each other. Facing the rock, each person experiences him/herself facing the rock.

THE IMPRESSIONIST MOMENT

A similar experience is described by the philosopher of art John Berger, who writes of the way that the subject of a painting may— breathtakingly—convince the viewer that it *has been seen.* The light-energy that is transmitted through the painted object "is the true subject of the painting."[54] Aglow with what lies behind the apparent, paintings interrogate appearances:

> Every artist discovers that drawing—when it is an urgent activity—is a two-way process. To draw is not only to measure and put down, it is also to receive. When the intensity of looking reaches a certain degree, one becomes aware of an equally intense energy coming towards one, through the appearance of whatever it is one is scrutinizing. . . . The encounter . . . is a ferocious and inarticulated dialogue. To sustain it requires faith.[55]

To sustain this meeting of two symmetrical energies, running between the eye and the work, requires faith. In our scene of potential revelation at the rock, the people are to be invited to see, to look hard, with eyes open wide. This, claims Meshech Chochmah, is precisely what Moses fails to do when he urges the people, *"Listen, now. . . ."* He is not merely neglecting their eyes: he is, in a sense,

obscuring a way of seeing that requires and generates *emunah*—
"Because you did not believe, trust Me. . . ."

Berger meditates on this faith-dimension of the painting:

> Paintings are prophecies received from the past, prophecies
> about *what the spectator is seeing in front of the painting at that
> moment*. . . . A visual image . . . is always a comment on an
> *absence*. . . . Visual images, based on appearances, always speak
> of *disappearance*.[56]

In another essay, Berger amplifies his thinking about the paradox
of the visible and the invisible in the work of art. "The Eyes of Claude
Monet" focuses on the sadness in Monet's eyes, which is not merely
personal but expressive of the melancholy that pervades his new
Impressionist school of painting. This sadness acknowledges that
"visibility itself should be considered flux." The history of painting
will never be the same again.

Impressionism was the term used to describe an early painting
by Monet, "Impression Soleil Levant." In the new painting method,
writes Berger,[57]

> . . . the optical truthfulness and the *objective* vagueness, all
> this renders the scene makeshift, threadbare, decrepit. It is an
> image of homelessness. . . . An impression is more or less fleet-
> ing; it is what is *left behind* because the scene has disappeared
> or changed. . . . An impression later becomes, like a memory,
> impossible to verify.

"A new relation between what you are seeing and what you have
seen" uncovers the meaning of other lilacs, other water lilies of one's
own experience. "What I want to represent is what exists between
the motif and me," Monet affirms.

The Impressionist painting no longer invites one into an "alcove"
of changeless time and space.[58] What it shows "is painted in such
a way that *you are compelled to recognize that it is no longer there*."
The viewer's memories are "often pleasurable . . . yet they are also
anguished, because each viewer remains alone." "*Memory* is the
unacknowledged axis of all of Monet's work. His famous love of the

sea . . . of rivers, of water, was perhaps a symbolic way of speaking of tides, sources, recurrence."

At the end of his essay, Berger singles out a late painting of a cliff near Dieppe. Here, Berger claims, Monet himself misunderstood the nature of his own achievement: he believed "that he was interpreting the effect of sunlight as it dissolved every detail of grass and shrub into a cloth of honey hung by the sea. But he wasn't, and the painting has really very little to do with sunlight. What he himself was dissolving into the honey cloth were all his previous memories of that cliff, so that it should absorb and contain them all."

In his paintings of the water lilies during the last period of his life, his aim was "to preserve everything essential about the garden. . . . The painted lily pond was to be a pond that remembered all." "More alone than even before, more ridden by the anxiety that their own experience was ephemeral and meaningless," painters wish "to save *all*."[59]

Let us now return to the eyes of the Israelites, and to the "Impressionist" moment staged by God in front of the rock. This is a scene about to disappear. Like Monet's cliff, the rock is the stone-hard repository of all previous memories of rocks, mountains, revelations; as well as of hands, eyes, rods, water, blood, snakes. What is to be done with this resistant but ephemeral object so that it will yield water? What the Impressionist painter does, says Berger, is infuse the seen in a new relationship with what has been seen. This acknowledges that the *impression* is what has been *left behind*— fugitive, impossible to verify. In this sense, it is "a comment on an *absence*"; such visual images speak of *dis*appearance.[60]

OF WORDS AND ROCKS

"Take the rod," God says, "and speak to the rock before their eyes." The address is to their eyes; the moment of faith will be known in that way of looking that acknowledges the fleetingness of the moment. What they will see is the rock, the rod—the visible objects; but also the *speaking to the rock*. This is to make a visual impression on them. It will absorb and contain all the memories of words, prophecies, commandments, decrees.

At a later time, the prophet will say: "Behold, My word is like fire—declares God—and like a hammer that shatters rock!"[61] And, at a still later time, the Sages will meditate on this rock and on their own interpretive activity: "Just as this hammer splits the rock into many fragments, so each word that issued from the mouth of God splits into seventy languages."[62]

Much later still, Kafka will relate the parable of Prometheus and his rock. He will offer four versions of the myth. The first is the traditional myth: Prometheus is clamped to a rock for betraying the secrets of the gods to men, and the gods send eagles to feed on his liver, which is perpetually renewed. In the second, Prometheus presses himself in agony into the rock until he merges with it. In the third and fourth versions, all the details are forgotten over the course of millennia; everyone grows weary of the story—even the gods, even the angels, even the wound, which closes wearily.

What remains after this? What is left behind? "The inexplicable mass of rock.—The legend tried to explain the inexplicable. As it came out of a substratum of truth, it had in turn to end in the inexplicable."[63] The substratum of truth underlies all the weariness of time; this is the timeless quality of the inexplicable that will, in Robert Alter's words, "eternally compel urgent questions."[64]

For Berger, Monet's rock is part of the future succession of images that are to be seen with the intense energy of the painter's desire to "save all." The substance of the rock is reduced to a frontier, with light coming from behind it toward one who looks with this visual desire.

We remember Walter Benjamin: "an experienced event is finite . . .; a remembered event is infinite, because it is only a key to everything that happened before it and after it."[65] Such a remembered event is the scene at Merivah: inexplicable, emerging from a substratum of truth. For the remembering mind, it is a key to everything that came before it and after it. From Mount Sinai to the rock at Merivah to Kafka's rock, an *aura* suffuses the vestiges of the sacred. For Walter Benjamin, this aura is the object steeped in memory. For those who stand in the presence of the rock at Merivah, a space is created in which each may see himself standing in that fraught presence. Like painters, the Israelites are to learn a way of seeing that involves receiving the revelations of the sacred. To be capable of this receptivity, involuntary memory must be allowed its sway.

"To see is to forget the name of the thing one sees," writes the poet Paul Valéry. Seeing in this way dissolves the rock and the rod into a stream of "impressions." The prophet Ezekiel speaks of change, flux, forgetting, as the marks of redemption: "And I will give you a new heart and put a new spirit into you: I will remove the heart of stone from your flesh and give you a heart of flesh" (Ezekiel 36:26). In this vision, the stony heart is an alien presence in human flesh. God's promise of a redeemed reality is to reconstitute the human being as *all flesh*—all impressible, receptive to impressions, responsive to the light-energy coming from behind the visible.[66]

HEART OF STONE, HEART OF FLESH

In the presence of the rock at Merivah, a critical developmental moment has arrived:

> When a child is small, his teacher hits him and educates him. But when he grows up, he corrects him with words. So God said to Moses: When this rock was young, you struck it, as it is said, "And you shall strike the rock . . ." (Exod. 17:6). But now, "You shall speak to the rock"—Recite over it a chapter of Torah and that will produce water from the rock![67]

God introduces Moses to a new way of understanding his own experience. Instead of regarding his earlier experience with the rock at Refidim as a precedent for future behavior, he is to regard it as an early stage of the people's development, to be transcended as the child-rock matures. What was once an effective teaching tool is now to be replaced by the use of language. The early memory is not cut in stone; it grows by opening to less concrete impressions. So, now, in memory—involuntary memory—the rock flashes back to the scene of an earlier self. It has become a holding space, preserving both the integrity of self-experience and the acute sense of transformation. The self has evolved. And the rock registers in imagination as capable of maturing; like the stony heart, it is seen in reverie as softening into flesh. If Moses speaks—a chapter, a law—the rock will, like Monet's cliff, essentially *dissolve*.

BEYOND MIRACLES

This developmental moment—reciting a chapter of Torah in the presence of the rock—becomes in the reading of Ha'amek Davar the central image of the narrative. In his view, the moment of Merivah is to prepare the people for the *post-miraculous* new epoch that they are now entering. This fortieth year of their wanderings sees a fading out of miracles and direct interventions by God in human life.

In tune with this process, Miriam's death also means the disappearance of her well, which provided water for the people throughout their travels. Strikingly, Ha'amek Davar claims that this well is not miraculous: it has become a "natural" resource for the people.[68] When it vanishes, this crisis is to be dealt with in the same way as, in the future, in the Holy Land, the people will deal with crises of drought: they will gather and engage in the dual activities of learning Torah and prayer.

The moment at Merivah is therefore a transitional moment; it is precisely *not* a miracle that is called for here, but a natural, organic human response to such situations of drought. Now, they are to learn how to reactivate natural water sources—engaging in words of study and prayer.

So God tells Moses, "You shall speak to the rock." Obviously, rock can't hear—Moses is to speak not *with* it but *in its presence*. He and Aaron are to speak in such a way as to move the people to inner growth and to prayer. In this way, the rock will—naturally, spontaneously—give forth its waters, its own familiar waters. In addition, as a kind of afterthought, "*You* shall bring forth for them water from the rock." In the case that the "natural" strategy of Torah and prayer does not work, Moses will act alone, in the old miraculous manner, using his rod to produce water. But, in this case, the miraculous is a fallback position; what God wants is to educate the people to their new post-wilderness lives in the Land, and to the practices that will enable them to live organically in a new place and time.

In this reading, the water that emerges from the rock after Moses has struck it twice is inferior to the natural resources that he fails to produce. The miracle of the rod is an anachronism. Moses loses the opportunity to teach the people the natural resources of *dib-*

bur, of generative language. His failure, in this view, is not that he did not speak. It is that he spoke—in the rock's presence—words of anger against the people. Instead of apprenticing them to Torah and prayer, he attacks them for their sins: they alone are responsible for the drought. His tone rings with angry scorn: "Listen now, you rebels, shall we produce for you water from this rock?"

The result is that instead of initiating the people into their own spiritual resources, instead of acting with Aaron, the man of peace, Moses acts alone, he speaks alone as old chagrins overwhelm him. He then performs the old, banal miracle that he remembers so well from the past; the rod, which had long been withdrawn from circulation, is now used not only on the rock but first—symbolically—against the people. In his exasperation, he *strikes* the people with his words.

In this startling reversal of conventional readings, Ha'amek Davar redefines Moses' failure. It is not that he fell short of a fully splendid miracle, but that he overshot the new "natural" mode of a life shaped by words. As Ha'amek Davar puts it, when it came to the moment, he "forgot" the law that he was about to teach the people—the words of Torah that would inspire them to prayer.

Forgetting the law is, in classic midrashic sources, associated with anger. Moses finds himself assailed by anger more than once in his life; at such moments, the midrash remarks, he forgets the law. Here, too, anger drives him off course, effacing the words that might have allowed the people to glimpse a new way of being.[69]

GENERATING HOLINESS

If the miracle of the rod has suddenly come to seem hackneyed, the alternative state of dynamic self-awareness, of being *drawn* by words toward a place of faith and holiness, could have been evoked only by words of a certain kind. Ha'amek Davar describes the desired use of words as *soft*, by contrast with the angry, rejecting words with which Moses in fact addressed them.

In the Merivah moment, then, Moses *does* speak to the people, but his language "misfires." His speaking was to have a *performative* power; words of Torah would have given birth to prayer and in turn to water from the rock. Language here was to be an *act*, not describing but transforming reality. Instead, Moses speaks so as to wither possibilities in the bud. As Rambam reads the scene, Moses' scornful speech misrepresents God's words. He "forgets" to address the inner lives of the people, the dynamic power of Torah and prayer to create a sense of holiness among them.

The Talmud offers guidance on how holiness may be generated: "And I shall be sanctified in the midst of the Israelites" (Lev. 22:32): How is God sanctified in the midst of the people? By speaking words of holiness in public.[70] So God turns immediately to Moses and Aaron: "Because you have not believed in Me so as to sanctify Me before the eyes of the Israelites . . ." They have not spoken words of holiness such as to create faith in the power of those words within them. Instead, Moses has wielded words as blunt weapons. The people remain unprepared for the gentler, more organic movements of self-awareness. The miracle that is not God's will drives a wedge between them and the future.

TWO-WAY PROCESS

"All language," writes Emerson, "is vehicular and transitive, and is good, as ferries and horses are, for conveyance, not as farms and houses are, for homestead."[71] Language is designed to move one, not to settle one; like ferries and horses, it "can lead me thither where I would be."[72] The poet takes things as occasions for words, as signs for words. In the presence of the inexplicable rock, words of Torah and prayer might have carried the people into their future lives, already knowing something of their own capacity for transformation. In his reading of the rock narrative, Ha'amek Davar carries us inward, to the impressionable heart of flesh that responds to language.

What, then, is the *emunah*, the faith that has sadly *not happened* here? Maharal[73] offers us a key: the experience of *emunah* is the experience of being *drawn* after God, willingly, by His word alone. This experience generates joy. And joy in turn demonstrates the existence of *emunah*. Moses is to speak to the rock, so that it will transcend its stony nature and be moved in attraction after God. To be attracted to an object is, paradoxically, to be at one's most free, at one's most autonomous.

We remember Berger's artist who discovers the two-way process in which, in one's intense gaze, "one becomes aware of an equally intense energy coming towards one."[74] "To sustain it [this dialogue] requires faith. It is like a burrowing in the dark, a burrowing under the apparent. The great images occur when the two tunnels meet and join perfectly.... It is like something thrown and caught."[75] This is the moment of most full and most free being—receiving and giving in one motion. This is achieved, says Maharal, by *dibbur* (language) alone, not by main force. A rock responding freely to words alone— the image will leave its trace on the people's imagination, creating a model for their own inner possibility.

Even rocks can discover their own power of response. Rabbi Yitzhak Hutner puts it like this: the miracle of the rock that produces water includes the miracle of its effect on the human soul.[76] In other words, the most miraculous thing is the movement of the soul in being drawn after God. Other images might have served to express the gift of water: heavy rains, or deep underground springs.[77] But the imagery of water from a rock has an intimate resonance for those before whose eyes it is enacted. It speaks to the possibility of a new, more responsive nature opening within them. As in a dream or a reverie, the stony heart gives way to the heart of flesh; a child grows to discover the power of language for *conveyance*. Through language, even a rock may be moved from here to there, from jagged dryness to vital flow. This is the joy of which Maharal writes. He calls it *emunah*—faith, trust, two-way processes of drawing and being drawn.

THE INEXPLICABLE ROCK

The narrative of the rock at Merivah yields its teaching *by negation*. After the drama has apparently reached resolution—the thirsty people have drunk their fill—God speaks and His words destabilize everything: "Because you did *not* believe in Me to sanctify Me before the eyes of the Israelites, therefore you shall *not* bring this congregation into the Land."

Ironically, there is perhaps no narrative biblical description of the process of faith and sanctification that conveys as much as this description of its absence. What has *not* happened here is an inward if public process that is evoked most powerfully in its failure. Here, we may say, the inexplicable rock comes to life in the text of the Torah.

The disjunction between the apparently happy narrative and God's dire sentence has mystified and provoked generations of readers. Like Kafka's rock, the story comes out of a substratum of truth in turn to end in the inexplicable. The desire to understand, to make the thing a sign of words, generates interpretations of both *belief* and *sanctification*. The words, inexplicable in this context, become a *thing* that entitles us to other words. But in the end, the mystery remains, focused precisely on that disjunction between the happy miracle narrative of a first reading and God's words that challenge future readings.

This gap is the place where Abarbanel finds his key to the meaning of the narrative. In his reading, the central reason for God's decree is not given in this narrative at all. The episode with the rock is a cover story. The true reason for the decree is repressed in this episode; it lies in the earlier major failures of Moses and Aaron. (Aaron made the Golden Calf; he did not resist the people's rebellion and die a martyr's death, in sanctification of God's name.[78] Moses shares responsibility for the disaster of the Spies, in that his questions to the Spies undermined their faith.) Abarbanel's provocative point is that the narrative of the rock is intended to obscure the true etiology of sin and punishment. If the reader finds the rock narrative of insufficient gravity to account for God's judgment, her impression is correct: the rock story screens other, graver narratives.

Abarbanel is well aware that his idea of repressed meanings is radical: why would the Torah hide its meanings, split the narrative of sin and punishment, and merge two separate sins—Moses' and Aaron's—into one? Abarbanel offers another example of this dynamic: the death of Aaron's two sons is "explained" in the text—"they offered strange fire that He had not commanded, before God" (Lev. 10:1). But this does not prevent the commentaries from searching far and wide for "other sins." The existence of these other interpretations indicates that the true cause of the priests' deaths may require further investigation.

Abarbanel does not offer a theoretical justification for his idea. However, such displacements, in which a simple, concrete explanation is regarded as a screen for other things, are familiar to us in modern literary and psychoanalytic texts. In the narrated life of Moses or Aaron or Aaron's sons, some preoccupation is being worked through; there emerges an arc that can only be suggested by the immediate objects of the narrative. In such a vision, the reader's search for unequivocal explanations misleads her. Moses is in the end unfound, unknown. He is both revealed and hidden. In each event of his life, there are "impressions"—something left behind. For the reader, too, there are impressions, such as those left by remembered events that are "a key to everything that happened before it and after it."[79]

The philosopher Kenneth Burke writes eloquently of the world of nature that "gleams secretly with a most fantastic shimmer of words and social relationships."[80] The midrashic literature deals with this "Impressionist" world of nature and the supernatural.[81] The Torah reveals and conceals. Implicitly, its enigmatic stories entitle the reader to read, and to speak.

A luminous midrash portrays Ben Azzai as such a reader and speaker:

> Once, as Ben Azzai sat and expounded Torah, fire flared around him. They went and told R. Akiva, "Rabbi, as Ben Azzai sits and expounds Torah, fire flares around him." He went to him and said, "I hear that as you were expounding Torah, fire flared around you." He replied, "That is so." He said, "Were you perhaps engaged in the secrets of the Divine Chariot?" He replied, "No. I was just threading words of Torah with one another, and then with the words of the prophets, and the prophets with Scriptures, and the words were as joyful as when they were given at Sinai, and they were as sweet as at their original utterance. Were they not originally given at Sinai in fire, as it says, 'And the mountain burned in fire'?"[82]

Encircled by fire, he teaches in the manner called *doresh* (in the genre of midrash)—interpreting, searching, soliciting the text for its hidden meanings. Word spreads like fire: "Ben Azzai is sitting and interpreting, with the fire flaring around him." Three times the words are repeated, like an incantation. The fire flickers and flares, making all space unstable. To Rabbi Akiva's accusation—"Have you been engaged in forbidden mystical practices?"—Ben Azzai serenely, almost domestically, replies: he is merely threading beads, bringing texts into electric contact with each other. What he is doing is—merely—remembering, reenacting the experience of Sinai. His activity generates joy and sweetness: this is the aura that flickers around him, as sweet and joyful as the original fire of Revelation.

What Ben Azzai is doing is no mystery, he says. As in Maharal's account of faith (*emunah*), he is being *drawn* into the otherness of God's words while at the same time he draws together the separate beads—out of context—into fiery new chains of meaning. This, he says, is sweetness and joy: the two-way process of human and divine energies meeting, so that something emerges from behind the appearances, becomes visible, and rejoices.

NINE

"Wherefore Could Not I Pronounce 'Amen'?": Balaam and Moses

THE THREE VICES

The episode of Balaam, the heathen soothsayer who is hired by Balak, king of Moab, to curse the Israelite camp, brings a shift in perspective. Suddenly, we focus on the world outside the Israelite camp, on protagonists who are alien to the Israelite story.

Against the background of Israelite victories over the Canaanites (Num. 21:3), the Emorites (21:24), and Og, king of Bashan (21:35), the Moabite king observes the sweeping triumphs of the Israelites and is appropriately anxious. The two superpowers of the region—Sihon and Og—have collapsed before the Israelites. He also sees that his own land, previously conquered by Sihon—Heshbon and its surrounding cities—is now in the hands of the Israelites, who show no sign of returning them. He turns to Midian for help. Speaking the vivid language of terror—"Now they will lick up the whole neighborhood as an ox licks up the vegetation of the field" (22:4)—he addresses first the Midianite elders and then Balaam son of Beor.

Who is this man who is clearly the last resort for the terrified king? No explanation is given at first, no professional qualification to justify the king's appeal. Only in the words of the royal invitation does Balaam's expertise appear: "Come now and curse this people for me" (Num. 22:6). Balaam is being hired to curse: not for his military skill but for his power of malediction. He clearly has credentials in this area: "For I know that whomever you bless is blessed and whomever you curse is cursed."

"Perhaps I will prevail if we smite them and I will drive them out of the land," says Balak, uneasily moving between singular and plural verbs—*I* and *we*. Each with his own talent, Balaam and Balak will collaborate in *smiting* the Israelites. Balaam's curses are war by other means.[1] It is true that Balak describes him as equally effective in *blessing*. But this seems to be a matter of courtesy, so as not to suggest that Balaam's talents are purely destructive—as in fact they are.[2] "Let us kill them, I and you—let us kill him with the tongue."[3] Balaam is the fit antidote to the oral fantasy of Israel who destroys by "licking up the whole neighborhood, as an ox licks up the vegetation of the field."

Balaam is hired, then, for a malign gift of the tongue. In essence, he is a destroyer, not a creator. He is a *kossem* and a *menachesh*,[4] a reader of omens, a diviner, a clairvoyant. His readings of God's will are accurate but based on an uncanny awareness of the weakness in people, of the rhythms of their spiritual lives. He can find the chink in time when his words will hit home.[5]

At the same time, he proclaims himself to be subject to God's will. He affirms God as "the Lord my God," and he faithfully and repeatedly obeys God's commands. In the end, after three attempts to fulfill Balak's demands, Balaam defends himself against the king's fury: "Did I not tell your messengers from the beginning, 'If Balak gives me his house full of silver and gold, I cannot transgress God's word [lit., His mouth] to do either good or evil of my own accord; whatever God speaks that I shall speak'" (Num. 24:13). Balaam emerges as a docile servant of God, honestly reporting to the messengers God's refusal, and acknowledging to the king at every stage that he can utter only what God puts in his mouth.

However, the midrashic tradition sees Balaam differently. Rashi's commentary on the narrative consistently "demonizes" Balaam, subtly undermining the manifest meanings of his words. In three passages, for instance, Rashi cites the midrash[6] to shed dark light on Balaam; in all three passages, Balaam describes his obedience to God, while Rashi reveals a world of unconscious meanings:

"God refuses to give me leave to go with you" (Num. 22:13): but only with princes greater than you. This tells us that he was of a proud nature and did not wish to divulge that he was under the control of God, except in arrogant terms. Consequently, "Balak sent yet again [more princes and more honorable than these]" (22:15).

Rashi emphasizes *imachem*—"to go *with you*"—hinting that the problem is not God's power over him but the low grade of the messengers. And, indeed, Balak responds by sending a new, higher-ranking delegation. Rashi reads this upgrade as a response to Balaam's hint.

In the second passage, Balaam answers the new delegation with their carte blanche offer ("Whatever you say I will do!"): "If Balak gives me his house full of silver and gold, I cannot transgress the word of the Lord my God to do anything small or large" (Num. 22:18). Rashi comments:

> "His house full of silver and gold": This tells us that he was avaricious and covetous of other people's wealth. He said, "He ought to give me all his silver and gold for he would otherwise have to hire many armies to fight against them. Even then, it is doubtful whether he would be victorious; but I would certainly be victorious."
>
> "I cannot transgress God's word": Against his own will he divulged that he was under the control of others, and he prophesied here that he would be unable to annul those blessings with which the patriarchs had been blessed by the mouth of God.

The house full of silver and gold is turned from an idiom of exaggeration ("If he offered me the moon!") to a genuine demand by Balaam. He is worth Balak's entire fortune. His limitless greed emerges at this moment.

In spite of this, *against his will,* he reveals that he is not a free agent, and that such a mission to curse the Israelites is doomed from the start—since the patriarchs were already blessed by God. There is no possibility, he acknowledges, of undoing God's words. We notice, indeed, that Balak's commission unconsciously echoes and parodies God's original blessing to Abraham: "And I shall bless those who bless you, and those who curse you I shall curse" (Gen. 12:3). Perhaps we can hear a note of regret in Balaam's refusal. In any case, he adds, "And now, please stay here for the night, you, too, so that I may find out what else God will tell me" (Num. 22:19). Balaam remains hopeful of a more congenial word from God. And indeed God responds to what the Talmud calls his *chutzpah*[7]—the insolence of asking again after God had said, "Don't go!"—by actually allowing him to go.

In another Talmudic comment, Rava says, "This teaches that in the way that a person wants to go, he is allowed to go."[8] Clearly, Balaam's desire is a factor in softening God's position. One is led, says Rava, in the direction of one's desire. Balaam becomes a paradigm of the desiring self, which is, in a sense, given its head. On the other hand, he is warned, what he says will be determined by God and not by Balak.

The question of obedience is ironically focused at this juncture. Balak has proclaimed that he is ready to do whatever Balaam requires; God, on the contrary, declares that Balaam will do whatever He requires. Balak defines his relation to Balaam as one of an obedient servant to a superior; God sets the terms in which Balaam is to be His obedient servant. Balak gives Balaam the power of *saying,* while God reserves that power for Himself.

What is interesting here is the dynamic of Balaam's relation to Balak. In Balaam's world of desire—of greed and arrogance—Balak is the one who desires Balaam's cooperation and is prepared to pay for it. Balaam, that is, desires Balak's desire. A relation is set up in which Balaam is apparently in control: he has what Balak wants. But such relations reverse easily, because the master is dependent on the slave's desire. From the outset, though, the essential axis of desire is drawn between Balak and Balaam. Balak sends to *call* Balaam (Num. 22:5). He addresses him out of his need; it is his need that inspires, for instance, the imagery of terror that he addresses to the Midianite elders and to Balaam (22:4-5).

Balaam, on his side, constantly addresses Balak. There is no moment when Balak is far from Balaam's sights; even when he praises and blesses the Israelites—when God has Balaam well under His control—he does so in the presence of Balak and against the grain of his desire for Balak's approval.

What does Balaam want of Balak? On one level, Rashi answers the question quite concretely: he wants honor and he wants silver and gold. In fact, Balak had not specifically offered him wealth— "We shall honor you exceedingly," he had said—but Balaam instantly translates the euphemism into concrete terms. In doing so, his idiom betrays his desire. His own words—"a house full of silver and gold"—reveal his fantasy.

Another level of desire, however, emerges from the third passage that Rashi singles out. Here, we read that Balaam, on his third attempt to curse the Israelites, "raised up his eyes" (Num. 24:2). Rashi comments:

> He wished to cast the evil eye upon them. Thus you have his three characteristics—an evil eye, as well as pride, and greed, which were mentioned before.

The midrashic character sketch of Balaam is now, essentially, complete. The third negative trait is different from the others, precisely because it does not seem to be driven by desire. The *evil eye* is *envy*. Envy, too, represents a desire; it is the wish to destroy even, or especially, good objects. Looking out over the Israelite camp, Balaam recognizes its goodness: "He saw that it was good in God's eyes to bless Israel . . ." "How goodly are your tents, O Jacob. . . ." (Num. 24:1,5). And yet his admiration, which issues in a classic poem of praise that the Jewish people have adopted into their own daily liturgy, is here understood to be inspired by that look-alike of admiration—envy. Rashi undercuts the apparent benevolence of Balaam's blessing; even at this moment of inspiration, a destructive impulse is at work.

In rabbinic thought,[9] indeed, Balaam becomes a paradigm figure for the three vices that we have just seen Rashi delineating in the narrative—pride, greed, and envy. These three vices characterize the "disciples of Balaam." One can observe the Balaam type, as well as the converse Abraham type, clearly in the world. These are two opposite ways of being human. The contrast particularly between Abraham's generosity of spirit and Balaam's envy, perhaps obscured in their own portraits, emerges most clearly in their disciples.

Beyond Balaam's concrete wishes for honor and wealth lies the truly tragic flaw of envy, with its eternal toxic insecurity. Envy wishes for the destruction of good objects; it represents a different level of desire. On this level, destroying the good object removes the goodness that threatens one's own power. What Balaam desires of Balak is the opportunity to triumph by exercising his resentful power. This strange human dynamic is seen in rabbinic thought as constitutive of Balaam's being, affecting and infecting even his greatest poetry.

CHARACTER TEACHES ABOVE OUR WILLS

We will later be discussing modern understandings of this dynamic. But first, we might ask, what is the basis of such an analysis of Balaam's character? *Lamadnu,* says Rashi; we *learn* Balaam's character traits from the way he speaks. But these traits might never have struck us without a process of *lemidah,* of interpretation. (Sometimes, in fact, character traits emerge more clearly in one's disciples than in oneself.) Apparently docile, obedient to God's commands, even humble, Balaam, in midrashic thought, becomes a case study of unconscious motivation. Arrogance, greed, envy, like other deadly sins, do not always proclaim themselves. Rather, they suffuse the physical being of the one who lives them.

Emerson touches on the unconscious aspect of this: "Character teaches above our wills. Men imagine that they communicate their virtue or vice only by overt action, and do not see that virtue or vice emit a breath every moment."[10] Stanley Cavell acutely remarks: this means that "with every word you utter you say more than you know you say."[11]

Freud, too, has a clinical observation on the same phenomenon: "He that has eyes to see and ears to hear may convince himself that no mortal can keep a secret. If his lips are silent, he chatters with his finger tips; betrayal oozes out of him at every pore."[12]

When the Rabbis *learn* about Balaam, they apply an almost psychoanalytic awareness of the indirections of passion. Take, for instance, the heart of the narrative, the drama of curses turned into blessings. Three times this turning happens. When Moses later revisits the narrative, he makes *turning* the essential dramatic move: "No Ammonite or Moabite may ever enter the community of God ... because he [Balak] hired Balaam ... to curse you. And God your God turned the curse to a blessing—for God your God loves you" (Deut. 23:4–6). God's desire was not to listen to Balaam's curse, which is suffused with hatred; His desire is concerned with love, not hatred. He therefore aborts the curse, *turns* it, so that He does not have to hear it, into blessing. Conversely, Balaam finds his spontaneous words *turning* in his mouth. But Balak, who is the kingpin of the action—who hires the hate-merchant—is banned with his people from "entering into the community of God."

CURSES AND BLESSINGS

To turn is to twist and twirl, to change direction. The Talmud records an extraordinary discussion of this moment of turning. Speaking of Balaam's third and most ecstatic blessing—"How goodly are your tents, O Jacob," R. Yochanan says:

> From the blessings of that wicked man you may learn his intentions. Thus he wished to curse them that they should possess no synagogues or houses of study—[this is deduced from] "How goodly are your tents, O Jacob"; that the Shechinah should not rest on them—"and thy tabernacles, O Israel"; that their kingdom should not endure—"As the valleys are they spread forth"; that they might have no olive trees and vineyards—"as gardens by the riverside"; that their odor might not be fragrant—"as the trees of lign aloes which God has planted"; that their kings might not be tall—"and as cedar trees beside the waters." . . .
>
> R. Abba b. Kahana said: All of them reverted to a curse, except the synagogues and houses of study, for it is written, "But God your God turned the curse into a blessing for you, because God your God loved you"—the curse, not the curses.[13]

God turns Balaam's desire—which is to curse—into words of blessing. But these words of blessing, R. Yochanan understands, are suffused with repressed hatred; they betray his malice at every turn. God inverts cursing into blessing; but the curse remains decipherable precisely in the turn of Balaam's phrases. The refrain echoes throughout the passage: "He sought to say . . . He said . . ." What he sought to say, he did not say. In the end, R. Yochanan re-turns every phrase of admiration into its negative, the primary impulse of envy. But there is the closest connection between his envious impulse and his admiring words. Merely a "not" separates the two.[14]

R. Abba b. Kahana adds yet another turn: all these words of toxic blessing revert ultimately to curses, except for one: the blessing of the "goodly tents," which signifies the intellectual and spiritual life of Israel—synagogues and houses of study. Even in this most poetic of Balaam's blessings, the venom of his envy suffuses his words: it is "the curse," till God turns it to blessing.

At this juncture, the biblical text gives us the impression that on this third occasion, Balaam is genuinely convinced of God's desire to bless Israel, that this time he does not turn to magical devices, that the spirit of God moves him (Num. 24:2), and that he composes his own utterance (*ne'um*) of blessing.[15]

But precisely here, in his lyrical masterpiece, he betrays his repressed hatred. He may have consciously decided not to curse the people, but he "turns his face *toward the wilderness*."[16] He draws his inspiration from the wilderness world that has been the intimate environment of Israel for forty years. With every word he utters he says more than he knows he says.

In another Talmudic passage, Balaam's language is not simply inverted to reveal its underside, but explored for the ambiguity of its imagery:

> Said R. Samuel b. Nahmani in the name of R. Yonatan: What is the meaning of "Wounds by a loved one are long lasting [lit., faithful, trusty]; the kisses of an enemy are profuse" (Prov. 27:6)? Better is the curse that Achiya the Shilonite cursed Israel than the blessing that Balaam the wicked blessed them. Achiya the Shilonite cursed them with the image of a reed, as it is said, "And God will strike Israel until it sways like a reed in water" (1 Kings 14:15)—This reed stands in a watery place and its stock changes and its roots are many, so that all the winds in the world cannot move it from its place, but it moves with the wind, and when the wind subsides the reed remains in place; but Balaam the wicked blessed them to be like a cedar—the cedar does not stand in a watery place,[17] and its roots are few and its stock does not change, so that when the south wind blows it immediately uproots it and overturns it.[18]

Balaam's blessings are more toxic than the curses of Achiya the Shilonite. As in the proof text from Proverbs, there is a profound paradox about this: even the sharp words of a friend are inspired by love, while the enemy's expressions of love are *ne'etarot*.[19] This term often translates as "profuse, manifold"; but perhaps here the meaning relates to the idea of *reversal*—as in the turning of the plow (*attar*).[20] The blandishments of an enemy are treacherous, ambiguous, unstable. Balaam's blessings are toxic because they are *reversible*: they turn colors as they are examined. Such volatile blessings are worse than unequivocal curses.

In this Talmudic text, one particular image is explored: the conceit of the cedar. Apparently benign, the image proves unstable: cedars turn out to be easy to topple in a storm, while Achiya's reed bends but does not break. Metaphors and similes may encompass contradictions. Undeclared passions may break through pleasant surfaces. Language does not provide a simple key to meaning. The question seems to be, Who says the words? And how are they inflected by passion?

EMBODYING ENVY

In a similar vein, Rashi reads the innocuous description of Balaam's departure with Balak's messengers. Balaam saddles his own ass (Num. 22:21), and Rashi comments,

> From here we learn that hatred disrupts order, so that Balaam saddled his own ass. God said, You wicked one, Abraham already preceded you, as it is said, "And he rose early in the morning and saddled his ass" (Gen. 22:3).

Two men, across a gap of centuries, saddle their own asses: the gesture expresses impulsive desire, impatience with social decorums. But one man is considered to be consumed with love, the other with hatred. How does one read the passion in the gesture? It is as though the gesture of that particular body in that particular situation would have spoken more powerfully than words.

In an arresting passage, Proust muses on the unconscious eloquence of the body and its gestures. The narrator of *In Search of Lost Time*, Marcel, contemplates a pregnant kitchen maid, who "was beginning to find difficulty in bearing before her the mysterious basket, fuller and larger day by day, whose splendid outline could be detected beneath the folds of her ample smock." He is reminded of Giotto's allegorical figures, associating the maid with the figure of Charity. But the kitchen maid carries the symbol of bounty before her, without seeming to understand its meaning.

Marcel draws on the Victorian art critic John Ruskin's discussion of Giotto's figure of Charity, where the woman's hand gesture is both expressive and banal: "she is holding out her flaming heart to God, or shall we say 'handing' it to Him, exactly as a cook might hand up a corkscrew through the skylight of her basement kitchen to someone who has called down for it."[21] Marcel then muses on the figure of Envy, who *"should have had some look of envy on her face"* (emphasis added); but who is depicted with a snake filling her mouth, so that "the muscles of her face are strained and contorted, like those of a child blowing up a balloon, and her attention—and ours too for that matter—is so utterly concentrated on the activity of her lips as to leave little time to spare for envious thoughts."[22]

The figure of Envy *embodies* the reality of envy. Marcel remarks on the *"étrangeté saisissante,"* the arresting strangeness of these figures. They have an allegorical force, which verges on the vulgar. As the literary scholar Gabriel Josipovici puts it, they are figures that "draw us *in* to reality": Charity does not look charitable, nor Envy envious. We see Charity in action, Envy in action; "Giotto has compressed into one image a whole state of being."[23]

I suggest that the midrashic view of Balaam bears some similarity to Giotto's and Proust's way of seizing character in action. Balaam, too, is Envy, struggling with the snake in his mouth. From the beginning, he ignores the will of God, so clearly expressed in his first encounter: "You shall not go with them" (Num. 22:12). He prefers to take up the license of God's later words: "Rise up and go with them" (22:20). He prefers God's word to His will.[24] A kind of docile formalism masks the true passion of his whole being, which turns toward Balak, not toward God; to envy, not love.

GOD'S MOUTHPIECE?

In a repeated act of poetic justice, God takes control of Balaam's mouth, in the most literal way. "And God placed a *davar* [word/thing] in Balaam's mouth" (Num. 23:5,16). The *davar* becomes in the rabbinic imagination either an *angel,* or a *bit.*[25] His mouth is invaded, twisted into the shape of blessing. He is, quite literally, possessed. This is the most intimate meaning of having one's curse *turn, twist,* into a blessing. This act of violence controls not only what comes out of his mouth but—like a bit in a horse's mouth—also his movements: "And He said, Return to Balak, and so you shall speak" (23:16). As Midrash Tanchuma puts it: "He twisted his mouth and pricked it like one who drives a nail into a board, making the animal go wherever the rider wishes."

The thing/word in Balaam's mouth reduces him to an object to be penetrated and mastered at will. If it is an angel who takes up residence in his mouth, editing and transforming his words, this expresses one level of reification; but, of course, the bridle-bit metaphor is considerably more horrifying. The effect is, as Seforno puts it, that Balaam's blessings become fully *involuntary* speech. "I am not the speaker of my own words."[26] Strangely, Balaam foresees from the outset that this will be his situation; he even announces it to Balak. Most strangely, it is he who coins the expression, "the word/thing which God shall place in my mouth," which the midrash interprets so concretely.

This condition—of possession, of speaking in tongues—Seforno implicitly also assigns to David, Psalmist, poet, musician. He quotes 2 Samuel 23:2: "The spirit of God spoke through me." To be God's mouthpiece can be imagined along a spectrum of possibilities. In the case of Balaam, there is an absolute tension between his desire and his words.

The imagery of the bridle bit piercing his mouth suggests the horror of the loss of personal autonomy. Prophets and poets also know about possession, perhaps value it as a privilege. But in the context of relationships such as those described in this narrative—of asses controlling and brutalized by riders, of kings manipulating and being manipulated by hired clairvoyants, Balaam's relation to God takes on a similarly dialectical tension. He is rider and ridden; his power, which lies in his mouth, takes on a life of its own, leaving him helpless to achieve his desires.

Even in the third blessing, which seems to emerge from a more autonomous place, there is a strange dissonance that infiltrates the biblical account. "Balaam saw that it was good in the eyes of God to bless Israel": he realizes that he will not be able to curse them. "There came upon him the spirit of God."[27] He becomes God's mouthpiece, like David; but unlike David, his own desire leaves some residual poison in his inspired words. "He turned his face toward the wilderness": to bless the people with reservations, with the sting of envy.

Like Giotto's Envy, Balaam struggles with the snake in his mouth. This is the reality of envy without the look of envy or even the conscious thoughts of envy. Repeatedly, Rashi remarks of him that he has to act *al korcho*—against his will, involuntarily. Against his will, he reveals to the messengers that he is under God's control, that he cannot undo God's promise to the patriarchs; against his will, he is warned that he will have to obey God; against his will, he is compelled to return to Balak; against his will, he admits to the angel, "I did not know that you were standing in front of me," despite his arrogant claims to "know supreme knowledge." "His mouth now testified against him." In spite of his conscious intentions, his mouth now speaks involuntary truth.

The picture that emerges is of a man forced to speak truths that are on some level known to him. But these are truths that he cannot own. He gives unwitting testimony to God's power, to his own greed, arrogance, and envy. Like Macbeth, he finds himself split from himself: "Wherefore could not I say Amen?" Macbeth asks helplessly, wishing to mobilize the "blessing" side of his mind. But his mouth is twisted out of shape. Balaam, more tormented, speaks the words of blessing but cannot prevent the seepage of malice that undermines them.

THE EVIL EYE

George Eliot writes: "Strange that some of us, with quick alternate vision, see beyond our infatuations, and even while we rave on the heights, behold the wide plain where our persistent self pauses and awaits us."[28]

This could almost be a portrait of Balaam—raving on the heights while beholding the plain; subject to the "quick alternate vision" that reverts always to the "persistent self." But George Eliot is describing "some of us"—perhaps referring to herself and her reader. This is a structure of paradoxical experience that she assumes will be recognizable to her reader: the phenomenon of alternate vision, in which the moment's madness, or inspiration, maintains awareness of the persistent self. By a kind of psychic mechanism, one learns to shut one eye in order to sustain a habitual way of seeing.

The Zohar says something similar about Balaam: "He blocked his *good eye* from them, so that blessing should not fall on them."[29] Ultimately, Balaam is hired for his way of seeing, for his gaze. When God first tells Balaam, "Don't go with them and don't curse them," Seforno reads: "Even if you do not curse them, don't even go with them, so that you don't lay eyes on them for evil," as in the expression, "He laid eyes on him, and he became a heap of bones."[30]

Distinguishing *going* from *cursing,* Seforno addresses the issue of Balaam's eye—the evil eye, which is envy. A malevolent glance of the eye has power to kill. A recurrent theme in Seforno's commentary, the good and the evil eye have power to affirm life and to destroy it. Later, when Balaam first attempts to curse the Israelites, he is led by Balak to a particular mountaintop from which he can *see* a section of the camp (Num. 22:41). His perspective is deliberately staged so that he may lay eyes on one aspect of the camp, bring a malevolent gaze to bear upon its population.[31] Similarly, Seforno refers to Moses' dying gaze at the Land as a proof text for the equivalent power of the eyes to bless.

Balak may trundle Balaam from mountaintop to mountaintop, seeking better visual angles. But even as God twists his mouth to blessing, even as he raves, his "persistent self," his evil eye, sustains its gaze. Balaam's envy is, for the Rabbis, a paradoxical strength that all but disables him.

In the thinking of the British psychoanalyst Melanie Klein, envy is a primary and universal emotion, which interferes tragically with the infant's first emotional relationship with the mother. For her, envy and gratitude are two sides of the same coin, one diminishing life, the other enhancing it. Unlike jealousy, envy represents a malign resentment of the *good* object: it "stems from within," is "insatiable," and "always finds an object to focus on." It is purely destructive, not least of the infant's own mental development, which requires the building up of a good object.[32]

In the midrashic view of Balaam, such an understanding of envy is implicit in the emphasis on his *evil eye*. He may be inspired to flights of rhetoric, but blessing sits awkwardly in a mouth twisted out of shape. Unwittingly, he testifies in every phrase to a truth that continues to escape him. In this sense, he is Everyman, struggling to control meanings that are not totally available even to himself. But the words themselves give birth to knowledge, if one could only hear them.

"MOSES WROTE THE STORY OF BALAAM"

According to the Talmud, the story of Balaam was written by Moses. "Moses wrote his book [Deuteronomy], the narrative of Balaam, and Job."[33] We have considered some of the complications of Moses as author of the book of Job.[34] The general notion of Moses-as-author is, of course, quite mysterious. But of the three attributed works, Balaam is the strangest. In the traditional view, this narrative was, like the rest of the Torah, written by Moses at God's dictation. Unlike Deuteronomy, moreover, there is no obvious relation between this text and Moses' experience. If Moses spoke many of the words recorded in Deuteronomy, a claim could be made for a kind of authorship, of authority, in relation to that book. But the Balaam story is entirely concerned with a foreign episode, recounting facts and conversations that must have been unknown to Moses. His only source for this material is God's narrative.

What can be meant by the claim that Moses wrote the Balaam story? It has been read to suggest that *even* this story, which is so alien to the historical experience of Moses and his people, was, like the rest of the Torah, inscribed by Moses. But this logic would not apply to the other two works attributed to him.

I suggest that, as in the case of Job, if we imagine Moses writing the story of Balaam, Moses' inner life becomes palpable to us, for an instant, as a mystery that can be intimated only through the indirections of the work of his own writing. If Job is a kind of alter ego, staging the forces at play in Moses himself, then Balaam, too, serves as a way of working through crucial aspects of Moses' own life struggle.

LANGUAGE AND CIRCUMCISION

Take, for instance, Moses' early struggle with his own mouth, his tongue, his lips. "I am not a man of words," he protests at the Burning Bush. "I am heavy of mouth and heavy of tongue" (Exod. 4:10). God promises to "be with your mouth; I shall teach you what to say"(4:12). When Moses continues to resist, God becomes angry with him. If God is angry, it is because Moses' "persistent self" shows no sign of being affected by God's speeches.

As Or Ha-Chaim[35] points out, God does not offer to cure Moses of his language problem. Instead, He asks him to trust the way that God has made him; and to know that "I shall teach you *that you can speak—asher te-dabber*." That is, once Moses assumes his role as God's speaker, he will find the words spontaneously arising within him, as though innately present. Or Ha-Chaim plays with the word *horeiti-cha* ("I shall teach you."), as though it is connected to the expression *harah* ("conception"): Moses will be born anew into the world of language.

The implication of this reading is that such impediments of mouth and tongue represent inner preoccupations whose tension can find release only if trust loosens the vocal chords. God is angry with Moses for refusing to allow himself to come to birth in language.

Moses' struggle with language thus can be understood as a reluctance to be born into the world of others. Even the strange episode at the *malon,* the lodging place where God attacks him (or his newborn son?), hints at its connection with the depths of Moses' inwardness. It has been suggested that the message he is to carry to Pharaoh ("You refuse to let them go—I shall kill your firstborn son" [Exod. 4:23]), is to be applied to Moses himself.[36] Moses is to speak words that have obvious reference to Pharaoh's recalcitrance; but that, on another level, refer to Moses. He is refusing to enable his people's redemption; and it is his own firstborn son who is now at risk.

Zippora saves her husband and/or her son by circumcising the child. This act of *milah,* of circumcision, represents a therapeutic opening into the world of others. *Milah* in Rabbinic Hebrew is the word for *word;* even the word *malon* plays on the same root, as yet another reference to language sown subliminally in this strange text.

After this, Moses refers once more to his speech problem, describing himself as *aral sefatayim*—of uncircumcised lips (Exod. 6:12). This grotesque metaphor is precisely expressive of a closed-in condition: lips webbed together—the essential space, the crack of vulnerability out of which language emerges, is blocked off. By this point, however, he is able to imagine his condition and, more important, its cure. He knows that he needs *milah*—that incision that opens a human connection with the other.

Rashi narrates the macabre scenario at the *malon* where God, in the form of a snake, envelops Moses' body head downward and then feet upward till the sexual organ. "Then Zippora understood that it was because of *milah*, circumcision."[37] He requires the act of *milah* to release him from his locked-in state and to generate the *milah*, the *word*. From the moment he utters his strange metaphor, *aral sefatayim*—"I am of uncircumcised lips"—Moses opens himself to this understanding.

Zippora calls Moses (or the baby) "a bridegroom of blood for circumcisions" (Exod. 4:26). Whatever this enigmatic expression means, clearly circumcision involves blood. Like the blood of birth, this has an ambiguous quality. It is, in Julia Kristeva's term, *abject*—evoking both repugnance and desire. When the prophet Ezekiel imagines the birth of the Israelite people in Egypt, he figures it as a female infant—"When I saw you wallowing in your blood, I said to you, In your blood you shall live. Yea, I said to you, In your blood you shall live" (Ezek. 16:6). *Mitbossesset* (wallowing) suggests defeat, degradation, soiling, kicking about—and *life*.

Strangely, these words are recited at the circumcision of a male infant, with *chayi*—"you shall live," in the feminine form, unselfconsciously quoted in this most masculine procedure. The passage from Ezekiel, which tells of the purely female experience of the birth of a female infant, is uncannily absorbed into the male symbolism of circumcision.

In spite of the repellent blood, God decrees that the infant shall live. Or—"*At the cost* of your blood, live." The phrase is repeated in allusion to the two bloods of circumcision and the paschal sacrifice:[38] self-sacrifice ensures life. The doubleness is also reflected in the unusual dual form, *damayich*—"your two bloods."

In another powerful midrash,[39] the Israelites in Egypt are seduced by the smell of the paschal offering and agree to be circumcised. In other words, the intimation of freedom rouses them to a desire to be fully born;[40] the act of circumcision—of conscious vulnerability, of full embodiment—is implicit in this desire. Another way of saying this is that a loss of power, a divestment of selfhood, is part of the movement into freedom.

To be born, or reborn, requires desire. The ambiguities of desire represent for Moses a dilemma that accompanies him through his whole life. The issues of circumcision, of blood, of connection and separation, play a significant role in his life. There is, for example, the following midrashic story about the blood of circumcision. Pharaoh angrily rejects Moses' demands: "God be with you, the same as I mean to let your children go with you! See, *evil is facing you!*" (Exod. 10:10). Rashi comments:

> Understand this as the Targum takes it: "See the evil you are about to do will turn against yourself." I have heard a midrashic explanation: There is a certain star the name of which is *ra'ah,* Evil. Pharaoh said to them, "By my astrological art I see that star rising toward you in the wilderness. It is an emblem of blood and slaughter."
>
> Consequently, when Israel sinned by worshipping the Golden Calf and God intended to slay them, Moses said in his prayer (Exod. 32:12), "Why should the Egyptians speak and say, He brought them forth together with *ra'ah* [i.e., under the influence of the star, *ra'ah*]; this is, indeed what Pharaoh already said, "See, the *ra'ah* is before you." At once, "God changed His intention about *ra'ah,*" and He changed the blood of which this star was an emblem to the blood of circumcision; and indeed Joshua had them circumcised. This is the meaning of "This day I have rolled off you the reproach of the Egyptians" (Josh. 5:9); for they said to you, "We see blood looming over you in the wilderness." (Yalkut 1:392; see also Rashi on Josh. 5:9)

Pharaoh's astrologers see evil and bloodshed in Israel's future; in fleeing to the wilderness, they run like lemmings to their doom. Moses makes use of this story to plead for mercy after the Golden Calf: if God massacres the people now, it will look as if the astrologers' prediction has come true. So God transforms the blood into circumcision blood. The narrative of despair is subverted—turned—when it is interpreted and redeemed by a genuine act of *milah*—an opening, a rebirth of the self that involves blood. Now, the blood is reframed as sacrifice or desire for rebirth.

Moses plays a central role in this midrashic narrative. It is his protest about the Egyptian narrative of doom, about the future as written in the stars, that moves God to *turn* the blood. For Moses, this moment of *turning*, which reconfigures the narrative, is of intimate concern. He "writes" Balaam's story because of it. For *turning* implies that a determined future may become an open future; the blood of slaughter can be rewritten as a different blood; God can *turn* Balaam's curses into blessings, "because He loves you." To write a story about *turning* is to choose a different meaning, to change its direction because one is implicated in the reading and in the writing.

MOSES AND BALAAM

Balaam's story represents the complexity of such turnings and re-turnings. How might Moses be implicated in the twists and turns of this story? There are a number of possible connections between Moses and Balaam. First, there is the classic view that Balaam is indeed a kind of alter ego for Moses: a counterweight among the nations, manifesting similar talents and powers. Of both, the midrash declares, "Their strength was in their mouth."[41] Both Moses and Balaam know how to discern the moment of God's anger, though each has a different desire in relation to it. For Balaam it is an opportunity to write the narrative of destruction; for Moses it is a call to protest.

There is also a strange parallel in the role of *makkot*—of blows, physical violence—in the story of Balaam and his ass, and in the larger story of Moses.[42] Moses' first conscious act is to strike the Egyptian taskmaster dead. He is instrumental in bringing down the Plagues (*makkot*) on the Egyptians; striking the river, raising his hand and his rod, he generates terror and violence in the violent world of Egypt. And at the end, he strikes the rock instead of speaking to it.

Balaam, for his part, is hired to speak hatred and destruction. But in the bizarre scene with the ass, when his own leg is crushed against the wall, he strikes the animal three times. When the ass protests, Balaam replies self-pityingly, "You have made a mockery of me! If I had a sword with me, I'd kill you" (Num. 22:29). The irony is that he is the prophet who is being hired to kill with his words alone, but this ass reduces him to impotence. His eyes (he fails to see the angel) and his mouth both fail him, so he brutalizes the poor animal who has served him so well.

Balaam's violence toward his ass is subtly mirrored in his relation with Balak. The king tries to control his hireling, whether by flattery, bribery, or threats. In the end, he "strikes his hands together" in anger (Num. 24:10)—a gesture that, at least in fantasy, destroys Balaam. Balaam is drawn into a master-slave relationship: the biter bit, the hitter hit, he plays out the destructiveness of such relationships. The pathetic desire for recognition turns yesterday's master into today's slave.

Having treated his ass as an object to be beaten into submission, he is now subjected in a similar way by the king.[43] Like the ass, he frustrates his master three times. In both cases, the "master" fails to understand—to see—what stands in his way. And the "slave," too, fails to comprehend the meaning of his own story.

Imagining Moses as the author, in some sense, of the Balaam story, we may think of Balaam's story as a kind of mise en abyme, a play within the play, embedded in the story of Israel for the purpose of self-reflection. Moses-writing-Balaam explores the themes of violence, of masters and slaves, of sensitivity to anger, of the turning of curses into blessings. But this kind of writing suggests that the writer is *implicated* in the tensions he stages.

CIRCUMCISION: BECOMING WHOLE

Perhaps most inwardly, however, the Balaam story, in the midrashic perspective, brings forward the question of circumcision and language. If Moses writes Balaam's story, it is the question that lies at the heart of his exploration. As we have seen, a form of circumcision,[44] of opening and rebirth into the world of relationship with others, is central to the inner history of Moses, who describes himself so graphically as "of uncircumcised lips." The arc of Moses' "to-be-circumcised" life is strangely mirrored in the figure of Balaam.

Balaam introduces his third and most significant blessing by describing himself, the speaker, as one who "sees the vision of the Almighty, *fallen with open eyes*" (Num. 24:4). The image of Balaam prophesying in some kind of cataleptic fit suggests a state of reduced moral agency. Rashi, however, comments that the fallen position indicates that Balaam's prophetic talents thrive by night, when he is supine—a dark, orgiastic spirituality. He then cites the midrash: "When God was revealed to him, he had no strength to stand on his legs: he fell forward onto his face, because he was uncircumcised and unfit to stand upright in God's presence."

Balaam becomes the type of the uncircumcised man who must collapse in the presence of God. What brings him down is an excess, which is, at the same time, an *insufficiency:* he has not the strength to stand in this state before God. A similar collapse is narrated about Abraham: "And Abram fell on his face" (Gen. 17:3). God has just told him, "Walk before Me and become whole!" God then speaks of the *brit,* the Covenant between Abraham and Himself, focusing on the commandment of circumcision. Rashi reads: "He fell down out of awe of God's presence: till he circumcised himself, he had no strength to stand upright before the Holy Spirit. . . . That is what is written about Balaam, 'fallen with open eyes.'"

Rashi's source, *Pirkei d'Rabbi Eliezer,* 29, focuses on the "power of circumcision." The paradoxes of this notion are fascinating. To circumcise is to cut away part of the male organ of sexual potency. It is at the least a symbolic gesture of castration. And yet, it is a source of power. Both Balaam and Abraham, the outsider and the quintessential insider, are, paradoxically, weakened by their *un*circumcised state. Because they have not diminished themselves in this way, their knees buckle, they fall over to cover the undiminished organ. The Hebrew word *arel*—uncircumcised—is a positive adjective describing a natural but unevolved state.

These paradoxes are reflected in midrashic literature. For instance: "Great is circumcision that with all the commandments that Abraham fulfilled he was not called whole until he was circumcised, as it says, Walk before Me and be whole."[45]

In Abraham's case, Meshech Chochmah makes an intriguing suggestion: God has spoken to him repeatedly before this juncture, without his falling down. What precipitates the collapse is the moment of the *commandment:* a new ideal of wholeness puts the past stability of his life into question. He now exists in a new narrative, in which circumcision constitutes a challenge to accustomed meanings. Self-consciousness changes his body sense. He now understands that his habitual condition is less masterful than he had imagined.

It is circumcision that gives one the strength to confront God.[46] The paradox of becoming whole by cutting off a part of oneself does not escape midrashic notice. For instance, Midrash Tanchuma has Abraham wonder: "Up to now, I have been whole; if I circumcise myself, I shall become defective." God answers, "What do you think? That you are perfectly whole?"[47] Abraham's potential wholeness is then explained as a matter of greater bodily integrity, represented by an augmentation in his name.

CONNECTING TWO THINGS

Falling on one's face, one cannot face the other. One is forced into a concealing, defensive posture. In this vein, Maharal carries the meaning of circumcision inward. This is, he says, an *inyan pnimi*—an esoteric matter—relating to mysteries not commonly understood. Writing of Balaam's uncircumcised state, he comments: Without circumcision, there is no *brit,* no covenant. And a covenant "connects two things." Without *brit milah,* the covenant of circumcision, the address of the Holy Spirit brings a man down; with it, one has peace, and love of God, and brotherhood, and one is able to stand.[48]

Circumcision makes it possible not to overwhelm or be overwhelmed in the presence of the other. Linking opposites, the covenant allows one to speak to and with the other. It generates love of God, brotherhood, and peace.

A psychoanalytic version of the deep structure that Maharal is intimating might invoke the Lacanian view of the structural role of castration in psychic life. Michael Eigen writes: "The neurotic clings to an enslaving imaginary castration to avoid a deeper, freeing castration. . . . Clinging to imaginary castration may heighten a master or slave position."[49]

By denying one's true vulnerability, one gains an illusion of strength, expressed in aggression and paranoia. Fear and defensiveness prevent one from achieving the experience of *jouissance,*[50] and of serving it in the Other.

Eigen describes the act of circumcision—as in Abraham's case—as an act that modulates one's tyrannical-servile sides. It brings Abraham closer to God, opens him to free-flowing *jouissance,* the bliss of aliveness. Surrendering the illusion of mastery, one is released to one's true self. If castration anxiety holds one rigid, circumcision opens one's heart, transforms it into a heart of flesh: "And I will give you a new heart and put a new spirit into you: I will remove the heart of stone from your body and give you a heart of flesh" (Ezek. 36:26).

How is this transformation to be achieved? "And God your God will circumcise your heart and the hearts of your offspring to love God your God with all your heart and soul, in order that you may live" (Deut. 30:6). The effect of circumcision is the ability to love God, for the sake of life. Such a circumcision of the heart is an act of covenant, creating connection between oneself and the Other, who is God; or between oneself and the other human being; or even between one's conscious self and the unknowable Other within. The aim is to achieve *lev echad,*[51] wholeness of heart.

Balaam becomes the very type of the uncircumcised. He lives the fruitless dramas of the imaginary ego, the fictions of power, the perversities of the master-slave symbiosis. He is Balak to his ass; he is the ass to Balak's desire. The unknowable has no place in his imagination. Clinging to his fantasy of knowledge and control, his immediate desires—for honor, wealth, the destruction of the Other—block him from the unlimited *jouissance* of surrender.

Such a midrashic-psychoanalytic view of Balaam is supported by a statement in the Zohar: "There is no condition of *sitra achra* [lit., the other side], of demonic evil, that does not have a slight, small spark of *sitra d'kedusha,* of the side of holiness."[52] Balaam becomes the type of one who cannot, in the words of Maharal, connect the two sides of himself. To open himself to God, to the potential beauty of the Israelite camp, to the reality of *jouissance,* would be to un-Balaam himself. Like the Giotto figure of Envy, he becomes an allegorical figure, his words twisting his mouth like a serpent.

The poetic justice of his fate is harsh. To speak words of blessing would require that he circumcise the grandiosity of his heart. It would mean that he open himself to his own insufficiency, to the gap that inhabits him and all human beings. From this gap, symbolic creativity flows; its *jouissance* lives in the twists and turns of language. But instead he inhabits a rigid place of selfhood, where he must collapse under the power of God's presence. He cannot connect opposite things: male and female, man and God, the divided human heart.

THE SINGER NOT THE SONG

Here is an intriguing midrash on the ambiguities involved in blessing:

> He [Balaam] began to turn to parables: "And he took up his parable. . . ." This bears on what Scripture says, "He that blesses his friend with a loud voice . . . it shall be accounted a curse to him" (Prov. 27:14). When Balaam came to curse Israel, God twisted his tongue and he began to bless them, as it says, "God your God would not listen to Balaam; but God your God turned the curse into a blessing" (Deut. 23:6). God put force into his voice so that it traveled from one end of the world to the other, so that the nations might hear that he was blessing them. How do we know this? R. Eleazar Hakappar explained: It is written in another place, "With a loud voice that did not cease" (Deut. 5:19), that is to say, it traveled from one end of the world to the other; and here it is written, "He that blesses his friend with a loud voice . . . it shall be accounted a curse to him." For Balaam had said to Balak, "Come, and I will counsel you" (Num. 24:14), and had thus slain twenty-four thousand men of Israel! Is there a curse equal to this?[53]

Blessing in a loud voice raises questions about hidden animosities. The lady doth protest too much methinks. . . . Strident benevolence is suspect. Balaam's blessings may resound from one end of the world to the other, but they are immediately followed by the fatal counsel that Balaam gives Balak:[54] to send Moabite women to seduce the Israelites, who then lose twenty-four thousand men.

This midrash invites us to consider human ambivalence in rela-

tion to the Other. Balaam utters extravagant blessing: perhaps blessing and cursing are closer than we think?

Even the righteous are not immune to this ambivalence. When,
for instance, Jacob takes Esau's blessing, Isaac strangely vindicates
him after the fact: "And indeed he shall be blessed!" (Gen. 27:27).
One midrash suggests[55] that Isaac's intention was to curse Jacob,
but, somehow ("God put it in his heart"), he found himself blessing
him instead. This turn seems to represent a benign transformation.
Sometimes, however, as our midrash implies, overhearty benevolence may compensate for resentment.

Another midrash reflects on the paradoxical speech acts of Moses
and Balaam:

> "These are the words": R. Aha b. R. Chanina said, It would have
> been more fitting for the rebukes to have been uttered by
> Balaam and the blessings by Moses. But had Balaam uttered
> the rebukes, then Israel would say, "It is an enemy who
> rebukes us"; and had Moses uttered the blessings, then the
> other nations of the world would say, "It is their friend who
> blesses them." Therefore, God commanded: "Let their friend
> Moses reprove them, and their foe Balaam bless them, so that
> the genuineness of the blessings and rebukes of Israel may be
> clear beyond question."
>
> Another comment: Had another said, "The Rock, His work
> is perfect" (Deut. 32:4), they might have said, "How can one
> who does not know the quality of God's justice declare, 'The
> Rock, His work is perfect'? But Moses, of whom Scripture says,
> "He made known His ways to Moses" (Ps. 103:7)—for him it
> was fitting to declare, "The Rock, His work is perfect."

It is as though both Moses and Balaam speak out of character.
Moses' critiques of his people and Balaam's blessings are equally
unexpected. If one's utterance is simply true to type—sweet words
from the friend, hostile from the foe—one's words can easily be
dismissed as personal prejudice. What gives words force and heft is
the sense of a large and complex experience backing the words. The
meeting of opposites, the surprise of blessings and rebukes emerging from unexpected mouths, invites serious thought in the listener.

The process of *birur,* of clarification, begins when one's assumptions about the Other are jolted. The blessing rings with the force of truth, when a Balaam speaks it against the grain, as it were. The singer creates the reality of the song; and the song reveals unknown dimensions of the singer.

The paradoxes of character and expression are picked up again in the next part of the midrash. Who is entitled to make grandiose statements like, "Now I know that God is great"; or "All is vanity"; or "The Rock, His work is perfect"?[56] Only someone who fully understands the difficulty of making such statements. If Moses justifies the ways of God, it is his knowledge of human suffering that gives his words their power. In another mouth, the same words would sound facile. But Moses speaks against the grain of his experience of the inexplicable. He has known the terror of God's anger; only he, therefore, can speak words that justify the ways of God.

These midrashic paradoxes play on the edge of the question: "Who is the speaker?" Who speaks? It is not just that character teaches above our wills, that "virtue or vice emit a breath every moment" (Emerson). It is rather that with every word, one says more than one knows. Control of one's meanings is precisely what one loses when one speaks. The desires of the speaker find expression in oblique ways, so that a full listening, or a full reading, opens one to the unique, and sometimes ironic, force of blessings, rebukes, even theological statements that come from *this* particular mouth.

MISRECOGNITIONS

The story of Balaam challenges us with the paradox of the hostile stranger who authors words that have entered the daily liturgy of the Jewish people. The mysterious blessings of an outsider unaccountably seize hold of the reader who is involved in the history of the Israelites in the wilderness. How does Balaam speak to us? What difference does it make to us that a heathen soothsayer is compelled to endure turnings and re-turnings, twistings and humiliations of language, in order to bless us?

The midrashic view of the narrative only sharpens the question, since it exposes a dark hinterland of motivation in this puppetlike figure. In the biblical text, Balaam first appears as one who is, in a real sense, converted to an appreciation for Israel's greatness: the appreciation of an enemy gratifies us. But in the midrashic readings, Balaam is reduced to something of an automaton. What is Balaam to us, or we to Balaam?

Balaam's story is largely composed of spoken utterances that become a written text; it is to be read, heard by the reader. Divided against himself, Balaam speaks these words of blessing. And Moses writes this text for us, because it speaks to our concerns, his concerns; perhaps because he finds dimensions of his own struggle uncannily mirrored—or caricatured—in the portrait of Balaam.

Perhaps the deepest reading effect of the Balaam story is to make us aware of how he fails to read his own reality. From the first arrival of the messengers, through the episode with the ass, through the triple humiliations of the curses-turned-blessings, Balaam maintains the illusion that he may yet have his way with God, that he may yet fulfill Balak's desire, which is his desire. In the end, instead of seizing hold of his desire, he becomes the object of Balak's furious gesture— "He struck his hands together"; at least in fantasy, Balaam is himself seized, annihilated.

His blindness perhaps never evolves into insight. He is the "nondupe" of whom Lacan writes: *Les non-dupes errent.*[57] What we read when we read Balaam is a trace of our own unconscious willfulness, our insistence on seizing meaning. What Balaam fails to recognize is how his own wayward desire ironically furthers the fulfillment of God's will. As in the famous legend of Death in Samarra,[58] Balaam is taken in precisely when he thinks to master the story. In that legend, the Baghdad merchant's servant encounters Death in the marketplace and tells his master that he is fleeing to Samarra. His master meets Death later in the day; Death explains, "I was astonished to see your servant in Baghdad, for I have an appointment with him tonight in Samarra."

The Oedipus myth similarly narrates the fulfillment of the prediction precisely by way of the attempt to evade it.[59] In such stories, attempts to elude prophecy become the very engine of its fulfillment. The subject of the story misrecognizes, mistakes the meaning of his own story; the error makes the truth come true. We overlook the way our act is already part of the process that brings the prophecy about.

The effect of the Balaam story is to generate in the reader a new

kind of reflexivity. Balaam's "madness," the ways in which he is different from his masterful self, evokes in the reader an equivalent
sense of ignorance. We are neither the same as him, nor his polar
opposite. What we recognize in reading him is the blind spot that
we, too, inhabit.

TWISTS AND TURNS

What, after all, distinguishes Moses from Balaam? Sefat Emet
repeatedly struggles with this question. In a characteristic passage,
he focuses on the *davar*, the word/thing/bit in Balaam's mouth, in
order to arrive at a more general understanding of the working of
language.

"God *placed* [*vayasem*] a word/thing in Balaam's mouth": *Vayasem*
has the meaning of "organizing, ordering." The righteous, says Sefat
Emet, are characterized by an ability to transform their prophetic
message for the better: all depends on the prophet's choice of language. Moses is, implicitly, the archetype of this creative power.
Sefat Emet uses the word *ta'amim* to make his point about transformations of meaning. *Ta'amim* refers to taste, meaning, sense, punc-
tuation marks, cantillation marks. The *ta'am* can turn the sense of
the words from one extreme to the other.

Balaam—who is set on interpreting God's words for evil, turning
his vision to Balak's advantage—is treated with a terrible poetic justice: God sets his words in unchangeable order, so that he becomes
incapable of *turning* his mouth at all. The "bit" in his mouth, the
involuntary words of blessing become rigid, irreversible. "My message was to bless: When He blesses, I cannot reverse it" (Num. 23:20).

Such is the fate of the wicked: "He takes away the reason [*ta'am*]
of elders" (Job 12:20)—the capacity to pursue meaning is withdrawn
from them. Sefat Emet here sharpens the notion of God's power to
disable the wisdom of the wise, to make them lose their reason. In
his reading, *ta'am* is not simply "reason" but the ability to "play" with
meaning. Balaam thus becomes the type of one who has forfeited
the true power of the poet-prophet—the musical flexibility that
gives new meaning to the words. Omnipotent, enviously distorting
meaning, he finds himself unable to inflect the words in his mouth.

If he has lost the *ta'am* of language, its taste in the mouth, he has become an automaton. He is like the "undead," possessed by an uncanny animation. Sefat Emet goes against the grain of the midrashic imagery: the bit that twists Balaam's mouth here *untwists* the spontaneous torsion of Balaam's malevolence. It counters the way his mind and body are already set to the mode of cursing; what God now does is switch him to the opposite mode, equally uncanny in its automatism. By this further turn of the screw, Balaam produces formulas of blessing.

READING BALAAM

The one moment, it seems, when this uncanny state cracks open is the moment of *Mah tovu—How goodly are your tents, O Jacob, your dwellings, O Israel!* (Num. 24:5). This is the one blessing that, according to R. Abba b. Kahana,[60] endured, unlike all the other blessings that eventually reverted to curses—to the original form of Balaam's desire. This is the crucial turn of the screw, the singular moment when "God turned the curse into a blessing." The tents of Jacob and the dwellings of Israel are classically interpreted to refer to houses of study and prayer, which, when all else failed, turned out to be most essential for Israel's survival. What makes this utterance different from all of Balaam's other doomed blessings?

I would suggest that the difference is that for the first time Balaam *addresses* Israel: he becomes an *I* addressing a *you*, in direct speech. *How goodly are your tents, O Jacob. . . .* He sustains this for one verse, then immediately reverts to the third person. This moment, which has entered the daily Jewish liturgy, holds the one true speech act of Balaam's many words of blessing. Here, he calls on Israel, changes their identity: their tents are the houses of prayer and study that they will become. He recognizes them, expresses perhaps a desire that they be what he says they are.

A kind of pact is implicit in this form of address. It constitutes a speech act, which transforms the other through the fact of its utterance.[61] Statements like, "You are my wife," or "I do," for instance, in themselves perform the act of marriage. They also, implicitly, transform the speaker. Jacques Lacan notes that in such acts of "full speech," or "founding speech," both self and other are invested with a new reality.

Balaam achieves this essential form of human speech in one moment of *Mah tovu—How goodly are your tents!* We, Israel, who will be the original readers of this text, are changed by his address. It makes a difference to us, to Israel, that Balaam "tasted" this essential freedom of the mouth. When Balaam invokes Israel in this way, a kind of metaphysical circumcision, a *brit,* a Covenant, takes place: two things are linked in a kind of pact.

The fact that these words are a singular moment in the story of a man who is otherwise locked in misrecognition does not diminish their power. For an instant, Balaam sees and speaks fully. He becomes the very type of Rava's statement: "In the way that a person desires to go, there he is led."[62] The way of transference, Balaam's way with Balak, is the painful, roundabout route through misrecognition. Balaam's singular act of full speech could not have happened without it. It implicates both himself and Israel, even though Israel is presumably not aware of the moment of speech. What remains for Israel, then, is to *read* the story of Balaam.

Moses, therefore, writes Balaam. He gives birth to a truth that he does not already possess. He writes, primarily, for himself and his people. He—and we—will read the story and, within it, the blessing, the last turn of the screw. Such reading may give us access to our blind spot, our place of not-knowing; our irreducible otherness.

TEN

To Be or Not to Be: A Tale of Five Sisters

THE FRAME NARRATIVE

In a signal act of courage, five sisters—daughters of one Tzelofchad—come forward and defend their right to inherit their father's portion in the Land. Their claim is accepted by God (Num. 27:1–7). Moreover, the law is framed in accordance with this precedent (27:8–11).

The most striking moment in this legal drama is the moment when God approves their plea: *Ken bnot Tzelofchad dovrot:* "They speak *ken* [rightly, justly]." Before instructing Moses to give the women the family land, God *speaks about their act of speech.* This unprecedented divine compliment resonates powerfully toward the end of a book in which so many unhappy acts of speech have been recorded. A cacophony of language rises up from the text of this book: after all the complaints of the people, the verbal fury and distrust, after Moses' complex failure to speak to the rock, after the Balaam narrative, with its murky projections of the problem of language as benediction and malediction, after forty years of misspeaking—five sisters achieve an act of *dibbur* that gains a gratified response from God, all the more intense for the misfires of the past. (*Ken,* God says—*Yes!* At last!)

This legal victory is recounted specifically as a *narrative* rather than simply as a formulation of the law. It makes its way into the text by way of a complaint, an appeal, and an apparent adjustment of the law.[1] More than that, instead of launching directly into the women's speech—"Our father died . . ." (Num. 27:3)—the episode begins with two verses of quite elaborate narrative scene-setting:

The daughters of Tzelofchad, of the family of Manasseh—son of Hepher, son of Gilead, son of Machir, son of Manasseh, son of Joseph—came forward. The names of the daughters were

Mahlah, Noah, Hoglah, Milcah, and Tirzah. They stood before
Moses, Elazar the priest, the princes, and the whole assem-
bly, at the entrance of the Tent of Meeting, and they said . . .
(Num. 27:1–2)

We notice that the framework of this episode is narrative from
start to finish. Time plays a role here. There is suspense and resolution; initial uncertainty, and tension tuned to the highest pitch, as
the case is referred upward to God, the "Supreme Court"; and gratification, as the divine *ken* is handed down.

More specifically, we notice the details of the introductory narrative. The two verbs—resonant in their unusual feminine plural
form—*va-tikravna, va-ta'amodna*—declare the significant acts of
the sisters. Before they even open their mouths, they *come forward:*
and they *stand* before all the dignitaries of the people. Both verbs,
each introducing a separate verse, express audacity: the root *karav*
("they came forward") signifies intimacy, struggle, sacrifice, possibly encroachment.[2] The wrong person in the wrong place may bring
down a thunderbolt from heaven. *Standing,* too, implies that they
stand their ground "in the presence of all of them," as Rashi puts
it. The roll call of dignitaries represents an intimidating forum—
perhaps a House of Study, an institute of advanced research into
the law.

Before a word has been spoken, therefore, the narrative has set
these sisters in a world that holds no obvious place for them. The
frame narrative introduces them by listing their ancestry: five male
names that link them back to Joseph; this is followed by the wom-
en's names—five names[3]—even though these have already been
listed among the clans enrolled for inheritance (Num. 26:33). Wom-
en's names in such a list is in itself unexpected, since censuses are
patrilineal by definition. The sisters' names are followed by specific
reference to the male members of the forum they approach: Moses,
Elazar, the princes, the whole *edah*—again, by definition, the male
assembly. The place in which the women stand, therefore, is framed
by male names. This structure gives us the sense of the world, the
field, in which the women speak: five women, heirs to sons who
become fathers, addressing an entirely male forum.

FORCE FIELDS

They speak in the name of their dead father, who begins and ends their speech:

> "Our father died in the wilderness. He was not one of the faction, Korach's faction, which banded together against God, but died for his own sin; and he has left no sons. Why should our father's name be lost to his clan just because he had no son? Give us a holding among our father's brothers!" (Num. 27:3–4)

Three times they refer to "our father." They speak in the name of a dead father who has been silenced by his lack of male heirs; sons represent and substitute for their father. Strangely, the sisters begin with an idiosyncratic description of their father's *sin* that blurs the clarity of their legal presentation. Only toward the end of their speech do they come to the legal core of the matter: "And he has left no sons. . . ." And only after that do they make their plea: "Why should our father's name be lost . . . ?" In other words, a narrative element—apparently redundant—infiltrates even into their legal plea. The text emphasizes that this is a speech given by specific women in a specific context and at a specific moment in time; and that their appeal calls on a specific, if obscure, biographical narrative.

The sisters' plea is in the plural voice: "Give *us* a holding. . . ." The tone of "Give us"—*t'na lanu*—evokes associations from narratives throughout the Torah and later scriptures: "Give us water," the people demand; "Give us meat" (Num. 11:13); "Give us seed that we may live" (Gen. 47:19); "Give me please of your son's mandrakes" (30:14); "Give me a burial site" (23:4); "Give me the girl as a wife" (34:12); "Give us a king" (1 Sam. 8:6); "Give me your vineyard" (1 Kings 21:2,6). The tone is imperious, expressing vital need, often existential need. It brooks no denial. In speaking in this way, the five sisters press their case with some force.

Similarly, when they pose their rhetorical question: "Why [*lamah*] should our father's name be lost?," *lamah* implies a challenge to show why it should be so; its connotations are emphatically negative ("It should *not* be lost"). The burden of proof is laid on the opposition.

Strikingly, it is with just such a *"Why"* that the people often prefaced their resentments and complaints during the wilderness journey. The sisters adopt the language of skepticism for their successful speech of protest. Why indeed should a man's name be lost *from the midst* of his family? His property should be given to his daughters, *in the midst* of his brothers. They emphasize their father's place within a social world, which represents a world of meaning. They speak as the only possible claimants and executives of their father's rights within a patriarchal society.

However, in spite of their assertive tone, these five sisters express no feminist aspirations. Even to describe them as "five sisters" is, in a sense, to skew the biblical presentation: they are *daughters* of a man, of a line of men, father and son; in the name of the father, of reason and order, they seek a place *within* the family, the clan, and the tribe. And yet, surprisingly, their names are listed, a female roll call. And the fact that they are five—counterbalancing their five illustrious ancestors—also has an ambiguous effect. Neither heroic individuals nor exactly a group, they speak without obvious leadership.[4] As sisters, they are neither identical nor fully differentiated. Does this diminish the impact of their dignity and courage? Or does it add gravitas to their position? Speaking with one voice, forming, as it were, their own female society, how do they affect the reader?

The reference to their father's sin is also mysterious: he did *not* belong to Korach's faction. The negative description seeks to exonerate him from having participated in Korach's rebellion; he died for a purely personal sin, which is never specified. Perhaps his daughters fear that Moses may be prejudiced against them if their father was party to that rebellion that was directed against the leadership of Moses and Aaron? On this reading, the women are aware of possible bias that needs to be neutralized.

In other words, they have a realistic sense of the political field in which they must stake their claim. A similar awareness informs the Zohar's explanation of Moses' referring the case to God (Num. 27:5): he recuses himself from the case, to avoid any suspicion of prejudice against Tzelofchad as a rebel against Moses' leadership. Here, again, is a reminder that truth is to be found within a force field of political power.

According to the *Concise Science Dictionary,* a field is a "region in which a body experiences a force as the result of the presence of some other body or bodies. A field is thus a method of representing the way in which bodies influence each other."[5] The field in which the women stand and speak is one in which passion may plausibly play a role, if only in the attempts of the protagonists to ward off suspicion. Justice must be seen to be done. The legal principle that registers the significance of this awareness derives from a biblical verse: "You shall be clear before God and *before Israel*" (Num. 32:22).

IMPLICIT TENSIONS

Against this background, let us look at Rashi's comments on God's accolade to the sisters:

> "And Moses brought their case before God": The law on this subject escaped him (*B.Sanhedrin* 8a). Here, he received punishment because he had assumed a "crown" (he had set himself as the supreme judge) by saying, "The case that is too hard for you bring to me" (Deut. 1:17). Another explanation: This chapter should have been written by Moses; but the daughters of Tzelofchad merited to have it written by them.[6]
>
> "The daughters of Tzelofchad speak right": Read the word *ken* as the Targum does: *ya-ut*—rightly, properly. God said: Exactly so is this chapter written before Me on high.[7] This tells us that their eye saw what Moses' eye did not see.[8]
>
> "The daughters of Tzelofchad speak right": They have made a fair claim. Happy is the person with whose words God agrees![9]

Why does Moses take the case immediately to God? The simplest answer is, Because he could not answer it himself: the law eluded him, was *hidden—nit'alma*—from him. This fit of forgetting is a punishment for the tone of superiority in Moses' long-ago words, in which he seemed to set himself up as the ultimate authority on the law. (It is striking that *takrivun*—"you shall bring to me"—is the same expression used in our narrative of the "approach" of the sisters to Moses for a legal decision.)

But there is another possibility: in this case, Moses loses the privilege of "having the Torah written through him"—"by his hand"—directly. Instead, the five sisters are granted that privilege; they are the catalysts of a page in Torah—in a sense, they are accredited with its authorship. To author is to initiate, to authorize, to assume responsibility. To have a section of Torah written through one's agency is a privilege that the women, in this case, take over from Moses. The sense of an implicit tension between Moses and the five sisters—his loss is their gain—is carried over into the next passage. "Their eye saw what Moses' eye did not see."

The theme of tension between Moses and the five sisters is, perhaps surprisingly, to be found in many midrashic sources. For instance, in *Midrash Rabbah*,[10] the women refuse to marry anyone who is not appropriate (*hagun*) for them. God brings the women into Moses' field so as to chasten any pride he might take in his own sexual abstinence. By force of their very being, they bring a moral perspective that in a sense makes Moses' self-control less remarkable.

Even more eloquently, the following section in the midrash[11] relates another version of the story about the law that is hidden from Moses. It eludes him (*hifli mimenu*). In the end, God charges him with hubris in his declaration, "What is too hard for you, bring to me!" And then God seemingly taunts Moses: "The law that you don't know, women discuss it!" The sarcasm slights Moses with its implication of *"Even* women . . ." This is, at least, the obvious way to read the midrash, again implying tension between Moses and the sisters. And yet, as we shall see later, there is another possibility: without sarcasm, God may be making a factual observation about the difference between Moses' vision and theirs.

TRUTH AND BEAUTY

God responds, *Ken;* strikingly, Rashi translates (after the Targum) *ya'ut*—rightly, properly—*exactly so* is this chapter written on high. The women have achieved an exact simulacrum of the ideal version written before God. This achievement, suggests Malbim, extends to the whole narrative framework—not just to the legal plea. All—the women's courage, their approach to the court, the way in which they live their moment—is "already written" before God on high. Follow-

ing the Sifre, he reads *ken* to suggest that God shows Moses his original version to demonstrate the rightness of the women's narrative.
It is a fine work of art; their story is just as it should be. The women's
speech is, one might say, the "happiest" act of *dibbur* in the book of
Bamidbar—the book of speakings and misspeakings.[12] It is as though,
quite simply, God can at last draw breath and say, *Ken!—Yes!*

This kind of fineness borders on the aesthetic. Indeed, Rashi's two
translations of *ken—ya'ut* and *yaffeh*—relate to beauty. He represents
this fine rightness as a matter of the eye: their eye saw what Moses'
eye did not see. Again, Moses and the sisters are placed in tension
with each other.[13] In some way, Moses' eye fails. And God celebrates
the felicitousness of the women's vision; He finds it beautiful. In
English, too, rightness and beauty meet in such expressions as nice,
fine, and fair. In his last sentence Rashi modulates God's aesthetic
acclaim—*ken!*—to the key of happiness: "Happy [*ashrei*] is the person
with whose words God agrees!" When God is in accord with one's
words, that is happiness! Here, Rashi interprets the exclamation *Ken!*
as both reporting the sisters' happiness and generating it.

The philosopher Elaine Scarry notes that the English word "fairness," which refers both to beauty and to the ethical requirement
of *being fair,* has traveled "from a cluster of roots in European languages (Old English, Old Norse, Gothic), as well as cognates in both
Eastern European and Sanskrit, that all originally express the aesthetic use of 'fair' to mean 'beautiful' or 'fit'—fit both in the sense
of 'pleasing to the eye' and in the sense of 'firmly placed,' as when
something matches or exists in accord with another thing's shape
or size."[14] Scarry argues that features of physical beauty, like symme-
try and equality, "act as a lever in the direction of justice."[15] "Beautiful things . . . hold steadily visible the manifest good of equality and
balance."[16]

In our story, Rashi reads God's accolade, "*Ken dovrot*—They speak
fairly," to suggest a similar pact between the aesthetic and the ethical. God acknowledges a perfect accord between the sisters' speech
and His script. *Ken* is *Kach*—Exactly so!; their words are aestheti-
cally and ethically pleasing. Rashi's lyrical conclusion celebrates
the felicity of those who speak so felicitously. Citing the Sifre, he
extrapolates from this narrative and opens up a new possibility for
human happiness: "Happy is the person with whose words God is in

accord!"[17] Here, Rashi goes beyond his usual brief. This is no longer commentary on the text: it is exhortation, creating a climate of aspiration. Rashi has made a personal appearance in his text; suddenly, he projects an imaginative world that he offers to his readers. What would it mean to fulfill this possibility?

The word *ashrei*, "happy," derives from a root meaning "going straight," "setting right," "on sure footing." This happiness is well grounded, stable; it is the experience of one who speaks *ken*—which also refers to stability. Speaking in a way that coincides with God's version of things generates true happiness. Both words, *ken* and *ashrei*, come together in Psalms 40:3, where the Psalmist praises God for stabilizing him in this way: "He lifted me out of the miry pit, the slimy clay, and set my feet on a rock, steadied my legs. He put a new song into my mouth. . . ." "He steadied my legs"—*Konen ashurai*—the two words are set on their firm common ground. Rashi evokes the emotional satisfaction of one who has found this ground of accord with the divine. Redemption now means finding a new song in one's mouth.

But what constitutes this state of accord? How might one experience this kind of happiness, short of hearing a heavenly voice proclaiming it? It is not, I suggest, that there exists a single, ideal utterance that one is called on to approximate. Only after the fact is the achievement of the daughters of Tzelofchad celebrated in this way. Wherein lies the exquisite felicity of their words?

TWO VIEWS OF GREATNESS

"The daughters of Tzelofchad came forward" (Num. 27:1): This was greatness for them and greatness for their father; greatness also for Machir as well as for Joseph, that such women came forth from them. They were wise and righteous women. What was their wisdom? They spoke at the appropriate moment, for Moses was engaged upon the subject of inheritances, saying: "Among these the land shall be divided" (26:53). They said to him: "If we have the status of a son let us inherit like a son; if not, let our mother perform the levirate marriage." Immediately, "Moses brought their case before God" (27:5).[18]

The midrash reverses our expectations: these women bring glory to their distinguished ancestors. They are wise, righteous: these terms, applied usually to men, are now inflected in the feminine form. In fact, they become classic epithets for the sisters, along with a third epithet: *darshaniyot*—expounders of textual meaning—this last term being the most unexpected praise for women. But this midrash aims to define their wisdom, grounding it in their fine sense of timing—*l'fi sha'ah dibru:* they spoke at the appropriate moment. Their wisdom, then, implies a kind of tact, a sense of decorum, of boundaries, which allows their plea to gain a hearing from Moses at just this moment.

This pragmatic wisdom characterizes the content as well as the timing of their intervention, and ensures its success. Their argument is cogent, well within the genre of such legal arguments: if they are considered their father's seed—"like sons"—they should inherit; or if their father left no seed, let their mother conceive from her dead husband's brother. Their reasoning gives them the title of *darshaniyot:* they know how to draw meaning from the text,[19] while their *chochmah*, their wisdom, teaches them when to speak and when not to speak. They have a case only in the present circumstances, where there are no male heirs: *l'fi sha'ah*, in accord with the reality of the moment, they plead their cause.

Another midrash, however, takes a different view of the greatness of these women. Also addressing the issue of time, this midrash makes a more radical claim:

These women rose up in the generation of the wilderness and merited to take the reward of all of them. This teaches you *at what moment* they stood before Moses—at the moment that Israel were saying, Let us appoint a leader and return to Egypt! Moses said, But Israel are demanding to return to Egypt, and you demand an inheritance in the Land! They answered, We know that in the end all Israel will claim their share in the Land; as it is said, "It is a time to act for God—they have transgressed Your Torah!" Don't read like this; read "They have transgressed Your Torah in acting for God!" . . . Where there is no man, try to be a man![20]

Here, the sisters' fine timing is expressed in their speaking against the grain of current prejudice. When the people are hankering to return to Egypt, these women affirm their desire for the Land. Their plea expresses more than its minimal meaning—"We want to be considered our father's heirs!" It also represents their love for the Land of Israel, an unfashionable love at that time.

But the midrash goes far in expressing the provocative force of the women's voice. *"It is a time to act for God"* has become an aphorism that carries a double meaning: When the Torah is being transgressed, this is the moment to act for God; but also "When it is time to act for God, one may even transgress Torah commandments." Here, the women transgress no formal commandments. But, inspired by the energy of loving conviction, they speak against the status quo of legal understanding. They speak with a fierce serenity. They represent an emergency ethic. Their passion becomes a paradigm for all human courage in the face of conformity.

"Where there is no man, try to be a man!" Of course, the midrashic authors are fully aware of the shock effect of this aphorism as applied to women.[21] Unmistakably gendered, "Try to be a man, a *gever*" evokes masculine might (*gevurah*) as the aspiration—and achievement—of these women. For a moment, the reader is jarred; the boundaries of gender slip.

If we look more closely at this midrash, the particular quality of the sisters' nonconformity emerges. Moses himself is astonished to hear such a different voice: "Everyone else wants to return to Egypt, and you desire inheritance in the Land!" The proof text refers to the narrative of the Spies, as though that was the historical moment of the women's declaration. However, the Spies' narrative took place in the second year in the wilderness, while Tzelofchad's daughters make their claim in the fortieth year. How then can the midrash claim that the women's speech is a direct response to the early rebellion? Pushing against obvious chronology, the midrash extends the meaning of *sha'ah*: the *moment* of the Spies' revolt remains the emotional moment of that "wilderness generation," even into the second generation. From start to finish, an emotional and spiritual undertow draws them back to Egypt. In the face of this, the women speak.

Here, then, to speak at the right moment is to speak precisely at the *wrong* moment. It is to speak without the support of conventional frameworks; to speak at the particular historical moment when one's speech will resound uncannily—when it may create change.

THE MOMENT OF EMERGENCE

This midrashic reading takes the daughters of Tzelofchad one step into the "masculine" world of *gevurah,* of the struggle against the stream as both an external and an internal struggle. In a different time and place, Ralph Waldo Emerson writes of the moment of self-creation, in which one authors oneself. In his essay "Self-Reliance," he describes it as the moment of *becoming:* "This one fact the world hates; that the soul *becomes.*"[22] Before this moment, the individual is, in a sense, uncreated: Emerson calls this state "conformity." Descartes's description of existence, "I think, therefore I am," becomes in Emerson's thought the continuing challenge to *say* "I am":

> Man is timid and apologetic; he is *no longer upright;* he *dares not say "I think," "I am,"* but quotes some saint or sage. He is ashamed before the blade of grass or the blowing rose . . . they are for what they are; they exist with God today.[23]

In conformity, the cringing posture of an individual prevents him from acknowledging his true existence. As the philosopher Stanley Cavell puts it, "I am a being who to exist must *say* I exist, or must acknowledge my existence—claim it, stake it, enact it."[24] The aim of such an existence is "not a state of being, but a moment of change."

Against a life of skepticism—of "world-consuming doubt"—Cavell, in Emerson's name, advocates the upright posture. The "life-giving power of words, of saying 'I,' is your readiness to subject your desire to words . . . to become intelligible, with no assurance that you will be taken up."[25] "You never know when someone will learn the posture, as for themselves, that will make sense of a field of movement, it may be writing, or dancing, or passing a ball, or sitting at a keyboard, or free associating."[26]

Good posture, it turns out, is the posture that allows one to create one's existence by performing it within a particular force field. One's ability to learn this is mysterious. After all the regulations have been

absorbed, there comes a moment when a new world falls into proper
focus.

The daughters of Tzelofchad come upon this moment when they
speak within the complex force field that constitutes their world.
They find their always-untimely, always-timely moment of "I am."
Not just their legal plea, but their whole narrative is, Malbim asserts,
"written before God on high." Beyond their legal astuteness, beyond
their tactical sense of timing, there is their primal, idiosyncratic passion. In a climate of ongoing skepticism—the climate of the Book
of the Wilderness—in which faith, trust, and love are constantly
challenged, these women speak, breathe a different language. In a
moment of emergency, they emerge from the swarm of life. Without assurance that they will be heard, they allow themselves to be
known.

Cavell writes: "'No one comes' is a tragedy for a child. For a
grown-up it means that the time has come to be the one who goes
first."[27] The daughters of Tzelofchad represent this form of adulthood or, as the midrash describes it, *gevurah*—the "masculine" self-
assertion that is self-conquest.

THE LANGUAGE OF DESIRE

"The daughters of Tzelofchad speak *ken*": the sisters' act of *dibbur* is
timely in yet another sense. According to the Talmud, at this same
historical moment, the word of God returns to Moses after a thirty-
eight-year hiatus:

> "And it was when all the men of war had ceased dying, God
> spoke to me": But from the narrative of the Spies till this point
> the expression *va-yidabber* is never used, but *va-yomer*—to
> teach you that all those thirty-eight years when Israel were
> in disfavor, the divine *dibbur* never addressed Moses—in the
> mode of affection, of a face-to-face encounter, and of tranquil
> communication. This teaches that God's presence rests on the
> prophets only for the sake of Israel.[28]

The word *dibbur* has been absent from the text since the sin of
the Spies, whose skepticism was so effective in undermining the

people's trust. World-consuming doubt wracks them during the long wilderness years, a melancholy that saps their ability to speak or to hear the language of love, intimacy, composure. Since Moses is deeply connected with his people, God addresses him, during these years, only in the muted tones of *amirah*—saying.

The new epoch of *dibbur* that begins at this point restores the possibility, particularly, of *chibah*, loving communication face-to-face. Both as presence and as absence, *dibbur* courses through the narrative of the *midbar,* the wilderness. At the beginning of the book, we read, "And God spoke [*va-yidabber*] to Moses in the *midbar,* in the wilderness of Sinai" (Num. 1:1). What is the quality of God's language? Again, Rashi treats it as an expression of *chibah:* "Because they were *dear* to Him, He counted them every now and then." The census, which is the first commandment in the book, represents tenderness, affection, familiarity—the gentler aspects of love connoted by *chibah*. Again, Rashi associates the full act of speech with a kind of mirroring intimacy—face-to-face, tranquil. This mode of relation vanishes and now again reappears.

On the surface of the text, the transitions—the loss and return of *dibbur*—go unnoticed. But for the Rabbis, who sense the secret pulse of life in the text, an ebb and flow has occurred. In this new period, *chibah* is restored. Perhaps God's command to Moses to *speak* to the rock evokes something of this old/new ethos. After so many losses, Moses and the people must again learn to put desire into language, without violence, and without the assurance of being heard.

At the turning point of the narrative, God enacts with Moses the new way of speaking: "Take Aaron and his son Eleazar and bring them up on Mount Hor. There Aaron shall be gathered unto the dead" (Num. 20:25–26). How is Moses to "take" Aaron to his death?

"Take Aaron": With consoling words. Tell him: *Happy are you* that you will see your crown passed on to your son, which I am not privileged to see![29]

One *takes* a human being with words: Moses is to speak words that will shift Aaron from his sadness to another way of thinking. "Happy are you [*ashrecha*] that your son inherits your legacy, unlike me!" *Ashrecha* is an example of a performative speech act. The word does not merely describe, it acts. It creates in language an alternative world, in which a different happiness becomes imaginable. It renames reality so that the unacceptable changes its color. Only in this way can one move another human being. By reframing Aaron's reality, Moses "takes" him to the mountaintop.

A similar usage occurs soon after the episode of Tzelofchad's daughters. Moses is told: "Take Joshua, and appoint him your successor." Again, Rashi comments: "Take him with words: Happy are you [*ashrecha*] that you are privileged to lead God's children!" (Num. 27:18).

Here, too, Moses is to move Joshua to a new ground of happiness. He invites him to contemplate leadership of a troublesome people from a different perspective. "Happy are you!" His words are to do the work of transformation.

In these and in many other cases of such "takings," a realistic expectation of death and sadness is to be transfigured by imaginative words. When a human being is to be "taken," Rashi often glosses the word in this way. A striking example is God's taking Adam and placing him in the Garden of Eden: "He took him with beautiful words and seduced [*pitahu*] him to enter the Garden" (Rashi to Gen. 2:15). Seduction, with its complex range of associations, recurs in Rashi's translation of such moments of "taking." For better and for worse, language has the power of captivating the other, moving him to unthought perspectives. To say *Ashrei!* particularly, is to recount experience; to create a vocabulary of transfiguration.

We remember Rashi's lyrical outburst: "Happy [*ashrei*] is the person with whose words God is in accord!" Here, too, *Ashrei!* acts as a performative—"The happiness of it!" It creates a confrontation of old and new values. And it brings onto the scene the voice of a speaker who creates this new perspective. In this case, the speaker is Rashi, or his midrashic forebear, who inflects the more limited meaning of the narrative. This is, in itself, an act of full speech, which the speaker implicitly hopes will be acknowledged by God.

In a sense, then, to say *Ashrei!* about a happy use of words is to wish happiness for oneself as well as the other. To find one's voice is to transform both speaker and other, to open up a register of tenderness, intimacy, and tranquil communication. When Rashi exclaims *Ashrei,* he is, in effect, extending his commentary on the word *ken:* in celebrating the women's language, God is Himself exclaiming *Ashrei!* The reader is initiated into a divine aspiration.

ON SLIPPERY GROUND

We have noticed that both *ashrei* and *ken* refer at root to stability, to the well-grounded step. In modern Hebrew, *l'asher* is to substantiate, verify, give strength, authorize. The peculiar strength of the *ashrei* usage is that in most cases the speaker speaks against the grain, in defiance of the commonsense view of stability. Why else would such a proclamation be necessary? "Happy is the man who has not followed the counsel of the wicked!" (Ps. 1:1); "Happy is the man who is always afraid!" (Prov. 28:14); "It is a tree of life to those who grasp it, and whoever holds to it is happy" (Prov. 3:18); "Her children rise up and declare her happy" (Prov. 31:28); "He lifted me out of the miry pit.... He steadied my legs. He put a new song in my mouth.... Happy is the man who makes God his trust!" (Ps. 40:3–5). *Ashrei!* holds a provocative power: it steadies one's steps with uncanny firmness in a world of slimy clay. Precisely in conditions of instability, an alternative stability is conjured—by a word.

At the end of his life, Moses blesses the people, and ends: "Happy are you, O Israel! Who is like you, a people delivered by God!" (Deut. 33:29). Again, Rashi gives great weight to *Ashrecha!*—"After Moses had given them the detailed blessings, he said, 'Why should I go into detail? *All is yours!* [*K'lal davar—Ha-kol shelachem!*]'" Moses leaves his people, not with specific blessings, but with a vision of fullness. Against the realities of their situation—about to lose their leader and teacher, facing a difficult war of conquest—he creates for them at one stroke the plenitude of *Ashrecha!*

Ashrei! resounds throughout the book of Psalms. The Talmud declares about one occasion when the Psalmist both begins and ends a Psalm with *Ashrei!*: "Every chapter of Psalms that was particularly cherished [*chaviv*] by David he began and ended with *Ashrei!*"[30] David's speech act is an expression of tenderness, doubly affirming the power of his own words. A situation where one's foot slips on the miry ground becomes a scene of salvation, of blessed grounding; *Ashrei!* itself sings the new song[31] in which a precious-precarious stability is affirmed. Suddenly, one is wholly present again.

STUMBLING AND STANDING

Perhaps we can go further. It is *only* in the act of falling, of failing, that such speech-acts become meaningful. In discussing the philosopher J. L. Austin's theory of the performative speech act, Shoshana Felman notes: "The capacity for misfire is an inherent capacity of the performative . . . the act as such is defined, for Austin, as the capacity to *miss its goal* and to *fail to be achieved,* to remain *unconsummated,* to *fall short* of its own accomplishment."[32] Uttering the formula of the marriage ceremony incorrectly, or if one is married already, would be an example of such a misfire. The utterance would then be void, without effect. In its subtler form, Felman argues, such a failure could be caused by a slip of the tongue, demonstrating "the human aptitude for fiasco."[33] Like a miner's lamp, in Austin's famous image, human intention illuminates only in a limited way: "It will never extend indefinitely far ahead."[34] In this image of the play of light and shadow, Felman suggests, Austin may be acknowledging the effect of the unconscious on the speaking body.

To speak in this transformative way is always to risk failure: this is the precarious reach of the *Ashrei!* language. Like the miner's lamp, it probes the dark with a stark, bravely playful light. The play of light and shadow constitutes its affirmation. *Ashrei! enjoys itself,* while knowing that it may fail to persuade. It may misfire; its beauty (the beautiful words that seek, according to Rashi, to seduce) may miss its mark.

Even so, even when the act is "infelicitous," as Austin puts it, its performance may still bring a "slippery" kind of pleasure. Slipping and sliding play an important role in language: "We may hope to learn something . . . about the meanings of some English words . . . philosophically *very slippery.*"[35] "We have discussed the performative utterance and its infelicities. That equips us . . . with two *shining new skids* under our metaphysical feet."[36] "'Vainly I strive against it,' writes Kierkegaard. 'My foot slips. My life is still a poet's existence.' The seduction of slipping is thus the seduction of poetry, of the *poetic* functioning of language."[37] "I must explain again that we are floundering here. To feel the firm ground of prejudice slipping away is exhilarating, but brings its revenges."[38]

The Talmud offers an aphorism that conveys its own version

of this notion of blessed slipping. "One never stands firmly on the words of Torah unless one has stumbled over them."³⁹ Error, failure, stumbling, slipping become the condition for stability. Only so, in such dismaying, exhilarating lurches, are prejudices transcended and a piece of Torah is *understood*.

To expose oneself to the slips of language is, undoubtedly, to move beyond the world of conformity. Here is the vertigo of lost footing, the instant fear of falling. Here, too, is poetry, humor, exhilaration. Here, one renounces playing God. And here, paradoxically, one may become aware of God acknowledging one's words; one may come to hear an *Ashrei!* ringing through them.

PAUL CELAN'S HEBREW WORD

The word *Ashrei!* endures its most testing moment in the poetry of Paul Celan. In 1966, Celan wrote a long poem called "Aschrei," writing the word in transliterated German. Now, he says, this is a "word without meaning." In a Europe where no Jewish community remains, what meaning can the word have? The word is quite literally *meaningless* to its German readers. Perhaps, as literary scholar John Felstiner suggests, Jewish readers will hear in it *a schrei*, "a scream" in Yiddish. Or, as he goes on to remark, we may remember "that in prewar Jewish prayer books, the German for *Aschrei* (in the sense of 'hale') was *Heil*."⁴⁰

The sarcasm of the *ashrei* word in such a world is lacerating. Celan writes of the "torn strings of a strident and discordant harp."⁴¹ His language is petrified, "a language of stone," he says. And yet, as Felstiner finely puts it: "Leaving Celan's Hebrew intact in English [as Celan did in the German (AZ)] preserves a communal bond against the muting of the Nazi years." In other words, the word still "does something"; it works, however ambiguously, against the silence. Felstiner soberly attests that in reading Celan, he has "felt a grim energy verging on elation. . . . Is elation akin to something the poet knew?"⁴²

COAUTHORING GOD'S TEXT

The daughters of Tzelofchad are celebrated by God for having reaffirmed God's original text on high. The unprecedented compliment transfigures an act that has taken place in the human field of uncertainty. The women speak without assurance of being taken up; the possibility of slipping and failing is inherent in their act. What prevents other speeches recorded in this book from attaining the high acclaim that God now accords these women?

Beyond the women's legal acumen, there is the question of *posture:* it is a matter of *how one stands* and moves within the field. As Cavell says, "You never know when someone will learn the posture, as for themselves, that will make sense of a field of movement."[43] It is hard to know how such learning happens. One might say of the Israelites in the wilderness that a habit of poor posture, a kind of *automaticity,* haunts all the complaints and hatreds of the people. Somehow, the women have learned how to shake off shrill voices, how to stand and how to move, as for themselves. This involves overcoming the rigidities of everyday life.

"They speak *ken,*" says God. Precisely at a moment of personal loss and instability, they dare to question the given world. But their skeptical question penetrates to another possibility. Their *Why?* implicitly envisions a "happier" world. If one speaks, in the full sense, one feels the firm ground of prejudice, of certainty, slipping away. When God congratulates them on the happy infelicity of their words, He, too, invokes a different kind of rightness.

The sisters speak in such a way as to *author* a passage in the Torah. Through them, and not through Moses, this passage in the Torah is written. Their instrumentality is necessary. To have a portion of Torah written "by one's hand" is to play on the edge of the notion of authorship. The traditional understanding is that Moses "took dictation" of the Torah text from God. But in this case, the midrash clearly implies some measure of direct involvement—whether by Moses, or by the five sisters. The hand by which Torah is written is privileged; the life of the writer has played a role in the creation of the text.

To be an author is to authorize something, to redeem it from muteness. From the Latin *auctor,* it means to validate a title, to ratify, to supplement and actualize something else that needs strengthening. As the European philosopher Giorgio Agamben puts it, "The act of the *auctor* completes the act of an incapable person, giving strength of proof to what in itself lacks it and granting life to what could not live alone. It can conversely be said . . . that the imperfect act completes and gives meaning to the word of the *auctor*-witness."[44]

In Hebrew, *Ashrei!* contains some of the same meanings as the Latin *auctor:* to validate, corroborate, affirm, authorize. To declare *Ashrei!* is to legitimize the other, to complete and give meaning to him. The daughters of Tzelofchad have their meanings amplified by God's words: *Ken dovrot*—"They speak with a just beauty, so as to realize My transcendent text on high." By saying *ken,* God supplements the power of the women's words. But similarly, one might say, by speaking as they do, by enacting their own existence in God's presence, the women give force to God's text on high. Through the prism of *ken,* the Creator and His creatures give life and authorship to one another.

ACQUIRING ONE'S WORLD

In such moments of change, a whole world may be brought into focus. "One may acquire/create one's world in one instant." In the Talmud, we find a cluster of stories that enact this axiom. In the best-known of these stories, a notorious libertine, Eleazar ben Dordia, suddenly and inexplicably[45] conceives the desire to change his life.[46] He beseeches mountains and hills, heaven and earth, sun and moon, to beg God for mercy. Finally, he realizes, "It depends only on me"; he puts his head between his knees and bellows in tears until his soul leaves him. A heavenly voice cries out, R. Eleazar ben Dordia is welcome into the life of the world to come! "On hearing of it, Rabbi (R. Yehuda Ha-Nassi) wept: "One may acquire one's world [eternal life] over many years, or one may acquire it *in one instant*! He added: Is it not sufficient that penitents are accepted, but they are also called Rabbi!"

Rabbi, the compiler of the Mishnah, the quintessential rabbinical figure, is deeply agitated, to the point of tears, by the notion of acquiring eternal life *in one instant*. The lives of the Rabbis, the sages of the Mishnah and the Talmud, stand as paradigms of spiritual work performed "over many years." How outrageous that the lifelong sensualist can access eternal life—acquire his world—in one instant of sacrificial passion! And, to top it all, to be welcomed into that world precisely as "Rabbi!" Both Rabbi and penitent weep; one deploring such a possibility—but in effect acknowledging it—the other soliciting it with his whole being.

Many centuries later, the nineteenth-century Hasidic master Sefat Emet,[47] sets this fraught paradox by the side of another statement about "the world": "Everyone has a world that is his alone." He cites a view that the word *olam*, the world, is linked with the notion of *he'alem*, of hiddenness. Every person has a specific form of *obscurity*, of resistance, that (s)he is challenged to confront in the world.[48] Eternal life, one's personal world, is created by the way in which one struggles to engage with this blind spot. "These are the struggles of human beings all their days in this world." The world that one creates is primarily constituted by one's confrontation with *he'alem*, with that which baffles and eludes one in this world. Imagination is required for this struggle. Only then can one speak of eternal life.

Acquiring one's world, then, involves "coming forward" and "standing": finding the movement and posture that makes sense of the field of this world. For the daughters of Tzelofchad, this means standing against the pressures of the field, against the resistances, external and internal, that are intended specifically for them. The question of creating a world is ultimately a question of enacting one's existence, of *being created*, of acknowledging one's place in the world. "To be or not to be, that is the question," says Hamlet: whether to be born, "whether to affirm or deny the fact of natality, as a way of enacting, or not, one's existence."[49] This means finding the posture that will allow them to stand up for an obscure love.

THE EMERGING ORDER

If the daughters of Tzelofchad have gained the felicity of such a moment, Rashi immediately transfers this possibility to the reader: "Happy is the person with whose words God is in accord!" On a different plane, in the Torah text, God declares the law in this particular case, and then declares it as a precedent for all future generations: "You shall *transfer* their father's share to them. Further, speak to the Israelites as follows: If a man dies without leaving a son, you shall *transfer* his property to his daughter . . ." (Num. 27:7–8).

The unusual expression, "You shall *transfer—ve-ha'avarta*—his inheritance," is repeated in the text. Rashi explains: "The expression *ha'avarah* applies to one who dies without a male heir. Another explanation: daughters *transfer* [*me'aberet*] the inheritance from tribe to tribe."

Citing *B.Baba Batra* 109a, Rashi links female inheritance with the idea of transferral. If a daughter inherits, the land goes with her when she marries. It adheres to her husband and to his tribe. Female inheritance, therefore, takes the ground out from under the stable division of the Land among the tribes. "Daughters transfer land": in effect, the feminine represents a fluid, even a *slippery* possibility. The firm ground of law slides away under their feet. Daughter becomes wife; and the land is lost to the tribe.[50] In spite of this, God ratifies the law of daughters' inheritance for future generations. He even calls it *ken*—as though, in its very instability, it establishes a different kind of grounding.

In a complex teaching, Sefat Emet[51] addresses the "slippery" quality that seems to characterize the feminine principle. If women are the vehicles of *transferral*, of *transition*, even in the case of something as stable as land, perhaps they embody the notion of a kind of *translation* principle?

The Hasidic master weaves into his text another use of the root *a-v-r* that occurs soon after: God tells Moses, "Ascend this Mountain of *Avarim*—of Transitions" (Num. 27:12). Transitions haunt this section of the Torah. Joshua is initiated into his new role as substitute for Moses. Moses lays (*ve-samachta*) hands on him in the presence of the whole community and invests him with some of his own authority (27:18–20). This laying on of hands—*semichah*—will in later generations characterize the conferral of rabbinic authority. At this moment, however, *semichah* means the transmission, the transfer of some of Moses' power, his *hod*—his radiance of authorship—to Joshua.

The Sages compare Moses to the sun and Joshua to the moon: Joshua receives all of his light from his master Moses.[52] In this sense, suggests Sefat Emet, Joshua can be seen as embodying the energy of the Oral Law, which draws on the Written Law, represented by Moses. The laying on of hands (*semichah*) relates, by a play on words, to the legal decisions that the Rabbis deduce from the written text (*asmachtot*).

A new epoch begins; the trajectory of the Oral Law emerges here. Sefat Emet associates the feminine principle with this movement into interpretation of given texts. What transpires in this section of the Torah is the transmission of Moses' Torah—the sun, the original source—to Joshua—the moon, representing the energy of the feminine, which receives and procreates. The law of inheritance, newly written "by the hand" of women, evokes the mythic notion of a movement from the age of the masculine to the age of the feminine. Now, in the time of Joshua, those who enter the Land will have their daughters inherit, when there are no male heirs. And women, as we have seen, shift boundaries: they transfer, translate, reframe realities.

This new ethos—initially disruptive of the status quo—is greeted by God with enthusiasm. It represents the movement and proliferation of genes and memes; it involves substitutions, metaphors, performative speech acts. Radically, it involves the creative imagination, which speaks the given world into transfigured being. What at first blush seemed infelicitous is now declared happy.

Most strikingly, Sefat Emet suggests that the shift from a masculine modality to a feminine one explains why this law of feminine inheritance is *hidden* from Moses. In answering the women's case, Moses finds himself at a disadvantage. He is unable to "see" the law that the women see so justly. Without sarcasm, Sefat Emet reads this midrash with a new lucidity: "The law that you don't know, the women frame," God tells Moses. The women see from a feminine perspective, which is the emerging order of the world. Your time is receding, God tells Moses. This moment is *for them:* it offers them an opportunity to enact their own existence, to *go first.* It represents their unique struggle to acquire their world.

But we may say, in another sense, that this moment is also for Moses. This is his moment of *he'alem,* of hiddenness, of blockage. Such moments of challenge, resistance, constitute the world of an individual. At this moment, when the law is hidden from him—the sun is, as it were, in eclipse—Moses knows that indeed he will not enter the Land. Here begins the regime of the Oral Law, signaled by the daughters of Tzelofchad, who embody the "moon" principle, carrying interpretations to full term.[53] The Sages will *author* Torah, completing and fulfilling what Moses has implanted in the world. Here, multiple interpretations, wordplays, slippages, will create networks of meaning. Moses, his face suffused with the light of God's word, is to ascend the Mount of Transitions, of translations and transmissions, and to contemplate this future.

In concrete terms, he will ascend Mount Nevo, months in the future, to look his first and last time on the Land. But for now, suggests Sefat Emet, it is the very experience of transition, the transference of masculine to feminine, that he must undergo. In this sense, the tension that the midrash traces between Moses and the daughters of Tzelofchad represents the turning point between the world in which Moses has acted until now—the world of miracles and revelations—and the world of his successors. A "feminine" epoch of passages, and translations, and fertile slippages of language will constantly reimagine the Torah of Sinai. For Moses, this paradoxically is the moment when he confronts his own blind spot and acquires his own world.

ELEVEN

"Let Me See That Good Land": The Story of a Human Life

SEVENTY LANGUAGES

In Jewish tradition, Moses is known as Moses our Teacher—*Moshe rabbenu*. Expressing the quintessential relationship between Moses and the Jewish people, the Hebrew term evokes respect and affection, a kind of living intimacy.

The irony is that, from the beginning of the narrative, Moses questions his own ability to transmit God's messages. Passionately, he protests against the role of speaker-intermediary that God has imposed on him. When he describes himself as "heavy of mouth, and heavy of tongue," as "of uncircumcised lips," he reveals a profoundly personal dimension of his life—perhaps the only information we receive about his inner life. Speaking of his language inhibition, he speaks of the interior of his mouth and of his difficulty in engaging with the world.

In the book of Deuteronomy, he speaks in a new way, reaching out to his listeners—and to his future readers—in the mode of *teaching*. Skeptical of his power to affect them, Moses stages for his students new teaching possibilities that are generated, I suggest, precisely by his inhibition.

Teaching, Freud declared, is the "impossible profession." Moses comes to confront that impossibility and to speak a language charged with unexpected force. The poetical power of a language that is not entirely transparent to itself—that reaches through ignorance and beyond it—comes to create the very possibility of teaching and of healing.[1]

The opening to language originates *in the wilderness*, even though its first manifestation is in the first verse of Deuteronomy: "These are the words that Moses spoke to all Israel on the other side of the Jordan, *in the wilderness*. . . ." In fact, says the midrash, it is the wilderness that generates the explosion of language that he experiences in the last months of his life:

> "These are the words that Moses spoke to the children of Israel": Israel said: Just yesterday you said, "I am not a man of words," and now you have so much to say! R. Yitzhak said: If you have a speech impediment, learn Torah and you will be healed! Moses had learned the whole Torah *"in the wilderness on the plains facing the Red Sea."* That is why it is written, "Then the lame shall leap like a deer, and the tongue of the mute shall exult" (Isa. 35:6).
>
> Come and see: When God told Moses, "Go on my mission to Pharaoh," Moses replied, "You do me wrong! I am not a man of words! Seventy languages are spoken in Pharaoh's palace, so that wherever a visitor comes from he is addressed in his own language. Now, if I go on Your mission, they will interrogate me, and when they find that I claim to be Your emissary and yet I am unable to speak freely with them, will they not mock me: 'Look at God's emissary who does not know how to discourse in all the seventy languages of the world!' You do me wrong! I am not a man of words! I am of uncircumcised lips!" Then God answered him: "But how did Adam, who had no teacher, learn seventy languages?—as it is said, 'He called them names' (Gen. 2:19)—not one name for each animal but *names* [seventy names]! And yet you say, 'I am not a man of words!'"
>
> Forty years after leaving Egypt, Moses began to interpret the Torah in seventy languages—"He explained [*ba'er*] this Torah" (Deut. 1:5). The mouth that had said, "I am not a man of words," now spoke "these [are the] words." And the prophet cried out: "Then shall the lame leap like a deer and the tongue of the mute shall sing aloud!" (Isa. 35:6). Why? "For waters shall burst forth in the desert, streams *in the wilderness.*" So, "These are the words that Moses spoke. . . ."[2]

Suddenly, it seems, Moses gains that access to language that was so long withheld from him. This means an ability to speak freely in all seventy languages—a minimum requirement for one who claims to speak for God! He can talk to everyone *in his own language;* he masters all possible codes of symbolic communication. He translates God's word into the terms of each human encounter. Like Adam, he discovers a primal genius for language; unprompted, like a spring in the desert, his voice resounds in the many words of Deuteronomy.[3]

The mysterious force of the analogy—language bursting forth like water in the wilderness—becomes more poignant when we consider the context and purpose of many of Moses' final speeches in Deuteronomy. These are, to a certain extent, retellings of Israel's forty-year history of wandering in the desert and of laws already promulgated in the earlier volumes of the Torah. Other passages contain new material. But these speeches, which occupy a large portion of the book, are understood, even by some of the traditional commentaries,[4] as bearing an unprecedentedly *personal* stamp. They are not simply mechanical transmissions of God's words, but the creation, to some extent, of the man Moses in the final months of his life. This assumption lies behind the midrash we have just quoted: the people are quizzically amazed at Moses' sudden eloquence, at the fertility of symbolic resonance that he now generates.

A TALE OF THWARTED DESIRE

What moves him to such expressiveness? These final speeches hold a peculiar pathos. They are, in a sense, deathbed speeches. In the most personal among them, Moses tells of his own failure to achieve his life's desire—to enter the Holy Land. This brief autobiographical passage is uniquely confessional in its content and in its timbre:

> "And I beseeched God at that time, saying, 'Lord God. . . . Let me, I pray, cross over and see the good land on the other side of the Jordan, that good hill country, and the Lebanon.' But God was wrathful with me on your account and would not listen to me. God said to me, 'Enough! Never speak to Me of this matter again! Go up to the summit of Pisgah and gaze about, to the west, the north, the south, and the east. Look at it well, for you shall not go across that Jordan. Charge Joshua with his instructions and imbue him with strength and courage, for he

shall go across at the head of this people, and he shall allot to them the Land you may only see.'" (Deut. 3:23–28)

Moses tells of a desperate plea to God, and of a cruel repudiation.[5] In a sense, he is telling the people of his failure to be heard by God, a failure that replicates his original failure of voice: "And God *would not listen* to me. . . ." God cuts his plea short, and closes off any future pleas in this vein: "Never speak [*dabber*] to Me of this matter [*davar*] again." God seals off his language in words that echo the description of his outburst of language at the beginning of the book: "These are the words [*devarim*] that Moses spoke [*dibber*]." With all the pathos he can command, Moses, the newly eloquent speaker, reports to his people how God interrupted his most passionate speech. As one to whom words come hard, Moses communicates his own frustration and humiliation.

Many questions arise from this poignant passage. This is, in fact, the only account we have of this encounter between Moses and God. There is no independent narrative of this painful moment. We know of it only because Moses chooses to tell the story to the people. Why does he do this? What would possess a leader, in his final speeches, to report such a crushing interaction with his God? What is his rhetorical purpose, the implicit demand he is making on his audience?

More concretely, *when* did Moses' prayer and God's denial occur? "I beseeched God *at that time*. . . ." The timing seems significant. Since there is no independent account of the moment, the midrash assumes that the prayer immediately followed on the conquest of Transjordan, just recorded (Deut. 2:26–3:22). Rashi finds in this sequence of events a hint of Moses' motivation:

"At that time": After conquering the land of Sihon and Og, I thought that perhaps the decree [that I should not enter the land] had been annulled. "To say": This is one of three occasions when Moses said to God: "I will not let You go till you tell me whether You will fulfill my request or not!"[6]

Rashi places Moses' prayer at the historical moment when Moses finds himself already, in a sense, inside the borders of the Holy Land. Having conquered the territories of Transjordan, he allows himself to hope that he will, after all, be permitted to cross the river and lead his people into their future. Perhaps the decree has been annulled? The moment of first conquest might plausibly have been a moment of personal hope for Moses; and this might well have issued in the urgent prayer that Rashi goes on to describe: "I will not let You go until You tell me whether You will fulfill my request or not!" The assertive pressure of his desire elicits God's trenchant response: "Enough!"

Another clue to the timing and motivation of Moses' prayer lies in the mysterious speech that God makes to Moses in Numbers 27:12:

> And God said to Moses: "Go up to these heights of Avarim [crossing places] and view the Land that I have given to the children of Israel. You shall see it, and then you too shall be gathered in to your people, just as Aharon your brother was gathered in."

This announcement of Moses' imminent death is strangely placed at the end of the book of Numbers, months before Moses dies. It occurs, in fact, immediately after the episode in which the five daughters of Tzelofchad successfully plead their cause and gain the inheritance of their portion of the land. At this juncture,[7] Rashi suggests, Moses sees a glimmer of hope in his personal case:

> "Go up to these heights of Avarim" (Num. 27:12): Why is this passage placed here? When God said, "You shall indeed give them [the daughters of Tzelofchad] a hereditary holding," Moses thought, "I was commanded to give them the inheritance— perhaps the decree has been annulled and I will after all enter the land?" Then God said, "My decree stands in place."
>
> Another view: When Moses entered the inheritance of the children of Gad and of Reuben, he rejoiced: "I think that the decree against me has been annulled." This is like a king who decreed that his son would not enter the palace. He entered the gate, left it behind him, and then the courtyard, till it was behind him, then the main hall, till it was behind him; when he was about to enter the living quarters, the king said, "My son, from here onward you are forbidden to enter."[8]

In two separate scenarios, Rashi tells his midrashic tale of thwarted desire. In the first scenario, Moses draws courage to pray from the wording of God's instructions: *"You* [personally?] shall give them possession of their inheritance. . . ."* He hears God's personal address as an invitation for prayer. Perhaps, too, he is inspired by God's acceptance of the plea of the daughters of Tzelofchad: the iron decree of male inheritance has been "transgressed."[9] Since one boundary has shifted, perhaps this is the moment to press his own case?[10] But God answers, "My decree *stands in place"*—inexorably blocking Moses' movement of hopeful imagination.

In the second scenario, as in the passage from Rashi that we have already seen, it is the geographical reality of his conquests that fuels Moses' plea. In neither case, however, is any prayer explicitly narrated in the biblical text. Yet in both cases, the midrash detects a movement of irrepressible desire triggered by the historical event. The prayer, if it existed, is repressed. Perhaps it was never uttered, a silent prayer, or a murmur?

Whatever shape it assumed, it is answered by God's enigmatic words: "Go up these heights of Avarim, of *transitions."* (Num. 27:12). The mountain from which he is to view the land before he dies is here named *Avarim*—the peak of *going across,* of *seeing across* to the far side of his desire. This moment of seeing and dying is set in the future. But it is the essential response of God *now.* As Moses will later tell the people in his account of his prayer, God answered him: "Raise your eyes and see with your eyes—for/that [*ki*] you will not cross over that Jordan" (Deut. 3:27). Moses' vision will take in two things: the vista of the land and the fact that he will not cross over. His vision will be informed by the deep knowledge that he will not make this crossing.

When God addresses Moses in this enigmatic way, blocking his desire—*E'evra na* ("Let me cross over and see")—yet cryptically offering him passage to some other form of vision, Moses replies by asking God to appoint an effective leader to succeed him. "And Moses spoke [*va-yidabber*] to God . . ." (Num. 27:15). *Dibbur* expresses a forceful, even aggressive act of speech. This is, in fact, the only occasion where the word is used when Moses addresses God. Rashi comments: "He spoke trenchantly to God. This tells the praise of the righteous who, as they depart from this world, set their own needs aside and involve themselves in the needs of the community." As the midrash puts it: "Anyone who speaks for the needs of the community, it is as though he comes with force [lit., with the power of his arm]."[11]

The irony is striking. Precisely at the moment when his personal hopes have been dashed, Moses speaks to God with the unprecedented confidence that his voice *will be heard*. What is the emotional logic of this moment of passage? How does the frustration of his desire to "cross over and see" the land metabolize into a new potency of language? "And Moses *spoke* these words": both in his speeches to the people and in his address to God, he who was not a man of words discovers a vein of powerful *dibbur*.

God's apparently ill-timed command ("Go up to the heights of Avarim") has, it seems, shifted the vector of Moses' desire. In the midrashic imagination, Moses—his energy of prayer harshly interrupted by God ("And God would not listen to me . . . 'Enough!'")—turns his energy toward his people's needs. That is, silenced on one subject, he speaks, with unprecedented force, on another. Silenced in speaking to God ("Never speak *to Me* again"), he speaks to the people, and on their behalf, with irrepressible power.

In Rashi's reading, then, Moses' new powers of language— following his repressed prayer and its sublimation—originate in the narrative of the wilderness, in Numbers, chapter 27. In Deuteronomy, chapter 3, in one of his farewell speeches to the people, he reports this most personal episode. The event and Moses' narration of it thus create a bridge between the two biblical books.

This framework raises questions about the mysterious absence of this prayer, in real time, from the text,[12] and, most radically, about his purpose in narrating this painful encounter with God to his people. This last question—why would he tell such a story of refusal and humiliation, which exists in the Torah *only* as part of his narrative?— evokes further questions about this uniquely autobiographical passage, its purposes, and its risks.

CROSSING OVER

In thinking about these issues and in reading the text of Deuteronomy, *crossing over* emerges as a leitmotif. Particularly haunting is the way Moses repeats the refrain of "You [Moses] shall not cross

over. . . . He [Joshua] shall cross over . . ." (Deut. 3:27–28).[13] This coun-
terpoint is sustained in relation not only to Joshua, his successor,[14]
but also in relation to the people: "For I am to die in this land; I shall
not cross over the Jordan. But you will cross over and take possession
of that good land" (4:22).[15] This is not simply an antithesis of (their)
life and (his) death, but, precisely, of *crossing over* and *not crossing
over.* ("I must die" is subsidiary to the main statement—*eineni oveir:*
"I am not to cross over.")

It is striking that, in many cases, this expression is not completed
by a reference to the Jordan River. *Crossing over* stands on its own in
almost metaphysical antinomy with *not crossing over.* The pathos of
Moses' harping on this theme provokes the reader to wonder about
the message that Moses may be conveying to the people. For once
God has repudiated his prayer; in some sense Moses lays his narrative at the door of his audience. What does he want of them? What
anger, or sadness, or envy, or spurned love do his words limn forth?

Another dramatic appearance of the *crossing over* theme occurs
in the speech of the two and a half tribes, Reuben, Gad, and half of
Manasseh, when they lay claim to the conquered lands of Transjordan. They forcefully plead with Moses: *"Al ta'avirenu*—do not make
us cross over that Jordan!" (Num. 32:5). These tribes want the conquered land for their cattle, but they just as strongly do *not* want to
cross over the Jordan. They appeal to Moses, whose deepest wish is
E'ebra na—"Let me, I pray, cross over."

In contrast to the daughters of Tzelofchad, who dare to speak
beyond convention, staking their claim to ancestral lands on the
far side of the Jordan—and drawing congratulations from God for
their strong reading, their happy act of *dibbur:* "They have spoken
finely" (Num. 27:6)—these tribes speak for what they already hold in
their possession, their *mikneh,* their cattle.[16] The word *mikneh,* with
its root meaning of "property" or "acquisition," of being attached to
pasture land, stands in some tension with the notion of *crossing over.*
For them, *crossing over* is anathema.

In his response, Moses excoriates them for demoralizing the people, precisely on this issue of *crossing over.*[17] He repeatedly refers to
their *crossing* of the Jordan with the rest of the people to fight the
wars of conquest: only on this condition may they inherit the pas-
tureland on *this* side of the river. What precisely is implied in the

tribes' reluctance to *cross over,* as it is played out against Moses' radical desire?

As Moses speaks, his desire to *cross over* becomes audible even in the prosaic context of his requests for safe passage through the territories of Transjordan. "Let me pass through [*e'ebra*] your land" (Num. 21:22), he begs Sihon, king of the Emorites; and in his last speeches to his people, he tells the story, repeating the word *e'ebra* (Deut. 2:27–28). Sihon's refusal leads to war. But for Moses the word and the desire it signifies hold a more than technical meaning. He is refused by Sihon, by Edom—and by God. And even among his own people, there are those whose language betrays a radical alienation from the structure of his desire: *Al ta'avirenu*—"Do not make us cross over."

A HEART TO KNOW?

In midrashic sources and in Hasidic appropriations of these sources, Moses' addresses to his people are informed by currents of implicit disappointment, even bitterness, which are intimated even as they are repressed in the biblical text.

One such moment occurs at the very beginning of Deuteronomy, in Moses' first speech to the people. God has commanded them to move away from Sinai and begin the journey into the Holy Land:

> "And I said to you, I cannot bear the burden of you by myself. . . . Pick from each of your tribes men who are wise, perceptive, and experienced, and I will appoint them as your heads. You answered me and said, What you propose to do is good." (Deut. 1:9,13–14)

Moses' expression, "I cannot bear the burden of you by myself," is read by the nineteenth-century Hasidic master Mei Ha-Shilo'ach[18] as a plea to the people to pray for him, to express their desire that Moses continue as their leader. Without their solidarity, he cannot lead them into the Land. Even before the explicit decree at Merivah, he realizes that, alone, he will not consummate the journey of exodus. Only if they *want* him to lead them will their prayers redeem his lonely wilderness death.

However, he can communicate his desire only obliquely. On the surface, he is instructing them to appoint to judicial roles an auxiliary group of "wise, perceptive, and experienced men." In fact, however, he is appealing to them to reject his proposal and to declare their unequivocal loyalty to him. But they, with magnificent obtuseness, respond: "What you propose to do is good." They fail to understand his meaning; they in fact declare their indifference to his leadership. For this reason, the new appointees are later described as "wise and experienced men," omitting the epithet, "perceptive" (*nevonim*). "Perceptive men did not find," says Moses in a sardonic midrash.[19] This is read by Mei Ha-Shilo'ach as a sad comment on the people's lack of emotional intelligence. They might perhaps have helped Moses through their prayers, but they could not intuit his real meaning, the desire that wordlessly animates his appeal to them.

This radical reading, with its play of implicit and explicit meanings, has Moses, in the opening speech of Deuteronomy, remind his people of a past failure in *understanding*. The gap between his desire and God's decree might have been bridged only by their unforced prayer. They might have helped him across the Jordan. Now, he tells his story—reproachfully, wistfully, bitterly?[20]

Such a failed dialogue is already adumbrated in midrashic sources. One midrash, for example, focuses on the theme of "You are crossing over—I am not crossing over.":

> Therefore, when they came to cross over the Jordan, Moses reminded them of every plea that he had made on their behalf, because he thought that now they would pray on his behalf, that he should enter the land with them. What is the force of "You are crossing over"? R. Tanchuma said: Moses prostrated himself before Israel and said to them: "You are to cross over, but not I." He gave them the opportunity to pray for him, but they did not grasp his meaning.
>
> This can be compared to a king who had many children by a noble lady. The lady was undutiful to him and he resolved to dismiss her. He said to her: "Know that I am going to marry another wife." She replied: "Yes, but will you not tell me whom it is that you intend to marry?" He replied: "So-and-so." What did the noble lady do? She summoned her children and said

to them: "Know that your father intends to divorce me and to marry So-and-so. Could you bear to be subjected to her?" They replied: "Yes." She then said to them: "Know what she will do to you." She thought that perhaps they would understand what she meant and would intercede with their father on her behalf, but they did not understand. As they did not understand, she said: "I will command you only for your own sake, be mindful of the honor of your father."

So it was with Moses. When God said to him: "Take Joshua the son of Nun . . ." (Num. 27:18); "For you shall not cross over that Jordan . . ." (Deut. 3:27), Moses said to Israel, "And it shall come to pass, when the Lord your God shall bring you into the land where you are going to possess it" (11:29); he stressed [the words], "You are to cross over this day, not I"; he thought that perhaps Israel would understand. As they did not understand, he said: "I will command you only for your own sakes, be mindful of the honor of your Father in heaven." How do we know this? For it is said, "That you may fear the Lord your God . . ." (6:2).[21]

In this poignant midrash, Moses simply tells the people the geography of his pain: "You are crossing over—I am not crossing over." Why can they not hear the appeal hidden within the words, especially in the context of his many prayers of intercession for them? The parable of the noble lady sharpens and deflects the anguish of misunderstanding. Across the generation gap, the lady probes her children's loyalty. They remain blithely insensitive to her need. Perhaps the prospect of a new mother has its attractions? In any case, they are incapable of realizing what the loss of their mother will mean. In the end, the lady darkly hints that it is their loss, rather than hers, that now concerns her. Where will they be without her intercession, without the dynamic family triangle of father, mother, children? But they cannot grasp their mother's crucial role in their lives. She can only warn them, somberly, "Be mindful of your father's honor." So Moses warns his people about the future without his loving mediation: "You are crossing over—I am not crossing over. . . . *Fear the Lord your God*—be mindful of the honor of your Father in heaven."

Midrashic sources offer many examples of explosive confrontations between fathers and sons. Here, the presence of the mother (Moses) displaces and diffuses some of the anger aroused by the unruly son. Without the symbolic complexity of this family triangle, such confrontations become dangerous. At first, Moses appeals to the people for his own sake; ultimately, his concern shifts to their welfare. How will they, unruly as they are, survive their father's unaccommodated anger? Without the mother's softening influence, the effect of her double love, they can survive only by dint of extreme caution: by fear, not love.

Ironically, it is their incomprehension that triggers the shift in Moses' feeling, from narcissistic to altruistic concern. Their obtuseness draws from Moses a final, devastating comment, shortly before his death: "God did not give you a heart to know, or eyes to see, or ears to hear, until this day" (Deut. 29:3). The midrash reads this as a personal reproach directed by Moses at the people:

> "God has not given you a heart to know": R. Samuel b. Nahmani said: Moses said this with reference to himself. How so? The Holy One, blessed be He, made two decrees, one affecting Israel, and one affecting Moses. The one affecting Israel was when they committed the unmentionable sin [the Golden Calf], as it is said, "Let Me alone, that I may destroy them" (Deut. 9:14). And the one affecting Moses? When Moses sought to enter the Land of Israel, God said to him, "You shall not cross over this Jordan" (3:27).
>
> Moses therefore entreated God to annul both decrees. He said to God: "Master of the Universe, Pardon, I pray, the iniquity of this people according unto the greatness of Your lovingkindness" (Num. 14:19), and God's decree was annulled while his own prayer was fulfilled; as it is said, "I have pardoned according to your word" (14:20). When he was about to enter the Land, Moses entreated: "Let me cross over, I pray, and see the good Land" (Deut. 3:25). And God replied: "Moses, on a former occasion you annulled My decree and I granted your prayer; I said: "That I may destroy them," and you prayed: "Pardon, I pray"; and your prayer was fulfilled. On this occasion, I wish to carry out My decree and to refuse your prayer." God added: "Moses, you do not know how to behave! You wish

to hold the rope at both ends. If you insist on 'Let me cross over, I pray,' then you must withdraw the prayer, 'Pardon, I pray'; and if you insist on 'Pardon, I pray,' then you must withdraw, 'Let me cross over, I pray.'

R. Joshua b. Levi said: When Moses our teacher heard this, he exclaimed before God: "Master of the Universe, let rather Moses and a hundred like him perish than that the fingernail of even one of them [Israel] should be injured!" R. Samuel b. Isaac said: When Moses was nearing his end and Israel did not pray that he should enter the Land, he assembled them and began rebuking them with the words: One man saved sixty myriads at the time of the Golden Calf, and yet sixty myriads cannot save one man! This is the force of "God has not given you a heart to know."[22]

Moses makes a radical choice between the people's interests and his own. It seems that he can prevail over only one of God's two decrees. Why should this be so? In a sense, there is nothing more natural than the desire to "hold the rope at both ends," as God puts it; and Moses in fact attempts to assert his will on both issues. But God interrupts him, as though some basic existential issue is at stake. Why, indeed, can Moses not save both himself and his people? Why is such a radical choice necessary?

The issue, I suggest, is one of language, of a combat of words between God and Moses: "your word" against "My word." Moses has won the first round ("I have pardoned *according to your word*"); now he must yield to God's word. There is a cryptic and relentless logic to God's demand; it is an elemental *emotional* demand. He must choose, either his people or himself, either the literal, narcissistic fulfillment of his words or a different use of words to express the play of a more imaginative desire.

Strikingly, in the midrash, God triggers a choice that for Moses is no choice: if the price of his own fulfillment is harm to even a fingernail of theirs, then his course is clear. In withdrawing his prayer, he is reading quite literally God's words: "Enough! Never speak to Me again of this matter!" God is telling him to *stop speaking,* to bite back his prayer, since the welfare of his people is inconsistent with it. There is a daring logic to this reading, since Moses has, precisely, asked God to withdraw His words of doom: "Pardon, I pray. . . ." At its core, the choice is between two worlds of words; each is constituted by a victory and a defeat.

The climax of the midrash, however, comes in its final lines: when Moses is close to death, he gathers the people and *tells them the story*. The tone and purpose of the story is named as *tochachah*—rebuke. He confronts them with a radical reproach, in the form of a narrative of satiric grievance: One man could save six hundred thousand, but six hundred thousand could not save one—"God has not given you a *heart to know*." He speaks about their insensitivity to his need, to his meaning. Presented in ironic, arithmetical terms, his speech creates an asymmetric history in which his "pleading for mercy" is set against their heartless obtuseness, their failure to find their own words of desire for his survival.

In other words, he is attacking their lack of imagination. He confronts them with this most radical reproach: they lack a knowing heart, they do not *understand* what is implicit, unspeakable. Their failure is a failure of imagination, which is the quality that is most vital for their future—the ability to see through the concrete, the obvious, and to recognize, to bring into full life, what is implicit.

His narrative is, in essence, *tochachah*—rebuke—which evokes the notion of *presence* (*noche'ach*). For this, perhaps, is what rebuke requires: the full presence of the speaker. If Moses is to reach them, if he is to achieve some lasting impact through his words, he must speak out of his own imaginative concern for them and their future. But he must also bring to bear the concentrated force of his own history. He must confront them with the movement of his desire.

EROS TRANSLATED

So he tells them: "I beseeched God. . . . 'Let me cross over, I pray.'" What is it to *cross over*? I suggest that the word *a-v-r* represents the very movement of desire, the movement to an elsewhere.[23] Its definition is *not-here, not-now*. When, for instance, God tells the people that His commandments are "not in heaven"—that is, not inaccessible, or mysterious—He elaborates: ". . . nor is it across [*me'ever*] the sea, that you should say, Who will go for us across [*ya'avor*] to that other shore [*el ever ha-yam*] and bring it back to us?" The word *ever*, used three times in one sentence, comes to express the unreachable terrain, which is set against God's triumphant closing note: "For it is very close to you, in your mouth and in your heart, to do it" (Deut. 30:13–14).

Here, the contrast is between the intimacy and concreteness of God's commandment, as against its alienation to ungraspable spheres. But Moses' desire—like all desire—is precisely for that place beyond place. To pass over, cross over, is, essentially, to disappear from present space and present time. In temporal terms, the past is referred to as *l'she'avar*—"that which is gone, lapsed, done with, over" (OED). Human life is compared to *tzel over*—a passing shadow. The moment of *passing* is fleeting: "My beloved slipped away and was gone [*avar*]. . . . I sought him but found him not" (Songs 5:6). The elusiveness of the lover is caught at the moment of his disappearance.

In the great epiphany where God appears to Moses by disappearing, He responds to Moses' desire:

"Let me see Your presence!" And He answered, "I will make all My goodness *pass* before you. . . . You cannot see My face, for man may not see Me and live. . . . See, there is a place with Me. Station yourself on the rock . . . and, as My presence *passes by*, I will put you in a cleft in the rock and shield you with My hand until I *have passed by*. Then, I will take My hand away and you will see My back; but My face must not be seen." (Exod. 33:18–23)

The "place with Me" in which Moses is positioned—the crevice in the rock—is the spatial equivalent of the fleeting moment of God's passing before Moses' covered eyes. To witness that moment would be perilous: "I will shield you with my hand *until I have passed by*." Seeing God's *back* is witnessing the *pastness*, the aftermath of God's presence. In space and in time, Moses is to know God as One who has already been here. "'I will make all My goodness *pass* before you.' . . . And God *passed* before him" (Exod. 34:6). The promise of the moment is withdrawn as it is given. To make His goodness pass in front of Moses is to remove it from his sight, to leave a space behind.

Here is the bittersweetness of Eros, which plays on the margin between the actual and possible. In her powerful meditation on

Eros, the poet and essayist Anne Carson describes the human desire that is "wooer of a meaning that is inseparable from its absence."[24] "'All men, by their very nature,' said Aristotle, 'reach out to know.'"[25] Moses reaches out to know God's glory and falls short. Desire makes a suitor of him, courting the unfathomable, eternally at the point of *ma'avar,* the crossing place to the unknown.

"Knowing and desiring entail the same delight, the same pain," writes Anne Carson. "Stationed at the edge of itself, or of its present knowledge, the thinking mind launches a suit for understanding into the unknown. So too the wooer stands at the edge of his value as a person and asserts a claim across the boundaries of another.... Something else. Think about what that feels like."[26] Eros is about boundaries and the desire to dissolve them: "Infants begin to see by noticing the edges of things. How do they know an edge is an edge? By passionately wanting it not to be."[27]

Eros becomes a verb; it acts. In a condition of acute tension, the mind moves into *metaphor,* which *transfers* meaning from the familiar to the strange. By an act of imagination, we bring two incongruent things together and notice a new congruence. This requires a "stereoscopic vision," an "ability to hold in equipoise two perspectives at once."[28] The fusion we desire can be attained only through this *metaphoric* action, which *carries meaning across.*

"Space reaches out from us and translates the world," as Rilke puts it (as cited by Carson). Moses' desire to *cross over* involves this desire to fuse the near and the far. He reaches out to meanings not known, he woos that which must dissolve in his grasp. Unlike the two and a half tribes, for whom such reachings, such acts of poignant and joyful imagination are intolerable (*al ta'avirenu*), for whom *mikneh*—the bird in the hand—is the thing, Moses yearns for the play of transcendence, of transition, of transference, of translation. He keeps returning to this restless place—to God's edict, "You shall not cross over," and to his desire, "Let me cross over." His wings will not be clipped.[29] If he cannot cross over this Jordan River, he will translate, transfer his desire to another extension of his being. At the very moment when God silences him, his soul grows new wings. Eros initiates a new metaphoric intensity.

Moses launches himself on a new movement of desire: to "come across" to his people, to reach out from the known to the unknown that they now constitute for him. "You are crossing over," he tells them, "I am not crossing over." "You are going into the unknown, you are leaving me behind, I no longer have the possibility of leaving anything behind. I will be your past, you are moving out of my sight." This is the impassable gap that opens up between himself and the people. Moses stages for them his surrender to the knowledge of this difference.

This is what it means to die:

> Palomar does not underestimate the advantages that the condition of being alive can have over that of being dead: not as regards the future, where risks are always very great and benefits can be of short duration, but in the sense of the possibility of improving the form of one's own past. . . . A person's life consists of a collection of events, the last of which could also change the meaning of the whole, not because it counts more than the previous ones but because once they are included in a life, events are arranged in an order that is not chronological but, rather, corresponds to an inner architecture. A person, for example, reads in adulthood a book that is important for him. . . . After he has read that book, his whole life becomes the life of a person who has read that book, and it is of little importance whether he read it early or late, because now his life before that reading also assumes a form shaped by that reading.[30]

In this description of learning "how to be dead," the novelist and essayist Italo Calvino conveys the power of each moment to transform the relation between the elements of one's past, its "inner architecture." Moses is, I suggest, telling the people that, unlike theirs, his life is a closed book, with no further movements into the unknown. But, at the same time, by narrating the story of his desire to "*cross over* this Jordan River," he is launching both himself and the people into a new narrative, a new history of desire. Even as he describes the impassable gap between his people's future and his own, he is attempting, by indirection, to bridge that gap.

"I am to die in this land; I shall not cross the Jordan. But you will cross and take possession of that good land" (Deut. 4:22). Ramban and Seforno read this: "Since I will not be crossing over with you, I need to warn you all the more powerfully about the dangers of disobedience." Moses' concern for his people is sharpened by his imminent death. His vision of their future without him is pessimistic, or perhaps realistic. ("For I know that after my death, you will corrupt yourselves" [31:29].) *Therefore,* he gathers them together and speaks to them of his frustrated desire to cross over. His effort now is to *get through* to them, to *come across* to them in language. For they now represent his unknown, unreachable desire.

He urges them: "But take utmost care and watch yourselves scrupulously, so that you do not forget the things that your eyes have seen and so that they do not fade from your mind as long as you live" (Deut. 4:9). But he knows that the people he is so passionately addressing, appealing to them to remember their own deepest experience, are a new generation. Only those who had been less than twenty years old at Sinai had actually seen it with their own eyes. A missing generation, numberless corpses fallen into the sand, now create a gap between Moses and his people that no sermons can bridge. As he speaks to them they are already "dys-temporaneous" with him; they live in a different time zone. How, then, does he hope to *come across* to them?

In the future, he instructs them, they will gather together every seven years and publicly read the Torah in God's presence, in Jerusalem—

in order that they may hear and learn to revere the Lord your God and to observe faithfully every word of this Torah. Their children, too, who have not had the experience [lit., do not know], shall hear and learn to revere the Lord your God as long as they live in the land that you are about to cross over the Jordan to possess. (Deut. 31:12–13)

Before he dies, Moses instructs those who have had the experience (who *know,* who *have seen*) to transmit their experience to their children, so that those who *do not know* may learn. This will not be a mechanical matter of providing information. For those who will be the teachers of the future are now, in Moses' presence, the already unknowing successors of a past generation that did know. How can

Moses transmit to them the essential knowledge that can then be transmitted, generation to generation, into the future?

A POETIC PEDAGOGY

Here is the problem of education, of the teaching project—Freud's "impossible profession"—in fact, one of three such professions (the other two being healing and governing). In Freud's words, in these professions, "one can be sure beforehand of achieving unsatisfying results."[31]

Shoshana Felman[32] provocatively reframes the issue. Freud, she claims, has instituted a "revolutionary pedagogy . . . It is precisely in giving us unprecedented insight into the impossibility of teaching, that psychoanalysis has opened up unprecedented teaching possibilities."[33] From a psychoanalytic perspective, it is precisely one's resistance to learning that sets the stage for a profound process of coming to knowledge. Paradoxically, what is transacted between patient and analyst or between student and teacher, disrupts knowingness. Reaching out beyond an ignorance of which one begins to take the measure, the student or the patient is possessed by an unnamable desire. Without this ignorance, or repression, or forgetting, there can be no passage, no crossing over.

"Come, *let yourself be taught!*" Freud adjures his readers, ". . . *learn first to know yourself!*"[34] The patient needs to reach out beyond her conscious intelligence. This new kind of knowledge is, in a sense, "unlearnable." Through "breakthroughs, leaps, discontinuities, regressions, and deferred action," the patient renews her understanding of what "not to know" may really mean. The analyst is to "learn the patient's own unconscious knowledge" and to return it, as a surprise, to the patient. Two partially unconscious speeches constitute a dialogue, in which "both say more than they know."

From this perspective, "the clear-cut opposition between the analyst and the analysand, between the teacher and the student" is radically subverted: "what counts, in both cases, is precisely the transition, the struggle-filled *passage* from one position to the other."

Knowledge is thus, in an important sense, "not in mastery of itself." Felman credits Lacan with understanding the radical significance of Freud's use of *literary* knowledge. This involves reading Freud as a literary text—which means that the author cannot exhaust the meaning of his own text. The poetic function of language becomes central, giving birth to genuine discoveries.

Ultimately, then, the Freudian pedagogical imperative is "to learn from and through the insight which does not know its own meaning, from and through the knowledge which is not entirely in mastery—in possession—of itself." Felman calls this a *poetic pedagogy*, which teaches "with and through the very blindness of its literary knowledge, of insights not entirely transparent to themselves."

Shoshana Felman's profound and brilliant discussion may serve us in reflecting on Moses' project in his last addresses to his people. I suggest that his aim is to overcome their active dynamic of negation, the active refusal that they have so often demonstrated. "The pathological factor is not his ignorance in itself, but the root of this ignorance in his *inner resistances*," Freud says of the patient in analysis.[35] There is a desire to ignore, a "passion for ignorance," a refusal to "acknowledge *one's own implication in the information*."[36] If Moses is to deal with ignorance of this kind, he must engage with it in such a way that the ignorance itself becomes instructive.

He does this by speaking to the people from the site of his own ignorance, from the very place of unconscious conflict. He tells the story of his own repudiation by God. Pleading for his desire and being denied his desire, he plays out his resistance, the sadness, envy, hostility of his relation to the people. At least in part, the conflicts he stages are unconscious, as he allows the people to learn from the process of his own unmeant knowledge. He tells an intimate life story, which is poetically framed for *this* audience, and for *this* moment.

Perhaps we can say that, as a teacher, he is, in some sense, like the *patient* in the analytic relationship.[37] He talks to a silent audience, which becomes the student of the patient's unknown knowledge. He who had begun life resisting language becomes a man who allows meanings beyond his conscious mastery to be released into the space between his audience and himself.

So great is his desire to reach out, to *cross over* to his people's inner world, that Moses puts on display, essentially, himself. Speaking beyond his means, by the poetic force of his language, he conveys to them the depths of his desire, its sheer humanity.

MAKING HISTORY

Kafka writes of Moses:

> He is on the track of Canaan all his life; it is incredible that
> he should see the land only when on the verge of death. The
> dying vision of it can only be intended to illustrate how
> incomplete a moment is human life, incomplete because a life
> like this could last forever and still be nothing but a moment.
> Moses fails to enter Canaan not because his life is too short
> but because it is a human life.[38]

A personal pathos is sublimated into a resonant demand in Moses'
last speeches. His human life, eternally incomplete, inspires his
words with intimations of an immortal desire. In a flood of language
("You said, *I am not a man of words,* and now you speak so much!"), his
text endlessly evocative, he conveys a *literary* knowledge, of which
he himself is not entirely aware. He remembers the past, he exhorts
for the future. The implications of his meaning resound through
the generations and between them. By retelling the past, he moves
across to his listeners, as he plays out the possibility of their having a
history, rather than merely repeating themselves forever.

He narrates in order to integrate and transcend the traumatic
effect of the facts of the past. The past, says the psychoanalyst Christopher Bollas, restricts our imaginative freedom, so congested is it
with "dumb facts" that arrest the play of our minds. There is something *unthinkable,* even traumatic, about such facts of life. They create a momentary blankness; moving beyond this blankness, we may
elaborate and interpret the facts. In this way, we may liberate our
own specific idiom that can counteract the intrinsically traumatic
effect of the passing of time.

In the work of the historian or of the psychoanalyst, the narratives of the past, its great events and figures, need, in a sense, to be
forgotten; the historian becomes absorbed in the minutiae of the
texts and allows the unconscious work of organization to transpire.
This work "surreptitiously defeats trauma and revives the selves that
had been consigned to oblivion."[39] Through the apparent minutiae,
the most profound secrets of a self or of an age are revealed. Here

are the "intensities of a lifetime, and history is the recovery of such moments."

In relating his past to his people, Moses, like the historian, or the analyst, immerses himself in his material. He does not use the authoritarian language of the original biblical account but, in a sense, he *makes history,* by allowing unconscious meanings to liberate him from the "bleakness of ordinary trauma." And like the good historian or analyst, he is "prepared for [his] own *undoing* each time [he] returns to the material."[40]

This deconstruction is particularly significant when Moses tells his own personal story and, by allowing imagination to work upon it, opens it to continuous revision. In this way, he transforms it into a history. Unlike the past, says Bollas, which sits in the self as a kind of lead weight, the work of making history "transforms the debris into meaningful presence."[41]

If Moses is *rebuking* (*tochachah*) the people when he retells the story of personal desire and rejection, he is, at heart, creating himself as a meaningful *presence* (*noche'ach*) for them. On one level, he may be reproaching them for not "asking for mercy" on his behalf— for ignoring, or resisting the knowledge of his meaning. But, more profoundly, he is staging for them his own life of aspiration, situated between knowing and not knowing: *"Let me cross over, I pray."*

When God asks him to withdraw his personal plea, a new energy is released in him: "And Moses *spoke to God.*" As his personal needs are sublimated, a language of unconscious force is liberated. In his speeches to the people, too, a personal voice reaches out from the debris of his desire. Implicitly, he is making a demand on them: that they find in themselves their own living process of *havanah,* of imaginative understanding.

This process is perhaps always unfinished, since it deals with something *else,* something essentially alien. In the past, they could not understand his private meanings, even as he pleaded with them to implicate themselves in his desire. However, like the children who cannot imagine the future, or the meaning of losing the mother, the people will come to understand his meanings, or at least to understand enough to ask: "What did he mean when he spoke so many words, mysteriously opaque even to himself, before he died?" For them, Moses *will have spoken.*

That is Moses' final desire, transmuted, imaginatively reworked from its original, literal form. Now, Moses wishes to traverse the gap that, more than ever, separates him from the people. His plea, *E'ebra na,* is displaced onto an unconscious plea to them. In narrating their past failure in understanding, he appeals to them to bring a transformed sensibility to bear on his silent desire. How effective is he in these last speeches? Does he indeed affect them at the depth he hopes for?

MOSES OUR TEACHER

A whisper of an answer can be heard in the critical words with which he summarizes their history: "God has not given you a heart to know, or eyes to see, or ears to hear, *until this day. . . .*" They have always been unaware, insentient; but does "this day" imply a shift toward understanding?

In a striking passage, the Talmud unpacks the implications of Moses' words:

Yet Moses indicated this [their ingratitude] to the Israelites only after forty years had passed, as it is said: "And I have led you forty years in the wilderness. . . . But God has not given you a heart to know. . . ." Said Rava: From this one can learn that it may take forty years to comprehend one's teacher.[42]

Even as he takes leave of them, Moses can do no more than hint at the narrative of their "ingratitude." With regard to their various sins and shortcomings, he is quite explicit. But by ingratitude, the Talmud refers to the insensitivity, the absence of intuition, or imagination, that is sketched in the verse: the unknowing heart, the blind eyes, the deaf ears. Moses is hinting that they have been incapable of receiving his transmissions, of registering the undercurrents of his desire that they pray for him. But—"It may take forty years to comprehend one's teacher," says Rava. This means that, as he speaks, Moses is recognizing that they are, indeed, beginning to transcend their obtuseness to what is implicit within his words. He has, perhaps, begun to "reach" them, to "come across" to them. This is the hopeful turn in Rava's reading: "till this day" opens up a possibility for a newly loving attentiveness.

Rashi translates: "'This day you have become a people': this day, I understand that you do passionately long for God."[43] The transformed consciousness that he now senses in them is the fruit of forty years' work, which issues in the concentrated work of Moses' many speeches in Deuteronomy. "You have become a people" implies that the heart has begun to know; a capacity for creative imagination now characterizes their inner life.

Rashi's expression may also suggest that Moses, too, is now in a state of evolved consciousness: *"Now, I understand* that you really do long for God."* Moses' imaginative consciousness of his people has undergone change in the course of forty years. The teacher, too, has gradually grown in his appreciation of the student's potential understanding. Before he dies, he brings a loving intuition to bear on the past that has given birth to this present. Through his many words, something has transpired between them.

These words model for them a process of coming to the knowledge that holds ignorance at its heart. This process represents the new form of his passion to *cross over,* to achieve *"l'amour de loin,"* the "love from a distance," of which the troubadours wrote. This reach of desire—transition, translation, transmission, transference—creates a world of poetic language, retrieved after long resistance: *E'ebra na* in a new voice.

Before he dies, Moses achieves one last transformation. His new intuition about his people's potential is expressed in his final song: *Ve-zot ha-brachah*—"This is the blessing that Moses, the man of God, blessed the children of Israel before he died." Before he dies, he becomes the *man of God* and bestows on his people an unprecedented blessing, unconditional, wholehearted.[44]

What is it to be the *man of God*? Daringly, the midrash reads the expression in a gendered sense:

> Just as a man, if he wishes to annul his wife's vow, he may annul it, and if he wishes to ratify it, he may do so—as it is said, "Her husband [ish-a] may ratify it and her husband may

annul it" (Num. 30:14)—so Moses said to God, "Rise up, O
God. . . . Come to rest, O God!"[45]

As God's *ish*, Moses has the "husbandly" power to confirm or
annul God's decrees. This means that after he has obeyed God's command to deliver His dire farewell warnings in Deuteronomy, chapter
32 (*Ha'azinu ha-shamayim . . .*)—sinister, doom-laden words—Moses
then takes the initiative and lavishes on his people the loving poetry
of "This is the blessing."

It is only at the end of his life that his relation to God is transfigured in this way. Before this, even in his successful interventions
with God on behalf of his people, he was in some way playing the
"wifely" role. Like all prophets, suggests the midrash, he plays the
wifely role of persuasion in the face of the angry father of her children.[46] Only at the very last moment, before ascending Mount Nevo,
does he become the *ish* of God. This is his moment of unequivocal blessing; in his farewell song, a transfigured imagination sees
through the many wilderness words of his people, as well as the catastrophic words of God. The last word is to be his: "Happy are you, O
Israel—a people saved by God!" (Deut. 33:29).

TRANSLATING THE WORLD

And yet, one last time, at the very moment of death, God reminds
Moses of His decree. At the summit of the Mountain of Transitions
(*Avarim*), Moses is shown the whole vista of the Holy Land:

> And God said to him: "This is the Land of which I swore to
> Abraham, Isaac, and Jacob, 'I will give it to your offspring.' I
> have let you see it with your eyes, but *you shall not cross over
> there.*" And Moses the servant of God died there. (Deut. 34:4)

Why does God revert in His last words to the painful core of
Moses' life? There is no practical force to the repetition of the decree
at this moment. He shows Moses the land, and then tells him that He
has shown it to him: why does He reiterate to Moses what has just
happened and already been narrated—only to add the final words:
"you shall not cross over there"?

Perhaps we can say that God is appointing Moses, at this last moment, as a messenger, a bearer of words beyond the edge. The last words Moses hears on earth are not about the past, but about history—a transmission, a translation, to be *carried across* the gap.[47] Perhaps the emphasis is on the last word—*shamah*—"You shall not cross over *there*": geographically, you will not cross over to the land of your desire; but you will achieve a different crossing.

Between Moses and his people, something significant, both personal and impersonal, has transpired. Moses' *tochachot,* his "rebukes," will leave their residue, will bear across to the people the interminable mystery of his presence. In the end, his love will reach through and beyond his anger, his rebukes will become songs, blessings. The desert will burst forth in streams, the lame leap like a deer, the tongue of the mute will sing aloud. And Moses, not a man of words, will have spoken these many words. A space will reach out and translate the world.

NOTES

PREAMBLE

1. Henceforth referred to as the Book of the Wilderness.
2. This is Gerard Manley Hopkins's expression.
3. Deuteronomy 1:19; 8:15.
4. The only exceptions mentioned are Caleb and Joshua, the "good" Spies, who are exempted from the national catastrophe. The census covered only male adults from the age of twenty.
5. *Shemot Rabbah* 2:5.
6. The difference is indicated by the following preposition: *le* or *be*, one suggesting a question of fact, the other a relationship.
7. See Ha'amek Davar to Numbers 14:11. He reads God's speech as relating to the depth of the people's skepticism, rather than to its duration.
8. See Exodus 4:31.
9. See Exodus 4:2–9.
10. Stanley Cavell, *Philosophy the Day After Tomorrow* (Cambridge, MA: Harvard University Press, 2005), 150.
11. Stanley Cavell, *In Quest of the Ordinary* (Chicago and London: University of Chicago Press, 1994), 128.
12. Ibid., 88.
13. Ibid., 172.
14. Ibid., 89.
15. Cavell, *Philosophy*, 151
16. Cited in Cavell, *Philosophy*, 151
17. Cavell, *Philosophy*, 151.
18. Ibid., 172. Cavell refers here to Freud's essay "Transience."
19. *Bamidbar Rabbah* 16:6.
20. Rashi to Numbers 13:2.
21. Exodus 16:15.
22. See *B.Yoma* 75b: "The manna was absorbed by the body and metabolized as pure energy." Psalm 78 refers to *lechem abirim*—bread for the mighty—which the Talmud reads as "bread absorbed into the *limbs* [*eivarim*]." Later, the people complain that the unnameable food is *ein kol*—that is, totally absorbed (*akul*) in the body. The people complain: Can a human

being bring in (food) without eliminating (waste)?—that is, bypass the digestive system of the human animal.

23. David Shulman, *More Than Real* (Cambridge, MA: Harvard University Press, 2012), 284.

24. Susan Stewart, *The Poet's Freedom* (Chicago and London: University of Chicago Press, 2011), 1–2.

25. See Exodus 16:29, Numbers 13:2, and multiple occasions. In each case, God "gives" (*noten*) the people the gift.

26. Mei Ha-Shilo'ach, vol. 2, *Be-ha'alotcha* (*Be-sefer ba-midbar . . .*).

27. *Shemot Rabbah* 2:5.

28. *Tanna d'bei Eliyahu Rabbah,* 29.

29. Mei Ha-Shilo'ach, vol. 2, *Shlach* (*Al inyan parshat nesachim . . .*).

30. Deuteronomy 1:27.

31. See chapter 3.

32. Jonathan Lear, *A Case for Irony* (Cambridge, MA, and London: Harvard University Press, 2011), 46.

33. Ibid., 50.

34. See ibid., 59.

35. *Shir Ha-Shirim Rabbah* 2:1.

36. The midrash continues with further "shadows": Sinai, the Exiles. The shadow of the Red Sea and of Sinai, which are positive, redemptive events, nevertheless, in midrashic sources, also imply menace: the Israelites might have drowned like the Egyptians, or been engulfed by Mount Sinai. See Rashi to Exodus 19:17: "The mountain was suspended over their heads like a bucket!"

37. *Shir Ha-Shirim Rabbah* 2:2.

38. *Shir Ha-Shirim Rabbah* 2:4.

39. Rashi to Numbers 33:1.

40. Rainer Maria Rilke, *Letters to a Young Poet,* trans. M. D. Herter Norton (New York and London: W. W. Norton, 1954), 53.

41. "*Zachor* means repeating with one's mouth" (*Torat Kohanim* 26:3).

42. This expression is used many times, particularly in Numbers, with concrete reference to performing duties of the Sanctuary.

43. The collection of his teachings from this period, published after the Holocaust, is called *Esh Kodesh.*

44. See Kalonymus Kalmisch Shapira, *Esh Kodesh* (Jerusalem, 1961), 105–8.

45. Tanchuma, *Tazria,* 6.

46. Rilke, *Letters,* 52.

47. Leo Bersani and Adam Phillips, *Intimacies* (Chicago and London: University of Chicago Press, 2008), 113–14.

48. George Eliot, *Scenes of Clerical Life,* cited in Neil Hertz, *George Eliot's Pulse* (Stanford, CA: Stanford University Press, 2003), 13.

49. See Hertz, *George Eliot's Pulse*, 13–19, for a fascinating discussion of this field of words in George Eliot's fiction.
50. Sefat Emet, Bamidbar, 20.
51. See Rashi to Numbers 11:15—"His strength flagged like a woman."
52. See John T. Hamilton, *Music, Madness, and the Unworking of Language* (New York: Columbia University Press, 2008), 15. Hamilton refers to Blanchot on the necessary movement of "unworking" the song, which consecrates the song.
53. See Deuteronomy 31:19—"Now write for yourselves this Song," which in some interpretations is understood to refer to the whole Torah.

ONE: FLAGS IN THE WILDERNESS

1. Sefat Emet, Bamidbar, 20.
2. *Mishnah Yoma* 7:1; *Menachot* 4:3.
3. The Hebrew root *p-k-d* means both "counting" and "absence."
4. *Shemot Rabbah* 2:5. The proof text is from Song of Songs: "Your lips are like a scarlet thread, and your mouth [*midbarech*] is lovely" (4:3). In context, *midbarech* obviously refers to the speaking mouth, but the midrashic genius senses the possibilities of the wordplay: "Your *wilderness* is lovely."
5. *B.Eruvin* 54a.
6. Frank Kermode, "The Plain Sense of Things," in *Midrash and Literature* (New Haven, CT, and London: Yale University Press, 1986), 180.
7. "The Snow Man," cited in ibid., 179.
8. Ibid., 180.
9. The forty-year time span in the wilderness becomes a thirty-eight-year wandering time, since approximately a year and a half have elapsed before God's decree, and another five months at the end of the wilderness time is after the decree has been consummated.
10. See Numbers 20:28; 33:38; 20:29; Deuteronomy 1:3. I am grateful for Jacob Milgrom's summary of this time frame. See *The JPS Torah Commentary, Numbers* (Philadelphia: The Jewish Publication Society, 1989), xi.
11. Rashi to Numbers 1:1. Cf. Rashi to Exodus 1:1.
12. *Bamidbar Rabbah* 1:9.
13. Annie Dillard, *For the Time Being* (New York: Knopf, 1999), 21.
14. Ibid., 72–73.
15. Stanley Cavell, *In Quest of the Ordinary* (Chicago and London: Chicago University Press, 1994), 88.
16. Ibid., 89.
17. Ibid., 100.
18. Stanley Cavell, *Philosophy the Day After Tomorrow* (Cambridge, MA, and London: Harvard University Press, 2005), 151.

19. See, for example, Leviticus 18:30; 22:9; Numbers 18:7.
20. *Bereshit Rabbah* 84:11.
21. *Bamidbar Rabbah* 2:3.
22. *Shir Ha-Shirim Rabbah* 7:2.
23. Cavell, *Quest*, 89.
24. *Pesikta d'Rav Kahana, Be-shallach (Gan na'ul . . .)*.
25. Rashi to Numbers 26:5.
26. Milan Kundera, *The Unbearable Lightness of Being* (London and Boston: Faber and Faber, 1985), 248.
27. Ibid., 254.
28. Ibid., 253.
29. Ibid., 254.
30. Ibid., 252.
31. Adam Phillips, *On Balance* (New York: Farrar, Straus and Giroux, 2010), 233.
32. Ibid., 236.
33. Ibid., 238.
34. Ibid., 239.
35. *Bamidbar Rabbah* 2:2.
36. Or Ha-Chaim to Exodus 25:8.
37. Cavell, *Quest*, 172.
38. *Bamidbar Rabbah* 2:2.
39. Seforno on Numbers 9:17.
40. Sefat Emet, Bamidbar, 3.
41. *Bamidbar Rabbah* 2:2.
42. *Esh Kodesh*, 98–99.
43. *B.Megillah* 21a.
44. *B.Taanit* 6a.
45. *Esh Kodesh* is based on sermons given in the outskirts of Warsaw during the Holocaust years leading up to 1944, when the Rebbe and his community were deported to Auschwitz.
46. *Esh Kodesh*, 113.
47. *Mo'ed Katan* 17.
48. *B.Shabbat* 25b.

TWO: MADNESS AND CIVILIZATION

1. Rashi to Numbers 26:64.
2. See Rashi to Numbers 27:7.
3. See Mary Douglas, *In the Wilderness* (Sheffield, UK: Oxford University Press, 1993), chapter 8, for an interesting discussion of "the laws for women" as metaphors for the faithful/faithless figure of Israel.
4. This central principle is often deduced from the biblical texts, "It is not in heaven" (Deut. 30:12), and "Follow the majority (even) in error"

(Exod. 23:2), as they are cited in the highly influential Talmudic text known as *Tanur shel Achna'i* (*Baba Metzia* 59b).

5. See *B.Sotah* 28a. In rabbinic law, the marriage cannot continue in the situation of doubt.

6. Rashi to Numbers 5:12.

7. Cf. the immediately preceding passage, introduced by the expression, "breaking faith with God" (Num. 5:6).

8. See Elchanan Samet, *Iyyunim Be-Parshot Ha-Shavua*, 2nd series, *Parshat Nasso*, 161.

9. *B.Sotah* 47a.

10. Peter L. Berger, *A Rumor of Angels* (Garden City, NY: Doubleday, 1969).

11. Ibid., 34.

12. *B.Sotah* 47b.

13. Rashi to Numbers 5:12.

14. Tanchuma, *Nasso* 5.

15. Cf. *B.Sotah* 3a: "One who goes to a married woman has gone out of his mind."

16. See also *Bamidbar Rabbah* 9:3. The root *s-t-h*, spelled with a *sin*, appears twice in Proverbs: 4:15 and 7:25.

17. Rashi to Numbers 6:2.

18. Tanchuma, *Nasso* 4–5.

19. Cf. the version of this midrash in *Bamidbar Rabbah* 9:1, where the fantasy of privacy is satirized.

20. I have not cited this passage.

21. There is a famous story about the Kotzker Rebbe who, when asked: "Where is the place of His glory?" answered, "Wherever you will let Him in!"

22. Cf. "Anyone who commits a transgression and repeats it, it becomes permissible to him" (*B.Yoma* 86b).

23. Biblical imagery of heart and kidneys refers to the hidden emotional and intellectual life of human beings.

24. It is striking that the midrash speaks of *mechilim*—the cavities that inhabit the human body psyche—which is related to the *challal panui*, the space that God vacates in world creation.

25. *Bereshit Rabbah* 87:5.

26. It is interesting that the same expression, *u-ma'alah bo ma'al*—which usually refers to transgressions against God—is used in the Sotah narrative.

27. Emmanuel Levinas, *Totality and Infinity* (Pittsburgh: Duquesne University Press, 1969), 213.

28. *B.Brachot* 8a.

29. Michel Foucault, *Madness and Civilization*, trans. Richard Howard (New York: Random House, 1965), 13–14.

30. Ibid., 16–17.

31. Shoshana Felman, *Writing and Madness*, trans. Martha Noel Evans (Ithaca, NY: Cornell University Press, 1985), 41.
32. Ibid., 41.
33. Ibid., 48.
34. Ibid., 55.
35. Ibid., 52n15.
36. Strikingly, *Amen* is derived from the Hebrew root for faith, trust. The Sotah must utter, as her only word, the double avowal of her acquiescence in this test of her fidelity.
37. Julia Kristeva, *Powers of Horror*, trans. Leon S. Roudiez (New York: Columbia University Press, 1982), 1–2.
38. Felman, *Writing and Madness*, 236.
39. *B.Brachot* 61a; *Bereshit Rabbah* 18:2.
40. See Deuteronomy 12:2–4.
41. See Rashi to ibid.
42. Exodus 17:14; Deuteronomy 29:19.
43. *B.Sotah* 17b.
44. *B.Chulin* 141a.
45. Felman, *Writing and Madness*, 235.
46. Ibid., 239.
47. This is a play on words—*"le nom du pere"* ("the name of the father")—represents a central concept in Lacan's thinking.
48. *Bamidbar Rabbah* 9:14.
49. The midrash amplifies the explicit meaning of the biblical text, in which the priest begins by dealing with the possibility of her innocence.
50. *B.Sotah* 32b.
51. Ibid.
52. *Likkutei Moharan* 4:5.
53. *B.Sotah* 7b.
54. In his final blessing to the twelve tribes, Moses addresses Judah immediately after Reuben (omitting Levi, the next son in order of birth), because both confessed their sins.
55. On this the Talmud soberly comments, "The words of a sage, even when they are conditional, are realized" (*B.Brachot* 14b).
56. See *B.Makkot* 11b.
57. See the end of *Bamidbar Rabbah* 9:14.
58. Foucault, *Madness and Civilization*, 16.
59. See Kenneth Gross, *Puppet: An Essay on Uncanny Life* (Chicago and London: Chicago University Press, 2011), 152.
60. See Felman, *Writing and Madness*, 232–33.
61. Elaine Scarry, *On Beauty* (Princeton, NJ: Princeton University Press, 1999), 52–53.
62. Cited in Felman, *Writing and Madness*, 242.

63. *B.Gittin* 43a.

64. Scarry, *On Beauty*, 15.

THREE: DESIRE IN THE WILDERNESS

1. Rashi reads this "goodness" as offering Jethro a share in the land. In the end, Jethro's children acquire the land around Jericho (see Judges, chapter 1).

2. See *Chizkuni*: 12:16.

3. Ramban suggests that their complaints are about the forced marches that have just been described. In other words, God's *tov*—the prospect of immediate entry into the Land—becomes for them a source of *ra*, of hardship.

4. See Seforno to Numbers 11:1.

5. See the Introduction by Ha'amek Davar to the book of Numbers.

6. Rashi identifies this group with the *erev rav*—the motley crowd who accompanied the Israelites out of Egypt.

7. *B.Shabbat* 116a.

8. Ramban to Numbers 10:35.

9. In fact, this expression is used in Isaiah 2:3 to refer to Mount Zion, the site of the Temple: "Come, let us ascend to the mountain of God!"

10. *Harchev Davar*: 11:4.

11. Cf. Rashi to *B.Shabbat* 116a. Ha'amek Davar bases this chronology on 11:4: "They returned to weeping." See also Seforno to Numbers 11:2, who sees a continuity between the "complaining" and the "desiring" sins.

12. It is striking that Ha'amek Davar is pursuing an idea that he has raised earlier in his commentary on the Nazirite. The choice of an ascetic life is justifiable only if a sensual pleasure is being renounced for the sake of a spiritual one. The pleasure principle is always at work, even in sublimated forms. In this narrative, the people's movement is in the opposite direction, from an experience of sublimation back to the concrete pleasure. (See Ha'amek Davar to Numbers 6:8–13. See also 17:3.)

13. *Bassar* is sometimes a generic term for food, for a "serious" meal (*se'udah*). It is so serious that, according to *Bereshit Rabbah* 67:3, its very mention makes Esau weep: "If Jacob received the birthright for making me a lentil soup, how much more serious is it if he brings his father *meat!*" (*Keivan she-hizkir bassar miyad bachah.*)

14. Jacques Lacan, *Ecrits* (New York and London: W. W. Norton, 1977), 322.

15. Michael Eigen, *The Psychoanalytic Mystic* (London and New York: Free Association Books, 1998), 136.

16. Lacan, *Ecrits*, 319.

17. Eigen, *Psychoanalytic Mystic*, 137.

18. W. R. Bion, *Cogitations* (London and New York: Karnac Books, 1992), 372.

19. Rashi to Numbers 11:1.

20. Rashi to Numbers 11:4.

21. Rashi to Numbers 11:5.

22. Rashi to Numbers 11:10.

23. Augustine called incest the sin of Avarice—"hoarding love in the family." It avoids the necessary expansive effort of love, its movement toward the other.

24. See Rashi to *B.Yoma* 75a.

25. Freud's view of the incest taboo is relevant here. He understands incestuous desire to be the primal, repressed desire, which every child struggles to manage and, ultimately, to sublimate. From this perspective, the Sinai Revelation might represent the advent of Law—the further development of a process that began at the beginning of human life in the stories of Adam and Eve and Noah.

26. *Avot d'Rabbi Nathan* 4:3.

27. Adam Phillips, *On Kissing, Tickling, and Being Bored* (Cambridge, MA: Harvard University Press, 1993), 71.

28. Adam Phillips, *On Flirtation* (Cambridge, MA: Harvard University Press, 1994), 56.

29. See *B.Kiddushin* 40b; Rambam, *Hilchot Teshuvah* 3:3.

30. Adam Phillips, *Promises, Promises* (New York: Basic Books, 2001), 205.

31. Donald Meltzer, *The Apprehension of Beauty* (Perthshire, UK: Clunie Press, 1988), 26–29.

32. Ibid., 19.

33. Ibid., 20.

34. Keats, *Letters* (London: Oxford University Press, 1954), April 1817.

35. Meltzer, *Apprehension of Beauty*, 28.

36. Melanie Klein, "Weaning," in *On the Bringing Up of Children*, ed. John Rickman (New York: Robert Brunner, 1952), 41.

37. Cf. a parallel passage in Exodus 5:22, where Moses complains of God's dealings with the people. In our narrative, his language conveys a more personal sense of grievance.

38. T. S. Eliot, *Selected Essays* (London: Faber and Faber, 1966), 17–19, 237–77.

39. Octavio Paz, *Alternating Current*, 68. Cited in Francis Landy, *Beauty and the Enigma* (Sheffield, UK: Sheffield Academic Press, 2001). See 273–74 for a discussion of metaphor in its integrative and disintegrative aspects.

40. *Shir Ha-Shirim Rabbah* 4:12.

41. Rashi to Song of Songs 4:5.

42. *B.Sotah* 12b.

43. It is striking that Winnicott's notion of *mirroring*, the way in which the mother reflects back to the baby his own face as lovingly experienced by her, also appears as powerful metaphor in the teachings of R. Nahman of Bratzlav. The oral transmission of the teaching of the Tzaddik (the righteous charismatic leader) is accomplished by gazing into his face and

seeing one's own face reflected as in a mirror. Furthermore, R. Nahman writes, the Tzaddik is called a mother who breastfeeds Israel with the milk of his Torah, arousing them from sadness, and drawing them away from their trivial passions to the true passion for the light of Torah, which is compared to milk. They are nurtured nonverbally through this visual connection (*Likkutei Moharan* 1:19 and 1:4). See Jonathan Garb, *Shamanic Trance in Modern Kabbalah* (Chicago and London: Chicago University Press, 2011), 92–93.

44. Sefat Emet, Bamidbar *Likkutim, B'Ha'alotcha.*

45. Maurice Blanchot, *The Space of Literature,* trans. Ann Smock (Lincoln, and London: University of Nebraska Press, 1982), 137.

46. Ibid., 147.

47. Ibid., 153.

48. On abjection, see Julia Kristeva, *Powers of Horror* (New York: Columbia University Press, 1980), 2.

49. *B.Yoma* 75a.

50. Hence *L'Sh'D*—an acronym for these three foods: *Le*chem, *She*men, *D'*vash.

51. Another midrashic passage explains the people's craving for the specific "Egyptian" foods they list in Numbers 11:5. These were not included among the many tastes of the manna, since they are "difficult for nursing mothers" (*B.Yoma* 75a). Here, manna and milk are not merely analogies; the taste of the manna affects the mothers' milk!

52. Cited in Herbert Fingarette, *The Self in Transformation* (New York and Evanston, IL: Harper & Row, 1965), 94.

53. *B.Gittin* 43a.

54. Mei Ha-Shilo'ach, vol. 2, *Be-ha'alotcha* 58–59.

55. *Torat Kohanim,* Vayikra 26:3.

56. Ralph Waldo Emerson, "Self-Reliance," in *Selected Essays,* ed. Larzer Ziff (Harmondsworth, Middlesex, UK, and New York: Penguin Books, 1982), 191.

57. T. S. Eliot, "Burnt Norton," in *Four Quartets* (San Diego, New York, and London: Harcourt Inc., 1943), 14.

58. See Jean Laplanche, *Essays on Otherness* (London and New York: Routledge, 1999), 190–91.

59. Julia Kristeva, *Tales of Love,* trans. Leon S. Roudiez (New York: Columbia University Press, 1987), 99.

60. Ibid., 100.

FOUR: "SING—NOW!—TO GOD": MIRIAM AND MOSES

1. For convenience, I will translate *tzora'at* as "leprosy," although it is now generally agreed that the biblical disease is not, in fact, leprosy.

2. Cf. other examples wherein a pair of subjects the woman is singled out in the verbal form: "And Esther . . . and Mordecai [she] spoke" Esther 9:29;

"And Devora and Balak [she] sang" (Judg. 5:1); and, without the gendered subject, "Then Moses and the Israelites [he] sang" (Exod. 15:1). In an apparently shared action, one protagonist takes the initiative.

3. See Rashbam, Bechor Shor, Yosef Kaspi, for attempts to provide the expression with historical or quasi-historical backing.

4. Rashi to Numbers 12:1–2.

5. *B.Sanhedrin* 17a.

6. Ibid.

7. See 1 Samuel 2:27 and Ezekiel 20:7, which are traditionally read as referring to Aaron's early prophetic role.

8. *B.Shabbat* 87a.

9. Ibid.

10. *Shemot Rabbah* 1:17.

11. Rashi to Exodus 1:15.

12. Ibid.

13. *Shemot Rabbah* 1:22.

14. S. R. Hirsch discusses the unusual grammatical form of *Va-tetatzav*, which suggests the reflexive mode—"She stood herself up."

15. *B.Sotah* 9b.

16. See Ramban and Seforno on Exodus 15:19 for this reading.

17. See Rashi to Exodus 15:1.

18. See, for example, *Shir Ha-Shirim Rabbah* 2:30.

19. There are a number of different views on the choral roles of Moses and the Israelites—ranging from Moses' dominating and the Israelites repeating line by line, to a responsive sequence in which the Israelites spontaneously continue Moses' words, to the tradition that *Shem Mi-Shmuel* draws on here, where even nursing babies sing spontaneously. See Tosefta *Sotah* 6.

20. *B.Brachot* 50a.

21. Donnel B. Stern, *Unformulated Experience* (Hillside, NJ, and London: Analytic Press, 1997), 235.

22. See ibid., 72, 74, 76.

23. *Shemot Rabbah* 23:12.

24. *B.Sotah* 11b.

25. In this version, the midwife is an angel, emissary of God from the highest heavens. But the expression, "God sent *one*"—*mi*—suggests that the midwife is in fact God Himself. In other versions, God is explicitly referred to as the midwife, who cuts the cord and cleanses and anoints the newborn. See *Shemot Rabbah* 23:9.

26. See Rashi to Exodus 15:20 *(With timbrels . . .)*.

27. *B.Sotah* 11b.

28. *Zeh* is understood to be the singular idiom of Moses, indicating a pre-

cision not available to other prophets. In the Song, however, the whole people, including babies, spontaneously sing, *"This is my God!"* See *B.Menachot* 53b; and Sifre on *Mattot*, 2.

29. Rashi to 15:20.

30. *Shemot Rabbah* 26:1.

31. See Catherine Clement, *Opera, or The Undoing of Women*, trans. Betsy Wing (Minneapolis: University of Minnesota Press, 1988).

32. Stanley Cavell, *A Pitch of Philosophy* (Cambridge, MA: Harvard University Press, 1994), 144.

33. Ibid., 146.

34. Ibid., 149.

35. Ibid., 150.

36. *Vayikra Rabbah* 11:9.

37. T. S. Eliot, "Burnt Norton," in *Four Quartets* (San Diego, New York, and London: Harcourt Inc., 1943), 15.

38. From the root *b-sh-sh*—as in Exodus 32:1: "And the people saw that Moses was late in coming down the mountain."

39. T. S. Eliot, ""The Love Song of J. Alfred Prufrock," in *Poems* (New York: A. A. Knopf, 1920), 47–48; 97–98.

40. *B.Shabbat* 87a.

41. See *Likkutei Anshei Shem* to 12:6.

42. Sefat Emet, Bamidbar, 83.

43. See Exodus 34:33–35.

44. According to the midrash, Aaron, too, becomes leprous ("God was angry with *them*") but is healed sooner. See *B.Shabbat* 97a.

45. Mei Ha-Shilo'ach, vol. 1, Be-ha'alotcha (end).

46. "He is our brother, our flesh," Judah says of Joseph (Gen. 37:27).

47. See Rashi to Numbers 12:12.

48. Moses had turned leprous at the Burning Bush when he expressed doubt about the Israelites' capacity for redemption (Exod. 4:1). *Tzora'at* is usually understood as the penalty for slander.

49. Numbers 12:10. JPS translates "struck with snow-white scales"— presumably to avoid translating *tzora'at* as "leprosy."

50. See *B.Baba Kama* 40a.

51. See Leviticus 13:5.

52. See Rashi to Numbers 12:15 and *B.Sotah* 9b, 11a.

53. Mei Ha-Shilo'ach, vol. 2, Be-ha'alotcha (end).

FIVE: BEWILDERMENTS

1. See, for example, Exodus 14:11; 16:3; 17:3; Numbers 11:20.

2. *Ta'anit* 4:6.

3. For instance: The destruction of the First and Second Temples, the crush-

ing of the Bar Kochba rebellion, the declaration of the First Crusade, the Expulsion of the Jews from the Iberian Peninsula; the beginning of the deportations from the Warsaw Ghetto to Treblinka.

4. *Efes* is used to refer to the end, extremity, nonexistence. As a verb, it means to "cease," "fail," "come to an end." Its use as a conjunction is quite rare. As here, it means "save that," "howbeit"—qualifying a preceding statement.

5. See Exodus 3:8,17.

6. See Genesis 6:4.

7. Tanchuma, *Shlach* 7.

8. See Beit Yaacov, *Vayera* 21.

9. See, for example, Jonathan Lear, *Happiness, Death, and the Remainder of Life* (Cambridge, MA: Harvard University Press, 2000), 118.

10. Seforno to Numbers 14:5.

11. *B.Sanhedrin* 19b.

12. See Numbers 13:27. Cf. Deuteronomy 1:25.

13. See Numbers 16:19; 17:7; 20:6.

14. Numbers 16:4,22; 17:10; 20:6.

15. *B.Sotah* 35a.

16. See *Torah Temimah* on 14:10. The sentence structure with the subject first is usually read in the pluperfect.

17. See Chapter 3, "Desire in the Wilderness."

18. This is the title of Emmanuel Levinas's volume of essays on Jewish topics.

19. Rashi to Deuteronomy 1:23.

20. Sifre 21.

21. Gur Aryeh to Numbers 13:2.

22. Ramban to Numbers 13:2.

23. See Sefat Emet, *Likkutim Shlach* on Numbers 13:28.

24. *Bamidbar Rabbah* 16:6.

25. Stanley Cavell, *In Quest of the Ordinary* (Chicago and London: University of Chicago Press, 1994), 128.

26. Ibid., 172.

27. Ibid., 88.

28. Ibid., 89.

29. See R. Hutner's interesting reading of Psalms 98:3: "All the ends of the earth shall see God's salvation." The Psalmist sings of the "edges," the end of time, the perspectives of the future that will read back now-absent meaning into the events of history. *Efes* describes a reality whose immediate relevance is obscure. (*Pachad Yitzchak, Purim,* 10)

30. Stephen Greenblatt, *Marvelous Possessions* (Chicago: University of Chicago Press, 1991), 14. See also Ilana Pardes, *The Biography of Ancient Israel* (Berkeley, Los Angeles, and London: University of California Press, 2000), 110–15.

31. The expression is a rabbinic construction. The word "sin" is never used in the biblical narrative.
32. See *B.Yevamot* 49b. Also see Rashi to Numbers 12:6.
33. See Rashi to the "unclear lens" passage in *Yevamot:* "Other prophets saw through an unclear lens and thought they saw, though they did not see. Moses saw through a clear lens and knew he did not see His face."
34. Ralph Waldo Emerson, "Nature," in *Selected Essays,* ed. Larzer Ziff (Harmondsworth, Middlesex, UK, and New York: Penguin Books, 1982), 38–39.
35. Mark Edmundson, *Towards Reading Freud* (Princeton, NJ: Princeton University Press, 1990), 131.
36. William Wordsworth, *Wordsworth: Poetry and Prose,* ed. W. Moelwyn Merchant (London: Rupert Hart-Davis, 1955), 153.
37. Cavell, *Quest,* 88–89.
38. W. R. Bion, *Attention and Interpretation* (Northvale, NJ: Jason Aronson, 1995), 16.
39. Lear, *Happiness, Death, and the Remainder of Life,* 46.
40. Ibid., 50–51.
41. Ibid., 102.
42. Ibid., 93.
43. Ibid., 90.
44. Ibid., 93.
45. Ibid., 94.
46. Ibid., 95.
47. Ibid., 96.
48. *Yalkut Shimoni* 16 (on Genesis 1:31).
49. *Bereshit Rabbah* 9:12. The midrash includes a play on *mavet* and *me'od.*
50. *B.Sotah* 35a.
51. D. W. Winnicott, *Home Is Where We Start From* (London and New York: W. W. Norton and Company, 1990), 82.
52. Ibid., 86.
53. Ibid., 87.
54. Ibid., 88.
55. Bion, quoted in Michael Eigen, *The Electrified Tightrope* (London: H. Karnac, 2004), 133.
56. *B.Brachot* 54a.
57. See Winnicott, cited in Eigen, *The Electrified Tightrope,* 114.
58. Jonathan Lear, *A Case for Irony* (Cambridge, MA, and London: Harvard University Press, 2011), 20.
59. See, for example, Sefat Emet, Bamidbar, 105.
60. See ibid., 92, 94–95, 105–6.
61. D. W. Winnicott, *Playing and Reality* (London and New York: Routledge, 1971), 24.
62. Lear, *Irony,* 43.

63. Ibid., 125.
64. Cf. Rashi on the parable of the stations of illness in the journey of the king's son—on Numbers 33:1. See my Preamble to this book.
65. See Abarbanel to Deuteronomy *Perush al HaTorah Devarim,* Bnei Arbel, 40–41.

SIX: BLACK SUN: MOSES AND JOB

1. Rashi to Deuteronomy 1:42.
2. Seforno to Deuteronomy 1:45.
3. See Levin Kipnis's famous poem, "Song of the *Ma'apilim,*" which became a Zionist hymn celebrating the movement of illegal immigration of 1934–1938.
4. See Ha'amek Davar to Numbers 14:40–44.
5. *Tzidkat Ha-Tzadik,* 46.
6. Julia Kristeva, *Black Sun,* trans. Leon S. Roudiez (New York: Columbia University Press, 1989), 41.
7. Ibid., 5.
8. Ibid., 6.
9. Ibid., 53.
10. *Bamidbar Rabbah* 16:20.
11. *B.Baba Batra* 15a.
12. *Bamidbar Rabbah* 16:25.
13. *B.Baba Batra* 14b.
14. Another such attribution from the same Talmudic text: Samuel is the author of the book of Judges and the book of Ruth. Moses himself is also credited with writing Deuteronomy ("his own book") and the story of Balaam. In European literature, the most famous example of character-turned-author is Proust's *In Search of Lost Time*—which is attributed to Marcel's authorship.
15. See *J.Sotah* v:6 on the idea that Job never actually existed. See also Maimonides's claim that Job is a parable—*Guide for the Perplexed,* 3:25.
16. Seforno to Deuteronomy 1:27.
17. Exodus 22:27.
18. Hatred, the curse, and the blow constitute a set in many biblical passages—the emotion and its verbal and physical expressions.
19. Leviticus 24:10–14.
20. Ramban to Leviticus 24:10.
21. According to Ramban, the blasphemer is "like a *mamzer.*"
22. *Vayikra Rabbah* 32:7.
23. See Numbers 14:14–16; and *Bamidbar Rabbah,* cited above in note 12 to this chapter.
24. "And now" is traditionally understood as an indication of repentance.
25. The incident when he "hits" (*makkeh*) the Egyptian taskmaster—that

is, he kills him—begins his life story; the incident when he "hits" the rock, rather than speaking to it, ends it. This framing of his history is suggestive.

26. William Blake, "The Marriage of Heaven and Hell," in *The Poems of William Blake* (London: Oxford University Press, 1913), 248.

27. Marion Milner, "The Sense in Nonsense (Freud and Blake's *Job*)," in *The Suppressed Madness of Sane Men* (London and New York: Routledge, 1987), 185.

28. Ibid., 183–84.

29. Ibid., 186–87.

30. Attributed to the Ba'al Shem Tov.

31. See Rashi to Exodus 2:2.

32. See Menachem Mendel Kasher, *Torah Shelemah*, vol. 9, *Shemot* (New York: Schulsinger, 1944), 197n.139. The notion that God is addressing Moses is dismissed by Ibn Ezra as "mad." However, as an ambiguous possibility, it bears consideration.

33. See *Midrash Ha-Gadol* to Exodus 6:2.

34. This meaning of *milah* is found mostly in postbiblical texts. See, however, Genesis 21:7.

35. Chapter 28.

36. *B.Niddah* 30b.

37. See Targum Onkelos and Rashi to Genesis 2:7.

38. The Talmudic expression is *makkeh be-patish*—the blow of the chisel—which signifies completion.

39. *B.Niddah* 30b.

40. See William Wordsworth, "Intimations of Immortality," in *Wordsworth: Poetry and Prose,* ed. W. Moelwyn Merchant (London: Rupert Hart-Davis, 1955), 577.

41. See *Shemot Rabbah* 5:22.

42. *B.Brachot* 7a.

43. See Mei Ha-Shilo'ach, vol. 1 to *Parshat Tissa*. The word *achar* can refer to "space" (behind) or to "time" (after).

44. See, for example, Job 9:11; 23:8. See Moshe Halevi Spero, "The Hidden Subject of Job: Mirroring and the Anguish of Interminable Desire," in *Hearing Visions and Seeing Voices,* ed. Gerrit Glas, Moshe Halevi Spero, Peter J. Verhagen, and Herman M. van Praag (Dordrecht, The Netherlands: Springer, 2007), for a fascinating Lacanian study of the book of Job.

45. In the Zohar, *amar* is often translated as "whisper."

46. Mei Ha-Shilo'ach, vol. 1, on *Parshat Emor*.

47. Alexander Nehamas, *The Art of Living* (Berkeley, Los Angeles, and London: University of California Press, 1998), 91–92.

48. Judith N. Shklar, *Ordinary Vices* (Cambridge, MA: Harvard University Press, 1984), 42–43.

49. Adam Phillips, *The Beast in the Nursery* (London: Faber and Faber, 1998), 95.
50. *Rachamim*—compassion—has as its root *r-ch-m*, the womb.
51. Mei Ha-Shilo'ach, vol. 2, on *Parshat Shlach*.
52. *Seder Eliyahu Rabbah*, 29.
53. *B.Yevamot* 49b.

SEVEN: "FROM ANOTHER SHORE": MOSES AND KORACH

1. There is some ambiguity in the narrative as to the fate of Korach and his people (Num. 16:32). See also *B.Sanhedrin* 110a.
2. *V'esh yatz'ah* is probably to be read in the pluperfect—"A fire *had gone* forth from God" (Num. 16:35).
3. This might be read more strongly as "not-God sent me." Some demonic force has been driving Moses to invent a narrative of divine calling?
4. It is striking that the other punishment is also described as "consuming": "a fire had gone forth from God and consumed the two hundred and fifty men" (Num. 16:35).
5. God's promise to dwell in their midst (Exod. 25:8) refers to the structure of the camp arranged around the Tabernacle. This is a physical reality, as well as a mystical idea, a project of aspiration for the people. Cf. the dancing circle of the righteous as an image of transcendent bliss in the world to come (*Vayikra Rabbah* 11:9; *B.Ta'anit* 31a).
6. It is striking that even the words *tallit she-kulo techelet* play on the theme of totality, both explicitly and implicitly—*techelet* contains *kol* (wholeness) at its center.
7. *Midrash Bamidbar Rabbah* 18:8.
8. Psalms 115:17. See also, among many other examples, Psalms 94:17; 88:12.
9. The biblical word *vayichar*, without the word *af*, is often translated in this way in the midrash, as though it refers to a generalized emotional agitation.
10. See Sefat Emet, *Shemot*, 84 (*U-bil'shon ha-passuk . . . kabbalat bnei yisrael*).
11. The Hebrew word for "two lips"—*sefatayim*—is also the word for "two edges."
12. The idiom, *le-hanik le . . . (nursing for . . .)* is used in Miriam's proposal and in the princess's speech to Moses' mother. Interestingly, when she nurses him, the text drops the *le-* idiom—simply, "she nursed him."
13. *B.Sanhedrin* 110a. See also Rashi to Numbers 16:12.
14. Rashbam reads this as refusing to submit to judgment.
15. See Or Ha-Chaim to Numbers 16:12.
16. Nineteen out of twenty biblical usages of the phrase have this meaning.
17. Jacques Lacan, Seminar XXI, as quoted in Shoshana Felman, *Writing and Madness*, trans. Martha Noel Evans (Ithaca, NY: Cornell University Press, 1985), 240.
18. See Rashi's translation of "uncircumcised" as "blocked," on Exodus 6:12.

19. See Gur Aryeh on Numbers 16:27.

20. Maurice Blanchot, *L'Entretien infini* (Paris: Gallimard, 1969), 13–14.

21. G. K. Chesterton, *Orthodoxy* (New York: Doubleday, 1990), 19–20.

22. *Likkutei Moharan* I, 64:4.

23. Walter Benjamin, *Understanding Brecht*, trans. Anna Bostock (London: Verso, 1983), 73.

24. Zohar, vol.1, 17a.

25. Cf. Nelson Goodman, *Ways of Worldmaking* (Indianapolis, IN: Hackett Pub. Company, 1978).

26. Mei Ha-Shilo'ach, vol. 2, *Korach* (*K'tiv* . . .).

27. See Marion Milner, *The Suppressed Madness of Sane Men* (London and New York: Routledge, 1988), 208.

28. Ralph Waldo Emerson, *Selected Essays*, ed. Larzer Ziff (Harmondsworth, Middlesex, UK, and New York: Penguin, 1982), 176.

29. "Alienated" holds the meaning of ghostly presences.

30. Stanley Cavell, *Conditions Handsome and Unhandsome* (Chicago: University of Chicago Press, 1990), 57.

31. Mei Ha-Shilo'ach, vol. 2, *Korach* (*Ki kol ha-edah* . . .).

32. This brings to mind the visionary image of the circle dance of the righteous. See *Vayikra Rabbah* 11:9. That, of course, is a vision of the world *to come*.

33. Emmanuel Levinas, *Totality and Infinity* (Pittsburgh: Duquesne University Press, 1969), 171.

34. Blanchot, *L'Entretien infini*, 74.

35. See Levinas, *Totality*, 207.

36. Ibid., 209.

37. Ibid., 197.

38. Sefat Emet, Bamidbar, 113.

39. *Bereshit Rabbah* 12:15.

40. Cf. Leonard Cohen's "Anthem":

> Ring the bells that still can ring
> Forget your perfect offering
> There is a crack, a crack in everything
> That's how the light gets in.

And W. B. Yeats, "Crazy Jane Talks with the Bishop":

> For nothing can be sole or whole
> That has not been rent.

41. See *B.Sanhedrin* 108a.

42. See *B.Sanhedrin* 109b. cf. *J.Sanhedrin* 10:4.

43. This is, in fact, an interrupted verse—a half verse, as it were. Perhaps the very form of the verse enacts its meaning: it serves to disrupt the

smooth flow of names and numbers of the national census, creating a suspension in the midst of the chronicle. Perhaps closure is not, after all, complete?

44. See Psalms 84, 85, 87, 88.
45. See *B.Sanhedrin* 110a.
46. "Revelation in the Jewish Tradition," in *The Levinas Reader,* ed. Sean Hand (Oxford, UK and Cambridge, MA:, Blackwell, 1989), 209.
47. My thanks to Sara Friedland, who drew my attention to this teaching.
48. *Sefat Emet, Vayikra* on *Pesach,* 79.

EIGHT: HEART OF STONE, HEART OF FLESH

1. Or Ha-Chaim to Numbers 20:8.
2. See Ibn Ezra to Numbers 20:6.
3. See Numbers 14:1; 16:19; 17:7.
4. Rashi to Numbers 20:12.
5. See Ramban to Numbers 20:7.
6. *Hakdamot Ha-Rambam la-Mishnah,* 240.
7. Ramban reads Korach's rebellion as an immediate offshoot of the narrative of the Spies, and therefore as happening in the second year in the wilderness.
8. Rashi to Deuteronomy 34:5.
9. Rashi to Deuteronomy 34:6.
10. Deuteronomy 33:1.
11. See *B.Sotah* 14a.
12. The Red Heifer law is called a—or the—*chukkah:* the quintessential pure decree, resisting normal rational inquiry.
13. *Yalkut Shimoni* 759.
14. The first narrative takes place near Horev, at Refidim; the second near Edom, on the plains of Moab, before crossing the Jordan.
15. Cf. Numbers 17:25. If this rod is identical with Aaron's rod, which flowered in the Korach narrative, its history becomes more complicated. I intend to follow the history of Moses' rod—called "the rod of God"—as it appears in the miracle stories in Exodus and in Numbers 20.
16. Exodus 16:33–34.
17. Meshech Chochmah cites Mechilta 6:3; and Rambam, *The Guide for the Perplexed* 2:29.
18. See *B.Horayot* 12a.
19. Rashi to Exodus 17:5.
20. *B.Rosh Hashanah* 29a.
21. Mechilta *Beshallach* 1 (17:11).
22. *Pirkei d'Rabbi Eliezer,* 44.
23. See Ramban to Exodus 17:9: "While he was praying with his palms outstretched to heaven, he grasped nothing in his hand."

24. Robert Alter, *Necessary Angels* (Cambridge, MA: Harvard University Press, 1991), 104.

25. Walter Benjamin, *Illuminations* (London: Collins Fontana Books, 1973), 204.

26. Or even including the plagues at the Red Sea. See Or Ha-Chaim to Exodus 11:9 for a psychological reading of Pharaoh's intransigence.

27. See Ramban to Exodus 7:16.

28. See Rashi: "Your words will be effective in liberating them."

29. *B.Shabbat* 97a.

30. This is the Jewish Publication Society translation.

31. See Exodus 2:7 with its repetition of the word *lach*—"for you."

32. Citing a midrash to be found in *Torah Shelemah*, vol. 8, *Shemot* 2:[51].

33. *B.Sotah* 12b.

34. Rashi to Exodus 4:8.

35. "He saw what he had done to him at home and in the field. . . . He saw that no future proselyte would be born of him" (Exod. 2:12).

36. *B.Sanhedrin* 58b.

37. See Rema on *Choshen Mishpat* 34:4. See also *Torah Temimah* to Exodus 2:13.

38. See Numbers 15:30.

39. Walter Benjamin, *Reflections* (New York: Schocken Books, 1986), 204.

40. See, for example, Rashi to Numbers 17:5: *"As God spoke by the hand of Moses:* in the same way as Moses was afflicted with leprosy." The dead metaphor is transformed into a specific moment of memory and judgment.

41. See Rashi to Genesis 42:24.

42. *J.Brachot* 5:1.

43. See *B.Shabbat* 87.

44. *J.Ta'anit* 4:5.

45. Michael Fried, *Realism, Writing, Disfiguration* (Chicago and London: University of Chicago Press, 1987), 99–100. See also Gillian Beer, *Open Fields* (New York: Oxford University Press, 1996), 14–15.

46. *B.Eruvin* 54a.

47. Yitzchak Hutner, *Pachad Yitzchak,* Chanukah, 36.

48. *B.Temurah* 16a.

49. *B.Menachot* 99b.

50. *Hamlet,* act 1, scene 5.

51. See Susan Stewart, *The Poet's Freedom* (Chicago and London: University of Chicago Press, 2011), 1–2.

52. See Rashi, "Seeing the audible."

53. *Bamidbar Rabbah* 19:5.

54. John Berger, *Keeping a Rendezvous* (New York: Random House, 1991), 129.

55. Ibid., 129–31.

56. John Berger, *The Sense of Sight* (New York: Vintage International, Random House, 1985), 206–7.

57. Ibid., 191–93.

58. Ibid., 194–96.

59. Ibid., 195–96.

60. Ibid., 207.

61. Jeremiah 23:29.

62. *B.Shabbat* 88a.

63. Franz Kafka, *Parables and Paradoxes* (New York: Schocken Books, 1961), 83.

64. Alter, *Necessary Angels,* 92.

65. Benjamin, *Illuminations,* 204.

66. S. R. Hirsch connects *bassar* (flesh)—with the verb *le-vasser* (to announce, proclaim), suggesting that "the human body is the herald of the spirit to the world"; it brings consciousness of the world and is the medium of impact on the world. (S. R. Hirsch, *The Pentateuch,* vol. 1, trans. Isaac Levy [London: Isaac Levy, 1959] on Genesis 2:21, 68.)

67. *Yalkut Shimoni* 763.

68. Naftali Zvi Berlin, *Ha'amek Davar: Torat Elohim,* vol. 4 (Jerusalem: Chemed, 1975), 174–75. Miriam's well is listed among the ten things created at twilight on the Shabbat eve of Creation (*Pirkei Avot* 5:8). These last-moment creations occupy a transitional space between the natural and the miraculous.

69. Sifra 60:12.

70. *B.Megillah* 23b.

71. Ralph Waldo Emerson, "The Poet," in *Selected Essays,* ed. Larzer Ziff (Harmondsworth, Middlesex, UK, and New York: Penguin Books, 1982), 279.

72. Ibid., 265.

73. Maharal, *Gevurot Ha-Shem* (Jerusalem: Yahadut, 1971), 44.

74. Berger, *Keeping a Rendezvous,* 130.

75. Ibid., 131.

76. *Pachad Yitzchak,* Pesach, 40.

77. See Jacob Zvi Mecklenberg, *Ha-K'tav v'Ha-kabbalah* to 20:8.

78. See Leviticus 22:32: "And I shall be sanctified in the midst of the Israelites," with its classical interpretation: "Allow yourself to be martyred for the sanctification of His name." (See Rashi to 22:32.)

79. Benjamin, *Illuminations,* 204.

80. Kenneth Burke, "What Are the Signs of What? A Theory of Entitlement," in *Language as Symbolic Action* (Berkeley, Los Angeles, and London: University of California Press, 1966). 379. See also Richard Poirier, "Frost, Winnicott, Burke," in *Transitional Objects and Potential Spaces,* ed. Peter L. Rudnytsky (New York: Columbia University Press, 1993), 216–28.

81. The idea of the *reshimu*—lit., the impression, the trace—is a major theme in the kabbalistic world of meanings.

82. *Shir Ha-Shirim Rabbah* 1:10.

NINE: "WHEREFORE COULD NOT I PRONOUNCE 'AMEN'?":
BALAAM AND MOSES

1. See Seforno to Numbers 22:6.
2. Seforno notes that Balaam is not hired, for instance, to *bless Balak* with military success.
3. See Hizkuni. See also Jeremiah 18:18. Here Jeremiah's enemies plot to lay charges against him to bring about his destruction.
4. See Numbers 22:7; 23:23; 24:1.
5. In the idiom of the Sages, "he knew how to intuit the moment when God is angry" (*B.Brachot* 7a).
6. Midrash Tanchuma, 6.
7. *B.Sanhedrin* 105a.
8. See *B.Makkot* 10b.
9. See *Pirkei Avot* 5:20.
10. Ralph Waldo Emerson, *Selected Essays,* ed. Larzer Ziff (Harmondsworth, Middlesex, UK, and New York: Penguin Books, 1982), 184.
11. Stanley Cavell, *In Quest of the Ordinary* (Chicago and London: University of Chicago Press, 1988), 116.
12. See Freud, *Fragments of an Analysis of a Case of Hysteria,* in *The Standard Edition of the Complete Psychological Works of Sigmund Freud,* ed. and trans. J. Strachey, vol. 7 (London: Hogarth Press, 1953), 77–78.
13. *B.Sanhedrin* 108b.
14. In Freud's famous case, the "Rat-Man," he compares his patient to "an inverted Balaam," because "something always inserted itself into his pious phrases and turned them into their opposite." Typically, it is the word "not" that is insinuated into his prayers. In view of the Sanhedrin passage, it is not clear whether Balaam and the Rat-Man are inversions of each other or replicas.
15. See Jacob Milgrom, "Diviner or Sorcerer?" in *The JPS Torah Commentary: Numbers* (Philadelphia and New York: The Jewish Publication Society, 1990), 473.
16. See Rashi to Numbers 24:1,3.
17. Rashi comments that it is an angel who adds the expression *alei mayim*— "by the water"—to Balaam's arid description of the cedar. Rashi is here referring to another midrashic scenario about the "turning" of Balaam's curse; an angel inhabits his mouth and edits all his curses. See p. 244.
18. *B.Ta'anit* 20a.
19. See the Soncino edition of Proverbs, which cites Eitan and Ehlich: *ne'etarot* has the meaning "deceptive," on the analogy of cognate Arabic roots.
20. See *B.Yevamot* 64a. See *Torah Temimah* 24n.12.

21. Marcel Proust, *Swan's Way,* trans. C. K. Moncrieff and Terence Kilmartin (New York: Random House, 1989), 87.

22. Ibid., 87–88.

23. Gabriel Josipovici, *Trust* (New Haven, CT, and London: Yale University Press, 1999), 182.

24. See Meshech Chochmah to Numbers 20:20–22.

25. See *B.Sanhedrin* 105b.

26. Seforno to Numbers 22:38.

27. See Rashi and Seforno to Numbers 24:1.

28. George Eliot, *Middlemarch* (London: Penguin Books, 1985), 182.

29. Zohar 3:147. See also *B.Sanhedrin* 108a: "Balaam was blind in one eye, as it says, 'the utterance of the man whose eye is open'" (Num. 24:3).

30. *B.Brachot* 58a. The story is told of R. Sheshet who is mocked for his blindness by a heretic and who promptly retaliates with the power of his blind gaze.

31. See both Seforno and Ramban to Numbers 22:41.

32. See Meira Likierman, *Melanie Klein* (London and New York: Continuum, 2001), 174.

33. *B.Baba Batra* 14b.

34. See Chapter 6, "Black Sun: Moses and Job."

35. Or Ha-Chaim to Exodus 4:12.

36. This is the reading of R. Yosef Kimchi, cited in Menachem Kasher, *Torah Shelemah,* vol. 9, *Shemot,* 197n139.

37. Rashi to Exodus 4:24.

38. *Pirkei d'Rabbi Eliezer,* 29.

39. *Shemot Rabbah* 19:6.

40. The aroma pervades over a distance of forty days' travel, the period in which the embryo takes on full human shape.

41. See Rashi to Numbers 22:4.

42. See Chapter 8, "Heart of Stone, Heart of Flesh."

43. The Talmud detects a sexual implication in the relation of Balaam and his she-ass. See *B.Sanhedrin* 105b.

44. According to the Midrash, Moses was born circumcised, as a sign of grace (*Shemot Rabbah* 1:24). However, his own words express a sense of blockage in the body openings—tongue, lips, mouth—that communicate with the world of others.

45. *B.Nedarim* 31b.

46. In *Pirkei d'Rabbi Eliezer,* 29, Abraham is even able to *sit* in God's presence, while He stands over him.

47. Tanchuma, *Lech,* 16

48. Gur Aryeh to Numbers 24:4.

49. Michael Eigen, *The Psychoanalytic Mystic* (London and New York: Free Association Books, 1998), 145.

50. The Lacanian term *jouissance* refers to sexual ecstasy, unlimited bliss.
51. See Ezekiel 11:19.
52. Zohar 2:69b.
53. *Bamidbar Rabbah* 20:20.
54. Midrashic sources connect Balaam's "counsel" to Balak (see Rashi to 24:14) with the following episode about the Moabite women and the Israelite idol worship.
55. *Ruth Rabbah* 6:1,2.
56. It is striking that the *Tzur,* the Rock, is the same word that is used to describe the "flint" with which Zippora circumcises her baby (Exod. 4:22), as well as the rock that Moses strikes to produce water (17:6). The root *tzar* evokes harsh, constricted, and bloody realities. Even *mitzrayim,* Egypt, is read, in a classic play on words, as *meitzarim*—the place of narrow straits. In kabbalistic language, this is the world of *middat ha-din,* strict judgment, incomprehensible fate.
57. This is a wordplay on *le nom du pere* and *les non-dupes errent* in Jacques Lacan's famous discussion of the role of the father in the symbolic order. See Jacques Lacan, *The Seminar of Jacques Lacan: The Psychoses,* trans. Jacques-Alain Miller and Russell Grigg (New York: W. W. Norton, 1997).
58. See Somerset Maugham's play, *Sheppey* (London: World Classics, 2003).
59. See Slavoj Zizek, *The Sublime Object of Ideology* (London and New York: Verso, 1989), 58–59.
60. *B.Sanhedrin* 108b. See my discussion on p. 240.
61. J. L. Austin coined the term "perlocutionary speech act" to describe such statements. They are also known as "performative speech acts."
62. *B.Makkot* 10b.

TEN: TO BE OR NOT TO BE: A TALE OF FIVE SISTERS

1. Cf. the case of the "second Passover" (Num. 9:1–12), which bears many similarities to our narrative, as well as important differences.
2. See, for example, Numbers 1:51 and Leviticus 10:1.
3. The two lists are in different order.
4. In fact, Rashi understands the changed order of their names as indicating that they are all equivalent (Num. 27:1).
5. Oxford and New York: Oxford University Press, 1984.
6. *B.Batra* 119a; *B.Sanhedrin* 8a.
7. Sifre.
8. Cf. Tanchuma, 8.
9. Sifre.
10. *Bamidbar Rabbah* 21:11.
11. *Bamidbar Rabbah* 21:12.
12. See Chapter 1, "Flags in the Wilderness," for a discussion of the classic pun on the double meaning of *midbar*—wilderness and speech.

13. It is interesting that Rashi is here piecing together readings from different sources: Sifre, Sanhedrin, Tanchuma.

14. Elaine Scarry, *On Beauty* (Princeton, NJ: Princton University Press, 1999), 91–92.

15. Ibid., 100.

16. Ibid., 97. Scarry brings the examples of the figure of the cube, equidistant in all directions, and of scales, equally weighted in both directions.

17. Rashi omits to refer to the speakers of this exclamation—"The *nations of the world* will in the future say, Happy is the person with whose words God agrees!" Without this attribution, the celebration becomes both more anonymous and more intimate.

18. *Bamidbar Rabbah* 21:11.

19. As the Talmud in *B.Baba Batra* 119b puts it: "The daughters of Tzelofchad were expounders of the text, for they said, If our father had had a son, we *would not have spoken.*"

20. *Yalkut Shimoni* 773.

21. This aphorism occurs at the end of another narrative of feminine timeliness.

22. Ralph Waldo Emerson, "Self-Reliance," in *Selected Essays*, ed. Larzer Ziff (Harmondsworth, Middlesex, UK, and New York: Penguin Books, 1982),190.

23. Ibid., 189.

24. Stanley Cavell, *In Quest of the Ordinary* (Chicago and London: University of Chicago Press, 1988), 109.

25. Ibid., 114.

26. Ibid., 115–16.

27. Ibid., 119.

28. Rashi to Deuteronomy 2:16–17. It is striking that "God spoke to me" is given a verse of its own. See *B.Baba Batra* 121a–b.

29. Rashi to Numbers 20:25.

30. The reference is to Psalms 1 and 2, read together as one long chapter.

31. See Psalms 40:4.

32. Shoshana Felman, *The Scandal of the Speaking Body,* trans. Catherine Porter (Stanford, CA: Stanford University Press, 2003), 55–56.

33. Ibid., 70.

34. Ibid., 71. Felman makes the interesting point that the adverb "inadvertently" has no antonym in English: there is no use, apparently, for *advertently*. A psychoanalytic intuition notes that such expressions stem from a discontinuity or a break in intention, which for Austin is "scarcely conscious."

35. J. L. Austin, *Sense and Sensibilia*, 4–5, quoted in Felman, *Scandal*, 85.

36. J. L. Austin, *Philosophical Papers*, 241, quoted in Felman, *Scandal*, 85.

37. Felman, *Scandal*, 85.

38. J. L. Austin, *How to Do Things with Words,* 61, quoted in Felman, *Scandal,* 92.

39. *B.Gittin* 43a.

40. John Felstiner, *Paul Celan: Poet, Survivor, Jew* (New Haven, CT, and London: Yale University Press, 1995), 232.

41. Paul Celan, "Winter," 1938. Cited in Felstiner, *Paul Celan,* 17.

42. Felstiner, *Paul Celan,* xix.

43. Cavell, *Quest,* 115–16.

44. Giorgio Agamben, *Remnants of Auschwitz* (New York: Zone Books, 1999), 150.

45. The trigger for his transformation is the provocative statement of the harlot—"You will never repent!" Her words change his world sufficiently to make him desire to change it entirely.

46. *B.Avodah Zarah* 17a.

47. Sefat Emet, Bamidbar, 173–74.

48. Kafka's story, "The Door of the Law," in *The Trial* (London: Penguin Books, 1953), 237, ends with a similar paradox: "No one but you could gain admittance through this door, since the door was intended only for you."

49. Cavell, *Quest,* 128.

50. This is the argument made by the women's male relatives later in Numbers 36:1–4. God's response opens with the same words as He had spoken to the five sisters: "*Ken,* rightly do they the clan of Josephites speak!" According to the Sifre, here, too, God gives the speakers the same praise of replicating the divine version of the narrative. However, this second *ken* does not have the same performative power as the first. The women created the precedent of such speech. God's response to them therefore does not draw the panoply of midrashic elaborations that we have noticed. The solution that God later proposes protects the stability of the land but leaves open the question of whether women in this position are prevented by law from marrying outside the tribe, or merely advised not to do so.

51. Sefat Emet, Bamidbar, 183.

52. *B.Baba Batra* 75a.

53. The root *a-v-r* is also connected with *ibbur*—pregnancy.

ELEVEN: "LET ME SEE THAT GOOD LAND": THE STORY OF A HUMAN LIFE

1. Healing and government are Freud's other two "impossible professions."

2. Tanchuma *Devarim* 2.

3. There may be a pun in the midrash on the word *be'er/ba'er*—"a well"/ "interpreting."

4. See, for example, *B.Megillah* 31b; Maharal, *Tifferet Yisrael,* chapter 43; the

commentaries of Abarbanel, Or Ha-Chaim, and the Dubno Maggid (*Ohel Ya'akov*).

5. See Rashi to Deuteronomy 3:26: "'Enough': so that people don't say, 'How harsh the teacher, how unruly the student!'" The apparent cruelty of God's repudiation can be countered only by assuming that Moses' plea is in some way egregious. The more eloquent he is, the harder it is for the reader to avoid the dilemma of judgment.

6. Rashi to Deuteronomy 3:23.

7. Numbers 27:12.

8. Rashi to Numbers 27:17.

9. See *B.Baba Batra* 109b on Numbers 27:8: "You shall *transfer* his property to his daughter": "Rav said, 'Everywhere the word *give* is used, only here is *transfer* used. No one *transfers* property from tribe to tribe but a daughter, since her son and her husband inherit her.'" See also Rashi on this verse.

10. See Rashi to Numbers 27:16: "The moment has come for me to plead my cause. . . ."

11. See *Bamidbar Rabbah* 21:15.

12. The mystery diminishes if we assume, in the wake of Ramban, a principle of literary economy in the biblical text. See, for example, Ramban to Genesis 42:21.

13. See also Deuteronomy 31:2–3.

14. Even before he tells the story of his prayer, Moses recounts how he charged Joshua with his future military role "among the kingdoms, where you are crossing over" (Deut. 3:21).

15. See also Numbers 33:51; 35:10; and Deuteronomy 4:14,26; 6:1; 9:1; 11:8,11,31; 30:18; 31:13.

16. The word *mikneh* opens and closes their first speech and occurs seven times in its course.

17. They are replaying, in a sense, the refusal of the Spies, the failure of desire that made that crossing unthinkable. This is Moses' retrospective analysis of their rebellion: "You had no desire to go up" (Deut. 1:26). It is striking that in Deuteronomy, *crossing over* largely replaces *going up* (*aliyah*) as the verb used to describe the movement into the Land. The latter was central to the story of the Spies; the former becomes the term of choice in Moses' parting speeches.

18. Mei Ha-Shilo'ach, vol. 1, *Devarim*.

19. *B.Eruvin* 100b.

20. See Rashi on Deuteronomy 1:14: Moses ironically notes the enthusiasm of their response to the idea of delegating leadership. Their eager assent betrays their secret intention of corrupting the future judges who, unlike Moses, will be open to bribery.

21. *Devarim Rabbah* 3:12.

22. *Devarim Rabbah* 7:11.
23. Abraham, the father of the Jewish people, is resonantly described as *ha-ivri* (the Hebrew) (Gen. 14:13): the one who came from the other side of the river (Rashi). Another midrashic reading: "The entire world was on one side of the divide, while he was on the other" (*Bereshit Rabbah* 42:13). This "Hebrew" identification becomes the primal epithet for Joseph in Egypt, for the Hebrew slaves in Egypt, and, in legal texts, for members of the Hebrew nation, as opposed to Canaanite or other foreign nationalities. The Hebrew language, too, is referred to in Talmudic and midrashic texts as *Ivrit;* this is, of course, the modern Hebrew word for the modern Hebrew language.
24. Anne Carson, *Eros* (London: Dalkey Archive Press, 1998), 75.
25. Ibid., 98.
26. Ibid., 71.
27. Ibid., 30.
28. Ibid., 73.
29. The biblical word for "wing" is *ever.*
30. Italo Calvino, *Mr. Palomar* (London: Picador, 1986), 110–11.
31. Sigmund Freud, cited in Shoshana Felman, "Psychoanalysis and Education: Teaching Terminable and Interminable," in *Yale French Studies* 63:401.
32. Felman, "Psychoanalysis and Education," 401.
33. Ibid., 401.
34. Sigmund Freud, cited in Felman, "Psychoanalysis and Education," 405.
35. Ibid., 407.
36. Felman, "Psychoanalysis and Education," 407.
37. See Roland Barthes, "Writers, Intellectuals, Teachers," in *Image/Music/Text* (New York: Hill and Wang, 1978), 194–96.
38. Franz Kafka, *Diaries 1914–1923*, trans. Martin Greenberg and Hannah Arendt (New York: Schocken Books, 1965), 195–96.
39. Christopher Bollas, *Cracking Up* (New York: Hill and Wang, 1996), 140.
40. Ibid., 141–42.
41. Ibid., 144.
42. *B.Avodah Zarah* 5b.
43. Rashi to Deuteronomy 29:3.
44. Cf. Balaam's forced blessings, and Jacob's qualified blessings.
45. Midrash Tehillim, Psalm 90. See also Zohar *Bereshit Vayechi,* 236b.
46. See Ha'amek Davar to Deuteronomy 5:24. He cites *Shir Ha-Shirim Rabbah* 1:44, which compares Moses to the "fairest of women." I owe this insight to Ari Elon, *Ba el Ha-Kodesh* (Tel Aviv: Yediot Achronot, 2005), 303.
47. See *B.Brachot* 18b; and Rashi to Deuteronomy 34:4.

BIBLIOGRAPHY

Agamben, Giorgio. *Remnants of Auschwitz*. New York: Zone Books, 1999.

Alter, Robert. *Necessary Angels*. Cambridge, MA: Harvard University Press, 1991.

Barthes, Roland. "Writers, Intellectuals, Teachers," in *Image/Music/Text*, 194–96. New York: Hill and Wang, 1978.

Beer, Gillian. *Open Fields*. New York: Oxford University Press, 1996.

Benjamin, Walter. *Illuminations*. London: Collins Fontana Books, 1973.

———. *Reflections*. New York: Schocken Books, 1986.

———. *Understanding Brecht*. Translated by Anna Bostock. London: Verso, 1983.

Berger, John. *Keeping a Rendezvous*. New York: Random House, 1991.

———. *The Sense of Sight*. New York: Random House, 1985.

Berger, Peter L. *A Rumor of Angels*. Garden City, NY: Doubleday, 1969.

Bersani, Leo, and Adam Phillips. *Intimacies*. Chicago and London: University of Chicago Press, 2008.

Bion, W. R. *Attention and Interpretation*. Northvale, NJ: Jason Aronson, 1995.

———. *Cogitations*. London and New York: Karnac Books, 1992.

Blake, William. *The Poems of William Blake*. London: Oxford University Press, 1913.

Blanchot, Maurice. *L'Entretien infini*. Paris: Gallimard, 1969.

———. *The Space of Literature*. Translated by Ann Smock. Lincoln and London: University of Nebraska Press, 1982.

Bollas, Christopher. *Cracking Up*. New York: Hill and Wang, 1996.

Burke, Kenneth. *Language as Symbolic Action*. Berkeley, Los Angeles, and London: University of California Press, 1966.

Calvino, Italo. *Mr. Palomar*. London: Picador, 1986.

Carson, Anne. *Eros*. London: Dalkey Archive Press, 1998.

Cavell, Stanley. *Conditions Handsome and Unhandsome*. Chicago: University of Chicago Press, 1990.

———. *In Quest of the Ordinary*. Chicago and London: University of Chicago Press, 1988.

———. *Philosophy the Day After Tomorrow*. Cambridge, MA, and London: Harvard University Press, 2005.

———. *A Pitch of Philosophy*. Cambridge, MA: Harvard University Press, 1994.

Chesterton, G. K. *Orthodoxy*. New York: Doubleday, 1990.

Clement, Catherine. *Opera, or The Undoing of Women*. Translated by Betsy Wing. Minneapolis: University of Minnesota Press, 1988.

Dillard, Annie. *For the Time Being*. New York: Knopf, 1999.

Douglas, Mary. *In the Wilderness*. Sheffield, UK: JSOT Press, 1993.

Edmundson, Mark. *Towards Reading Freud*. Princeton, NJ: Princeton University Press, 1990.

Eigen, Michael. *The Electrified Tightrope*. London: H. Karnac, 2004.

———. *The Psychoanalytic Mystic*. London and New York: Free Association Books, 1998.

Eliot, George. *Middlemarch*. Harmondsworth, UK, and New York: Penguin Books, 1985.

Eliot, T. S. *Selected Essays*. London: Faber and Faber, 1966.

Elon, Ari. *Ba el Ha-Kodesh*. Tel Aviv: Yediot Achronot, 2005.

Emerson, Ralph Waldo. *Selected Essays*. Harmondsworth, Middlesex, UK, and New York: Penguin Books, 1982.

Felman, Shoshana. "Psychoanalysis and Education: Teaching Terminable and Interminable." *Yale French Studies* 63 (1982): 400–420.

———. *The Scandal of the Speaking Body*. Translated by Catherine Porter. Stanford, CA: Stanford University Press, 2003.

———. *Writing and Madness*. Translated by Martha Noel Evans. Ithaca, NY: Cornell University Press, 1985.

Felstiner, John. *Paul Celan: Poet, Survivor, Jew*. New Haven, CT, and London: Yale University Press, 1995.

Fingarette, Herbert. *The Self in Transformation*. New York and Evanston, IL: Harper & Row, 1965.

Foucault, Michel. *Madness and Civilization*. Translated by Richard Howard. New York: Random House, 1965.

Fried, Michael. *Realism, Writing, Disfiguration*. Chicago and London: University of Chicago Press, 1987.

Garb, Jonathan. *Shamanic Trance in Modern Kabbalah*. Chicago and London: Chicago University Press, 2011.

Goodman, Nelson. *Ways of Worldmaking*. Indianapolis, IN: Hackett Publishing Company, 1978.

Greenblatt, Stephen. *Marvelous Possessions*. Chicago: University of Chicago Press, 1991.

Gross, Kenneth. *Puppet: An Essay on Uncanny Life*. Chicago and London: Chicago University Press, 2011.

Hamilton, John T. *Music, Madness, and the Unworking of Language*. New York: Columbia University Press, 2008.

Hertz, Neil. *George Eliot's Pulse*. Stanford, CA: Stanford University Press, 2003.

Josipovici, Gabriel. *Trust*. New Haven, CT, and London: Yale University Press, 1999.

Kafka, Franz. *Diaries, 1914–1923*. Translated by Martin Greenberg and Hannah Arendt. New York: Schocken Books, 1965.

———. *Parables and Paradoxes*. New York: Schocken Books, 1961.

———. *The Trial*. London: Penguin Books, 1953.

Keats, John. *Letters*. London: Oxford University Press, 1954.

Kermode, Frank. "The Plain Sense of Things." In *Midrash and Literature*, 179–94. New Haven, CT, and London: Yale University Press, 1986.

Klein, Melanie. "Weaning." In *On the Bringing Up of Children*. Edited by John Rickman. New York: Robert Brunner, 1952.

Kristeva, Julia. *Black Sun*. Translated by Leon S. Roudiez. New York: Columbia University Press, 1989.

———. *Powers of Horror*. Translated by Leon S. Roudiez. New York: Columbia University Press, 1982.

———. *Tales of Love*. Translated by Leon S. Roudiez. New York: Columbia University Press, 1987.

Kundera, Milan. *The Unbearable Lightness of Being*. London and Boston: Faber and Faber, 1985.

Lacan, Jacques. *Ecrits*. New York and London: W. W. Norton, 1977.

———. *The Seminar of Jacques Lacan: The Psychoses*. Translated by Jacques-Alain Miller and Russell Grigg. New York: W. W. Norton, 1997.

Landy, Francis. *Beauty and the Enigma*. Sheffield, UK: Sheffield Academic Press, 2001.

Laplanche, Jean. *Essays on Otherness*. London and New York: Routledge, 1999.

Lear, Jonathan. *A Case for Irony*. Cambridge, MA, and London: Harvard University Press, 2011.

———. *Happiness, Death, and the Remainder of Life*. Cambridge, MA: Harvard University Press, 2000.

Levinas, Emmanuel. *Totality and Infinity*. Pittsburgh: Duquesne University Press, 1969.

Likierman, Meira. *Melanie Klein*. London and New York: Continuum, 2001.

Maugham, Somerset. *Sheppey*. London: World Classics, 2003.

Meltzer, Donald. *The Apprehension of Beauty*. Perthshire, UK: Clunie Press, 1988.

Milgrom, Jacob. "Diviner or Sorcerer?" In *The JPS Torah Commentary: Numbers*, 473. Philadelphia and New York: The Jewish Publication Society, 1990.

Milner, Marion. *The Suppressed Madness of Sane Men*. London and New York: Routledge, 1987.

Nehamas, Alexander. *The Art of Living*. Berkeley, Los Angeles, and London: University of California Press, 1998.

Pardes, Ilana. *The Biography of Ancient Israel*. Berkeley, Los Angeles, and London: University of California Press, 2000.

Phillips, Adam. *The Beast in the Nursery*. London: Faber and Faber, 1998.

———. *On Balance*. New York: Farrar, Straus and Giroux, 2010.

———. *On Flirtation*. Cambridge, MA: Harvard University Press, 1994.

———. *On Kissing, Tickling, and Being Bored*. Cambridge, MA: Harvard University Press, 1993.

———. *Promises, Promises*. New York: Basic Books, 2001.

Poirier, Richard. "Frost, Winnicott, Burke." In *Transitional Objects and Potential Spaces*. Edited by Peter L. Rudnytsky, 216–28. New York: Columbia University Press, 1993.

Proust, Marcel. *Swann's Way*. Translated by C. K. Moncrieff and Terence Kilmartin. New York: Random House, 1989.

Rilke, Rainer Maria. *Letters to a Young Poet*. Translated by M. D. Herter Norton. New York and London: W. W. Norton, 1954.

Scarry, Elaine. *On Beauty*. Princeton, NJ: Princeton University Press, 1999.

Shklar, Judith N. *Ordinary Vices*. Cambridge, MA: Harvard University Press, 1984.

Shulman, David. *More Than Real*. Cambridge, MA: Harvard University Press, 2012.

Spero, Moshe Halevi. "The Hidden *Subject* of Job: Mirroring and the Anguish of Interminable Desire." In *Hearing Visions and Seeing Voices*. Dordrecht, The Netherlands: Springer, 2007.

Stern, Donnel B. *Unformulated Experience*. Hillside, NJ, and London: Analytic Press, 1997.

Stewart, Susan. *The Poet's Freedom*. Chicago and London: University of Chicago Press, 2011.

Winnicott, D. W. *Home Is Where We Start From*. London and New York: W. W. Norton and Company, 1986.

———. *Playing and Reality*. London and New York: Routledge, 1971.

Wordsworth, William. *Wordsworth: Poetry and Prose*. Edited by W. Moelwyn Merchant. London: Rupert Hart-Davis, 1955.

Zizek, Slavoj. *The Sublime Object of Ideology*. London and New York: Verso, 1989.

INDEX

PERMISSIONS ACKNOWLEDGMENTS

Grateful acknowledgment is made to the following for permission to reprint previously published material:

Faber and Faber Ltd: Excerpts from "The Love Song of J. Alfred Prufrock" and "The Waste Land" from *Collected Poems 1909–1962* by T. S. Eliot. Reprinted by permission of Faber and Faber Ltd.

Houghton Mifflin Harcourt Publishing Company and Faber and Faber Ltd: Excerpt from "East Coker" from *Four Quartets* by T. S. Eliot, copyright © 1940 by T. S. Eliot, copyright renewed 1968 by Esme Valerie Eliot. Print rights in the United States are controlled by Houghton Mifflin Harcourt Publishing Company. Print and electronic rights outside the United States from *Collected Poems 1909–1962* administered by Faber and Faber Ltd., London. Reprinted by permission of Houghton Mifflin Harcourt Publishing Company and Faber and Faber Ltd. All rights reserved.

Random House, an imprint and division of Random House LLC: "The First Elegy," translation copyright © 1982 by Stephen Mitchell; from *Selected Poetry of Rainer Maria Rilke* by Rainer Maria Rilke, translated by Stephen Mitchell. Reprinted by permission of Random House, an imprint and division of Random House LLC. All rights reserved.

Random House of Canada Limited: Excerpt from *Stranger Music: Selected Poems and Songs* by Leonard Cohen. Copyright © 1933 by Leonard Cohen and Leonard Cohen Stranger Music, Inc. Reprinted by permission of McClelland & Stewart, a division of Random House of Canada Limited, a Penguin Random House company.